AF840879

'For readers who value long-term universal human wellbeing over short-term narrow goals, Mikdashi provides a blueprint for progress. Readers will be inspired to support the author's call for a periodic impartial and comprehensive State of the Globe assessment.'

John Gault, economist, Co-Director of and Lecturer in the Executive Masters Program, Oil and Gas, Graduate Institute of International and Development Studies, Geneva

'Zuhayr Mikdashi has worked tirelessly to introduce new perspectives to provide policymakers with a meaningful opportunity to pursue their development aims while, in the meantime, meeting the aspirations of the populations involved. Zuhayr Mikdashi's rich and diverse academic, research and practice covers many fields which reflect the expansion of the range of challenges facing the globalized world. It also corresponds to the inflated content of commitments in the agendas of intergovernmental negotiations. In this respect, given the complexity of the issues, fresh avenues, which imply holistic and multidisciplinary approaches, as well as precise definitions, are indispensable.'

Antoine Basile, Former UN Interregional Adviser on Investment and Technology

'A moving and cultured cri de coeur of a Levantine humanist and intellectual.'

Michel Habib, University of Zurich, Switzerland

The Evolution of Economic Wellbeing

Throughout history, humans have sought to enhance their wellbeing across various domains. Though the spectrum of factors responsible for wellbeing has widened considerably and advances have been realized in scientific-technological fields, significant failures have been encountered in establishing peaceful relations among various communities, and the natural environment has been degraded inconsiderately by humans since the Industrial Revolution.

This book identifies the key factors that influence changes in wellbeing – both positively and negatively – within a framework of socio-economic globalization, instantaneous interconnectedness, and rising environmental risks. These 'clusters of progress' comprise essentially the following seven areas: bolstering peace and security; respecting universal fundamental values; satisfying personal and social basic needs; expanding knowledge and managerial-technological skills; promoting arts and culture; husbanding natural resources and protecting the environment; and concerting actions for the global common good.

The term 'progress' is used here to mean an all-embracing sustainable advancement towards desirable goals (be they material or non-material), offering higher levels of wellbeing to individuals and to society at large, compared to previous or current conditions.

In unravelling the 'progress conundrum', the author draws on his own original research and field work experiences which dovetail with those of other scholars by complementing their findings and/or by offering different appraisals. The author adopts an inter-disciplinary approach that overcomes the 'silo-like compartmentalization' of fields of study. The said approach enables us to reach a better understanding of the complex reality of progress (or regression) in various domains.

Zuhayr Mikdashi is the founding Director of the Institute of Banking and Financial Management, now the Institute of Banking and Finance, at the University of Lausanne, Switzerland.

Routledge Studies in the Modern World Economy

176 **China and Japan in the Global Economy**
Edited by Tomoo Kikuchi and Masaya Sakuragawa

177 **Exports, Trade Policy and Economic Growth in Eras of Globalization**
Edward M. Feasel

178 **Chinese Trade**
Trade Deficits, State Subsidies and the Rise of China
Rich Marino

179 **The Evolution of Economic Wellbeing**
Progress-Driven Economic Policies in the Era of Globalization
Zuhayr Mikdashi

180 **Entrepreneurship and Local Economic Development**
A Comparative Perspective on Entrepreneurs, Universities and Governments
Edited by Bruno Dallago and Ermanno Tortia

181 **The Future of the Economy**
East-West Perspectives on Pathways Through Disruption
John Powers and Vikram Khanna

182 **Regional Government Competition**
Chen Yunxian and Gu Wenjing

183 **The Dynamics of Growth in Emerging Economies**
The Case of Turkey
Edited by Arzu Akkoyunlu Wigley and Selim Çağatay

For more information about this series, please visit
www.routledge.com/Routledge-Studies-in-the-Modern-World-Economy/book-series/SE0432

The Evolution of Economic Wellbeing

Progress-Driven Economic Policies in the Era of Globalization

Zuhayr Mikdashi

Routledge
Taylor & Francis Group
LONDON AND NEW YORK

First published 2019 by Routledge

2 Park Square, Milton Park, Abingdon, Oxfordshire OX14 4RN
52 Vanderbilt Avenue, New York, NY 10017

Routledge is an imprint of the Taylor & Francis Group, an informa business

First issued in paperback 2020

British Library Cataloguing-in-Publication Data
A catalogue record for this book is available from the British Library

Library of Congress Cataloging-in-Publication Data
Names: Mikdashi, Zuhayr, author.
Title: The evolution of economic wellbeing progress-driven economic policies in the era of globalization / Zuhayr Mikdashi.
Description: 1 Edition. | New York: Routledge, [2018] | Series: Routledge studies in the modern world economy | Includes bibliographical references and index.
Identifiers: LCCN 2018015396 | ISBN 9781138594661 (hardback) | ISBN 9780429488702 (ebook)
Subjects: LCSH: Sustainable development. | Economic policy. | Quality of life. | Globalization–Social aspects.
Classification: LCC HC79.E5 M4675 2018 | DDC 338.9–dc23
LC record available at https://lccn.loc.gov/2018015396

ISBN: 978-1-138-59466-1 (hbk)
ISBN: 978-0-367-66299-8 (pbk)

Typeset in Goudy
by Wearset Ltd, Boldon, Tyne and Wear

Contents

Exhibits

Biographical notes

Zuhayr Mikdashi (D.Phil. & M.Litt. Oxford; B.A. & M.A. American University of Beirut) is the founding Director of the Institute of Banking and Financial Management (now the Institute of Banking and Finance) at the University of Lausanne, Switzerland. He has also been a tenured Professor of Business Administration at the American University of Beirut, and Distinguished Visiting Professor at the Business School of the American University in Cairo. In addition, Mikdashi was Research Fellow at the Center for International Affairs at Harvard University, and at the Japanese Institute for Developing Economies, Tokyo. He has also served as an advisor or consultant for numerous institutions, including the World Bank, UN agencies, the OECD Development Centre, and the Arab Monetary Fund. Mikdashi was Resident Advisor to the Minister of Finance and Oil of the State of Kuwait, and Economic collaborator to a Prime Minister in Lebanon.

These experiences have all enriched the development of his reflections over many years.

Academic background

- Graduate studies/degrees at Oxford University – St Catherine's College (M. Litt. in Economics, 1958 and British Council Scholar) & (D.Phil. in International Economic Relations, 1971); Stanford University Graduate School of Business (International Center for the Advancement of Management Education); the American University of Beirut (B.A. & M.A. in Economics); Université de Lyon (Certificat d'études littéraires générales); École nationale supérieure du pétrole et des moteurs/Institut Français du Pétrole – Rueil-Malmaison (stage de chercheur).
- Author or co-author of over ten books and monographs. His latest are: *Regulating the Financial Sector in the Era of Globalization* (Palgrave Macmillan, 2003, 275p.); and *Progress-Driven Entrepreneurs, Private Equity Finance and Regulatory Issues* (Palgrave Macmillan, 18 December 2010, 216p.).
- The author has also contributed chapters to various books. Among the most recent is: Zuhayr Mikdashi, 'Entrepreneurs as Heroes of Development', in

Entrepreneurship and Innovation in Egypt, eds Nagla Rizk and Hassan Azzazi, American University in Cairo Press, 2016, pp. 7–28/215p.

- Over recent years, the author has been invited to join the boards of several small and medium-sized companies located in Continental Europe.

Relevant field experiences

My interest in this book's themes has been particularly reinforced by my consulting experiences, most notable of which are the following five episodes in my professional career:

The first goes back to the summer of 1958 when I was invited to join a mission set up by The International Bank for Reconstruction and Development (The World Bank) at the request of the Libyan government. The mission's mandate was to prepare a developmental programme for Libya which happened, in the late 1950s, to be amongst the world's poorest countries, and heavily dependent on foreign aid. My assignment was that of assistant to the Mission's Chief, P. S. Narayan Prasad, with the duty of scouting for data and soliciting interviews needed for the World Bank's Report. The World Bank Mission comprised 13 experts of nine different nationalities, whose expertise covered various socio-economic sectors relevant to Libya's development. We visited several localities scattered over a vast territory (Libya had in the mid-1950s about 2.5 million inhabitants spread over a territory that covers about 1.8 million square kilometres or 700,000 square miles – mostly desert or arid land).

By the time the World Bank mission came to write its report, *The Economic Development of Libya*, oil had been discovered in considerable commercial quantities. Oil revenues, thereafter, freed Libya's budget from dependence on foreign aid. The World Bank Report was re-drafted and its publication by the John Hopkins University Press was delayed till 1963 to have the Mission's recommendations take account of the oil bonanza discoveries, in the hope that these would be a *boon* for society. Improperly or selfishly used by a despotic ruler, oil would turn out to be a *bane* – as subsequent events in Libya after 1969 have painfully shown.

Libya won its independence in 1951 with the eviction of the Italian colonial regime. The country had then an impoverished population of some 2.5 million nationals (compared with about 6 million in 2018). Given its arid climate and subsistence agricultural economy, Libya had to depend on donors' aid to alleviate endemic poverty till the mid-1950s. Thanks to oil concessions granted to foreign companies since that period, and the discovery of commercial oil deposits in 1959, the country became economically viable (see, for example, *The Economic Development of Libya: Report of a Mission* [in which this author was a member], organized by the International Bank for Reconstruction and Development at the request of the government of Libya [then a constitutional monarchy], published by the John Hopkins Press, Baltimore, September 1960, pp. xvii & 524).

The second episode concerned consulting in the field of natural resources. In particular, one of my assignments in the oil-rich State of Kuwait in the late

1960s (as resident adviser to the Minister of Finance and Oil) offered me a fecund source of experiences (in matters of government-business relations). My principal responsibility was to prepare the requisite documentation that would enable the State of Kuwait to 'acquire' the oil concessions granted earlier on its territories to foreign transnational companies. The largest concession (that of the Kuwait Oil Company, KOC) was originally granted in 1934 by the Emir of the State of Kuwait when the country was a British protectorate. KOC was then equally owned by the British 'Anglo-Iranian Oil Co' (later renamed British Petroleum, BP) and the U.S. 'Gulf Oil' company.

Other consultancy works in the field of petroleum were carried out for the Organization of Petroleum Exporting Countries (OPEC), which was created in Baghdad in mid-September 1960 by an inter-governmental conference of major oil exporting developing countries – namely Iran, Iraq, Kuwait, Saudi Arabia, and Venezuela (joined later by other countries, comprising Algeria, Angola, Ecuador, Libya, Nigeria, Qatar, and United Arab Emirates). The OPEC Secretary General Francisco Parra asked this author in 1973 to study the economics of pricing oil. Oil price levels were considered in the 1960s and prior to 1973 as too low by OPEC countries. With their discovery of vast oil reserves in the post-Second World War period, the international petroleum oligopoly, comprising a few large transnational private companies, had realized that their commercial interest then was to expand their sales – given the vast oil reserves they have discovered – via relatively low prices to whittle away the dominance of coal in the global energy market.

The OPEC secretariat was also interested in finding out whether other developing countries relying on the export of raw materials to developed industrial countries could improve their terms of trade – using the OPEC model as a producers' association capable of flexing their oligopolistic muscles. Among the issues raised were three important ones:

- Can private transnational oligopolies be effectively counterbalanced by governmental cartels of major raw material exporting countries?
- Are commodity agreements (jointly governed by large producer and consumer nations) more effective in moderating price volatility within a jointly agreed optimal range of prices and with the help of market transactions executed by the manager of a buffer stock equally funded by both parties?
- Would it be more efficient to have a level-playing field in an openly competitive market that allows for dynamic forces to operate freely without governmental intervention?

The third episode was concerned with interregional business meetings. This happened upon the invitation of Klaus Schwab in 1975 (the President of the *European Management Forum*, later re-named the *World Economic Forum*), to join him in mobilizing business and political leaders from Arab countries to meet their peers from Western countries in an international symposium for business cooperation. The first Symposium was held on 25–27 October 1976 in

Montreux, Switzerland, when Europe was still recovering from an acute economic crisis triggered by the quadrupling of crude oil export prices over 1973–1974.

This dramatic increase in petroleum prices, mostly provoked by the disruption of transport means (with the blockage of the Suez Canal and the destruction of oil terminals in the East Mediterranean) due to the outbreak of military hostilities in the Middle East, had then led to oil rationing in several Western economies which were hooked on oil as their major source of energy. The ensuing shortages of oil supplies provoked a widespread closure of industries, and a dramatic rise in unemployment in oil-importing countries. It was hoped that the above-mentioned Symposium discussions could help in furthering *mutual understanding*, *dialogue*, *compromises*, and *cooperation* among policy- and decision-makers of (a) northern developed and technologically advanced countries that had hitherto held the upper hand in the international economy, and (b) newly independent southern countries, especially those endowed with strategic natural resources. Discussions covered: (i) sharing in know-how with transfers of technology at reasonable terms, (ii) creating and developing business opportunities and jobs through joint ventures, (iii) involving actively nationals alongside expatriates in a level-playing field, (iv) balanced partaking in value created among partnering parties, (v) protection of foreign investments from confiscation or other discriminatory measures, and (vi) respecting the legitimate rights and obligations of various stakeholders.

The first Arab–European Business Cooperation Symposium was attended by some 1,000 business executives, political leaders, and senior representatives of international/regional organizations. Prompted by mutual interest, protagonists had sought *balanced* relations among stakeholders to forestall gridlocks and promote synergies (see summary proceedings by this author, published by the European Management Forum, Geneva, March 1977, 199p.; this was followed by a second symposium held on 29–31 May 1978 in Montreux and whose proceedings were published by Kommentator-Kluwer under the title of *Partners in Development through Resources and Technology*, Z. Mikdashi, ed., 1978, 285p.).

The fourth episode relates to my involvement with United Nations agencies and other international organizations that enabled me to do research for my book *The International Politics of Natural Resources*. Written under the auspices of the Center for International Affairs at Harvard University, then directed by Professor Raymond Vernon of the Harvard Business School, the book was first published in 1976 by Cornell University Press, and was later translated into Japanese and published in Tokyo.

The opportunity to function as an Expert Advisor for the UN Commission on Transnational Corporations (UNCTC) proved a fertile intellectual arena. The UNCTC was created in 1973 at the UN headquarters in New York following the deliberations at the United Nations regarding the establishment of a New International Economic Order. Its Board of Expert Advisors comprised a constellation of non-remunerated representatives from academia, from member governments of both developed and developing countries, and from transnational corporations. The advisor function I assumed over 1983–1986, along with other consulting work for UN agencies, offered me a fertile opportunity for the exchange of views with a variety of thinkers and practitioners hailing from different backgrounds. The Commission's ultimate objective was to draft a Code of Good Conduct for these corporations. In 1994, the UNCTC programme was transferred to the United Nations Conference on Trade and Development (UNCTAD), based in Geneva.

The fifth episode was related to an academic sojourn in 2012 at the American University in Cairo (AUC) as a *Distinguished Visiting Professor*. During that stint, I greatly benefited from thought-provoking exchanges with faculty, students, and practitioners in seminar sessions I had addressed, at the initiative of Professor Shawki Farag. It was also my opportunity to actively participate then in the 2012 AUC Research Conference on '*Entrepreneurship and Innovation: Shaping the Future of Egypt*' with a lecture on key aspects of entrepreneurial creativity. In particular the Conference's organizers and co-chairs, Professors Nagla Rizk and Hassan M. E. Azzazy, invited this author to address the Conference as the main speaker and as the moderator of the session on strategies of *Social Entrepreneurship*.

As member of the *three-jury* panel entrusted with screening several entrepreneurial projects submitted by AUC students, the panel had to evaluate and choose the three best laureates. My background as a non-executive board of directors' member of small-medium sized companies has helped me in the evaluation process. The AUC Conference has been a landmark that inspired several participants to explore new avenues for business development and for wellbeing.

Preface

Humans across time and space have had a widespread urge to enhance their personally perceived wellbeing during their life span. This book sheds new light on a subject that will remain fundamental to human behaviour. To the non-specialist, the book reveals key facets of this complex phenomenon illustrated by examples and case studies, while the specialist will find areas that deserve her/his further probing to attain fruitful results.

The pursuit of wellbeing has been anchored in the coherent/synergetic working of key categories of factors, hereafter referred to as 'clusters of wellbeing'. Fundamental core clusters of wellbeing can be classified into several important categories. We propose seven key groups: bolstering peace and security; respecting universal fundamental values; satisfying basic personal and social needs; expanding knowledge and capabilities; promoting cultures; husbanding resources and protecting the natural environment; and concerting actions for the global common good.

The foregoing clusters of wellbeing constitute a *multifaceted whole* that is essential to the vibrancy of planet Earth, perennially, and for the benefit of its diverse stakeholders.

Humankind, as the dominant species on our planet, should guard against poaching other species or exploiting *nature* for its selfish current interests, to the detriment of future generations. The premise of our analyses is that the human species can only prosper on a healthy planet in which diverse stakeholders are reasonably protected.

This work should appeal to a wide spectrum of academics (scholars, students, researchers, educators), and practitioners (government officials, business leaders, and other economic agents), along with non-governmental organizations (NGOs – such as think tanks, gatekeepers, and philanthropic groups). In an increasingly interdependent, interconnected, and globalizing complex world, the uninitiated and the specialist – concerned with sustainable wellbeing that *protects* and *improves* life's quality on planet Earth for existing and future generations – will welcome the book's non-esoteric style.

Essence of the book

The book's keystone contribution is in its novel approach that advocates a comprehensive understanding of personal and collective *wellbeing*, coupled with mapping out tracks for enhancing that phenomenon. The book examines *wellbeing's* components (the material and the non-material, the objectively measurable and the subjectively estimated). Components of wellbeing vary across time and geography. Nevertheless, their bedrock values rest on the protection of human rights. By offering a few original case studies and narrating certain events, the book seeks a dialogue with the reader on paths that could *avert* or *contain conflicts* and *promote fruitful cooperation for people's wellbeing*. Progress in that domain presumes the underpinning of science and ethical values working *in tandem*. Otherwise, humanity will remain vulnerable to various traps of poverty and other calamities.

Catchwords

Alterity, biodiversity, business and country competitiveness, business leadership, capabilities' enhancement, dysfunctional finance, economic crises, ecosystems, empirical studies on development, entrepreneurial leadership, ethics, financial crises, globalization, governance, Gross Domestic Product (GDP), growth, happiness, human development, inequalities, international cooperation, international finance, management of natural resources, migrations, political economy, pollution, poverty, predatory behaviours, profligacy, progress, public goods, quality of life, resilience, scarce resources, scientific-technological advancement, security, social entrepreneurship, socio-political emancipation, socio-political inclusiveness, solidarity, sources of conflicts, state of the globe, sustainability, transhumanism, tyrannical regimes, value creation, universal human rights/values, wellbeing, welfare.

Acknowledgements

This book's analyses are based on the author's research and experiences in economic and business fields. Many scholars' and practitioners' works cited in the text have proved quite helpful. Several people have been particularly generous with their time over the years to exchange with the author reflections on this book's themes. The cogency of their views has helped the author to sharpen his analyses. Obviously, the author remains solely responsible for the contents of his work.

The author reiterates here his thanks to those who have offered advice, notably with respect to his earlier publications, and in particular on the following books: (1) *The Community of Oil Exporting Countries – A Study in Governmental Cooperation* (jointly published by Cornell University Press, and George Allen & Unwin Ltd, 1972, 239p.); (2) *The International Politics of Natural Resources* (written under the auspices of the Center for International Affairs at Harvard University, then directed by Professor Raymond Vernon of the Harvard Business School – and first published in 1976 by Cornell University Press, 214p.; also translated into Japanese and published in Tokyo); (3) *Transnational Oil: Issues, Policies and Perspectives* (published by F. Pinter, London, 1986, 184p. – under the General Editorship of Susan Strange, then Professor of International Relations, London School of Economics and Political Science); and (4) his more recent books: *Regulating the Financial Sector in the Era of Globalization*, Palgrave Macmillan, 2003, 275p.; and *Progress-Driven Entrepreneurs, Private Equity Finance and Regulatory Issues*, 2010, 222p., also published by Palgrave Macmillan. In the last-mentioned book, I have had an eminent contribution on 'Private Equity as a Wealth Recycler' by my colleague Dr Benoit Leleux, S. Schmidheiny Professor of Entrepreneurship and Finance at the International Institute for Management Development (based in Lausanne, Switzerland).

The quality of this book has been enhanced by the fine multiple editorial services provided under the aegis of Senior Executive Editor Kristina Abbotts at Routledge. I am particularly grateful to Kristina and to her Editorial Assistant Christiana Mandizha for their painstaking efforts and their efficiency in managing the complex publication process. Kristina has, furthermore, called on the competence of David Whitehouse for the copy-editing function of the manuscript. I also wish to recognize the fine quality of the final stage of copy editing provided by Steph Allison. She deserves my deep-felt gratitude for her scrupulous scrutiny. The supporting staff in the book's production process, though not personally known to this author, also merit to be duly recognized for their contributions.

Finally, I would be remiss not to mention the unwavering support offered by my family throughout the time I devoted to this monograph; their empathy deserves my loving recognition.

Acronyms

BIS	Bank for International Settlements
CEO	Chief Executive Officer
FAO	Food and Agriculture Organization of the United Nations
FDI	Foreign Direct Investments
FSB	Financial Stability Board
GAC	Gaps of 'Aspirations vs Capabilities'
GCC	Gulf Cooperation Countries (Bahrain, Kuwait, Oman, Qatar, Saudi Arabia, and United Arab Emirates)
GDP	Gross Domestic Product
GEM	Global Entrepreneurship Monitor
GNI	Gross National Income
GNP	Gross National Product
GSI	Global Subsidies Initiative
HLY	Happy Life Year
HPI	Happy Planet Index
ICC	International Chamber of Commerce
ICC	International Criminal Court
ICRC	International Committee of the Red Cross
ILO	International Labour Organization
IMF	International Monetary Fund
IOM	International Organization for Migration
IPE	International Political Economy
MSME	Micro/Small/Medium sized enterprises
NATO	North Atlantic Treaty Organization
NGO	Non-Governmental Organization
OECD	Organization for Economic Co-operation and Development
QOL	Quality of Life
SIPRI	Stockholm International Peace Research Institute
SME	Small and Medium-sized enterprises
SPV	Special Purpose Vehicle
SRA	Society for Risk Analysis
TNC	Trans-national Corporation
UDHR	Universal Declaration of Human Rights

UNCTAD	United Nations Conference on Trade and Development
UNDP	United Nations Development Programme
UNEP	United Nations Environment Programme
UNESCO	United Nations Educational, Scientific and Cultural Organization
UNICEF	United Nations International Children's Emergency Fund
UNU	United Nations University
WHO	World Health Organization
WTO	World Trade Organization

Introduction

Throughout history, humans have sought to enhance their wellbeing in multifarious domains – with mixed results. This monograph recognizes that (i) the spectrum of factors responsible for wellbeing has expanded considerably, (ii) advances in the scientific-technological fields have favourably impacted wellbeing, (iii) important failures have been encountered in fortifying peace among various human communities, and (iv) the natural environment has been degraded considerately by humans since the *Industrial Revolution* (circa 1750). Indeed, some natural disasters are not strictly *natural* since they are provoked or exacerbated by human activities that produce CO_2 and other greenhouse gases. Increases in these emissions have been largely associated with a growing world population and increased economic activities in agriculture and industry that use intensively fossil fuels (and their derivatives), and/or resort to deforestation.

Interpreting the behaviour of economic agents has generally relied on models that use simple postulates. These cover such axioms as: self-interest of private economic agents; rational behaviour aimed at maximizing utility; established fixed preferences; ready and continuous access to a comprehensive flow of authentic information; perfectly competitive markets that have self-balancing mechanisms; absence of rigidities or obstacles to remedy imbalances, etc.

In recent economic analyses, some of the above-mentioned postulates have been reformulated or nuanced to reflect complex reality. Indeed, humans could be confused or muddle-headed, and subject to irrational or arational *herd-like behaviour* – for example, in such domains as consumption or investment. Contemporary economists who make judicious use of advances in other disciplines (psychology, sociology, anthropology, biology, neurology, etc.) seek to improve and deepen our comprehension of human behaviour. An inter-disciplinary approach is deemed increasingly productive in probing the essence of *wellbeing* and of changes related to that condition within a framework of socio-economic globalization, instantaneous interconnectedness and interdependence, and rising environmental risks.

The term '*progress in wellbeing*' used in this monograph refers to the perennial enhancement of humankind's overarching goals of wellbeing (in economic, social, physical, mental, emotional, cultural, and/or ethical conditions), in symbiosis with a healthy *natural environment*. *Wellbeing* overlaps with other terms, such as:

happiness, quality of life, fulfilment, pleasure, self-realization, meaningfulness, hedonism, welfare, wellness, utility, virtuous life, plenitude, joy, quality of environment, contentment, comfort, and/or other conditions of lasting or fleeting personal satisfaction. Among the foregoing concepts, *wellbeing* is closest to *happiness-quality of life*. Indeed, surveys on the evolution of happiness

> continue to highlight people's own reports of the quality of their lives as measured on a scale with 10 representing the best possible life and 0 the worst … [that comprise]: GDP per capita, healthy life expectancy, social support, freedom, generosity, and absence of corruption.[1]

In unravelling the conundrum of 'progress in wellbeing', the author draws on his own original research and field-work experiences, and complements certain aspects of *existing scholarship*. The book's *interdisciplinary approach* attempts to overcome the *silo-like compartmentalization* of the field under study. The said approach enables us to reach a *holistic* understanding of the complex reality of wellbeing that views humans (the *prosperous* and the *destitute*) and their natural environment as a *single system* on planet Earth.

Arguments about caring for the *destitute*[2] worldwide are reinforced by the self-interest of protecting the wellbeing of the *well-to-do* individuals or communities. Indeed, pandemics, air and water pollution, climate and ecological upheavals, toxic materials, spoiled nutritional inputs, lethal conflicts, cyber and space wars, and other dangers cannot be confined to limited localities. They can spread over vast areas beyond *national boundaries* more or less easily, and destroy life, wealth and wellness of the hitherto prosperous communities.

Notes

1 See *World Happiness Report 2017*, John F. Helliwell, Richard Layard, and Jeffrey D. Sachs, eds, New York: Sustainable Development Solutions Network, p. 37/185p.; and http://worldhappiness.report/.

2 The United Nations General Assembly declared 17 October 'the International Day for the Eradication of Poverty' (resolution 47/196 of 22 December 1992).

1 Unravelling the 'wellbeing conundrum'

This introductory chapter seeks to identify the significant *clusters* of factors conducive to driving forward an *all-embracing progress in wellbeing*, and to probe their determinants. Other scholars define 'progress' narrowly to comprise (i) advancements in science and technology, and (ii) institutional change that would encourage commerce, capital accumulation, and innovation.[1]

In the process of unravelling the components of progress – the economic, the non-economic, and the hybrid, our analysis identifies *seven categories of fundamental clusters of wellbeing* whose significance will be examined in the following chapters. The categories of 'wellbeing clusters' are susceptible to being split into sub-categories. Moreover, the relative weights of these clusters are not uniform; they depend on the values and goals of individuals and communities (including the global community).

The seven major categories of 'progress in wellbeing' proposed in the *normative archetype* represent goals that need to be implemented synergistically through appropriate mechanisms. Such mechanisms already exist for a few of the constituent components of wellbeing. Other mechanisms are essentially at the budding stage and are 'talking shops' for the time being, as they are lacking in effectiveness or efficiency. Hopefully, their empowerment can be developed – since establishing 'peace and security' and protecting 'universal fundamental values' constitute the primordial ethical bedrock of global wellbeing. Indeed, the normative values proposed in the proposed *archetype* are ethically superior to laws, rulings, mores, or traditions that any society or state could espouse.

Conceptual tools and views

Humans down the ages have generally sought to *advance* and *protect* what they perceive to be their *wellbeing* – a condition that comprises both objective and subjective components. In this monograph, we have chosen to examine the scope for enhancing 'wellbeing' whose core 'prerequisite components' are identified in Exhibit 1.1. *Wellbeing* appears to some onlookers at first sight *nebulous* or *fuzzy*, indistinguishable from wellness, welfare, happiness, utility, good life, pleasure, joy, fulfilment, hedonism, standard of living, satisfaction of self-interest, enhanced per capita GNP/GDP/NDP/NNI, etc.

Exhibit 1.1 A normative archetype of 'global wellbeing'.
Source: author.

The foregoing terms happen to have some overlapping content. At the outset of this monograph, we distinguish between two commonly used concepts, namely (i) *wellbeing* and (ii) *welfare*. The *first* concept is used in this book to refer to comprehensive improvements in the *material* and *non-material conditions* of humans, while the *second* concept refers to the provision (by the public authorities and/or by philanthropic institutions) of a minimal level of social *support for citizens* whose current means fail to cover their basic needs. In the quest to improve their wellbeing, many people have emphasized the material dimensions (such as disposing of higher levels of wealth, income, consumption, or expenditures) while others have emphasized personal feelings (such as harmonious personal and social relations, affection, or equanimity).

Among economists, Amartya Sen and Mahbub ul Haq link *wellbeing* to 'human development', defined as the process of enlarging people's freedoms and opportunities to decide who to be, what to do, and how to live.[2] Expressed succinctly, 'Human development is a process of enlarging people's choices – as they acquire more capabilities and enjoy more opportunities to use these capabilities. Human development is also the objective'.[3]

The World Health Organization (WHO) defines *wellbeing* as 'a state of complete physical, mental and social wellbeing and not merely the absence of disease or infirmity'.[4] This document acknowledges that the state of *wellbeing* or *happiness* – though largely based on the subjective feelings of individuals – cannot be solely determined by 'income per capita'. It quotes (on p. 104) a United Nations commissioned report:

> Happiness seems far too subjective, too vague, to serve as a touchstone for a nation's goals, much less its policy content. That indeed has been the traditional view. Yet the evidence is changing this view rapidly. A generation of studies by psychologists, economists, pollsters, sociologists, and others has shown that happiness, though indeed a subjective experience, can be objectively measured, assessed, correlated with observable brain functions, and related to the characteristics of an individual and the society.[5]

In our analyses, *wellbeing's* components are split into two broad categories – the *objectively measurable* vis-à-vis the *subjectively evaluated*. Indeed, individuals may well include a variety of desiderata in their hierarchy of wellbeing components, and could well assign different weights to each of these. These differences in wellbeing reflect intrinsic or acquired personal predispositions that are influenced by prevailing traditions and mores, cultural and historical backgrounds, changing contexts of the communities under study – among other determinants. The *objectively measurable* components are observable and quantifiable. They include access to: potable water, nutrition, years of schooling and training, health care, salubrious housing, employment opportunities, etc. *Subjectively evaluated* components of wellbeing convey feelings of individuals or communities at a given moment of time and/or over a stretch of time covering a whole range of emotions.

Researchers and educators, policy- and decision-makers in government and business, as well as non-governmental organizations (NGOs) and more generally laypersons have been increasingly concerned with sustainable wellbeing that *protects* and *improves* life's quality on planet Earth for the sake of existing and future generations. Indeed, humans – and notably the poor – need not be necessarily locked up in any predetermined particular destiny. Many could have the opportunity of exiting the poverty trap and improving their lot through the development of their latent talents and capacities, should socio-political institutions and business organizations assume a catalytic positive role.

Possibly the most comprehensive and ambitious proposal for global wellbeing is that of the United Nations *Sustainable Development Goals [SDG] for 2015–30*. It follows-up on an earlier UN document *Millennium Development Goals [MDG]* that sought to reduce over 2000–2015 the global number of people living in dire poverty by half. SDG has several global goals to be realized by 2030. Chief among these goals are the following: ending poverty and hunger; ensuring healthy living conditions; providing inclusive and equitable quality education; striving for gender equality; sustainable management of water, sanitation, and energy; decent work for all; resilient infrastructure; fostering of productive innovations; control of climate warming; conservation of sea resources; protection of ecosystems from harmful activities; and promotion of peaceful relations and inclusive societies.[6]

Ranking potential calamities which are largely attributable to human activities differs from one socio-geographic area to another. For a developed country (namely the United States) one group of thinkers has emphasized the following challenges: the fragility of financial systems; disruptions in global trade; crying multiple inequalities among and within countries; massive casualty-prone unregulated migrations; degradation of ecosystems that hurt food production, potable water, air quality,[7] climate protection, etc.; violation of business ethics; deterioration of health and education; excessive or ill-advised governmental interventionism in business; terrorism and armed conflicts; pandemics; and delinquencies or ineffectiveness of national or international institutions.[8]

Domains for global cooperation have considerably expanded over the years. They include, for example: banning certain types of arms (nuclear, chemical, biological, etc.), control of money laundering from criminal sources, funding of terrorist activities (enforced under the aegis of the *Financial Action Task Force*), combating bribery of foreign public officials in international business transactions (as established by conventions reached at the *Organization for Economic Development*, OECD and the *World Bank Group*), stabilization of financial markets and systems (through the *IMF* and the *Financial Stability Forum*), consolidated supervision and solvency of transnational banks (as recommended by the *Basle Committee on Banking Supervision*), avoiding famines and alleviating starvation (with the help inter alia of the *Food and Agriculture Organization*, FAO), open non-discriminatory multilateral trade (within the framework of the *World Trade Organization*, WTO), the protection of workers and employees (with the support of the *International Labour Organization*, ILO), prosecution persons responsible for genocides and/or crimes against humanity (through the *International Criminal Court*), and the protection of health (with the help of the *World Health Organisation*, WHO) – are examples of more or less effective mechanisms that are relevant to the normative archetype of wellbeing proposed in Exhibit 1.1. The effectiveness of a few of these mechanisms leaves much to be desired, as sovereign member states with political clout try to elude them.

The humanitarian argument of caring for the *destitute* worldwide is reinforced by self-interest and self-preservation arguments of protecting the wellbeing of the *well-to-do* individuals. Indeed, pandemics, air and water pollution, climate and ecological disturbances, toxic materials, spoiled nutritional inputs, spread of lethal conflicts, cyber-attacks, and other dangers affect wellbeing beyond *national boundaries* more or less easily. This was eloquently expressed with respect to one key component of basic needs, namely health, thus:

> In our globalised world, where there is increased travel across borders, it is apparent that emerging infectious diseases and environmental threats are on the rise, and do not respect national boundaries. Without concerted international efforts, there may be grave impacts on all countries. No matter how wealthy or militarily powerful they may be, no country is 100 per cent safe, as epidemics such as SARS and the ongoing threat of avian influenza have demonstrated. These self-interest and self-preservation arguments may ultimately be more convincing than humanitarian arguments, although one would hope world leaders, and not just philanthropists, care about alleviating human suffering by improving health.[9]

The desire for life satisfaction is generally a perennial quest, with some people underlining material dimensions (such as their quests for higher levels of wealth, income, consumption, or expenditures) while others emphasize positive personal feelings (such as harmonious personal and social relations, trust, empathy, love, or equanimity). Although uncertain to realize fully the sought-after goal of *wellbeing* or *happiness* during our earthly life, such a quest has been fundamental to a variety of polities and civilizations. The United States is notably the first modern nation to enshrine in its Declaration of Independence of 1776 the inalienable rights of 'preservation of Life and Liberty, and the pursuit of Happiness'. Currently, researchers, governmental leaders, and legislators in developed and developing countries (e.g. the United Kingdom, Canada, France, Thailand, Bhutan, and other countries) have sought to formulate and implement policies and programmes aimed at the 'betterment of people's life' (i.e. their *wellbeing* or *happiness*).[10]

Disciplines other than economics have also seen their research and publications on *wellbeing* and *happiness* soar reflecting the *zeitgeist* of the twenty-first century. This applies to management, psychology, neurology and other medical sciences, biology, behavioural sciences, philosophy, ethics, religious studies, etc.[11] Indeed, as put by one research organization:

> Economic resources, while important, are not all that matters for people's well-being. Health status, human contact, education, jobs, environmental quality, civic engagement, governance, security and free time are all fundamental to our quality of life, as are people's subjective experiences of life – including, for example, their feelings and emotions, and their satisfaction with life as a whole.[12]

Increasingly, analysts and policymakers use the concept of 'sustainable development' as an indicator of *wellbeing*.[13] It is:

> ...development that meets the needs of the present without compromising the ability of future generations to meet their own needs. It contains within it two key concepts (1) the concept of 'needs', in particular the essential needs of the world's poor, to which overriding priority be given, and (2) the

> idea of limitations imposed by the state of technology and social organization on the environment's ability to meet present and future needs.[14]

Furthermore, certain aspects of *wellbeing* – such as harmony within family life, social trust, solidarity, feeling of security, and others – cannot be accurately measured similarly to the conventional measures of per capita gross domestic product (GDP), gross national product (GNP), gross national income (GNI), or net national income (NNI).[15]

In decoding economic facts or events, several economists seek complementary tools to those traditionally used in their discipline. They envy scholars working in the *exact sciences* – such as physics or biology – for their ability to explain the dynamics of phenomena in quantitative formulae. Economists often seek to emulate these scientists by resorting to regression analyses to ascertain the main determinants of economic activities, in order to recommend policies conducive to progress in wellbeing.

High levels of correlation between two or more factors in the economic field do not necessarily imply the existence of stable and deterministic cause-to-effect relationships between these factors. The correlation could merely represent links (of concomitance, juxtaposition, or lead-lag relations) that may not be valid for other social groups, or may not replicate in the future. Indeed, economic, social, political or geographic conditions evolve or mutate over time.[16]

The diversity of hurdles encountered by the poor (the inherited intergenerational poverty or the sudden new poverty) requires differentiated empirical analyses and solutions. This was expressed pointedly thus:

> If we resist the kind of lazy, formulaic thinking that reduces every problem to the same set of general principles; if we listen to the poor people themselves and force ourselves to understand the logic of their choices; if we accept the possibility of error and subject every idea, including the most apparently commonsensical ones, to rigorous empirical testing, then we will be able not only to construct a toolbox of effective policies but also to better understand why the poor live the way they do. Armed with this patient understanding, we can identify the poverty traps where they really are and know which tools we need to give the poor to help them get out of them.[17]

Several studies have found that there is no direct linear-cum-high correlation between increases in per capita income, and the improvement in the *perceived level of wellbeing*.[18] Layard relies on statistical data compiled over the 1990s by R. Inglehart and H-D. Klingemann (using a threshold per capita income of US$15,000). The threshold of 'adequate income' could vary across time or geography. What is *adequate* in an emerging economy at a given point of time (say India in 2017) is very likely to prove inadequate for an advanced economy (e.g. the U.S. in 2017).[19]

An increase in the real per capita income for people who are below the 'poverty line' is generally closely correlated with a rise in individuals' perception of improved wellbeing; this implies that the marginal utility of income for the 'lowest income brackets' of people is higher than that for the remaining population. This situation calls for a governmental policy of *income redistribution* in favour of the very poor – other things remaining equal – in order to enhance the overall welfare of the community. The scope of alleviating poverty through a policy of *income redistribution* may prove constrained in several poor countries with hardly any significant number of rich persons.

Within a socio-political environment of peace and dialogue that allows for democratic changes and compromises without upheavals, judicious policies of boosting quality growth by privileging public spending on developmental projects along with income redistribution can considerably alleviate poverty. In particular, as planned in 2000 by the United Nations Conference on *Millennium Development Goals* [MDG] the global number of people living in dire poverty was effectively reduced by half in the year 2015. Dire poverty was defined by MDG as less than $1.25 per capita per day. In 2007, the World Bank's yardstick for absolute poverty was set at $1.90 consumption per person per day at the 2011 purchasing power parity.[20]

Bolstering peace and security

Human beings cannot prosper and enjoy life unless they are assured that their personal physical-cum-moral integrity or that of their families and communities are properly protected. It is inconceivable to have societies prosper during periods of conflict. The World Bank estimated that more than 1.5 billion people (one in four of the people on planet Earth in 2011) live in vulnerability, affected by messy conflicts or large-scale high levels of criminal violence.[21] Among prerequisites of human development, one should emphasize the fundamental role of the binomial concept of *freedom-security* calling for *balanced compromises* in matters of *personal freedom* to attain a desirable level of *security provided by the legitimate authorities*.

Historical chronicles abound with events of violence across the ages. Upheavals and wanton destructions (of communities, patrimonies, natural sites, and cultural heritages) have been carried out (and continue to be) by those who ill-use their power. Across history, many civilizations have been obliterated, transformed, or re-composed under more powerful domineering forces. Ruinous conflicts (often associated with crimes against humanity; exploitation of minorities; stark inequalities; violent upheavals; plunders and destruction; and other abuses) continue to plague contemporary society.

Since the first atomic explosion over Hiroshima in 1945, the potential for the obliteration of life has increased through the continuous development of weapons of mass destruction. Unable to distinguish between enemy forces and innocent civilian populations, these weapons include thermo-nuclear bombs, killer robots, cluster munitions, landmines, blinding lasers, provoked pandemics, poisoning by toxic biological or chemical products – to mention a few. Moreover, the militarization of space (via aircrafts, drones, rockets, missiles, satellites, space ships, etc.) make the dangers of conflicts ubiquitous.

It is evident that *war* and *wellbeing* are antonymic. The extreme violence of wars produces death, handicaps, and indelible traumas and suffering; their physical, psychic, emotional, and moral scars cannot be fully healed. Their after-effects show-up in physical handicaps, severe mental illness, or emotional disturbances resulting from acts of torturing till an agonizing death, and sexual violence inflicted on innocent victims. The impact of the foregoing sufferings is often permanent, despite therapeutic efforts to cure them. To remind people of the tragedies of war and the benefits of peace, the United Nations General Assembly set-up in 1981 (by resolution 36/37) the 21st of September as the Peace Day devoted to strengthening the ideals of peace, both within and across the world's nations.

Exhibit 1.2 illustrates the tragedies encountered by the people of a country in the throes of war for several years in the 2010s, namely Syria. It reflects on the costs of the conflict, and the daunting task of re-building a shattered country, whose surviving civilian population has been sacrificed (displaced as internal refugees or forced to flee into foreign countries with no means to care for the basic needs of their children, women, or the aged).

Exhibit 1.2 War's ravages: Syria in 2011–2018

Across the ages, many conflicts have fragmented and destroyed communities or civilizations. In the Near-Middle East region, the hecatomb that has befallen Syria in the second decade of the twenty-first century has proved amongst the most tragic in humanity's history. It has produced large-scale wanton massacres of civilians (women, children, elders, minorities, and other innocent non-combatants); huge displacement of populations within and beyond national territories; vast destructions of cultural heritages and historical splendours; the obliteration of vital infrastructures, and personal properties; vandalism and looting of irreplaceable treasures; and other calamities that have brought wrath on current and future generations.[22]

Starting on 15 March 2011, Syrian unarmed pro-democracy demonstrators had initially sought peacefully reforms to live in dignity and freedom, rejecting extremism. The regime resorted to indiscriminate brutal force to quell these demonstrations. By the end of 2011, these violent confrontations turned into a full-fledged festering civil war that kept on raging till 2018. Many villages, towns and cities have been destroyed and their populations killed, maimed, and forced out of their homes. The 'regime vs rebels' confrontations remind us of Goya's masterpiece of mutual destruction of the two rival protagonists – mercilessly bludgeoning each other to death over moving sands (see Chapter 5, p. 222).

The Syrian regime was governed over the period of 1971–2017 by a family dynasty belonging to a religious minority group, the Alawites (a branch of Shi'a Islam living in a society that belongs predominantly to Sunni Islam). The founder of the dynasty, Hafez al-Assad, who ruled Syria from March 1971 till June 2000, was succeeded by his son Bashaar al-Assad [still ruling at the time of the final writing stages of this book in late 2018]. They had resorted to massive indiscriminate lethal power in defence of their regime, supported by their henchmen and a ruthless security apparatus, as well as by powerful regional or international actors – notably Iran (with its client Shi'a militias: Iranian, Iraqi, Lebanese, Afghani, Pakistani), Russia with long-standing strategic interests (through naval, land, and air-force bases – in addition to arms sales and military-training programmes), and China. A few regional and international powers have created zones of influence in Syria with little consideration for the country's overall national interest.

Other countries have generally shown little interest in mediating to solve through diplomacy the Syrian chaos and enable rival factions to reach pragmatic compromises before matters worsened. Initially peaceful, confrontations consequently slid into armed conflict between an authoritarian regime and adamant protesters who gradually fragmented into radical rebel bands that sought to control swathes of territories in Syria. Human rights organizations (UN agencies and NGOs such as Amnesty International, Médecins sans frontiers, along with other credible sources) have reported on atrocities inflicted by the regime and by extremist rebels – with tens of thousands of Syrian civilians arbitrarily detained incommunicado, tortured, starved to death, denied vital health care, or summarily liquidated without due process of justice and without informing their families.[23]

The Syrian deflagration in 2011–2018 has been amongst the worst of regional military conflicts in this first quarter of the twenty-first century. Massacres, and destructions in Syria have been fuelled by regional or international powers entering the fray – thereby rendering the Syrian conflict more intractable. In view of political rivalries and conflicting interests among regional powers (Iran, Turkey, Saudi Arabia, etc.), the League of Arab States, the United Nations Security Council and in particular the five permanent members who wield veto power (namely the United States, Russia, France, the United Kingdom, and China) were at odds, and impotent or deliberately unwilling to reconcile their divergent interests in order to reach workable compromises and stop the Syrian mayhem. They allowed the regime and its warlords, along with armed rebels (supported by external parties, among which a few with nefarious motives) to indulge in the relentless destruction of cities and historic sites, and the decimation of civilian people to proceed unabated over several years. Humanitarian corridors under UN agencies and international philanthropic agencies to deliver medicine, food and other vital necessities for stranded civilians (notably children, women or elderly persons) have been often blocked by belligerents. Analysts have likened the blockage of essential medicine (such as the immunization of children against polio or other viruses) or the rupturing of clean water supplies to 'biological warfare'.

Despite international prohibitions, deadly *land and aerial* warfare have been indiscriminately waged against civilian citizens by belligerents, including chemical weapons such as the nerve agent Sarin, cluster bombs and barrels of explosives.[24] The ravages of war have led to massive loss of life and vast destructions without the least compunction for trapped innocent civilians. Vast movements of populations within the national territory, and into neighbouring countries (and beyond) have occurred. UN sources reckon that about one-half of the population has been dramatically affected (death and/or handicaps, loss of homes and sources of livelihood, and absence of security).

The battlefield in Syria claimed a heavy toll of casualties. Besides regular soldiers and rebels, victims included innocent people, detainees tortured to death, sick and injured persons who were denied medical treatment, etc. United Nations and NGOs sources estimate war fatalities at some 500,000. Other deaths have resulted from hunger, diseases, lack of medicine and health care, and exposure to the natural elements without proper shelter – besides the drowning of refugees escaping via in the Mediterranean Sea seeking safe abode in Europe.

The social tissue of solidarity among the different components of the Syrian population had badly disintegrated over 2011–2018 as extremism, racketeering, and gangsterism have been fomented by a mosaic of unscrupulous parties with shady interests. War lords with their private armies of mercenaries had unscrupulously fed on others' misery and murky politics. By 2018, belligerents encompassed diverse groups with respect to ethnicity (Arabs, Kurds, Turkmen), religion (Sunnis, Alawites, Shias, Christians), ideology (liberals, radicals, fundamentalists, jihadists), or nationality (Middle Eastern, West European, Russian, and American). The monstrous carnage of innocent people (in schools, hospitals, playgrounds, business markets, and residential areas) has been widely reported. Several hundreds of thousands of displaced families and struggling refugees, within the country or in neighbouring countries, live since March 2011 in appalling conditions and struggle for survival.

Scorched-earth practices have destroyed cities, villages, and neighbourhoods, forcing millions of Syrians to flee in terrible conditions – with little food, hardly any medical care and precarious shelter (e.g. tents pitched in inhospitable or desert stretches of land devoid of basic amenities and exposed to the harsh elements of nature) leading eventually to high mortality rates. Much of Syria's economic life has been paralyzed and the national-cum-social fabric has been torn out dramatically. Families have been broken down with loss of parents and children (UNICEF estimated in 2014 that 5.5 million Syrian children were in dire need of protection and care in matters of health, nutrition, and schooling). Whoever wins in this civil war will have a pyrrhic victory with such a devastating cost that it is tantamount to defeat.

Cynical foreign governments, motivated by self-interest, had intervened to support, financially and/or militarily, a client tottering regime or subservient factions of the fragmented Syrian society. Their involvement had a dramatic impact on Syria's descent into ruin, as evidenced by: the tearing-up of the social fabric; the massive destructions of infrastructures, habitat, and historical patrimonies; the internal displacement of populations, and the exodus of nationals into foreign lands. By stoking Syria's civil war, a few rival powers, regional or international, could insidiously work for the dismantling of the Syrian state, and the subjugation or deportation of its people. Foreign powers or fighting factions absolve themselves from wrong-doing or blame, and often claim that information on their intentions is faked.

Neighbouring countries (Jordan, Turkey, Lebanon, Iraq, and Egypt) have allowed, more or less grudgingly, sizeable flows of Syrian refugees into their territories. Overwhelmed by such inflows of refugees, the hostility of certain segments of host countries' populations has grown towards these refugees. Other countries have refused to host Syrians – despite the dangers encountered by these hapless people fleeing the atrocities committed in their country in the throes of a devastating civil war.[25] Among hosting countries of Syrian refugees, Lebanon has admitted, relative to its population, the highest number.[26] Dreading being drawn into the Syrian 'tornado', a few occidental democratic powers have espoused *isolationist policies*. *With inadequate means of intervention*, they tend to prevaricate to avoid costly involvement so long as foreign calamities do not impinge directly on their countries' wellbeing and interests. Engrossed by national issues and having already considerably suffered from earlier military adventures, pragmatic foreign political leaders could well prioritise staying aloof and be concerned with domestic issues – despite their watching daily massacres of innocent civilians and the blatant flouting of universal ethical values. Should foreign powers intervene to aid or mediate in resolving lethal conflicts, they often do so belatedly after considerable suffering has been inflicted on the embattled people, and after ensuring that their perceived national interests are fully protected as interpreted by their ruling leaders. '[President] Obama generally does not believe a president should place American soldiers at great risk in order to prevent humanitarian disasters, unless those disasters pose a direct security threat to the United States'.[27] It is possible that political leaders of any given country could have different views or strategies on what is *national interest* in a globalized inter-dependent world. This turned out to be the case when comparing the *Democratic* President Barak Obama and his *Republican* successor President Donald Trump.

One needs to emphasize that blunders could be made by egomaniacal leaders regarding *national interest* and their decisions about getting militarily involved. Leaders' decisions could be based on false information and flawed reasoning. This was clearly presented by a researcher on recent U.S. military foreign interventions. He argued:

> that a consolidation of war-making power in the executive poses significant foreign-policy risks to the United States. As witnessed in the planning process in the lead-up to the Iraq War, multiple mistakes were made, most notably in the kind of information provided to the president, the pronounced biases the president brought with him into the White House, the manner in which the president received information, and how the president himself organized key advisory roles. Moreover, it has been well established that American generals can make significant mistakes in their own war-planning processes and advisory roles to the president. American generals, including those in the Bush administration, have suffered from an inability to think strategically about the purpose and objectives in warfare.[28]

The evaluation of *Syria's war costs* is a challenging exercise. It covers not only physical destruction of towns and cities, but also cultural-cum-human destructions and injuries. Vast forcible displacements of populations internally and externally have impacted more than half of the Syrian population. The Syrian toll-of-war estimates by international organizations, as this book went to press in 2018, have exceeded a trillion U.S. dollars.[29] Civilian deaths resulting directly from military operations are reckoned to have exceeded half a million individuals over 2011–2018.

The country after seven years of war stands in 2018 fragmented and torn apart subject to warring factions, often supported by foreign rival governments or parties (regional and global) – each seeking to satisfy partisan interests in the Syrian quagmire. A former Swiss attorney general who had probed war crimes in Rwanda and ex-Yugoslavia, served for some five years the UN Commission of Inquiry on Syria whose mission was to investigate war crimes and crimes against humanity. She decided in August 2017 to resign from the Commission owing to lack of political support. Indeed, the Commission has failed to obtain from the UN

Security Council the referral to the International Criminal Court in the Hague of authors of horrendous crimes against humanity perpetrated in Syria. These crimes included chemical weapons attacks, genocide against the Yazidi community and other defenceless populations, bombing of aid convoys, siege and shelling of civilian populations, torture and extrajudicial killings, etc., as reported by Reuters, BBC News, and other media.

Indeed, national interests have predominated as illustrated by the handling of the Syrian civil war's atrocities which proceeded unabated over 2011–2018, with large scale massacres and deaths of innocent civilian populations estimated at over 500,000. Displaced Syrians (internally and externally) have been estimated at 12 million (over half the total Syrian population) trying to escape the vast destructions of towns, cities, neighbourhoods – including medical facilities, schools, markets, and irreplaceable world cultural heritages.

Surviving innocent victims do not expect adequate reparations from belligerents or from philanthropic institutions for the death of family members, and the destruction of their livelihoods.

Respecting universal fundamental values

Respecting universal fundamental values is generally considered an integral part of virtuous behaviour. Nevertheless, humans continue to encounter unacceptable violations of basic human rights in several developing and developed societies. These violations comprise: the detention and liquidation of innocent persons without trial; practices of slavery, serfdom, or poorly remunerated forced labour (imposed on adults and children); torture, rape, or other brutal degrading ignominious treatment; the subjugation or eviction of communities and the grabbing of their lands and the scorched-earth destruction of their habitat; formal or informal apartheid; gender discrimination and abuses;[30] ghettoizing of communities by blocking the opportunity of social mixing and advancement, assigning them to subaltern statuses, and/or confining them in desolate geographic areas or fenced camps; and other forms of monstrous cruelties (e.g. denial of food, potable water, medicine and medical assistance, salubrious housing, etc.). Some of the most pernicious atrocities have occurred with general indifference or impunity, with authorities and civil society reneging on their moral-cum-legal obligations of assistance to people in distress.

Observance of 'universal fundamental values' is the acme of factors that move forward the wellbeing process. In modern times, these values are mostly encapsulated in the *Universal Declaration of Human Rights (UDHR)* that was consensually adopted by a vote of 48 in favour, eight abstentions, and none against at the UN General Assembly.[31] This complements the United Nations Charter whose primary purpose is to maintain international peace and security (art.1). UDHR is generally considered universally and morally superior to various legal corpuses, mores, traditions, or codes of conduct, past or present, and anywhere on Earth. UDHR is at the basis of *global development* and *wellbeing*. It specifically bars the exploitation of human beings, and calls on all authorities to protect the dignity of *all humans* (regardless of socio-economic status, gender, beliefs, ethnicity, culture, colour, or other differentiating factors). Its implementation has been nevertheless uneven and patchy among nations and communities.

The protection of *human dignity* is underlined in the very first sentence of the UDHR's preamble: 'Whereas recognition of the inherent dignity and of the equal and inalienable rights of all members of the human family is the foundation of freedom, justice and peace in the world…'. Also, article one of the UDHR highlights the fundamental timeless axiom that 'All human beings are born free and equal in dignity and rights'. One can therefore consider the maxim of *human dignity* (namely mutual respect for our shared humanity) to represent the bedrock foundation of our 'global wellbeing'. Many factors could hurt human dignity, chief among which are: war crimes and crimes against humanity, enslavement and subjugation, wanton cruelty, torture, cultural exclusion, gender discrimination, denial of basic needs (for food, health care, salubrious housing, education, work opportunities, etc.), and other cruelties.[32] UDHR's principles have been included in the constitutions of several states and have influenced international jurisprudence in such domains as justice, freedom, political representation, power devolution, equal opportunities, acceptance of cultural diversity, and the protection of planet Earth. The UDHR is the most overarching global code of ethical conduct. It is particularly notable for its universality by covering all humans, all generations, everywhere, and at all time. Yet several democratic countries claiming to have lofty humane values have in fact betrayed UDHR's principles on various occasions.

Best practices for UDHR's implementation have been enunciated in *Good Governance for the Protection of Human Rights*.[33] While generally recognized as a code of 'superior moral values', the UDHR's principles are not enforceable by any supranational authority across the world. Indeed, many governments and decision-makers give precedence to their sole egocentric interests in full equanimity, even if these trample on UDHR's principles. Certain parties espouse a neutral stand towards moral considerations. They question the reasons justifying the acceptance of UDHR, deemed a utopian vision of a homogeneous universal society. A few political leaders and thinkers openly or tacitly espouse a *realpolitik* approach.[34]

Some countries' constitutions even prefer to be essentially inspired and guided by their own religious-cultural-traditional values, some of which could be at variance with those of UDHR. This is the case of the Cairo Declaration of Human Rights in Islam (CDHRI), adopted on 5 August 1990 by the 45 member states of the Organization of the Islamic Conference (later renamed Organization of Islamic Cooperation). CDHRI gives precedence to *Shari'ah* (i.e. Koranic law) over UDHR. One should note that 'this declaration was conceived as universal for Muslims, although there are significant divides within that category along socioeconomic, ethnic, gender, sectarian, and other lines' – as reported by some researchers.[35]

A few Asian leaders (notably those of China, Singapore, and South Korea) have also questioned the UDHR's focus on individuals' rights ahead of states' rights. They 'defended authoritarian arrangements on the ground of their alleged effectiveness in promoting economic success … [although] systematic empirical studies give no real support to the claim that there is a conflict between political rights and economic performance'.[36]

Governments, civil society thinkers and activists, along with 'think tanks' organizations have also proposed ethical charters or codes of conduct. One can refer to the *Declaration Toward a Global Ethic* by the Parliament of the World's Religions (issued on 4 September 1993 in Chicago, U.S.A.); the *Manifesto of Global Economic Ethic – Consequences for Global Business* (launched on 6 October 2009 at the UN Headquarters in New York); and the Code of Globethics as approved by its Board of Foundation on 25 March 2017 in Geneva.[37] Moreover, several regimes, organized groups, or individuals have constructed their own legal-ethical codes of conduct independently from international conventions or codes. Some have opted to give 'spiritual', 'divine', or 'traditional' commandments absolute precedence over the UDHR.

Till today, rhetorically adhering to *human rights* principles has not prevented democratically elected politicians in certain intellectually sophisticated, technologically advanced, and culturally developed societies from transgressing these principles.[38] It is not uncommon to find in the twenty-first century so-called 'enlightened' parties that intentionally and remorselessly inflict on various communities or individuals inhumane degrading treatment, and authorize the liquidation of hapless civilian victims.[39]

The observance of 'universal fundamental values' in a given community (i) enhances the motivation of *economic agents* to create wealth, and (ii) fends off potential stalemates or conflicts among protagonists. Compliance with the UDHR standards can then serve to measure the ethical standing of governments, organizations, or individuals. Nevertheless, one should not belittle the difficulties encountered in establishing an index for 'fundamental universal values', mostly in view of the absence of comprehensive, objective, comparable, and reliable information. Moreover, as stated by a researcher on this subject, 'An overall measure cannot adequately reflect state performance on actions as diverse as providing universal primary education and avoiding torture'.[40]

To estimate the degree of observance of *universal human values* or *similar codes of ethical behaviour* by individual countries, communities, and/or institutions, researchers, think tanks, and governmental and non-governmental organizations have addressed this subject by building appropriate analytical tools.[41]

The evaluation of wellbeing is a delicate exercise especially with respect to such intangibles as the extent of free choice, fair justice, tolerance towards others, protection of human rights, or access to group solidarity. Indexes' methodologies regarding compliance with the UDHR have to be clearly presented to the scrutiny of researchers to ascertain the soundness of their assumptions and the accuracy of their calculations.[42] The shortcomings of indices could be due to one or more factors, such as irrelevance of data, doubtful or fragmented information, lacunas, inaccuracies, faked information, etc. One could complement the human rights' index with other indices, such as those on 'modern slavery' (www.globalslaveryindex.org/report/), on corruption (www.transparency.org), or on gender inequalities as proposed by the UNDP or the World Economic Forum (www.weforum.org).

Social *inclusiveness* can be considered a logical corollary for the observance of *fundamental human rights*. The *inclusiveness* feature calls for a reasonably level-playing field for all parties who partake equitably in economic, social, political, civic, and other matters. Effective *inclusiveness* unfurls into a web of balanced relationships with respect to sharing in responsibilities, risks, benefits, and burdens based on the *fair* treatment of all parties concerned (regardless of ethnicity, gender, age, race, culture, etc.). Stakeholders would then bond together to build institutions and adopt strategies that generate benefits to all parties, including the hitherto marginalized. By comparison, privilege for the few and discrimination against others would weaken community ties, enhance the risks of social upheavals, and undermine stability and prosperity for all.

The United Nations Declaration on the Right to Development (DRD) acknowledges the existence of fundamental links between *development* and the UDHR. The UDHR is considered fundamental, universal, and perennial for all humanity (that is not dependent on local or transient laws, customs, cultural backgrounds, or belief systems). These rights-cum-obligations are deemed vital to the wellbeing of all humans (notably respect for everyone's life; protection from barbaric practices of enslavement, torture or rape; freedom of expression, beliefs, and association; etc.), and are inalienable. Most modern states' constitutions and basic laws recognize UDHR, though few are those that observe scrupulously the enshrined principles.

Certain rights (such as the mandatory right to development or the right to work) do not command an unreserved consensus among member states of the United Nations system. For example, the Declaration on the Right to Development, adopted by the General Assembly resolution 41/128 on 4 December 1986, does not obligate wealthy states to commit resources to the development of poor states.[43]

A momentous event with respect to the protection of human rights through hunting down authors of heinous deeds (such as crimes against humanity) and bringing them to justice was the creation on 17 July 1998 of the permanent Hague-based *International Criminal Court*, ICC-CPI. Other ad-hoc *specific* international tribunals have been set-up to protect or do justice to victims of genocides[44] and other mass killings during armed conflicts or terrorist attacks in certain countries (e.g. ex-Yugoslav republics, Rwanda, Cambodia, Lebanon, etc.). Some specialized organizations are known for alleviating the suffering of victims of wars, despotic regimes, and natural calamities (for example, the *International Committee of the Red Cross* – ICRC; Médecins sans frontières, MSF; Amnesty International; Human Rights Watch; Oxfam; amongst others).

In modern times, several parties make use of the UDHR as a 'universal moral compass' for the evaluation of human behaviours and practices. That compass is premised on our shared humanity which is more fundamental than citizenship, or other affiliations. Nevertheless, the objective observer cannot naively consider that the clauses of the UDHR, such as the prohibition of torture, are universally implemented by signatory states. Several states that claim to be democratic and virtuous have occasionally failed to abide by UDHR principles which remain a compendium of ideal goals to which virtuous progress-minded individuals and societies generally aspire to reach.[45]

The principles enshrined in the UDHR have emphasized the vital importance of protecting human dignity. Respect for *human dignity* in a society offers the key fulcrum for *human development* (see Exhibit 1.3 below).

Exhibit 1.3 The tipping power of 'flouted dignity': the case of Tunisia

One could trace the origins of Tunisian discontent to the riots of 2008 in Tunisia's central region of Gafsa, which ran over several months. The large pool of unemployed (some 30 per cent of the adult population) had then protested peacefully against governmental corrupt practices of parcelling jobs in state-run phosphate mines in favour of cronies and henchmen, to the exclusion of well-qualified and deserving persons.[46]

The tipping point that ignited the spread of Arab revolts in the 2010s was the self-immolation tragedy on 17 December 2010 of Mohamed Bouazizi in Southern Tunisia. He had been harassed and bullied by agents of the local municipality for his so-called '*unauthorized*' peddling of his fruit-and-vegetable merchandise. He died on 4 January 2011 in excruciating pain. His ordeal, extensively covered by the media, lit the fuse of revolt in other Arab countries. The hitherto 'weak and meek' would not remain indefinitely docile under dictatorial regimes.[47] Tunisian tolerance for exploitation by despotic brutal regimes reached a paroxysm with the Bouazizi's suicidal action – itself preceded by less mediatized suicides of protesters seeking work opportunities and social justice.

Bouazizi was a destitute despairing person in quest of honest work to sustain his family with a decent livelihood. Orphaned by the death of his father at the age of three, he reportedly started working since the age of six in the agricultural town of Sidi Bouzid, to provide for his mother and her seven siblings. Forced to quit school at the age of 14, he became a pedlar of fresh produce of vegetables and fruits – without being able to afford to pay the fee of a work licence for that activity from municipal officials (who were prone to graft practices). Bouazizi was unremittingly harassed until the day when his produce, along with his cart and his pair of scales, were confiscated by the local police on that fateful day of 17 December 2010. Frequently scorned and vilified in public by venal officials, and dispossessed of an honest means of livelihood (for him and his family), utter anger and despair drove him to commit the irreversible act of self-immolation on that date; he died in extreme suffering a couple of weeks later, without any declared intent or desire to act as a revolutionary hero or martyr.[48]

Bouazizi's self-immolation was widely reported in the media and the social networks. His death sparked riots among the young (men and women), the poor, the unemployed, the intellectuals and artists, and the trade unionists – in Tunisia and beyond. That breaking point produced vast popular protests against the heavily policed regime of president Zine el-Abidine Ben Ali. To impose his autocratic rule, Ben Ali had manipulated the state apparatus (security services, state-owned enterprises, compliant tribunals, a venal monolithic bureaucracy, and others) aided by a circle of corrupt family members, subservient cronies, and parasitical sycophants. Official evidence has revealed the vast extent of President Ben Ali's plundering of the national economy for the self-serving interests of his family and acolytes.[49]

Tunisia's Truth and Dignity Commission created 9 June 2014 and headed by Ms. Sihem Ben Sedrine invited Tunisians who suffered abuse (torture, rape, maiming, murder of family members, etc.) under Ben Ali to air their grievances live on TV during three sessions (in November and December 2016, and in January 2017) to a panel of commissioners, and to representatives of national and international civic groups.[50]

Popular protests culminated on 14 January 2011 with the demise and escape of Ben Ali with his family overseas. For a scholar in international relations:

> Mohamed Bouazizi's act of setting himself on fire arose not only from the loss of his livelihood, but from feeling humiliated by the authorities. His act touched the experience of so many others in his social environment that it unleashed a storm of emotion in the public realm which brought thousands in the street and emboldened them to engage in acts of resistance. The brutalization of the state in response brought the everyday experience of humiliation into public view, while transforming it into an expression of dignity.[51]

The unfolding events following the tragic death of Bouazizi in Tunisia inspired numerous people in Arab countries ruled by despotic regimes; these included the oppressed or marginalized who sought jobs, allowing for a decent livelihood. His action prompted his likes to overcome the paralysis of fear from authoritarian regimes by demonstrating in favour of work, freedom, social justice, and dignity.

The young Tunisian democracy of the 2010s has had its ups and downs. Demonstrations have been generally peaceful until the assassination on 6 February 2013 of Chokri Belaid, a human rights lawyer and left-wing opponent of the Islamist-led government (under the aegis of the Ennahda party) that ruled after the collapse of the Ben Ali regime. Mr Belaid had frequently criticized the foregoing government of Ben Ali, as well as the Islamist-led Government of Ennahda. Some wayward revolutionaries of the post-Ben Ali era did commit heinous acts (such as the killing of foreign tourists in 2015), thereby undermining the stability and growth potential of the economy in which tourism represented 7 per cent of GDP. Corruption, nepotism, cronyism, and political exclusion have remained common practices. More Tunisian households have fallen into utter poverty, and social unrest among the unemployed population has continued to simmer until this book's publication.

Tunisia's democratic process, nevertheless, has survived and consolidated. Proponents of that process (Tunisian associations representing labour, business, human rights, and the legal profession) received the Nobel Peace Prize for 2015.

> The Quartet was formed in the summer of 2013 when the democratization process was in danger of collapsing as a result of political assassinations and widespread social unrest. It was thus instrumental in enabling Tunisia, in the space of few years, to establish a constitutional system of government guaranteeing fundamental rights for the entire population, irrespective of gender, political conviction or religious belief.[52]

The resilience of Tunisian democratic institutions will depend mainly on the growth in the economy, the eradication of corruption, and a fair sharing in national prosperity among all components of the Tunisian society. The nightmare of Tunisians in the 2010s has been the *risk of terrorism* (aiming at killing liberal politicians, foreign tourists, and security forces). That risk thrives among the destitute seeking 'work opportunities, social justice, and political participation'. The riots of January 2018 in Tunisia protested against the non-realization of this triad demonstrate the vulnerability of the Tunisian democracy in an environment of stagflation, exacerbated by budgetary austerity with a large pool of Tunisians seeking work.

Within the 'universal fundamental values' and besides the key role of *protecting human dignity*, one should mention *open sensitivity to spiritual values*. For an edifying example of the said openness, we analyse the case of a couple of Afro-European social entrepreneurs whose spirituality is underpinned by the core values of dedication to peace, enlightenment, tolerance, toil, and inclusiveness (see pp. 194–198).

Satisfying basic personal and social needs

Assuming the primordial conditions of peace and social harmony do exist, individuals' basic needs have to be adequately satisfied for the sake of enjoying a 'decent life'. The latter situation is premised on the availability of adequate resources that should enable individuals and groups to build-up and expand their potential capabilities.[53] Indeed, an individual cannot realize her/his potential of wellbeing to the full if she/he is deprived of adequate nutrition, salubrious shelter, health care, education and training, positive inter-personal/social links, and decent employment opportunities. Among the currently deprived, many could flourish to become notable contributors to science, art, business, or other fields of human achievements – once their basic needs are reasonably met.

There is no paradox in the fact that a country can rank among the highest in the world for *childhood malnutrition*, namely India, and boast equally *cutting-edge scientific-technological expertise* capable of launching on 5 November 2013 a spacecraft to Mars. Freed from malnutrition, illness, and ignorance, hitherto marginalized Indians (and other communities trapped in poverty) could then enhance their capabilities and ultimately their wellbeing. Such freedom from want would indeed enable the concerned individuals to stoke dormant talents in all wakes of life available to them. The pretence of *stupidity* or *incompetence* attributed to poor people is far from true. Poor parents are unable to offer their children good educations, and these children cannot access stable and well-paid jobs. Moreover, their low incomes expose them often to vulnerable health conditions or insalubrious precarious living conditions.[54]

Health and socio-economic development are considered the vital twin factors of wellbeing. This is the definitive conclusion of researchers in the field who stated:

> As contributors [to a research project] have emphatically shown, health and development are synergistically connected. The health status of a population in any place influences the economic and social development of the region; so too, development initiatives can offer the economic traction needed to introduce health-enhancing interventions such as better sanitation or more widespread immunisation or health promotion.[55]

Unless a person is not deprived of a satisfactory access to resources to meet her/his basic biological and social needs, their *latent capabilities* are likely to remain dormant. Measured by multidimensional criteria, Sabina Alkire and Maria Emma Santos have proposed an index for acute poverty, based on three areas and their subcategories. They are: *health* comprising levels of child mortality and nutrition (equally weighted at 1/6); *education* comprising years of schooling, and child enrolment (equally weighted at 1/6); and *standard of living* comprising electricity, drinking water, sanitation, flooring, cooking fuel, and assets – equally weighted at 1/18.[56]

Besides basic biological needs, humans seek to satisfy their emotional needs. The latter comprise feelings of harmony, empathy, and/or affection vis-à-vis other humans – notably at the level of the family, the working environment, and more generally the community within which they live. Once the primary basic needs are reasonably satisfied, people can aspire to realize their potential capabilities, in order 'to lead the kind of lives they value' – using Sen's own wording, and assuming that what 'they value' does not hurt others' fundamental rights. Resource deprivation along with serious physical, psychic, emotional, and mental ailments constrain human beings' chances of enhancing their wellbeing.

The basic needs of individuals vary greatly. The benchmarks for the optimal satisfaction of an individual's needs (e.g. for food intake) could be influenced by personal intrinsic conditions of the individual (such as her/his health), as well as by geographic conditions (temperate, cold, hot, tropical, or arid) and the socio-cultural environment. This was eloquently expressed by Amartya K. Sen as follows:

> The need for income to achieve any specified living conditions can, in fact, vary greatly with various physiological, social, cultural, and other contingent features. For example, to reach the same level of nutrition as another, one needs a larger command over food if one has a higher metabolic rate (or a larger body frame), or if one is pregnant (or breast feeding), or if one has a disease that makes absorption more difficult, or if one lives in a colder climate, or if one has to toil a lot, or if food has other uses (such as for entertainment or festivals).[57]

Underpinned by an appropriate income redistribution policy and governmental investment programs in 'infrastructure for civic renewal', the hitherto deprived can overcome the root causes of their poverty. They should then be enabled to break through the vicious circle of poverty by being able to provide good education for their children, take care of their health, health care, and access salubrious living conditions. Such support for the destitute could be shored up by 'conditional cash transfers'. It has been demonstrated that 'the biggest conditional transfers (Brazil's Bolsa Familia and Mexico's Oportunidas) are credited with cutting poverty and boosting literacy in Latin America's largest countries for tens of millions'.[58] Such 'conditional cash transfers' can trigger the willingness of distressed people to exit their poverty traps.

Through his pamphlet on *Agrarian Justice* (1797), Thomas Paine (1737–1809), became one of the leading political philosophers and revolutionary activists to have cogently argued in favour of universal and long-term solidarity among humans. He advocates in his *Agrarian Justice* pamphlet that every human being has an equal legitimate right to the earth's bounties. This would come in the form of a basic universal guaranteed minimum income, and an old-age pension. He called on governments to:

> ... create a national fund, out of which there shall be paid to every person regardless of her/his condition, when arrived at the age of twenty-one years, the sum of fifteen pounds sterling ($2,000 in U.S. dollar terms in 2015, equivalent to half the annual earnings of a farm labourer in England and Wales in 1797), as a compensation in part, for the loss of his or her natural inheritance, by the introduction of the system of landed property. And also, the sum of ten pounds (about $1,333 in U.S. dollars) per annum, during life, to every person now living, of the age of fifty years, and to all others as they shall arrive at that age.[59]

For the sake of social justice and social cohesion, one would expect welfare payments through safety nets for those living in wretched conditions. The reasons for satisfying basic needs by lessening inequalities have been clearly expressed thus:

> ... there are further reasons that we should be concerned about growing inequality than just a sense of social justice. It can lead to increased political and social instability. There is, moreover, a growing understanding, even within the IMF, that inequalities may lead to lower economic growth, more economic instability, and a weaker economy.[60]

Besides satisfying one's basic needs, personality characteristics impact *wellbeing*. These characteristics cover inter alia introversion vs extroversion, sobriety vs exuberance, neuroticism vs evenness, emotional volatility vs equanimity, stable vs unstable biological conditions, and other inherent or acquired psychological/physiological/physical characteristics. Moreover, professional occupations can also influence wellbeing. Thus unskilled routinely-run risky physical activities – e.g. in the industries of construction or mining works – generally rank in *satisfaction/wellbeing/happiness*[61] below the reflective or inventive ones – e.g. academic or technological research. Marital status can have also its impact on wellbeing, with married status topping cohabitation, being single, separated, divorced, or widowed.[62]

Expanding knowledge and capabilities

In their pursuit of *wellbeing*, humans are generally guided by personal and/or collective *goals*. Their wellbeing will then be raised by a process that combines (1) the enhancement and the diversification of *individuals' capabilities*, along with (2) the productive *matching of these capabilities with opportunities* that dovetail with people's *competencies and desiderata*. Such matching will

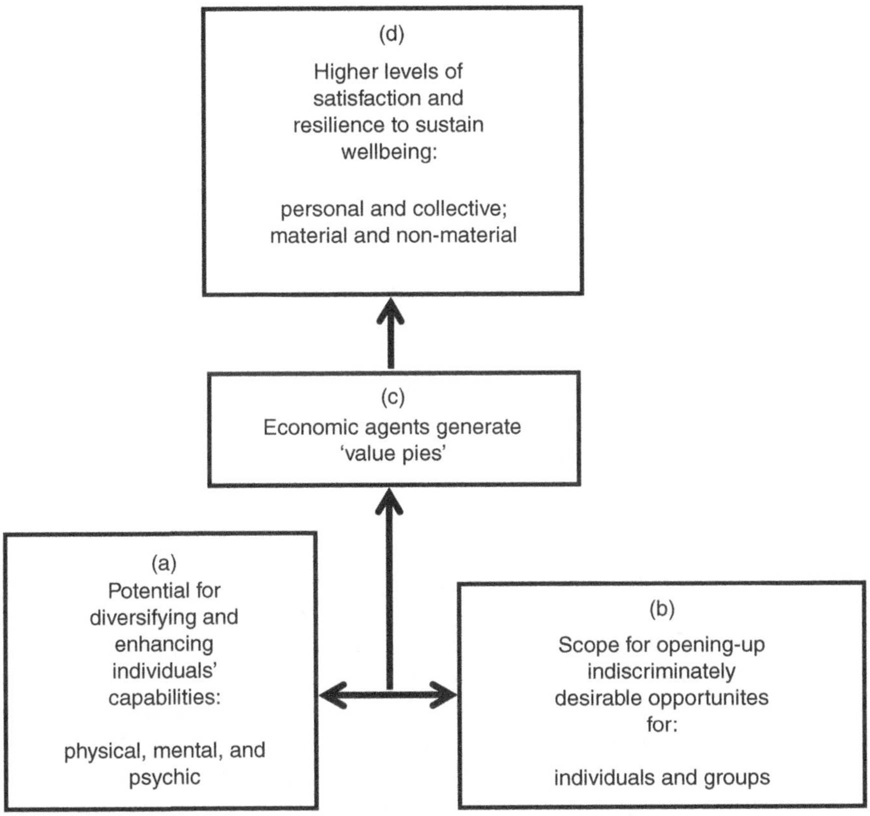

Exhibit 1.4 Capabilities and opportunities: links to wellbeing.

Source: author.

Notes
Value Creation and *Wellbeing improvements* are the product of a binary process that enhances *capabilities* (a) in tandem with the expansion of desirable and available *opportunities* (b).[63] The outcome of the joint synergetic functioning of (a) and (b) leads to the generation of 'value pies' (c) and eventually to improvements in *wellbeing* (d).

raise the 'value pies' created by economic agents. The split of gains from the said value pies among economic agents or community members will depend on the bargaining power of protagonists (e.g. employers/owners vs trade unions/employees), the socio-economic policies of public authorities, and/or the governance of rulers.

It is vital for the wellbeing of a community to build up capabilities for its members along with opening up opportunities. Human development through 'quality education' at all levels is crucial for that purpose. Reputable institutions of learning, in various parts of the world, need to be more readily accessible – regardless of wealth or relation to centres of power – to enable people to realize their potential.[64]

The democratization of learning – along with the development of research, training, and extension programs – figure importantly in unlocking opportunities for value-creation to a wide range of people. The cross-fertilization of ideas is a source of progress, and contributes to an expanding kit of know-how that offers – when put to productive use – opportunities for innovation and wealth creation. The overall wellbeing of society should then improve – assuming that the hitherto excluded or marginalized have access to these opportunities. Nevertheless, analysts' research has reproached reputed centres of learning for privileging the wealthy and the well-connected in their admissions of new students. As per an academic researcher (senior fellow at the Century Foundation) of on this subject in the United States, Richard D. Kahlenberg, 'the dirty secret of elite colleges is that all the positive talk about the importance of racial diversity, low-income students of all races are essentially shut out'.[65]

The pursuit of knowledge could well be for its own sake, without the knowledge-seeker being eager for lucre. Several academic institutions extolled knowledge and wisdom with logos such as *Sapientia et Felicitate* or *Knowledge is felicity*.[66] An open access to *know-how* and *culture* in a context of universal inclusion and tolerance can serve as a vital conduit for cross-fertilization of ideas and eventual emancipation from poverty traps.

Avenues to knowledge and its applications are multiple, and several branches of learning have been developed over the last few millennia, with many scholars worldwide contributing. They comprise disciplines or sub-disciplines that dovetail to fill in lacunas. To obtain a better understanding of complex and changing reality, greater trans-disciplinary porosity offers several advantages. It is bound to help us widen our perspectives, deepen our comprehension of complex phenomena, enable us to view things in their relative importance, and help us avoid *partial* or *skewed* interpretations that could lead to flawed judgements and faulty decisions. Such a multi-disciplinary approach provides us with several 'tool boxes' potentially valuable in decompartmentalizing analyses, and opening-up new perspectives for creativity of global significance. Venturing beyond one's area of specialization or expertise into unchartered territories could produce ingenious ideas or insights.

As eloquently put by a mathematician and professor of Public Understanding of Science:

> Rather like the brain which shows extraordinary integration to create that sense of one identity out of many millions of neurons, the way to crack the big problems is not to use ideas from a single discipline, but to integrate modes of thinking from across disciplines.[67]

Research centres, such as the Oxford Martin School (United Kingdom) and the Santa Fe Institute (United States) host a variety of talents with polyvalent functions that use different approaches and tools of analysis. Insatiable curiosity and discussions among researchers hailing from different intellectual backgrounds stimulate creativity.[68]

Many phenomena are too complex and indecipherable to be explained by sole reliance on a single analytical approach. Indeed, in comprehending and solving any of the world's complex problems and/or in creating value out of potential opportunities, pervious multidisciplinary approaches that break down the silo-like separateness of disciplines, become necessary. For economists, some disciplines (namely psychology, neuroscience, anthropology, and others) offer valuable analytical tools for the advancement of knowledge; their decompartmentalization could spark to serendipitous discoveries.

Although integrating multiple tools and approaches to decode and solve complex conundrums is a challenging endeavour, the potential rewards for pursuing that path are superior to the alternative of concentrating solely on probing particular aspects of such problems. As pointedly expressed by one connoisseur of this domain, HIA (health impact assessment) within an EIA (environmental impact assessment) has been described as:

> ... an ideal platform to assess the potential health impacts of development actions ... It encourages people to look at impacts of developments and policies as a whole (covering besides the impact on the environment, other impacts: sustainability, social issues, economic and business issues, human rights, gender, law and order, equality, etc.) rather than think in their professional silos. It avoids the need for staff to answer the same questions in several separate impact assessments and reduces the risk of '*impact assessment fatigue*'. It insures that consistent methods and assumptions are used for all types of assessment. It allows health staff to make alliances with those interested in other types of assessment rather than competing with them for priority. Finally, it allows the decisions which do not raise major health issues to be rapidly dealt with while the few where health impacts are a major issue can be identified.[69]

Thanks to the eagerness to know (with an open-minded questioning of existing hypotheses or postulates) and the continued scientific investigation of various domains using more adapted tools, the frontiers of human ignorance or opacity are likely to recede. Nevertheless, humans are constrained or bounded by the human species' mental-physical-psychic-sensorial constitution. Indeed, some living creatures could have certain senses that are absent in the human species. This is the case of homing pigeons that are able to hear very-low-frequency sound waves, and are able to navigate by the sun and by the Earth's magnetic field.[70] Given their constitution, humans do have 'blind spots' (i.e. domains that cannot be directly apprehended under existing circumstances); such blind spots deny humans direct knowledge of phenomena that elude their senses and/or intellectual comprehension. Nevertheless, humans can overcome limitations in the reach of their senses by resorting to indirect tools that their intelligence is capable of producing. This was expressed eloquently by John Hands as follows:

> ... While humans may have some characteristics that are superior to those of other species such as large brains and manual dexterity, other species have their own superior characteristics. Thus bats are superior echolocators, birds are superior navigators, and so on for other species ... While humans may not be good echolocators, they invented radar, which performs that function for them. While humans may not be good navigators, they have invented the Global Positioning System that provides them with precise navigation capability. It is difficult to think of any superior animal characteristic the function of which has not been enabled for humans by their creativity and invention. No other species has transcended its natural physiological characteristics in this way.[71]

Scientific truths can:

> ... change with and according to our increasing knowledge and shifting perspective ... Consequently, scientists talk mainly about relative truth. So does everyone, all the time. But absolute Truth is a whole different matter. It is beyond temporality, beyond the world, and ultimately immutable. God, moral law, and ultimate reality are all expressions of Truth.[72]

Scientists and technicians can indeed enrich over time their tool kits of instruments that enable them to grasp *directly* or *indirectly* multiple aspects of vast domains that have so far eluded them. These tools have been used for example in various realms, stretching from astronomy and cosmology to that of the infinitely small (for example the Higgs boson particles). Nevertheless, certain domains – such as metaphysics – are likely to remain inaccessible *scientifically* to the human mind.[73]

Knowledge's potency is evident: its applications can be used to serve progress, or conversely to destroy wealth and life. For some scholars, 'poor countries are poor because those who have power make choices that create poverty. They get it wrong not by mistake or ignorance but on purpose.'[74] The pursuit of knowledge needs therefore to be protected against its misuse. Ethical watchdogs are often elected or sponsored by professional associations (e.g. in the medical professions) with the aim of protecting against dangerous drifts.

Although fundamentally *equal in dignity*, humans are, nevertheless, *not equal in capability*, *opportunity*, or *resilience*. Investments that prop up the capabilities of individuals and foster their resilience contribute to their wellbeing.[75] The actual or potential capability and resilience vary considerably among peoples, for multiple reasons. These reasons belong to personal factors (physical, mental, psychic, and emotional factors) as well as to opportunities available to humans in their respective socio-economic-political environments.

Capability enhancement increases the scope for humans to make choices based on sound judgement and for implementing appropriately their decisions. The 'capability' approach of Amartya Sen comprises a person's entire capabilities of freedoms to lead their lives as they *deem good or valuable* to them among the set of options they can access. In Sen's words,

> A person's 'capability' refers to the alternative combinations of functionings that are feasible for her to achieve. Capability is thus a kind of freedom: the substantive freedom to achieve alternative functioning combinations … For example, an affluent person who fasts may have the same functioning achievement in terms of eating or nourishment as a destitute person who is forced to starve, but the first person does have a different 'capability set' than the second (the first can choose to eat well and be well nourished in a way the second cannot).[76]

Besides the '*affluent person who chooses freely to fast*', one can also illustrate the concept of *capability* by reference to a rich person who chooses *freely* to live modestly. This is the case of a Canadian couple (Allen and Violet Large, 74 and 78 years old respectively) who won the equivalent of US$10.9 million in July 2010 in a lottery and gave away $10.2 million to philanthropic organizations. The couple had the *capability* of living more opulently, but they chose to continue their non-ostentatious modest life.[77] Their *ethical/spiritual satisfaction* (as spontaneous-cum-low-profile philanthropic donors) appears to exceed their eventual *material pleasure* of using their windfall wealth in additional personal material comfort or consumption. Other philanthropists (whether institutions or individuals) are not disinterested; they look for ostentatious publicity for themselves, and some may seek to cover up their past misdeeds or questionable sources of their wealth.

We can consider that the *process of development* consists of raising the capabilities of humans, and expanding their choices of things they value best. Obstacles or handicaps to free choice (referred to by Sen as 'un-freedoms', [*sic*]) can be lifted through appropriate socio-economic-political development. A Human Development Index (HDI) was originally introduced in 1990 as a composite indicator of the level of social and economic development. Constructed by Amartya Sen and Mahbub ul Haq for the United Nations Development Programme's Reports, it is prepared annually for surveyed member countries using (a) average life expectancy at birth, (b) educational attainment (adult literacy rate and mean years of schooling), and (c) real Gross National Income (GNI) per capita. All three components are equally weighed. Two of its components, life expectancy at birth and educational attainment, represent long-term *capabilities*. The 'GDP per capita' that was originally used has been replaced in later years by the measure of 'real GNI per capita' which reflects more accurately changes in the levels of standard of living. HDI should be considered as a rough shortcut proxy for the level of human development (see: www.undp.org). On the basis of HDI, Indian Economist Amartya Sen has developed his 'capability approach' regarding what people are able to *be* and *do* things they desire. The 2010 Human Development Report introduced an Inequality-adjusted Human Development Index (IHDI).

The HDI index has been fine-tuned by enlarging its components and sharpening their measurement, and by disaggregating national groups into sub-groups in order to reveal the different conditions and levels of human development within any given country – for example by reference to relative income, geographical or administrative regions, urban vs rural residence, gender, or ethnicity.[78]

Some scholars have considered Amartya Sen's version of the capability approach as 'inadequate', in so far as its telos focuses on the 'individual living well'. They call for a modified telos of 'living well together' which:

> includes consideration of social structures and institutions that enable people to pursue individual freedoms in relation to others. The policy significance of the capability approach can be further strengthened by paying greater consideration to the political economy of policy-decision making processes and the ways in which conflicts and distributions of power are institutionalized.[79]

Martha C. Nussbaum argues that:

> Given a widely shared understanding of the task of government (namely, that government has the job of making people able to pursue a dignified and minimally flourishing life), it follows that a decent political order must secure to all citizens a least a threshold level of these ten Central Capabilities.

She summarizes the latter as follows: a normal length life; bodily health; bodily integrity; being able to use senses, imagination, and thought; being able to have attachments to things and people outside ourselves; being able to form a conception of the good and to engage in critical reflection about the planning of one's life; being able to live with and towards others, and having the social bases of self-respect and non-humiliation; being able to live with concern for other species; being able to participate in political choices, and to have equal rights in holding property.[80]

Capabilities standards

Capabilities' development of individuals consists of the education/training process that kindles dormant talents. Nevertheless, there are limits to such enhancement, since no human being is perfectible (physically, emotionally, mentally, morally, spiritually, aesthetically, or otherwise). We are constrained by our innate natural/biological conditions, and by complex other factors acquired or encountered during our life in the context of our socio-physical environment. These factors cover non-rational *behaviours* (e.g. *addictions* to toxic products, games, and other high-risk activities) and human rights' abuses. Indeed, some individuals could derive pleasure from physical, psychic, or mental torturing of innocent persons – driven by envy, fanaticism, sadism, or other base sentiments. They delight in *schadenfreude* (in lieu of feeling compassion or empathy) or rejoice in inflicting gratuitous *pain* on others without any remorse. Such irrational, heinous or morbid behaviours are an integral part of some humans with an intrinsically deviant nature. Researchers and decision-makers need to continuously examine, monitor, and control malefic behaviours in order to avoid their disastrous impact on society and the natural environment.

The differentiation between 'healthy' conditions versus 'troubled' or 'pathological' conditions is constantly evolving, and has been a subject of debate and controversy. For the run of the mill individuals, *normal* patterns of behaviour are diverse and are generally influenced by differing mores and environments. Frontiers between the *normal* and the *anormal* or *pathological* conditions of individuals are often tenuous, porous, blurred, and far from being clear cut. Indeed, these frontiers as set by professionals have changed over time, and are likely to change in the future. Individuals may have characteristics that belong to both categories, the *normal* and the *anormal*. Users of evanescent pleasures (for example through stimulants or euphoric products) can become addictive, with serious negative side-effects on their personal condition and their social relations. Intemperance and addiction inevitably lead to grave disorderly behaviours, acute health problems, and premature death. The affected individuals thus fail to function in their 'long-term best interest'. Such persons' deleterious behaviour makes them go downhill and ends their life prematurely. They are also very likely to burden their families or friends, as well as society at large.

Several analysts have attempted to define norms of healthy, normal or rational behaviour. Indeed, establishing a rigid dichotomy between the 'healthy' and the 'non-healthy' in human behaviour cannot be done without subtle nuances, and is bound to evolve along with our know-how and the zeitgeist of society.[81] Certain individuals could be handicapped at birth (for example due to genetic reasons); others could become disabled later on during any phase in their life cycle for other reasons (such as accidents, illnesses, geographical environments, or socio-political impediments). Even wide differences can exist between parents and siblings.

Paranormal factors – such as a natural inclination for violence, hatred or domination – are part of human nature's grim side. Flawed decisions in governmental institutions, various business professions, or other activities can be a source of calamity. The timely identification of these persons could help society ward off their potential blunders or misdeeds. To the extent that their wayward behaviour is incorrigible, they constitute sources of danger for themselves, for their communities, and/or for society at large. Indeed, so many political leaders have been responsible for horrendous crimes and genocides for which they have had no remorse. In business activities, several have been responsible for accidents which could have been avoided were those in command enjoying sound judgement. Some professions call for the close scrutiny and evaluation by respected accredited gatekeepers (such as medical doctors, independent civic rights representatives, ethical boards' delegates, vetted national regulators, etc.). Citizens of certain democratic states have sought and obtained from their political leaders the requirement of disclosing periodically the 'state of health' of their leaders. Their aim is to verify the capacity of these leaders to exercise their high responsibilities with equanimity.

Among risky activities, one could mention transporters of passengers (by air, sea, or land). For an illustration, the European media widely reported on the deliberate destruction of a German airliner on 24 March 2015 by its copilot Andreas Lubitz who had locked out the senior pilot after he had left momentarily the cockpit to the passengers' side of the plane. Lubitz is accused of deliberately crashing the Germanwings Airbus, killing 150 persons on a steep mountainside of the French Alps. The copilot reportedly was suffering then from depression with suicidal inclinations. Treating doctors did not communicate to management or to the concerned regulatory authorities his health situation (for reasons of medical confidentiality?!) despite the potential dangers of his suicidal tendencies. Lubitz successfully managed to hide his medical problems from his superiors, and very few were apparently well informed about his psychic vulnerability.

The perennially moot question remains 'what criteria to use in defining and judging *normality*'. Put differently, is the maverick or 'black swan' necessarily anormal or paranormal? In order to reach a full understanding of phenomena relating to human behaviours, a cross-disciplinary approach could serve to improve our grasp of normality.[82]

Heterogeneous, complex, arcane, or ambivalent mixtures of feelings (the noble and despicable) could co-exist consciously or unconsciously within the psyche of many individuals. Besides intrinsic personal characteristics or idiosyncrasies, multiple external factors of differing importance exercise their influence on human behaviour. These factors belong to: family or clan; mores and traditions; doctrinaire ideologies; education and culture; work versus leisure time; community relations and politics; the media; systems of beliefs; and others. Noble sentiments – such as *friendship*, *sympathy* or *altruism* – could well alternate or rival with egotistic interests in a jigsaw of abstruse ambivalence within the same person.[83] Obviously, the Manichean interpretation of human nature oversimplifies complex reality.

Contemporary thinkers have tended to lean towards one of the following two main streams of views on human nature – that of the *realists* vis-à-vis that of the *liberals*. As summed-up by Andrew Heywood, in the *realists'* view:

> ... the essential core of human nature is fixed and given, fashioned by 'nature' (biological or genetic factors) rather than by 'nurture' (the

influence of education or social factors generally) … Liberals have a broadly optimistic view of human nature … Humans are self-seeking and largely self-reliant creatures, but they are also governed by reason and are capable of personal self-development … By contrast with the realist image of humans as ruthless power maximizers, liberals emphasize that there is a moral dimension to human nature, most commonly reflected in the doctrine of human rights.[84]

Promoting cultures

Among the key building blocks of wellbeing for an individual or a community are *cultures*. Cultural works (literary, music, plastic arts, monuments, etc.) represent sources of 'creative wealth' that produce subjective enjoyment. It is, however, difficult to estimate their commercial value.

The importance of culture for the wellbeing of people has been recognized by many communities, countries, and international organizations (such as the United Nations Educational, Scientific, and Cultural Organization – UNESCO). In promoting culture, Italy and France offer two different models. The erstwhile Italian Prime Minister Matteo Renzi had offered the young Italians born in 1998, and for two years beginning in 2016 and ending in 2017 'cultural tickets' free of charge for all types of artistic or cultural events. French President Emmanuel Macron, as confirmed by his Prime Minister Edouard Philippe, promised each young French person 500 euro on the day of her/his reaching the age of 18 years. The money can be spent on fees for museums, historical monuments, shows, concerts, movies, books, musicals and other artistic/cultural events. The funding of the Italian scheme came totally from the state budget, whereas the French model is largely funded by the distributors and the social networks (Google, Apple, Facebook, Amazon, etc.).[85]

At the apogee of their prosperity, various socio-political groups have built up notable seats of learning and scholarship boasting richly endowed libraries consisting of outstanding collections of know-how, art works, and artefacts. Their curators took care of gathering erudite works, whether produced by nationals or others, and of preserving such works for transmission to future generations. Seats of learning and culture had existed since ancient times and had sought to expand, conserve, and diffuse knowledge and artistic works in various domains. Indeed, beginning with the 3rd millennium BC, the treasures of knowledge have covered historical chronicles, hymns, poems, scientific and religious texts, commercial annals, and other mementoes. They were recorded in the Sumerian and Akkadian languages on clay tablets (using the cuneiform alphabet) by the kingdoms of Babylon, Uruk, and Nippur.[86]

Other centres of cosmopolitan scholarship and learning (ancient or modern) had collected, and actively developed and spread know-how. This was the case of Alexandria's famed Royal Ptolemaic Library, founded in the third century BC Bayt al-Hikma [or House of Wisdom] was another case of a global hub of comprehensive knowledge. It consisted of a library that hosted intellectual works of various civilizations, a translation institute, and a research-cum-teaching centre. Founded in Baghdad in the eighth century AD during the Golden Age of the Abbassid dynasty (notably during the reign of Harun al-Rashid [AD 786–809] and further developed by his son al-Ma'mun [who reigned over [AD 813–833]), it boasted then the largest repository of literary and scientific books in the world (in the fields of humanities, mathematics, astronomy, medicine, chemistry, zoology, geography, cartography, and the arts. Following the Mongol invasion and the siege of Baghdad led by Hulagu Khan in AD 1258, Bayt al-Hikma was vandalized, looted, burned and destroyed. The Mongol's scorched-earth invasion of the Middle East broke-up brutally the Abbasside realm at the height of its cultural splendour.

Causes for the ruin of once flourishing communities or civilizations are not limited to (i) *internal oppressions and/or dissensions* that could tear-up the social tissue, and/or (ii) *external aggressions*. Adverse situations could also include natural *environmental causes* – such as chronic droughts, flooding, hurricanes or earthquakes. Descendants of ruthless conquerors could turn later on into 'civilized' rulers who greatly appreciate cultural creativity. This had happened with the brutal scorched-earth Mongol invaders whose descendants formed in later years, in the Indian sub-continent and beyond, the culturally-rich and sophisticated Mogul Empire with its multiple luminous dynasties ruling from the sixteenth till mid-nineteenth centuries: these dynasties allowed for the peaceful and harmonious cross-fertilization of diverse traditions and cultures (drawing on Mongolian, Turkic, Persian, Hindu, Urdu, and Arab cultures).

Needless to say, the wilful destruction or looting of antiquities, ancient manuscripts, artefacts and historic monuments has continued unabated across the ages by predators and aggressors in different regions of the world, and until the twenty-first century. Among the motives for such actions, one can mention the desire to subjugate other humans and obliterate their culture, vandalism, bigotry, venal illicit trading in stolen artefacts, and other ignominious motives.[87] Existing vestiges of ancient famous cities, temples and monuments built over the past millennia stand witness to flourishing past civilizations that were destroyed by various calamities, among which one could single out notably protracted ruinous wars.

As historical events have shown, democratic systems are fragile and can be easily overwhelmed by authoritarian leaders of different backgrounds (e.g. autocrats, oligarchs, plutocrats, aristocrats, theocrats, etc.). Among contemporary thinkers, Francis Fukuyama warns that:

> No one living in an established liberal democracy should therefore be complacent about the inevitability of its survival. There is no automatic historical mechanism that makes progress inevitable, or that prevents decay and backsliding. Democracies exist and survive only because people want and are willing to fight for them ...[88]

Husbanding resources and protecting the natural environment

A community's wellbeing cannot be extricated from its setting. *Setting* is defined here to include multiple dimensions. These dimensions cover geography and other conditions (social, geopolitical, historical, cultural, family, work relations, political systems, etc.). The foregoing factors have a potentially significant impact on the wellbeing of individuals and the society in which they live.

Analysts, researchers, policy- and decision-makers need to examine the multiple different layers of settings that influence individuals or communities. They can then formulate and implement relevant and appropriate measures that could render settings more hospitable and productive. Researchers have found that 'levels of relational, organizational and communal well-being, as measured by different methods and indicators, have a potent influence on the well-being of a particular individual'.[89]

Some settings are unchangeable or slightly changeable if judged by reference to the time horizon of an individual's life cycle (e.g. settings dictated by geography-cum-climate of a country and/or its endowment in natural resources), while others are amenable to transformation thanks to the effective commitment of the people concerned. Among the remarkable transformations of settings, one could refer to the Netherlands which has expanded its liveable and productive national territory by gaining land at the expense of the sea, protected by dykes and barrages. Its low-lying territory (below sea level) has currently reached about one quarter of the country's total land surface.

Settings, if properly organized and operated, are conducive to the wellbeing of individuals and their communities.[90] Health settings, as defined by the World Health Organization (WHO), stands for:

> The place and social context in which people engage in daily activities in which environmental, organizational and personal factors interact to affect health and wellbeing … where people actively use and shape the environment and thus create or solve problems relating to health. Settings can normally be identified as having physical boundaries, a range of people with defined roles, and an organizational structure.[91]

Referring specifically to the Earth's crust, some countries have large commercial supplies of economically valuable natural resources (such as arable land, forests, minerals, oil and gas, water, gems, etc.) while others have mostly arid or barren lands improper to economic exploitation. Benefits from natural resources could be considerable, assuming that (a) both the national regulatory authorities and operators (foreign or domestic) adopt wise strategies in managing these resources for the benefit of current and future generations, and that (b) these resources are not subject to the covetousness of powerful foreign predatory interests (that could operate with the complicity of local corrupt influent parties). Autocratic rulers have tended to waste their country's wealth on such operations as (i) 'white elephant' projects that glorify rulers, (ii) accumulation of excessive military arsenals, (iii) fuelling and/or intervening in external conflicts, (iv) burdening their populations with confiscatory taxation, (v) resorting to graft and/or coercion in order to muzzle and loot their populations.

Upon the discovery of the Americas and other territories, and possibly until the Industrial Revolution era, many thinkers and policy-makers considered 'Nature' a boundless resource. Conquerors and their communities could then have access to pristine land to exploit for profit without constraint, as it was then *plentiful*. Moreover, pollution was limited and of little concern. As such, nature was deemed practically an inexhaustible resource to be *freely exploited* – often disregarding the legitimate rights of indigenous populations. Today, practically all the Earth's resources (whether exploited or not) are known. The supply of arable land, sub-soil minerals, liveable habitat, clean air, and water cannot be considered limitless.

Most if not all of the Earth's resources are subject to depletion[92] or deterioration. They require the husbanding (i.e. the prudent and efficient management, exploitation or conservation) of planet Earth's finite resources. Nature cannot cope fully with the process of absorbing sizeable wastes, often toxic, generated by human activities. Polluting factors have therefore to be abated, and eventually neutralized if salubrious living conditions on planet Earth are to be protected perennially for the benefit of humans and other living creatures over the very long term.

Husbanding the Earth's resources requires therefore appropriate planning focusing on families, communities, and territories that protect healthy sober living conditions on planet Earth. Global *wellbeing* includes the protection of biodiversity, and more generally 'nature's living creatures',[93] as enunciated in the *UN Guiding Principles on Business and Human Rights*.[94] These guidelines have also been adopted in the *OECD Guidelines for Multinational Enterprises* dated 25 May 2011.[95] *Not-for-profit* institutions have been established to protect living creatures on planet Earth, in a harmonious relation between humans and non-humans. Indeed, humans who are currently 'masters of nature' should avoid predation pressure on their natural environment, lest they harm their own quality of life and possibly their existence.[96]

Exhibit 1.5 Protecting bio-diversity

International conventions (e.g. the Action Programme of the Convention on Biological Diversity adopted at the United Nations Conference of Nagoya-Japan, held on 29 October 2010) need treaty-like political commitment by signatory countries, enforcement through accredited agencies, and funding in relation to monitoring and controlling. Otherwise, their recommendations would remain vacuous lip service. Biting accountability and effective remedial actions need therefore to apply to deforestation, over-fishing, poaching, water/land/air pollution, protection of coral reefs, and preservation of animal and plant species. Polluters should pay for, or carry out clean-ups. Highly polluting activities whose damages are irreparable should be barred, and be subject to prosecution.

Animals (whether domesticated or not) have indeed been subjected to questionable practices (e.g. cruel treatment, industrial rearing in limited spaces, or forced feeding to increase their productivity – see the Universal Declaration of Animal Rights, proclaimed in Paris on 15 October 1978 at the UNESCO headquarters). Some persons have become vegetarian to avert their being involved in animal suffering through inconsiderate slaughtering for personal consumption or use. In the field of rights, thinkers and policy-makers have generally 'ordered' rights within a hierarchy which prioritizes humans over other living creatures. Though not endowed with consciousness, intelligence or reason comparable to humans, many categories of living creatures are sentient and experience *feelings* or *sensations*.

The European Union's Lisbon Treaty, effective since 1 December 2009, has recognized that animals are 'sentient beings'. In an article of the Treaty, it states:

> ... the Union and the Member States shall, since animals are sentient beings, pay full regard to the welfare requirements of animals, while respecting the legislative or administrative provisions and customs of the Member States relating in particular to religious rites, cultural traditions and regional heritage.

The hierarchy and degrees of sentience among diverse animals has yet to be accurately established.

With the rise in the popular sentiment for the protection of animals in Europe, the wanton killing of domestic animals has been sanctioned by the judiciary. One could mention the conviction of a 28-year old French recidivist in the ill-treatment of animals to a six-month firm imprisonment for killing a cat, along with prohibiting him from owning any animal in the future.[97]

Wastes from human activities and/or the use of unsafe new technologies (e.g. in nuclear power plants) have hurt neighbouring communities and condemned their lands to become sterile and uninhabitable by various species. One should add that past testing of nuclear weapons had already irradiated vast territories rendering them permanently dangerous for centuries, while debilitating the health of communities residing close-by and exposed to high levels of radiation. Nuclear weapons, along with other radio-active, toxic or poisonous products, could proliferate among belligerent nations or illegal groups; they could be used to inflict irreversible lethal damage on all living creatures and destroy hitherto fertile ecosystems of planet Earth. The use of these dangerous products is deemed in effect akin to an *ecological crime*.

Among the unwarranted destruction of the Earth's vital commonly-shared resources, one could refer to climate warming. The use of fossil fuels is a major source of that change. One example of malpractices in this respect is the development of 'golf courses' in hot rainless desert lands. These courses have to be abundantly watered daily with soft water, itself distilled from salty sea water using depletable gas- or oil-powered energy-intensive desalination plants whose fuel produce carbon dioxide (CO_2). The latter is a critical factor for the deterioration of our *common vital good*, namely the Earth's fragile climate system.[98]

Indeed, CO_2 contributes to climate warming, severe droughts, increasing the acidity of oceans and seas (which account for 70 per cent of our planet), massive thawing of ice glaciers and caps, rising levels of oceans with vast large inundations, and other upheavals in the global weather and the ecosystem. These natural disturbances hurt habitat, affect adversely food production, overflow low-lying coastal areas, harm marine life, exacerbate inequalities and impact disproportionately the poor (see, for example, United Nations, *World Ocean Assessment I*, 2015, 1400p.; and Solomon Hsiang and Robert Kopp *et al.*, *American Climate Prospectus – Economic Risks in the United States*, Rhodium Group, October 2014, 201p.).

Another aberrant example is the decision of FIFA (Fédération Internationale de Football Association) to choose in 2012 as host country of the 'summer 2022 World Cup Games' the desert country of Qatar where summer temperatures reach 50 degrees Celsius in the shade. This environmentally inimical decision has called for constructing exorbitantly-costly air-conditioned stadiums and housing quarters fuelled by extracted natural gas that produce the climate-warming carbon dioxide (CO_2). Another example of questionable use of natural resources is the allocation of the world's limited arable lands to produce agro-fuels, at the expense of food products needed to feed populations (locally or internationally). One could mention the cultivation of sugarcane for biofuel at the expense of pomegranate trees that were the main source of income in the rural Indian dry state of Maharashtra. Sugarcane currently uses 70 per cent of that state's irrigation water while accounting for 4 per cent of the land under cultivation. Underground aquifers are getting dangerously depleted driving many desperate farmers to end their life.[99]

The deliberate and systematic irreversible destruction of large areas of the Earth's natural environment inclusive of its biodiversity, referred to as *ecocide*, has been considered equivalent in gravity to *genocide* by ecological activists. Rational policies should therefore exclude ravenous exploitation of natural resources. Protecting the ecosystem (from deforestation, erosion, desertification, pollution, and waste accumulation that lead to loss of food production and the deterioration of life's quality) has become imperative, to avoid impairing living conditions. Analysts have resorted to the measure of 'ecological footprint' to evaluate the impact of human demand on the Earth's ecosystem. It considers factors relating to the availability of: food and household water; minerals, fuels, metals; salubrious air, living space, and arable land; biodiversity, among other resources, along with the Earth's capacity to regenerate these resources. Ideally, noxious materials produced or used by humans (e.g. pesticides that could harm other living creatures of high value, such as bees) need to be barred and substituted by other *non-harmful* materials.

Should certain communities encroach on, or dilapidate resources that belong to the common good (e.g. clean water, green land, breathable air, etc.), conflicts could arise. As expressed by a researcher,

> Conflicts associated with the 'green grab' are receiving increasing attention, notably with respect to the dispossession of 'small holders' by large-scale agro-industrial investments and food production regimes. More recent topics likely to receive growing attention include conflicts associated with urban political ecology, broadly defined bio politics in the 'Anthropocene', the political ecology of 'de-growth', and dispossession and environmental degradation in '*emerged* economies'.[100]

The deterioration of the environment has been well-established, as conveyed by various scholarly works. Succinctly put, 'The message from a scientific analysis of the state of the environment over the course of four decades has been precisely this, that we are living beyond the planet's capacity to provide resources and to absorb waste.'[101] By protecting the environment and biodiversity for the sake of current and future generations, the human species is likely to flourish and prosper along with other species.[102]

The steady increase in world population has prompted many communities to resort to deforestation for the sake of expanding their farming land to meet rising demand for food. This can be illustrated by reference to India, Africa and other developing countries whose populations in the twentieth century and until today have soared with a concomitant decline in wild-life natural habitat. Besides deforestation, poaching and the illegal trade in wild animals has had a considerable impact on the decline – or even the extinction – of many wildlife species.[103]

Concerting actions for the global common good

Collective volition for advancing balanced progress in wellbeing at the global level is likely to be stimulated and sustained when stakeholders expect benefits to be fairly shared and risks to be jointly controlled. Such progress will be realized through international agencies that command resources to offer help, and wield power to enforce sanctions. The world community already boasts several such agencies. They extend over motley fields (health, food and agriculture, education and culture, ecology, arms' control, human rights, trade, finance, labour relations, control of criminality, etc.). Some of these organizations are essentially talking shops (e.g. those dealing with the prohibition of torture), while others lack significant resources or political will faced by the blockage of member states (e.g. those dealing with migration). Nevertheless, certain international organizations (e.g. the World Bank or the International Monetary Fund) command sufficient financial resources to enable them to influence the behaviour of member countries soliciting their aid.

To sustain the 'wellbeing' process, the cumulative wills of individuals and groups should converge and deploy coherently for the sake of protecting global public goods such as climate and health. *Lip service* or *obiter dicta* without determination to realize desired objectives are ineffectual. For the implementation of such collective *volition*, humans need to be psychologically motivated.[104]

Comprehensive wellbeing calls for an indefectible *volition* on the part of protagonists in any given community aimed at protecting *human rights*. This requires *courage* in the unfaltering prosecution of individuals or groups worldwide who have committed grave offenses (through, for example, such international institutions as the ICC). It is of paramount importance to global prosperity to prompt all parties concerned (in business, government, academia, and civil society) to *harness wills* effectively aimed at mobilizing resources that sustain development and stave off possible calamities. One needs to bear continuously in mind that we live in a precarious world comprising multiple stakeholders with rival interests and dependent on circumstances beyond their control. Dangers are not always susceptible to proper forewarning, assessment, or containment (e.g. the destructive forces of nature, technological disasters, economic crises, and protracted lethal conflicts). Many governments are ill-prepared to face such crises – nationally or internationally.

Some individuals have the will and stamina to sacrifice their leisure time, money, and security in order to improve society's wellbeing. This was notably the case of Narendra Dabholkar, a medical doctor who belonged to the Indian rationalist movement. He had been for over 30 years courageously and unfalteringly battling against charlatans who claimed magical powers. Followers of these phoney persons managed to eliminate him on 20 August 2013, at the age of 67.[105] Many in India, forcefully trapped by tradition into a socially despised status since their birth (e.g. low castes, tribal people, and religious minorities) have become gullible preys to these self-styled 'god-men' or 'marabouts' who pretend to remedy endemic distress and misery through fraudulent practices of 'miracle cures'.

Thanks to their volition, determination, courage, and ethical values, those endowed with potential characteristics of leadership and creativity would then have the task of realizing the transformation needed for a safe and prosperous planet Earth. The flowering of hitherto untapped capabilities would then generate for humanity additional inventors, innovators, entrepreneurs, managers, scientists, literary personalities, philosophers, artists, philanthropists, etc. – thereby contributing to society's enrichment, harmonious relations, and sustainable progress in wellbeing.

In conclusion, progress is realizable perennially subject to the planetary willingness of individuals and communities to operate harmoniously the various clusters of prerequisites, notably those relating to the 'common good' mentioned above in the proposed normative archetype (ref. Exhibit 1.1). Reflecting on the problematic of voluntary collective action in favour of protecting such common good as the world's climate, one ethicist admitted the existence of a tragic dilemma for humans to implement *collective actions for the common good* that surmount *egocentric interests*. He argued:

> Assigning contributory responsibility for collectively produced harms requires a consideration of the tragedy of the commons. The modern interpretation of the tragedy of the commons comes from Garrett Hardin's [his

> article published in 1968] analysis of the depletion of a shared resource by the individualistically rational decisions of those who utilize that resource. As any cost (damage) to the commons is distributed across all users and any benefit from using the commons is held by the individual user alone, there is a rational incentive for individuals to exploit the resource. As all members are subject to this incentive structure, the rational consequence is the depletion of that resource … Without constraint on individual freedom to use that common resource, environmental harm is the result. What is in our common interest is not necessarily what is in an individual's interest.[106]

Clusters of factors aiming for the collective goal of protecting humanity's well-being should be continuously fine-tuned to produce the 'right balance' that optimizes the outcome. For example, the component of 'individual freedom' should be allowed to expand up to the point of avoiding *solipsism* (i.e. extreme egocentrism) and should be carefully dovetailed with 'community solidarity' to avoid the drawbacks of mandatory *collectivism*. This was conveyed by Dallmayr thus:

> Is freedom compatible with a strong sense of solidarity and solidarity compatible with a strong sense of freedom? My basic answer is 'yes' because both are constitutive of each other … As previously indicated, freedom can decay into solipsism and solidarity into collectivism.[107]

An all-embracing enhancement of wellbeing (economic and non-economic) is most likely to be achieved by observing overarching policies of non-discrimination with open opportunities for all members of society – an ideal often proclaimed but seldom attained. The normative categories of 'clusters of wellbeing' presented at the outset of this book (Exhibit 1.1) can serve as a basis for constructing an all-embracing benchmark for measuring progress in well-being. This could apply to individual countries, as well as to group of countries and the whole planet Earth. There are many challenges for attaining such a goal – chief among which is the absence of reliable data. Nevertheless, adamant researchers bent on collecting reliable data could be collectively rewarded with greater reliability in formulating productive policy recommendations for the ultimate benefit of the global good.

Notes

1 Joel Mokyr, *A Culture of Growth – The Origins of the Modern Economy*, Princeton University Press, 2017, p. 259/403p.
2 See the United Nations Development Programme, *Human Development Report* of 1990; and Selim Jahan [Director and lead author], *Human Development Report 2015*, 274p.; see also Douglas Beal, Enrique Rueda-Sabater, Su En Yong, and Shu Ling Heng, *The Private-Sector Opportunity to Improve Wellbeing – The 2016 Sustainable Economic Development Assessment*, The Boston Consulting Group, July 2016, 49p.
3 Selim Jahan [Director and lead author], *Human Development Report 2015*, p. 2/274p.

4 *Constitution of the World Health Organization*, 1948, http://apps.who.int/gb/bd/PDF/bd47/EN/constitution-en.pdf; see also: Enrique Loyola, Ritu Sadana, and Claudia Stein, *The European Health Report 2012: Charting the Way to Well-Being*, WHO, Regional Office for Europe, 2013, 142p.

5 J. Helliwell, R. Layard, and J. Sachs, eds, *World Happiness Report*, The Earth Institute, Columbia University, 2012; see also William Davies, *The Happiness Industry – How the Government and Big Business Sold Us Well-Being*, Verso, 2016, 314p.; Fiona Nunan, *Understanding Poverty and the Environment – Analytical Frameworks and Approaches*, Routledge, 2015, notably pp. 105–134/206p.; Chu Kim-Prieto, Ed Diener, Maya Tamir, Christie Scollon, and Marissa Diener, 'Integrating the Diverse Definitions of Happiness: A Time-Sequential Framework of Subjective Well-Being', in Antonella Delle Fave, ed., *The Exploration of Happiness – Present and Future Perspectives*, Springer, 2013, pp. 47–75/340p.

Among researchers, economists' recent boom of interest in the domain of wellbeing, happiness, and other closely related themes can be illustrated by reference to writings on this subject: 'The number of published articles referenced in EconLit in any given year that mention happiness, life satisfaction or subjective well-being in the title or abstract has increased from 3 in 1986–90 to 146 in 2011' (see Bruno S. Frey and Alois Stutzer, eds, *Recent Developments in the Economics of Happiness*, Edward Elgar Publishing 2013, p. ix/524p.; see also Daniel L. McFadden, 'The New Science of Pleasure', *National Bureau of Economic Research*, January 2013, 51p. As conveyed by a researcher on the subject,

> the concept of *happiness* [and other similar concepts, one should add, such as *wellbeing, pleasure*, and/or *flourishing life*] is a bit like a mirage to social scientists – it shimmers on the horizon as an appealing object of study, but often has a tendency to slip away when it is most closely approached.
>
> (Daniel Nettle, *Happiness – The Science Behind Your Smile*, Oxford University Press, 2005, p. 6/216p.)

6 http://sustainabledevelopment.un.org/focussdgs.html; see also: The Report of the Oxford Martin Commission for Future Generations, *Now for the Long Term*, Oxford Martin School, October 2013, 85p.

7 In an estimate released on 25 March 2014, the World Health Organization (WHO) reported that in 2012 around 7 million people died – one in eight of total global deaths – as a result of air pollution exposure, and confirms that air pollution has become the world's largest single environmental health risk. A sizeable body of research has been conducted around the themes of expanding and sustaining global wellbeing (see, for example, Nicole Bates-Eamer, Barry Carin, Min Ha Lee, and Wonhyuk Lim, with Mukesh Kapila, *Post-2015 Development Agenda: Goals, Targets and Indicators – Special Report*, The Centre for International Governance Innovation; and the Korea Development Institute, Ontario-Canada, 2012, 63p.; www.cigonline.org; www.kdi.re.kr; see also 'Development – The Economics of Optimism', *The Economist*, 24 January 2015, pp. 57–59).

8 See Joseph L. Bower, Herman B. Leonard, and Lynn S. Paine, 'Global Capitalism at Risk – What Are You Doing About It?', *Harvard Business Review*, September 2011, 9p. – reprint R1109H.

9 Anne Andermann, *Evidence for Health – From Patient Choice to Global Policy*, Cambridge University Press, 2013, p. 9/206p.

10 The International Day of Happiness is celebrated throughout the world on the 20 of March. It was established by the United Nations General Assembly on 28 June 2012 by Resolution A/RES/66/281 which states in pertinent part:

> The General Assembly, [...] Conscious that the pursuit of happiness is a fundamental human goal, [...] Recognizing also the need for a more inclusive,

equitable and balanced approach to economic growth that promotes sustainable development, poverty eradication, happiness and the well-being of all peoples, Decides to proclaim 20 March the International Day of Happiness, Invites all Member States, organizations of the United Nations system and other international and regional organizations, as well as civil society, including non-governmental organizations and individuals, to observe the International Day of Happiness in an appropriate manner, including through education and public awareness-raising activities.

11 See, for example: Guy Fletcher, ed., *The Routledge Handbook of Philosophy of Well-Being*, Routledge, 2016, 529p.; Antonella Delle Fave, ed., *The Exploration of Happiness – Present and Future Perspectives*, Springer, 2013, 340p.; and Hans Henrik Knoop and Antonella Delle Fave, eds, *Well-Being and Cultures – Perspectives from Positive Psychology*, Springer, 2013, 221p.

12 OECD, *Measuring Well-Being and Progress: Well-Being Research*, 2017; ref. www.oecd.org/statistics/measuring-well-being-and-progress.htm.

13 For an extensive coverage of *development* concepts, see: Sylvia Chant and Cathy McIlwaine, *Geographies of Development in the 21st Century – An Introduction to the Global South*, Edward Elgar, 2009, pp. 6–24/364p.

14 The World Commission for Environment and Development [known as the Brundtland report] 1987; see also Dieter Birnbacher and May Thorseth, eds, *The Politics of Sustainability – Philosophical Perspectives*, Routledge, 2015, 236p.

15 The above-mentioned feelings are estimated through polling (see e.g. Betsey Stevenson and Justin Wolfers, *Brookings Papers on Economic Activity*, Spring 2008, 102p.: Richard Easterlin, 'Diminishing Marginal Utility of Income? Caveat Emptor', *Social Indicators Research* 70, no. 3, 2005, pp. 243–255; and 'Life Satisfaction: Can We Produce It?', in Wolfgang Glatzer, Susanne Von Below, and Matthias Stoffregen, eds, *Challenges for Quality of Life in the Contemporary World*, Kluwer Academic Publishers, 2004, pp. 347–357; other articles in Bruno S. Frey and Alois Stutzer, eds, *Recent Developments in the Economics of Happiness*, Edward Elgar Publishing 2013, p. ix/524p.).

16 See Sir John Hicks, *Causality in Economics*, Basic Books, Inc., 1979, 124p.; also Rodney Ramcharan, 'Regressions: An Economist's Obsession', *Finance & Development*, IMF, March 2006, pp. 36–37 – updated on 29 July 2017.

17 Abhijit V. Banerjee and Esther Duflo, *Poor Economics – A Radical Rethinking of the Way to Fight Global Poverty*, Public Affairs, 2011, p. 273/304p.

18 See, for example: Richard Layard, 'Happiness: Has Social Science a Clue?', *Lionel Robbins Memorial Lectures*, London School of Economics, March 2003.

19 Sabina Alkire has illustrated the absence of deterministic relations between *wealth* on one hand, and *wellbeing* on the other hand, by giving the eloquent example of the 'ill millionaire' in comparison to the 'vivacious millionaire'. She commented as follows: 'Perhaps the 'basic functioning' that her illness prevents is the physical ability to be nourished; thus issues of energy and indeed survival re-emerge constantly. Clearly this capability deprivation is caused by some condition other than resource deprivation' (Sabina Alkire, 'Poverty and Wellbeing', in UNDP, *What Is Poverty? Concepts and Measures*, December 2006, p. 22/23p.). In the foregoing example, absence of wellbeing for the 'ill millionaire' is not due to 'resource deprivation'; it is due to 'good-health deprivation'.

20 See: Martin Ravallion: *Benchmarking Global Poverty Reduction*, September 2012, 33p., and *How Long Will It Take to Lift One Billion People Out of Poverty*, January 2013, the World Bank Working Papers 6205 and 6325 respectively; Laurence Chandy, Natasha Ledlie, and Veronika Penciakova, *The Final Countdown: Prospects for Ending Extreme Poverty By 2030*, The Brookings Institution, April 2013, 21p.; and ILO, *World Social Protection Report 2014–15: Building Economic Recovery, Inclusive Development and Social Justice*, ILO, xxiv/337p.

21 The World Bank, *World Development Report 2011 – Conflict, Security, and Development*: www.worldbank.org/publications.
22 See, for example, 'Destroying History – The Loss of Arab HERITAGE', *The Economist*, 19 August 2017, pp. 23–24; also World Bank Group, *The Toll of War – The Economic and Social Consequences of the Conflict in Syria*, July 2017, 121p.
23 See, for example, UN News Centre, 'All Sides in Syria Killing Thousands of Detainees in Crimes against HUMANITY', 8 February 2016; Chibli Mallat and Edward Mortimer, 'The Background to Civil Resistance in the Middle East', in Adam Roberts, Michael J. Willis, Rory McCarthy, and Timothy Garton Ash, eds, *Civil Resistance in the Arab Spring – Triumphs and Disasters*, Oxford University Press, 2016, pp. 1–29/339p.; and Human Rights Council, *Out of Sight, Out of Mind: Death in Detention in the Syrian Arab Republic*, 3 February 2016, 25p., A/HRC/31/CRP.1.
24 See www.hrw.org/ report of 17 June 2014; and the Organisation for the Prohibition of Chemical Weapons [OPCW], Report on Khan Sheikhoun's Exposure to Sarin on 4 April 2017 in Syria – Reuters and BBC, 6 September 2017.
25 See, for example, Oxfam Briefing Note, *Resettling 10 Percent of Syrian Refugees – The Commitment Needed at the Geneva Conference*, 29 March 2016, 8p.: www.oxfam.org.
26 'Lebanon's Mood towards Refugees Darkens', *Financial Times*, 2 August 2017, p. 4.
27 'President Obama's Interview with Jeffrey Goldberg on Syria and Foreign Policy', *The Atlantic*, April 2016.
28 Ryan C. Hendrickson, *Obama at War – Congress and the Imperial Presidency*, University Press of Kentucky, pp. 127–128/171p.
29 Based on United Nations' agencies, and notably: The World Bank Group, *The Toll of War – The Economic and Social Consequences of the Conflict in Syria*, July 2017, 121p.
30 On abuses against women, see David L. Richards and Jillienne Haglund, *Violence against Women and the Law*, Routledge, 2016, 190p. For the sake of protecting women's human rights worldwide, the UN General Assembly invited member states in 1977 to celebrate every year on the 8th of March as the 'UN Day for women's rights and world peace'.
31 Resolution 217 A/III of 10 December 1948; see also: www.humanrights.com.
32 See, for example: K. C. Calman, 'Evolutionary Ethics: Can Values Change', *Journal of Medical Ethics*, 30, 2004, pp. 366–370.
33 Office of the United Nations High Commissioner for Human Rights, New York and Geneva, 2007, 79p.
34 See, for example, Ragnar Redbeard [pseudonym], *Might is Right or the Survival of the Fittest*, Dil Pickle Press, 1890.
35 Amy Elizabeth Young, 'Irreconcilable Differences? Shari'ah, Human Rights, and Family Code Reform in Contemporary Morocco', in Kamari Maxime Clarke and Mark Goodale, eds, *Mirrors of Justice – Law and Power in the Post-Cold War Era*, Cambridge University Press, 2014, pp. 191–207/344p.
36 Amartya Sen, 'Human Rights and Asian Values', *Carnegie Council on Ethics and International Affairs*, New York, 25 May 1997.
37 See Christoph Stückelberger, Walter Fust, and Obiora Ike, *Global Ethics for Leadership – Values and Virtues for Life*, 2016, 435p. www.globethics.net.
38 See, for example, U.S. Senate Select Committee on Intelligence's Report on the Central Intelligence Agency's Detention and Interrogation Program, 525-page summary, 3 December 2014.
39 Some analysts have considered that the U.S. Government's massive monitoring and storing of communication data worldwide (as evidenced by leaks to the media made in 2013–2014 by Edward Snowden, formerly a Central Intelligence Agency employee and later a National Security Agency contractor) a feature of the Big Brother's phenomenon. George Orwell in his dystopian allegorical novella [*Nineteen Eighty-Four* published on 8 June 1949] has used the term 'Big

Brother' as the personification of excessively intrusive power in a totalitarian brutally repressive state or party. The tyrannical ruler(s) seek to format individuals (by denying them individual freedom, shaping their thoughts, and secretly directing and manipulating their behaviour), using comprehensively falsified of facts and deception. Other reputed dystopian novels on transgressions of personal freedom include Franz Kafka's *The Trial* (1925), Aldous Huxley's *Brave New World* (1932), Ray Bradbury's *Fahrenheit 451* (1953), Margaret Atwood's *The Handmaid's Tale* (1985), Suanne Collins' *The Hunger Games* (2008), and Dave Eggers' *The Circle* (2013) – see Thomas Widmer, 'Dark Premonitions', in *Privacy: The Balancing Act Between Security and Freedom*, Credit Suisse Bulletin, 2, 2017, pp. 58–61/72p.

40 See Sally Engle Merry, 'Human Rights Monitoring and the Question of Indicators', in Mark Goodale, ed., *Human Rights at the Crossroads*, Oxford University Press, 2014, quoting from p. 149 in article on pp. 140–150/from the cited book of 236p.

41 www.universalhumanrightindex.org/.

42 See ref. www.universalhumanrightindex.org/.

43 See Bonny Ibhawoh, 'The Right to Development: The Politics and Polemics of Power and Resistance'; and Jeremy Sarkin & Mark Koenig, 'Developing the Right to Work: Intersecting and Dialoguing Human Rights and Economic Policy', in *Human Rights Quarterly* 33, 2011, The Johns Hopkins University Press, pp. 76–104, and 1–42 respectively; also Kenneth E. Goodpaster, 'Corporate Responsibility and its Constituents', in George G. Brenkert and Tom L. Beauchamp, eds, *The Oxford Handbook of Business Ethics*, Oxford University Press, 2010, pp. 126–157/733p.

44 A *genocide* refers to the deliberate and systematic destruction (partial or total) by a regime of an ethnic, racial, religious or national group – as defined by the United Nations Convention on the Prevention and Punishment of the Crime of Genocide of 9 December 1948.

45 Literature on *human rights* is profuse. Controversies abound with respect to the omnipresence of *morality* in human behaviours. Some thinkers (e.g. Hannah Arendt in her book *Eichmann in Jerusalem: A Report on the Banality of Evil*, 1963) have argued that in totalitarian states, those in power do not recognize limits to their authority as they strive to regulate all aspects of public and private life. Horrendous crimes could be organized or implemented by individuals who seek to function 'efficiently and zealously' [*sic*] by obeying the leader [Hitler, according to Arendt] without questioning their conscience on the criminal-cum-evil finalities of their actions. These individuals' ultimate objectives could well be '*professional advancement*' (!?). Her views regarding the absence of awareness for the evil they have committed have been contested by other scholars (see, for example, Bernard J. Bergen, *The Banality of Evil – Hannah Arendt and 'The Final Solution'*, Rowland & Littlefield Publishers, Inc., 1998, 167p.).

46 For an insightful analysis of the genesis of the Tunisian revolution, see Sami Zemni, 'Returning to the Tunisian Revolution: Some Reflections on Political Change during the Arab Spring', in Christopher K. Lamont, jan Van Der Harst, and Frank Gaenssmantel, eds, *Western Encounters with Democratization – Imagining Democracy after the Arab Spring*, Ashgate, 2015, pp. 51–65/241p.

47 Unlike the taming of animals (refer to the beautifully sculptured *taming of wild horses* of Pyotr Klodt, currently crowning the four corners of St. Petersburg's Anichkov Bridge), humans cannot indefinitely acquiesce to the trampling of their dignity.

48 See, for example, Marc Lynch, *The Arab Uprising: The Unfinished Revolutions of the New Middle* East, Public Affairs, 2012, 269p.

49 See the documents of Tunisia's *Commission nationale d'investigation sur la corruption et la malversation*, presided by Abdelfattah Amor, report published on 11 November 2011.

50 See, for example, articles in: www.jeuneafrique.com/.

51 K. M. Fierke, 'Human Dignity, Basal Emotion and a Global Emotionology', in Linda Ahäll and Thomas Gregory, eds, *Emotions, Politics and War*, Routledge, 2015, pp. 44–57/239p.
52 Norwegian Nobel Committee, *Press Release*, 10 October 2015.
53 See, for example, Théodore H. Macdonald, *The Global Human Right to Health – Dream or Possibility*, Radcliffe Publishing Ltd, 2007, 219p.
54 See John Smyth and Terry Wrigley, *Living on the Edge – Rethinking Poverty, Class and Schooling*, Peter Lang Publishing, Inc., 2013, 239p.
55 Robin Kearns and Pat Neuwelt, 'Healthy Development/Developing Health', in Issac Luginaah and Rachel Bezner Kerr, eds, *Geographies of Health and Development*, Ashgate, 2015, p. 300/310p.
56 For details, see: Sabina Alkire and Maria Emma Santos, *Acute Multidimensional Poverty: A New Index for Developing Countries*, Oxford Poverty & Human Development Initiative, Working Paper 38, 132p., available at www.ophi.org.uk; see also UNDP, *Human Development Report 2011*.
57 In: The Standard of Living, The Tanner Lectures, Cambridge University Press, 1987 – reproduced in note 1 of Sudhir Anand and Amartya K. Sen, 'Human Development Index: Methodology and Measurement', Human Development Report Office, July 1994, p. 1/19p. To quantify the 'burden of morbidity', WHO uses the metrics of 'Disability-Adjusted Life Year' (one DALY is equivalent to one lost year of 'healthy' life: ref. WHO, *The European Health Report 2012*, p. 36).
58 See: 'Cash to the Poor', *The Economist*, 26 October 2013, pp. 61–62; and www.economist.com/cashstrings.
59 See Anthony B. Atkinson, *Inequality – What Can Be Done?*, Harvard University Press, 2015, pp. 169–170/384p.; documentation on this subject is available at: www.economist.com/basicincome15.
60 Joseph E. Stiglitz and Bruce C. Greenwald, *Creating a Learning Society – A New Approach to Growth, Development, and Social Progress*, Columbia University Press, 2014, p. 360/380p.; see also James K. Galbraith, *Inequality – What Everyone Needs to Know*, Oxford University Press, 2016, 211p.
61 The International Day of Happiness is celebrated throughout the world on the 20th of March. It was established by the United Nations General Assembly on 28 June 2012 Assembly Resolution A/RES/66/281 states in pertinent part:

> The General Assembly, [...] Conscious that the pursuit of happiness is a fundamental human goal, [...] Recognizing also the need for a more inclusive, equitable and balanced approach to economic growth that promotes sustainable development, poverty eradication, happiness and the well-being of all peoples, Decides to proclaim 20 March the International Day of Happiness, Invites all Member States, organizations of the United Nations system and other international and regional organizations, as well as civil society, including non-governmental organizations and individuals, to observe the International Day of Happiness in an appropriate manner, including through education and public awareness-raising activities.

62 Daniel Nettle, *Happiness – The Science behind Your Smile*, Oxford University Press, 2005, p. 71 and 79/216p.
63 The aphorism 'Capability is of little account without opportunity' is generally attributed to France's Napoleon Bonaparte (1769–1821). It encapsulates the process of wellbeing, driven by the tandem of capabilities-cum-opportunities.
64 See, for example, the researched book of Pulitzer Prize laureate Daniel Golden, *The Price of Admission: How America's Ruling Class Buys its Way into Elite Colleges – And Who Gets Left Outside the Gate*, Crown Publishers, 2006, 323p.
65 Cited in 'Colleges and Inequality', *The Economist*, 28 January, 2017, p. 35.

66 See, for example, John Tepper Marlin, 'What's Your Blazer?', *Oxford Today*, Michaelmas Term 2015, pp. 45–48.

67 Marcus du Sautoy, 'No More Isolation', *Oxford Today*, Trinity Term 2013, p. 31/30–33; see also Gillian Tett, *The Silo Effect: The Peril of Expertise and the Promise of Breaking Down Barriers*, Simon & Schuster, 2015, 304p.

68 See, for example, Jonah Lehrer, *Imagine: How Creativity Works*, Houghton Mifflin Harcourt, 2012, 304p.; and Jan Wouters, Antoon Braeckman, Matthias Lievens, and Emilie Bécault, eds, *Global Governance and Democracy – A Multidisciplinary Analysis*, Edward Elgar, 2015, 289p.

69 John Kemm, ed., *Health Impact Assessment – Past Achievement, Current Understanding, and Future Progress*, Oxford University Press, 2013, p. 95/311p.

70 See, for example, Jon Hagstrum, 'Atmospheric Propagation Modelling Indicates Homing Pigeons Use Loft-Specific Infrasonic', *Journal of Experimental Biology*, 2013, pp. 687–699; also 'Avian Navigation', *The Economist*, 2 February 2013, p. 66.

71 John Hands, *Cosmosapiens – Human Evolution from the Origin of the Universe*, Duckworth Overlook, 2015, p. 532/674p.

72 Paul Froese, *On Purpose – How We Create the Meaning of Life*, Oxford University Press, 2016, pp. 101–102/245p.

73 See, for example, Marcus du Sautoy, *What We Cannot Know*, 4th Estate, 2016, 440p.

74 Daron Acemoglu and James A. Robinson, *Why Nations Fail: The Origins of Power, Prosperity, and Poverty*, Random House Inc., 2012, p. 68/529p.

75 See, for example, Gregg Braden, *Resilience from the Heart – The Power to Thrive in Life's Extremes*, Hay House, 2015, 297p.

76 Amartya Sen, *Development as Freedom*, Oxford University Press, 1999, p. 18 and 75 respectively/366p.

77 As reported by *BBC News*, United States and Canada, 4 November 2010; and other news agencies.

78 See Joseph E. Stiglitz, Amartya Sen, and Jean-Paul Fitousi, *Report by the Commission on the Measurement of Economic and Social Progress*, set-up by the French President Nicolas Sarkosi, Paris 2009, 291p. (www.stiglitz-sen-fitousi.fr); also the Nobel Lecture of Amartya Sen on 8 December 1998 'The Possibility of Social Choice', reproduced in *Economic Sciences 1998*, pp. 178–216; *Human Development Report 2011* (http://hdr.undp.org); and Axel Börsch-Supan, Martina Brandt, Karsten Hank, Mathis Schröder, eds, *The Individual and the Welfare State – Life Histories in Europe*, Springer, 2011, 285p.; UNDP – Human Development Report 2011, *Sustainability and Equity: A Better Future for All*, 2012, 180p.

79 See, for example, Séverine Deneulin and J. Allister McGregor, 'The Capability Approach and the Politics of a Social Conception Of Wellbeing', *European Journal of Social Theory*, November 2010, vol. 13, no. 4, pp. 501–519.

80 *Creating Capabilities – The Human Development Approach*, Harvard University Press, 2011, pp. 32–34/237p.

81 See, for example, the *Diagnostic and Statistical Manual of Mental Disorders* of the American Psychiatric Association, in: www.dsm5.org.

82 See, for example, OECD, *Society at a Glance 2011, OECD Social Indicators*, 101p.; also Trevor R. Parmenter, 'Quality of Life as a Concept and Measurable Entity', *Social Indicators Research*, Kluwer Academic Publishers, 1994, pp. 9–46.

83 See, for example, Dan Ariely, *The Honest Truth about Dishonesty*, HarperCollins, 2012, 255p.

84 Andrew Heywood, *Global Politics*, Macmillan, 2nd ed., 2014, p. 59/590p.

85 Claire Bommelaer, 'Edouard Philippe confirme un pass culture de 500 euros pour les jeunes', *Le Figaro*, 4 July 2017.

86 See: N. K. Sandars, *The Epic of Gilgamesh*, Penguin Classics, revised edition, September 1987, 128p.

87 The President of France Emmanuel Macron admitted in a speech (28 November 2017) to African students at the University of Ouagadougou in the capital city of Burkina Faso that a significant portion of African cultural artefacts have been plundered by colonial powers and their nationals (among which France). He promised to restitute from France much of such patrimonies to the African states to which they belong.

88 *Political Order and Political Decay – From the Industrial Revolution to the Globalisation of Democracy*, Farrar, Straus and Giroux – Profile Books, 2014, p. 548/658p.

89 Issak Prilleltensky and Ora Prilletensky, 'Webs of Well-Being: The Interdependence of Personal, Relational, Organizational and Communal Well-Being', in John Haworth and Graham Hart, eds, *Well-Being – Individual, Community and Social Perspectives*, Palgrave Macmillan, 2012, pp. 61 and 61–78/298p.

90 See, for example, Angela Scriven and Margaret Hodgins, eds, *Health Promotion Settings – Principles and Practice*, SAGE Publications, 2012, 258p.

91 Cited by Mark Dooris, 'The Settings Approach: Looking Back, Looking Forward', in: Angela Scriven and Margaret Hodgins, eds, *Health Promotion Settings – Principles and Practice*, SAGE Publications, 2012, p. 20/258p.

92 Humans currently emit in 2018 more carbon than the oceans and forests can absorb in a year, we caught more fish, felled more trees, harvested more, and consumed more water than the Earth was able to produce in the same period (ref. overshoot day.org).

93 One scholar hypothesizes

> that most environmental ethicists do not engage the sustainability literature because they take the emphasis on economic development goals for humans among political actors and scientific advocates of sustainability as revealing a commitment to anthropocentricism. In fact, it would be possible to challenge that emphasis and to advocate a nonanthropocentric version of sustainability, which would argue for the sustenance of natural processes of the good of *all living things*.
>
> (Ref. Brian G. Norton, 'Sustainability as the Multigenerational Public Interest', in Stephen M. Gardiner and Allen Thompson, eds, *The Oxford Handbook in Environmental Ethics*, Oxford University Press, 2016, pp. 355–366/593p. – emphasis on the three last quoted words is added by Z. Mikdashi)

94 See 'Implementing the Guiding Principles on Business and Human Rights', General Assembly, UN Doc. A/HRC/17/31, 21 March 2011; the document was unanimously endorsed by the UN Human Rights Council in June 2011.

95 See Tadahiro Asami, 'Towards the Successful Implementation of the Updated OECD Guidelines for Multinational Enterprises', *Columbia FDI Perspectives*, no. 56, 17 January, 2012.

96 See, for example, www.humanite-biodiversite.fr/; also Exhibit 1.5.

97 *Le Figaro*, 15 September 2017.

98 See World Meteorological Organization, *Greehouse Gas Bulletin*, Bulletin no. 13, 30 October 2017, Geneva, 8p.: www.wmo.int/.

99 See Simon Mundy, 'India Farmer Suicide Rates Soar as Water Supplies Dry Up', *Financial Times*, 11 May 2016, p. 2.

100 See Philippe Le Billon, 'Environmental Conflict', in Tom Perreault, Gavin Bridge, and James McCarthy, eds, *The Routledge Handbook of Political Ecology*, Routledge, 2015, pp. 606/598–608/646p.

101 Ernest Garcia, Mercedes Martinez-Iglesias and Peadar Kirby, eds, *Transiting to a Post-Carbon Society – Degrowth, Austerity and Wellbeing*, Palgrave Macmillan, 2017, p. 275/285p.

102 The Paris Agreement reached in December 2015 aims to strengthen the global response [excepting the United States of America] to the threat of climate change by keeping a global temperature rise in this century 'well below' 2 degrees Celsius above pre-industrial levels and to pursue efforts to limit the temperature increase even further to 1.5 degrees Celsius. Additionally, the agreement aims at strengthening the ability of countries to deal with the impacts of climate change. To reach these ambitious goals, appropriate financial resources and new technologies will be made available in support of developing countries and the most vulnerable countries (namely the poor low-lying countries).

103 See, for example, 'Conservation and Nature – A Tiger's Tale', *The Economist*, 23 December 2017, pp. 67–70.

104 See, for example, Anastasia Efklides and Despina Moraitou, eds & authors of Chapter 1, 'Introduction: Looking at Quality of Life and Well-Being from a Positive Psychology Perspective', in *A Positive Psychology Perspective on Quality of Life*, Springer, 2013, pp. 1–14/299p.; also Christopher Peterson, *Pursuing the Good Life – 100 Reflections on Positive Psychology*, Oxford University Press, 2013, 341p.

105 *India Times*, 20 August 2013; *Wikipedia*; and *antisuperstition.org*.

106 Kenneth Shockley, 'Individual and Contributory Responsibility for Environmental Harm', in Stephen M. Gardiner and Allen Thomson, eds, *The Oxford Handbook of Environmental Ethics*, Oxford University Press, pp. 265–275/593p.

107 Fred Dallmayr, *Freedom and Solidarity – Toward New Beginnings*, University Press of Kentucky, 2016, p. 196/232p.

2 GDP growth versus wellbeing

Gauges of wealth and wellbeing

As already presented in Chapter 1, *wellbeing* is a composite phenomenon whose multiple components comprise *objectively* measurable material elements (such as nutrition and shelter), and *subjectively* evaluated non-material or intangible elements (such as freedom of belief and expression). Various surveys provide information about the importance of a range of factors that affect wellbeing, covering income, health, marital status, employment, and civic trust.[1] Expressed differently, the five essential elements of wellbeing (that differentiate a *thriving* life from one spent *suffering*) revealed by Gallup's research are dependent on the positive conditions of: an attractive career, personal love-relations, financial/economic prosperity, good health, and engagement within one's community.

Gauging changes in wellbeing is often done through polling. This is the case with World Values Survey which make worldwide comparative analyses of answers to such questions as 'All things considered, how satisfied are you with your life as a whole these days?'[2] This type of survey requests interviewees to situate themselves within a scale of 1 to 10. The answers are bound to be approximate depending on the moods of the polled persons at the time they are contacted. Moreover, sentiments expressed at a given period could be influenced by *memories* (nostalgic versus tragic) of past periods, and *expectations* (optimistic versus pessimistic) regarding the future.

Researchers continue to design or refine existing 'happiness indicators', generally focusing on the selection of a few relevant key variables to produce country rankings. This is the case of the 'The New Economics Foundation' which relies on three variables – namely perceived life satisfaction, life expectancy, and the depletion of natural resources – in order to produce a composite index of happiness.[3] Other researchers analyse the state of wellbeing by focusing on specific contexts. These contexts could be those of: work, family, friends, community relations, political affiliation, leisure, sports, etc.[4]

Some analysts have chosen to limit their empirical research to countries sharing, broadly speaking, the same cultural background and socio-economic organization, in order to be able to make valid comparisons. One study measures and compares the *level of wellbeing* among 22 advanced market economies, using multiple indicators. They include: trust among fellow western citizens, absence of endemic corruption, low unemployment, education, adequate income, economic freedom, and others. Available data in this field suffer from lacunas and/or imprecision. Moreover, differences among researchers – even flaws and controversies – exist with respect to issues of relevance, inclusion/exclusion of certain factors, methods of measurement, and/or the weighting and ranking of these factors. Such differences could get magnified across cultures and over time[5] – depending on each society's preferences.[6]

Definitions and measurements of *wellbeing* differ depending on the analysts' metrics.[7] Views on key indicators of wellbeing differ, although most analysts in the twenty-first century broadly agree on the prominent importance of the following: physical and mental health, knowledge, stable employment, satisfaction of material necessities, freedom and self-determination, and harmonious interpersonal relationships.[8]

Challenges in making valid comparisons across time and space are many. They concern the availability of pertinent, reliable and quantifiable data; the use of relevant indicators; the weights to be assigned to each indicator; and the proper interpretation of available information. *Reductive* theories that seek to explain complex conditions by reference to a few factors are fraught with risks of distortions in conjecturing or hypothesizing. Referring specifically to quality of health, one informed source concludes that 'quality is complex to measure, and all data sets have their limitations. Most indicators are just that – pointers rather than absolute markers of performance.'[9]

Among conceptual and assessment challenges is the measurement of a country's wealth or income. Wealth, for example, encompasses a wide variety of constituent components. Notable among these are the following categories of assets: (a) *built-up physical capital* (machinery, buildings, infrastructures, etc.); (b) *human capital* (levels of education, lifelong learning and training, research, scientific-technological discoveries, health care, etc.); (c) *natural resources* (e.g. arable land, fisheries, forests, water, fuels, minerals, touristic scenic attractions, clean and salubrious environment, and a fecund ecosystem); (d) *financial capital* (comprising savings, investments, financial markets, financial intermediaries and products); (e) *social capital* (civic values, harmonious relations and mutual respect among members of the community); and (f) *cultural-recreational capital* (that includes museums, antiquities, monuments, galleries, artistic works, leisure-cum-sport facilities, etc.). The economic value of some of these assets can only be approximated. Other assets' valuation – such as those in the social, cultural, or ethical fields – are subject to speculation and surmise.[10]

Having defined above *wealth* in the widest possible sense, the basic query can be expressed as follows: 'Is wealth readily fungible into wellbeing?' The answer depends on the use to be made of that wealth. With the concern of providing for future generations, one has to recognize that some assets (e.g. mineral resources) are finite and subject to depletion, degradation, or obsolescence. Espousing a long-run perspective spanning over several generations and with the concern of protecting life on planet Earth, it will be beneficial for humanity to favour the use of *renewable* and *clean* natural resources (e.g. in the field of energy: wind, solar, tidal, hydro, etc.). The last-mentioned sources of energy should replace polluting sources of energy (e.g. fossil fuels that accumulate greenhouse gases responsible for global warming) or accident-prone ones (e.g. nuclear power that could produce fatal radioactive fallout). The exploitation of the foregoing sources of energy could eventually imperil ecosystems, climate, and/or the health of humans and of other living creatures.

Pollution is a negative externality that hurts society by decreasing the quality of life. It is not accounted for in the private cost of users/consumers, or in the private return of producers/sellers. Pollution is an indirect cost borne by society as a whole (in the form of higher health expenditures by residents next to the polluting sites, and/or forgone opportunities of business/touristic activities in the said sites) and not by the private polluter. The social or total cost of polluting transactions are therefore superior to the private cost or returns.[11]

Some economic activities offer both types of externalities, the *positive* and the *negative*. This is the case of hydroelectric or irrigation dams that provide concomitantly – besides their basic core activity – positive externalities that are not earned by the builders or users of these dams (e.g. control over eventual floods, or opportunities for the development of touristic attractions), and negative externalities that are not paid for by the builders or users of the said dams (e.g. threats to stocks of migratory fish, arrest of nutrient sediments reaching downstream farms, possible incursion of salt water in rivers' deltas, destruction of vegetation and animal species, inundation of habitat, obliteration of historical-archaeological sites, etc.). Negative externalities that affect health and ecosystems (such as those of fossil fuels) need to be properly assessed and fully internalized in market prices. For a corollary, public authorities should induce economic agents to replace their use of polluting materials by non-polluting ones through appropriate policy instruments (e.g. fiscal measures, administrative rules, financial incentives-cum-sanctions, etc.).

An annual reporting of the above-mentioned categories of wealth in a given country permits to compare changes over time with respect to the: (i) net *accretion* of wealth to the people of that country (e.g. through innovations that offer valuable products or reduce the cost of existing products), or conversely (ii) net *destruction* or *diminution* of wealth (e.g. through mismanagement, pollution, accidents, social and political conflicts, crises, noxious waste, pandemics, depletion of resources, or obsolescence – to mention a few factors). Such information is bound to help researchers, policy makers, and decision-makers in formulating and adopting productive strategies or practices aimed at: the preservation and development of wealth; the reduction of waste and pollution (produced by habitat, industry, agriculture, or other sources); the recycling, re-use, storage, or final proper disposal of discarded or noxious products.[12] Concern for the wellbeing of future generations, through the efficient sustainable husbanding of planet Earth's resources over the long-term horizon, should be considered of top importance for current and future generations.

Among the notable historical research studies in the field of *wellbeing*, one could mention OECD's *How Was Life* (a collective research work produced under the aegis of Jan Luiten van Zandem, published in October 2014). It spans over the period 1820–2013 and covers 25 major countries representing 80 per cent of the world's population. The indicators used are: GDP per capita, average wages, average education, life expectancy, individuals' average height (as a surrogate for the quality of people's physical health and nutrition), personal security, political institutions (as measured by competitive electoral participation), environmental quality, income inequality, and gender inequality.

Material wellbeing (or its proxy of *standard of living*) can be roughly approximated by the use of per capita measurements of: GDP/GNP/GNI/NNI. The often-used concept of GDP measures market activity of officially recognized finally transacted goods and services (regardless of their utility) within a country over a given period of time (usually a calendar year). It can be calculated by using any of the following approaches for the country under consideration: (a) *total production value*, (b) *total expenditures*, or (c) *total incomes of factors of production*. The most common expression of GDP comprises: C + I + G + (X-M) where C is consumer spending, I is investment spending, G is government spending, X is exports, and M is imports.[13] For inter-year comparisons, it is important to use inflation-adjusted real GDP or GNP. GNP stands for GDP that specifically accrues to residents of the country concerned. NNI is equivalent to GNP after making allowance for the depreciation of the country's capital stock and cross-border movements of income.

Economic historian Angus Maddison estimated world GDP and world populations over the past two millenniums. His calculations show that in AD 1, world GDP was about 1/500th of what it was in 2008, and that the world's per capita income was practically unchanged from around 1000 till 1820. Since that later date, the world economy grew significantly in wealth, and life expectancies have surged considerably.[14]

For another scholar who has examined changes in worldwide economic inequality over global human history (broadly, from the Stone Age till today), the gap between the rich and the poor narrows with the occurrence of major calamities encountered by society. He singles out four such calamities. He concludes that: 'Throughout recorded history, the most powerful levelling [of income and wealth] invariably resulted from the most powerful shocks. Four different kinds of ruptures have flattened inequality: mass mobilization warfare, transformative revolution, state failure, and lethal pandemics.'[15]

To measure a country's GDP across time, one should ascertain that competitive market prices used are in constant/real terms (i.e. adjusted for inflation), and 'reasonably competitive' (i.e. excluding situations of bubble, dumped sales, or monopolistic practices). Another serious problem with the GDP is that wellbeing could increase with a decline in GDP. As eloquently put by Erik Brynjolfsson and Andrew McAfee:

> If the cost of creating and delivering an encyclopaedia to your desktop is a few pennies instead of thousands of dollars, then you're certainly better off.

> But this decrease in costs *lowers* (italics by the authors) GDP even as our personal wellbeing increases, leaving GDP to travel in the opposite direction of our true wellbeing.[16]

Indeed, in assessing the evolution of living standards, analysts often use expediently and inappropriately shortcuts: increases in per capita *GDP*, *GNP*, *GNI* or *NNI*. Constituents of the foregoing concepts include – beside items that directly relate to people's wellbeing (e.g. health care and education) – other items such as the construction of ostentatious monuments extravagantly expensive built for the satisfaction of rulers' egos, or national prestige. Conventional GDP also includes negative factors such as expenditures on such activities as those linked to the: control of criminal actions, aftermath of accidents and their repairs, depletion or degradation of natural resources, destruction of ecosystems and of bio-diversity, expenditures on white elephants, etc.[17]

One should caution that it is advisable to be cagey about splitting categories of poverty with exactitude by reference to the lowest tiny fraction of a monetary unit (here one U.S. cent), since we are dealing with estimates. Ranges (say of 25 U.S. cents or multiples thereof) would then be more realistic. In lieu of monetary figures on poverty, it would be more meaningful in our evaluation of poverty's evolution for any given community to compare over time in-kind figures of 'basic goods and services' consumed by low-income individuals or households per year.

The above-mentioned monetary aggregates do not account properly for activities that are not commercially transacted (e.g. household works, do-it-yourself activities, or country folks who cultivate and consume their own products); changes in the quality (improvements or deterioration) and/or efficiency (cost) of products; the underground, grey, black, informal or shadow economy in which economic activities are not recorded in official statistics.[18] Indeed, conventional GDP statistics do not account for collateral *negative* factors (such as pollution, desertification, or other degradations of ecosystems) or *positive* factors (e.g. improved infrastructures or elimination of waste/pollution) generated during the process of producing, transporting, stocking, using/consuming various products; etc.

Moreover, the proceeds from the sale of exhaustible natural resources should not be considered revenues in their totality, as the stock of these extracted commercial resources has to be replaced or compensated by equivalent assets (referred to as a depletion allowance) in order to maintain the productive capacity of the economy. Finally, there is little authentic or accurate data on illegal activities in such domains as: funds that evade regulation or fiscal/social charges; addictive drugs; prostitution; forced labour; corruption exactions; smuggling and trade in stolen goods; fraudulent transactions; unauthorized gambling; undisclosed commissions paid to intermediaries for arms' deals, etc. (see also Exhibit 2.1).

Exhibit 2.1 Gross domestic product and wellbeing

Even if we act to erase material poverty, there is another greater task, it is to confront the poverty of satisfaction – purpose and dignity – that afflicts us all.

Too much and for too long, we seemed to have surrendered personal excellence and community values in the mere accumulation of material things. Our Gross National Product, now, is over $800 billion dollars a year, but that Gross National Product – if we judge the United States of America by that – that Gross National Product counts air pollution and cigarette advertising, and ambulances to clear our highways of carnage.

It counts special locks for our doors and the jails for the people who break them. It counts the destruction of the redwood and the loss of our natural wonder in chaotic sprawl.

It counts napalm and counts nuclear warheads and armoured cars for the police to fight the riots in our cities. It counts Whitman's rifle and Speck's knife, and the television programs which glorify violence in order to sell toys to our children.

Yet the gross national product does not allow for the health of our children, the quality of their education or the joy of their play. It does not include the beauty of our poetry or the strength of our marriages, the intelligence of our public debate or the integrity of our public officials.

It measures neither our wit nor our courage, neither our wisdom nor our learning, neither our compassion nor our devotion to our country, it measures everything in short, except that which makes life worthwhile.

And it can tell us everything about America except why we are proud that we are Americans.

If this is true here at home, so it is true elsewhere in world.

Source: Robert F. Kennedy, Speech at the University of Kansas, 18 March 1968

A few authors have considered that the principal objective of progress consists primarily of *material wellbeing* (for example as reflected by: increases in per capita GNP or disposable income, households' average consumption of goods and services, and/or net wealth per capita). Others, including this author, opt for a more *comprehensive definition* of 'wellbeing'. This concept comprises a broad range of indicators: objective and subjective, material and non-material, economic and non-economic, personal and societal, etc.[19] As expressed by a United Nations agency: 'development is about changing a society to enhance people's wellbeing across generations – enlarging their choices in health, education and income and expanding their freedoms and opportunities for meaningful participation in society'.[20]

A scholar in the field of national accounts, Diane Coyle, stressed that: 'Gross Domestic Product (GDP) definitely does not attempt to measure welfare or well-being.'[21] According to an official U.S. history of the national accounts, 'before GNP was made available, projected defense expenditures were sometimes *erroneously* [*sic*] subtracted from projected national income, producing a residual that was interpreted as the amount of production left for non-war goods and services ...'[22]

Unsatisfied with the *GDP/GNP/GNI/NNI* per capita and other macroeconomic monetary measures, a few governments, legislators, economists, and various other researchers have been mulling over the use of non-monetary measures for *wellbeing* geared to individuals or households of a given community. Notable among these measures are regular surveys of individuals' or households' consumption patterns aimed at evaluating their perceptions of 'life satisfaction'. It is argued that such microeconomic information (in contra-distinction to economy-wide monetary aggregates of *GDP/GNP/GNI/NNI* per capita) could help public authorities to fine-tune national policies and programs aimed at enhancing the wellbeing of poor people.[23]

The decline of *GDP/GNP/GNI/NNI* per capita in a given period could well be accompanied by a genuine improvement in the quality of life – if the said decline is more than compensated for by lesser required spending on abating criminality, accidents, health problems and distress, social disturbances, conflicts, and other negative factors that affect adversely wellbeing. Some of the 'health problems' (such as stress, burnout, depression, health accidents or other hardships) could be reduced through: *flexible* work hours, *tele-work*, *part-time work*, or *early retirement* in order to accommodate employees' particular needs. These needs would cover: *sufficient* time to rest and recuperate, to attend to household work, to care for children or senior persons, to do physical exercises, to spend time with family and/or friends, or other enjoyable leisure activities.[24]

Aggregate measures of *standard of living* (such as GDP/GNP/GNI/NNI per capita) suffer notably from various shortcomings. Among these limitations, one should mention the (i) failure to account adequately for the deterioration in the quality of life or of the ecosystem resulting from accidents and pollution, (ii) the depletion of non-renewable natural resources without commensurate replacement by substitutes or other productive assets, (iii) the impact of toxic materials, (iv) exorbitant expenditures on military activities that impair the civilian economy, (v) the omission of certain activities, such as home work, and the informal (or underground/black) economy, (vi) neglecting changes (improvement or degradation) in the quality of goods and services, (vii) involuntary unemployment, and/or (viii) dangerous working conditions that affect physical and mental health. 'Standards of living' comparisons over long periods of time for the same country pose challenges with respect to the composition and quality of the basket of goods and services *representative* of the general average consumption. Thanks to innovation, some goods and services become obsolete and get replaced by new ones.

National accounts' figures should therefore be treated with caution. They are often revised and updated in later periods to correct previously collected data, to fill in lacunas, or adjust for such factors as changes in the quality or utility of goods and services. Moreover, measurement methodologies and their hypotheses are not standardized worldwide to permit faultless and meaningful international comparisons.[25]

Numerous 'wellbeing' indexes currently exist covering various domains, extending from the subjectively perceived phenomena (feeling of happiness, or control of corruption), and the objectively measurable ones (such as infant mortality or average life longevity). Some interested parties may resort to building indices that serve to justify their preconceived hypotheses. We need therefore to scrutinize the validity of assumptions used and the logic behind the construction of each of these indices. Thanks to their discernment and capacity of separating the 'wheat from the chaff, several scholars have already questioned the validity of quantitative data offered by a few indexes.[26]

In-kind measurements

Monetary measures (namely GDP, GNP, GNI or NNI per capita) are often used as short-cuts for assessing changes in the wellbeing of a country or a community. As we have seen, they have shortcomings that could be addressed by using 'in-kind' indicators that apply to a representative individual of sub-groups of a community's population. This will enable the analyst to evaluate the discrepancies that exist among various segments of a society's population – stretching from those whose lot is *best* to those whose lot is *worst*. *Wellbeing's components* are multifarious. Some could be *objectively measured* (e.g. the satisfaction of basic needs for food and shelter), while others are *subjectively estimated*, *surmised* or *guess-estimated* (e.g. the protection of human rights).

Hereafter, we seek to probe the main in-kind contributors to the state of *illbeing/poverty*. *Poverty* exists in all parts of the world – however with varying degrees of importance. In benchmarking poverty, one could distinguish three broad categories by comparing resources available to individuals in relation to their needs:

a *dire* or *extreme poverty* that stunts people's normal growth – for example due to acute endemic famine or starvation level diets when individuals are deprived of the necessary minimum vital requirements to avoid health impairment and premature death;

b the *subsistence* level which offers individuals the bare minimum for their survival, without the scope to improve their conditions in order to fortify themselves against eventual vulnerabilities resulting from accidents or crises; and

c the *frugal* level with relatively limited comfort or leisure. Global standards for these levels of poverty expressed in constant 'purchasing power' standard monetary units (e.g. U.S. dollars) per day per person are reference points and are not necessarily valid across countries in view of the difficulties of collecting or interpreting data.[27]

Once decent work and adequate income enable a person to reasonably satisfy her/his basic needs (i.e. safety, nutrition, shelter, health care, educational requirements, etc.), an increase in income could be used to expand one's personal capabilities as wished by those concerned. It is too simplistic to convey a complex phenomenon such as *poverty* by a single figure (such as per capita income). It would be preferable to address the multiple dimensions of *poverty* and *wellbeing* via a synthesis of multiple key indicators.[28]

Dire poverty can also be a source of negative externalities, such as pollution generated by insalubrious habitat and improper disposal of waste. Such negative externalities lead to public health problems by affecting adversely the quality of water, land, and air. Poverty could drive communities to deforest their land (by using timber for fuel) – thereby leading to soil erosion, flooding, climatic disorders, and/or desertification. Finally, poverty could be exploited by some unscrupulous parties and lead to increases in ill-being and social costs caused by such activities as illicit human trafficking, drug addiction, forced labour, and other criminal activities.

Recommended thresholds of 'in-kind' basic requirements have to be calibrated by reference to geography, climate, and the health-cum-physical constitution of individuals or communities.[29] For the sake of comprehensiveness, some indices comprise both *objective* and *subjective* measures of progress in wellbeing. The proposed normative components of the archetype in Exhibit 1.1, appropriately weighed, can serve to build *composite benchmarks* to measure and judge the performance of individuals and groups in various parts of the world.

Nevertheless, one should point out to certain difficulties of interpretation of 'wellbeing indicators'. For example, an increase in the regular food intake by an individual beyond a certain level 'x' does not mean necessarily that the said individual is commensurately better off (compared with her/his previous state). On the contrary, her/his health could become worse because of obesity.[30] Furthermore, it is important to bear in mind that components of wellbeing interact, and the chemistry of the *whole* is different from that of the simple addition of *individual components*. Finally, several components of wellbeing cannot be fully fathomed and accurately gauged. This applies particularly to indicators relating to the protection of basic human rights (such as freedom of expression and belief, people's sovereignty or autonomy, democratic elections, social justice, etc.), harmonious personal-social relations, enjoyment of cultural activities, and others.

Preferences of individuals or groups do diverge: for example from (i) objectively and rationally set health-based 'nutrition and shelter' to (ii) selected vices of alcoholism or drug addiction. Indeed, one can find in certain societies spending on officially approved addictive products exceeding the size of funds allocated to worthy programs (such as the eradication of illiteracy through mandatory schooling or the fight against malnutrition through supporting domestic food crops). For an example, chewing *qat* is ubiquitous in countries of the horn of Africa where arable land and water are particularly in short supply. Citizens of a few countries (namely Yemen, Djibouti, Somalia, Ethiopia and Kenya) spend significant sums of their meagre income on it. The leaves of the shrub *Catha edulis* contain a euphoric stimulant and are chewed like tobacco or coca leaves in South America. Some 90 per cent of Yemeni males and over a third of Yemeni women chew its leaves habitually. Apparently, Yemenis give *qat* cultivation and consumption priority over basic food crops (namely cereals). Some of Yemen's best farmland is allocated to the cultivation of *qat* – despite the prevailing protracted famine, pervading epidemics, and a three-year brutal civil-cum-regional war ravaging the whole county – from North to South.[31]

Exhibit 2.2 offers a spider's cobweb diagram of key components that measure changes in the level of 'in-kind wellbeing' of a representative individual in a given community or country over two periods of time (t1 and t2). For valid comparisons over time, the analyst has to adjust figures for changes in quality, efficiency, utility, and/or variety. Exhibit 2.2 is illustrated with six in-kind basic *clusters of wellbeing* that could typically apply to a 'representative' person or a household of a given community. They are:

1 security and justice,
2 nutrition and potable water,
3 salubrious shelter and proper clothing,
4 health care and public sanitation,
5 schooling and training, and
6 decent job opportunities.

By comparison with conventional GDP and similar monetary aggregates, our cobweb approach focuses on key items vital to individuals' wellbeing such as *nutrition*. The said items do not include expenditures on 'white elephants' (e.g. ostentatious monuments that glorify existing rulers; highways to 'nowhere' serving scant traffic; costly housing projects that have been lying idle for several years; non-usable, obsolete, or rusting military hardware; etc.). Such expenditures are excluded since they do not contribute to the wellbeing or protection of the people concerned. Moreover, our in-kind analysis can measure objectively the salubriousness of living conditions (e.g. sanitation, control of pollution, absence of noise, living space, etc.).

Symmetrically to the above-mentioned *clusters of wellbeing*, we could also propose *clusters of ill-being* using the cobweb approach. Major *ill-being* factors for which humans are responsible could comprise the following six categories: (1) insecurity and criminality, (2) human rights abuses, (3) pervasive pollution, (4) plundering of resources, (5) vices (alcohol, addictive drugs, gambling, etc.), and (6) insalubrious slum-type habitats. Factors of wellbeing will then have to be compared with those of illbeing over time to ascertain the degree of progress accomplished over the years. For detailed analyses, categories of indicators can be split into sub-categories.

Wellbeing components are split into ten equal ranges starting from 0 to 10, the last figure (namely 10) standing for the optimal level for the indicator under study. The cobweb diagram could be rendered more realistic by including additional components and by varying their relative weights in accordance with the conditions of communities under examination and their environment.[32]

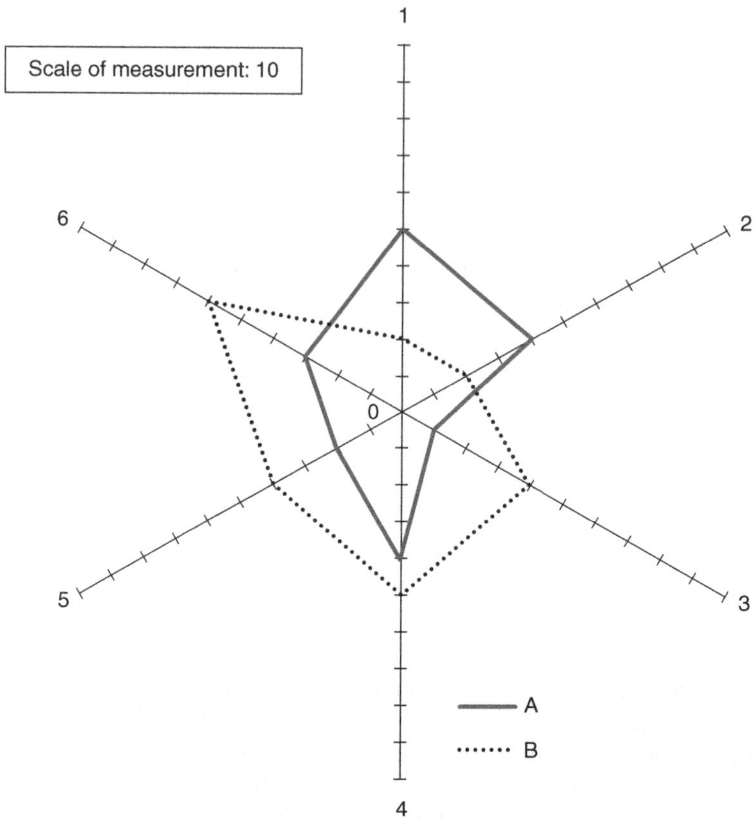

Exhibit 2.2 A cobweb diagram of key in-kind indicators of basic needs.

Source: author.

Notes

The in-kind components of 'basic needs' need not have equal weights. Thus, for a drought-afflicted country that depends heavily on subsistence agriculture, the component of 'nutrition-cum-potable water' warrants a higher weight in the proposed index (by comparison with a country that has plenty of soft water through rivers and rainfall). Other analysts are cagey regarding the production of a single measure for multifarious factors. They would prefer a 'dashboard approach' of multiple dimensions that convey realistically the evolution of individual wellbeing components – thereby avoiding lumping-up heterogeneous factors.

In Exhibit 2.2, a larger area of the polygons (**A** = for year **t1**) compared with (**B** = for year **t2**) would then represent graphically an enhancement in the overall wellbeing level for 'basic needs' of a typical individual in two selected years, t1 and t2, respectively. One can also compare the performance of an individual indicator over the two selected years (for example, for the 'nutrition-cum-potable water' component bearing no 2 in the cobweb diagram, year **t2** has *regressed* in comparison with year **t1**).

The conventional measures of economic growth (namely those based on GDP, GNP, NNP, or NNI) could well decline over a given period of time (notably for a decline of expenditures on white elephants), while the wellbeing of people could remain stable or even improve (e.g. owing to a concomitant decline in pollution generated by these white elephants). This will generally happen when economic activities with high negative fallout shrink considerably and are more than compensated for by 'improved salubrious living'.

Certain research entities or think tanks use additional indicators to measure more comprehensively 'better life'. For example, the OECD uses 11 variables covering housing, income, jobs, community relations, education, environment, civic engagement, health, life satisfaction, safety, and work-life balance.[33]

Some analysts have attempted to measure *happy life years* (HLY) for an individual. Yet, the methodology and results of such 'HLY years' assessments are still imprecise, in view of the lack of uniformity in measuring happiness felt by individuals over their life, and the difficulties of estimating *cumulative* HLY, even by discerning individuals. Furthermore, those who account for their HLY need to deduct *suffering* they may have already encountered.[34]

Human beings do not necessarily give the same weight or priority to such factors as: improvements in physical comfort, expansion of knowledge, accumulation of wealth, mix of work-leisure time, production of material goods, artistic creation, alleviation of anxiety – to name just a few. Moreover, the exact measurement of such factors could well prove too difficult or complex to ascertain. Finally, what is considered pleasurable or attractive to a particular individual is not immutable, and could well vary over time, and differ from the conventional norms of 'what is good or valuable' for her/him, as judged by society.[35]

Composite indices (e.g. the Human Development Index, the OECD Better Life Index, the Genuine Progress Indicator, the Ecological Footprint, the Happy Planet Index, The Economist Intelligence Unit's quality-of-life index, the Legatum Prosperity Index, etc.) have emphasized particular aspects of progress in wellbeing. Their declared objective is to prod the parties concerned to introduce measures and incentives susceptible of encouraging the laggard to move forward. One should nevertheless acknowledge that what makes the *wellbeing* of one party in a given region and/or in a given period of time is not necessarily transposable to other parties, as different contexts have diverse impacts.[36]

Differentiation of risks

Risks permeate human life. The verb 'to risk' is defined as 'to hazard, endanger; to expose to the chance of injury or loss' (*Oxford English Dictionary*). It can be assigned a probability (e.g. with respect to the timing of its occurrence, and/or regarding its relative weight), while *uncertainty* cannot be determined or measured accurately and is subject to surmising. Risk-taking in a *business project* is usually assumed in the expectation of net gain.

Risks originate from multiple sources. They pertain to diverse domains: ill-health and diseases, absence of personal safety, abuse of human rights, natural resources' mismanagement, economic and financial faulty operations, dangerous technologies, lack of protection from the elements, geopolitical upheavals, malignant cyber-attacks – to mention a few.[37]

Risk events can be classified by reference to the gravity of their potential impact on various parties. These parties could cover: individuals, communities, particular economic sectors, individual countries or regions of these countries, business projects, enterprises, the global economy, and planet Earth (see Exhibit 2.3). The mitigation of risks has been receiving the earnest attention of researchers and decision-makers. What is needed is a continuous, thorough examination of existential risks and of means of warding them off.[38]

The above-mentioned risks can be illustrated by reference to the natural resources sector. Judiciously used, natural resources can enhance people's wellbeing. Otherwise, they can be a source of ill-being, should benefits from their exploitation fall into the hands of vicious rulers or incompetent people.

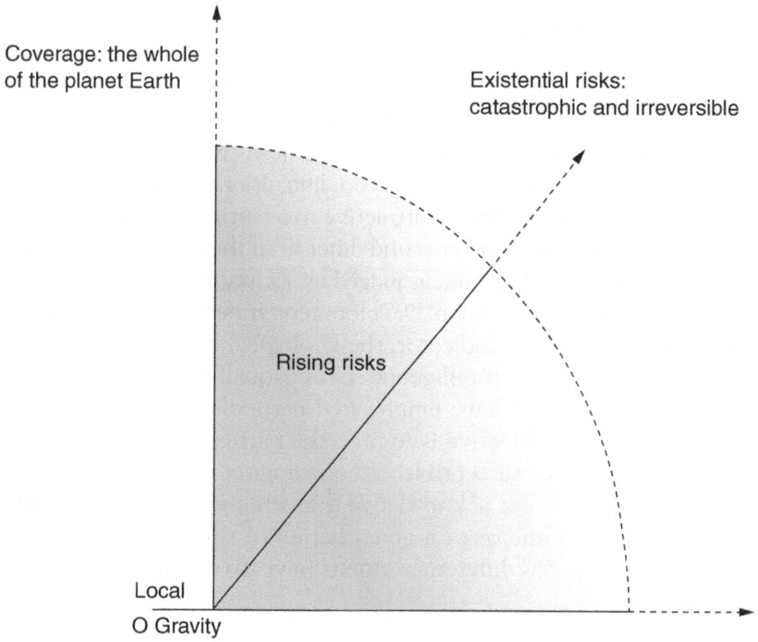

Exhibit 2.3 Extent and gravity of risks.

Source: author.

Notes
1 Vertical axis = an indicator of *coverage of risks*.
2 Horizontal axis = an indicator of the *gravity of risks* which starts with (i) trivial risks (i.e. limited to one or few persons and that last over a brief moment), and ending-up with (ii) comprehensive risks that generate multiple and irreversible damages.
3 Oblique axis = combines the above-mentioned categories of risks. Risks rise from the levels of local/ephemeral in significance (i.e. levels close to the point of origin O in the graph of Exhibit 2.3) to the levels of total obliteration (i.e. levels beyond the shaded area).

Misconduct could produce a variety of risks such as (i) rising pollution that injures the health of humans, and degrades ecosystems, (ii) practices of greed and predation in the illegitimate grabbing of resources for their selfish interest and those of their clans, and (iii) the generalization of corruption and kleptomania. Indeed, corruption, extortion, and other abuses in some resource-rich countries have left their social fabric in tatters and have sapped the ethos of honest and productive work. This has generally led to idleness and moral degeneration of those who capture undeservedly such unearned wealth.

Malpractices have been resorted to by private operators who skim resources. For example, some oil producers exploit the best deposits available to them in their concessions/leases and burn the 'associated gas' that accompanies the extraction of crude oil from the subsoil. That gas could have been used economically: (i) by domestic or foreign consumers of energy, (ii) as a raw material for petrochemical industries (plastics, synthetic fibres, fertilizers, medicine, perfumery, etc.), or (iii) stored for future usage. Besides being a wasteful practice, the flaring of associated gas damages the environment and the livelihood of local communities through acid rain (leading to the destruction of land's fertility and crops, pollution of ground water, respiratory and skin diseases, rusting of local roofing material, and other problems).

Public-minded and enlightened host governments in various countries have managed to obtain from their concessionary/lease-holder companies certain guarantees. These consist of (i) substantial commitments to invest in the extraction, refining and industrialization of raw materials, (ii) competitive royalties and other fiscal payments, (iii) relinquishment of unexplored areas, (iv) employment of nationals, (v) procurement of goods and services from domestic markets, and (vi) access of local communities to concessionaires' infrastructures (namely company roads, ports, water desalinization plants, medical facilities, training centres, and other amenities).

Dramatic disasters in the chemical-petroleum field have caused immense suffering; they include Union Carbide Bhopal's plant explosion in India in 1984, the gravest industrial accident so far in which several thousand died after being intoxicated instantaneously, and several additional thousands became incurably sick or were permanently maimed [estimated deaths by the year 2014 reached 22,000. Another calamitous event was BP's rapture of its deep-sea oil drilling platform and wells in the Gulf of Mexico on 25 April 2010 producing history's largest oil spill so far: this has affected the ecosystem of large areas of sea and coastlines – destroying fisheries, beaches, coral reefs, and mangroves. Compensation offered to victims and/or rehabilitation of ecosystems (such as animal and vegetal life) often proved inadequate in re-establishing the pre-disaster quality of life of affected communities.[39]

Negative externalities can readily spread their noxious effects globally across international frontiers. This is the case of carbon dioxide (CO_2) and methane pollutants generated by the extraction and use of fossil fuels which are responsible for greenhouse global warming and climatic upheavals on planet Earth – leading eventually to the extinction of many species. Hydrocarbons come from different sources (coal, oil, natural gas, bitumen, tar sands, petroleum-bearing schist rocks, etc.) and have different degrees of noxiousness or collateral damages. Tools for estimating the costs of health damage and health-relevant adaptation for climate change are continuously being improved.[40]

Nuclear power faces also multiple grave risks. These cover radioactive contamination at the various stages of that industry. They include (a) mining uranium, (b) processing nuclear fuel; (c) operating-cum-decontaminating sites; (d) transporting, storing and recycling nuclear materials; (e) maintenance and repair of installations; (e) security and accidents' prevention and control; (f) decommissioning/dismantling power plants; and finally (g) the storage of nuclear waste whose lethal radioactivity may last for tens of thousands years.[41] Nuclear contamination can condemn hitherto fertile regions to permanent sterility – thereby jeopardizing definitively the existence of life on impacted regions of planet Earth. It may take up to 30 years to decommission a nuclear plant, with a cost – admittedly difficult to ascertain – superior to that of its construction (according to French sources). France is the second biggest country (after the U.S.) that produces electricity from nuclear-power plants in the 2010s.[42]

Moreover, nuclear power plants are potentially subject to grave accidents. These may result from human errors, technological shortcomings in safety measures, and/or the impact of natural catastrophes (such as earth quakes, tsunamis, hurricanes, blizzards, tornados, typhoons, floods, etc.). Nuclear-radioactive contaminations can be deadly for humans and other living creatures, with fatal effects stretching over several centuries. This happened at Three Mile Island in the United States.[43] Since that accident, no nuclear power plant has been built in the U.S. By far more important and catastrophic is the accident of Chernobyl in Northern Ukraine, then part of the former Soviet Union. Its nuclear power plant explosion and fire on 26 April 1986 killed 31 workers and contaminated large areas around the plant. It also affected several European countries with radioactive particles. Over 500,000 people living around Chernobyl have been hurt.[44]

Even Japan (which had suffered tens of thousands of civilian victims from two atomic bombs dropped over Hiroshima and Nagasaki at the end of the Second World War) has resorted massively to nuclear electric power generation, with the approval of its population. Nevertheless, Japan could not avoid nuclear pollution generated by dysfunctions and destructions encountered by the Fukushima Daichi plants – following the earthquake and tsunami of early March 2011. Indeed, one could argue in retrospect that the Japanese population has been lulled by 'seals of technical security' offered by their *public regulators* and/or *handsomely-paid consultants* who had compromised their principles of objectivity. They had thus vetted the private-sector nuclear plants operators (Tokyo Electric Power) in order to spare them spending on costly, but necessary, investments to protect against possible risks of natural catastrophes in the densely populated Japanese archipelago. Skimpiness in this field (prompted by generating for private owners' profits at the expense of tight security) has been the principal cause responsible for the contamination of the hinterland (and its system of underground drinking water), as well as the shores and a portion of the contiguous Pacific Ocean whose water was used to cool the damaged reactors to prevent the risks of explosions.

Notwithstanding the gravity of the Fukushima accident, some countries have nevertheless persevered with the implementation of their civilian nuclear energy programs. Others have reacted by shutting down or phasing out their reliance on nuclear power stations. Many people worldwide, however, 'look forward to a safe, secure, and sustainable energy future with minimized risks of dangerous forms of pollution, particularly radioactive pollution that can impact the global community, an issue that Fukushima Daiichi has rivetingly drawn our attention to'.[45] It behoves therefore the public authorities to bar technologies and means of production or consumption that are potentially harmful to living creatures. This standard of prudence is generally advocated but unfortunately often flouted, or belatedly and partially observed. Risky technologies can, indeed, impact indiscriminately the human species along with other living species, notably the sentient ones (through the destruction of their eco-systems on land, sea, and/or air).

Resources and resourcefulness

Several countries, though richly endowed in natural resources, have a significant proportion of their populations living for a long time in poverty and insecurity. This has been the case in a few countries in Africa and Asia. Among these resource-rich countries, one could mention Nigeria, Zaire (also called Democratic Republic of Congo), Zimbabwe, and Libya in Africa, and Afghanistan, Iraq, and Myanmar in Asia. Their populations have suffered from governmental mismanagement, social upheavals, or lethal conflicts.

Factors responsible for poverty in resource-rich countries are diverse – chief among which is the absence of *good governance* (already defined in Chapter 1). The foregoing term encompasses respect of laws and regulations founded on public interest. This would require accountability of decision-makers; fair treatment of stakeholders; honesty and transparency of operations; and ready adaptability to dynamic situations. The foregoing principles are likely to be effective if they are underpinned by a rational system of sanctions/incentives.[46]

In contrast to troubled resource-rich countries, other countries which are poorly endowed in natural resources have managed to attain high levels of prosperity in the twenty-first century. This applies to small countries (e.g. the Netherlands, Singapore, South Korea, Switzerland, Luxembourg, Taiwan, Bahamas, etc.) or bigger countries (e.g. Japan and Finland). Their prosperity derives, inter alia, from the vision, talent, creativity and commitment of their people – notably those at the helm of policy- and decision-making processes in public and private institutions. Operating in a peaceful environment, they have been able to develop opportunities in domains deemed of value to individuals and to society at large.[47] The World Bank's 'data show that countries with poor endowments or geographical constraints can overcome bottlenecks to trade [and more generally to development]' thanks to judicious policies properly implemented.[48]

Singapore offers a role model. It:

> … is one of the world's most obvious examples of successful FDI-driven economic development. Since the 1980s, the focus of FDI promotion policies gradually moved away from lower-end manufacturing to knowledge-intensive activities. In addition to targeting innovative MNEs, in recent years the government has launched new programs to attract foreign universities into the country, building a competitive science hub. The Global Schoolhouse initiative, launched in 2002 to attract campuses of foreign universities, aims at improving the national education system and attracting international scholars and students. Complementing these efforts, the Campus for Research Excellence and Technological Enterprise (CREATE) program was set up in 2008 to attract foreign universities' research-and-development (R&D) centres. As a result, nine universities in total (including MIT and Cambridge University), from six countries, have established new research centres in Singapore, and are now collaborating closely with local universities and firms. However, Singapore's experience is a unique success story, with a confluence of historical, geopolitical and institutional circumstances (not easily replicable by other countries), enabling the development of a world-class international science hub.[49]

Over the long term, the wellbeing of a community is likely to be less dependent on *natural resources' endowment* and more dependent on the *resourcefulness* of policy-cum-decision-makers. Natural resources can be a *blessing* or a *curse* for the countries richly-endowed with such wealth – depending on the wisdom (or lack of it) available to persons entrusted with their management. Historical evidence shows that citizens of countries richly endowed in natural resources are not necessarily better off in wellbeing – compared with resource-poor countries relying on human skills, ingeniousness, or industriousness for their development. Commenting on the misappropriation of oil revenues by the few in Nigeria, one researcher noted that

> oil revenues combined with systemic corruption, embezzlement, and capital flight has created huge benefits to the ruling elite. Private enrichment is glaring, with former president Abasha embezzling US$2.5 billion during his reign, and at least three out of the five Nigerians on Forbes' 2015 list of billionaires have their wealth from combining their political influence and connections with oil revenues.[50]

For an example of wasteful management of natural resources, it was estimated that Nigeria had flared 20 billion cubic metres per annum of 'associated gas' accompanying the extraction of crude oil; that flared gas could have earned the country some $800 million annually. Also in Nigeria, major oil producing companies, notably Shell, accepted liability for some of the oil spills which were estimated at hundreds of millions of dollars. Local communities (in Bodo – Ogoniland) suffered considerably from the poisoning of their drinking water, creeks, arable land, fishing stocks, mangroves, breathing air, and more generally their habitat.[51]

By 2017, oil companies have not completed their mopping up of spilled crude oil they were responsible for, or rehabilitated the polluted environment to enable local dwellers, fishermen, peasants, and others to have back their traditional healthy sources of livelihood. Moreover, the Nigerian authorities have not secured oil installations (pipelines, reservoirs, or tankers) from pilferage or pirating by local activists, disaffected inhabitants, and security forces – all operating in an environment of corruption and impunity. The stolen crude oil was estimated to exceed 100,000 barrels a day. Such thefts have produced collateral damage such as devastating fires, kidnapping, and deaths.[52]

Similarly to Nigeria, a few other oil producing countries have suffered from oil spills and the flaring of associated gas. Iraq of the mid-2010s is another example of a country richly endowed with natural resources that has squandered its oil wealth. Commenting on the Iraq's major sea outlet, *The Economist* remarked that:

> ... it [Basra] has Iraq's only ports, and oil production that generates around 95% of the government's oil revenues ... [nevertheless] Power cuts last most of the day. The water is stickily saline. The air is acrid from oil plumes and from sewage that dribbles into collapsed canals that once saw Basra called 'the Venice of the East'. Cholera is back.[53]

Iraq and Libya – despite their vast petroleum resources relative to their populations – have suffered considerably from civil and regional wars over the past half century that disrupted their economic lifeline of petroleum exports, and plunged their people into deep poverty and suffering.

Among those who worried about the earth's capacity to feed world's population is the English political economist and demographer Thomas Robert Malthus (1766–1834). In his *Essay on the Principle of Population* (1798), he questioned the likelihood of improvements in the standard of living of the world's population. His argument is based on the hypothesis that growth in world population tends to parallel the growth in world's food supplies – thereby precluding improvements in standards of living. Malthusian argumentation was further developed by several thinkers.[54] Malthus' gloomy argumentation that population would always grow as fast as food production has earned 'economics' the epithet of 'dismal' discipline – as reported by historian Thomas Carlyle in 1839.

For a rebuttal of Malthus, one can quote Gary S. Becker:

> Malthus's conclusion that [human] fertility would rise and fall as incomes increased and decreased was contradicted by the large decline in birth rates after some countries became industrialized during the latter part of the nineteenth century and the early part of the [twentieth] century.[55]

At variance with the Malthusian *mono-causal* dogmatic grim prediction of global starvation (premised on population growth outstripping food production), several analysts have demonstrated that *multiple* factors of varying importance could influence *progress* and the *wellbeing* of individuals and communities. Thus, scientific-technological innovations judiciously developed and used could increase the productivity and quality of agricultural products, prevent and/or reduce waste, and protect the ecosystem. The foregoing factors have not been taken into consideration by the Malthusians and neo-Malthusians.

Several economists and political scientists have addressed the issue of overpopulation relative to the Earth's natural resources. They include notably Kenneth E. Boulding. In his pioneering essay,[56] Boulding explained that the planet Earth's economy is bounded, necessitating the careful husbanding of its resources. In his words: 'The closed economy of the future might similarly be called the 'spaceman' economy, in which the earth has become a single spaceship, without unlimited reservoirs of anything, either for extraction or for pollution, and in which, therefore, man must find his place in a cyclical ecological system…'.

Planet Earth is the only hospitable *liveable planet* in the cosmos known to humanity currently and for the foreseeable future. Nevertheless, most of its resources (animal, vegetal, mineral, aquatic, air-cum-space, etc.) are finite, exhaustible, or subject to deterioration owing to wasteful or harmful human activities. This situation calls for parsimony in the use of the planet's finite resources for the benefit of current and future generations. It also calls for adding value to these resources through appropriate and safe scientific/technological know-how. In this respect, global codes of *good governance* and/or *good conduct* have been elaborated under the auspices of United Nations' agencies and other organizations to serve perennially global wellbeing.

Other economists, so-called members of the *Club of Rome* (by reference to the venue of their initial conference), have expounded on the subject of a planet Earth with its bounded resources and its limited capacity to absorb waste.[57] The above-mentioned authors and many others emphasized the finiteness of our planet's natural resources (covering arable land, drinking water, breathing air, valuable minerals, clean energy, and other basic resources) in the face of rising world population, and the risk of evanescence for these resources. This situation would call for policies aimed at careful husbanding of vital scarce resources, by containing profligacy and favouring family planning and parsimony. Such an approach would spare mankind potential violent conflicts resulting from population pressures that could lead some parties to grab or plunder others' resources.

Contrarian views to the Malthusian or neo-Malthusian hypotheses of impending shortages and catastrophes on planet Earth have been expressed by certain scholars who argue that human creativity would solve the problem of scarcity of resources through greater efficiency in producing, transforming, transporting, storing, and consuming existing products, and through the development of substitutes brought into production thanks to human ingenuity.

Science-cum-technology has yielded better quality seeds, irrigation of arid lands, fertilizers, pesticides, mechanization, and other practices that have increased the productivity of farming.[58]

Death from hunger (deficiency in nutrition with respect to quality and/or quantity) hitting millions of humans annually are less due to the absence of food crops on planet Earth than to the disastrous consequences of *certain conditions*. Among these conditions, one could mention: natural disasters such as droughts, inundations or diseases; inefficient planting, storage, processing, and/or transport; misallocation of arable land (e.g. to produce bio-fuels at the expense of basic food products); monopolization of agricultural land or commodities; speculative trading; the hoarding of agricultural products or inputs; the evisceration of national wealth by despotic rulers; and/or lethal conflicts. Planet Earth has the potential to feed its inhabitants properly if the foregoing ills are properly addressed, along with implementing appropriate measures regarding the protection of food quality, stopping the erosion of arable land, and assuring the safety of inputs (fertilizers, herbicides, antibiotics, genetically modified plants or animals intended for human consumption, etc.).

Indeed, for a leading philanthropic NGO, Oxfam, hunger is not due to shortage of food supplies worldwide for reasons of production failures. It is principally due to: (a) *logistical inefficiencies* of transporting and storing *surplus* food products available in certain regions for delivery to other regions encountering *shortages*, or (b) food production patterns *incompatible* with needs. Moreover, some poor countries suffering from unhospitable environment due to drought (e.g. those in the Sahel and the Horn of Africa regions) cannot afford to buy at market prices all their nutritional requirements. They have accordingly to solicit some foreign aid (whose availability is often volatile or conditional on political strings). UN bodies and other international conferences have recommended that governments of rich countries contribute voluntarily 0.7 per cent of their GNP to foreign aid.[59] Seldom, however, has such a level been reached, while spending on armaments in many countries, poor and rich, has outstripped 2.0 per cent of GNP.

To sum up, the causes of deprivation are attributable to a variety of principal causes, natural and man-made. These comprise such factors as: (i) natural catastrophes (e.g. drought, flooding, earthquakes, pandemics, pests, viruses, parasites, or other calamities), (ii) insurgencies, foreign aggressions, and civil wars, (iii) socio-political problems (e.g. abuses of human rights, mismanagement of public affairs, social conflicts, widespread criminality, monopolistic practices, corruption, plunders, predation, enslavement, etc.), (iv) skewed relations among trading parties, (v) flawed organization and management of food production, transport, storage, conservation, etc., and/or (vi) lack of international solidarity and donors' stinginess or fickleness. It is generally recognized that violence, and more specifically wars, constitute the principal source of poverty. Starvation policies have been used by belligerent as an effective primary weapon for defeating opponents.[60]

Reflecting on the effective protection of the planet Earth's global environment, the judgement of various researchers has been circumspect. In the words of seasoned experts: 'Global environmental issues are becoming more critical as more serious, complex, and long ranging problems surface, but attempts to address them remain a low priority for governments feeling the impact of economic challenges.'[61] By making good use of scientific-technological progress, existing resources of planet Earth can reasonably meet the needs of future generations – assuming human behaviour is guided by a general ethos of sobriety.

Inequalities, vulnerabilities, and resilience

Several empirical studies have sought to analyse the probable causes that contribute to the prosperity (or to the poverty) of a country's population by comparison to other countries. These causes are referred to as 'horizontal inequalities' among countries. 'Vertical inequalities' focus on individuals' socio-economic mobility (upward or downward) within a single community.[62]

While it is ethically understandable to postulate that all humans are born equal in dignity, the fact remains that individuals' opportunities and living conditions are unequal. Differences can be explained by reference to (a) innate or acquired characteristics (mental, physical, emotional, etc.), and/or (b) geographical and socio-political environments. Destitution is often beyond the control of individuals in so far as it could result from the fallout from negative events (e.g. violent domestic conflicts, economic crises, natural catastrophes, rogue regimes, foreign aggression, unfair trade, dearth of resources, etc.). Aspirations of capable individuals could become, within their life-time, realities – assuming a propitious environment.

Viewed from the perspective of society-at-large, a very high concentration of wealth among the few would constrain overall socio-economic growth – with many people suffering from marginalization and undeveloped potential capabilities. Economic historians have established that, over the past two centuries, wealth concentration in Western economies has considerably increased.[63] For example, Piketty's central argument is that 'the process by which wealth is accumulated and distributed contains powerful forces pushing towards divergence, or at any rate an extremely high level of inequality'.[64]

A governmental policy of taxing a significant portion of individuals' built-up wealth for income redistribution and safety nets to benefit the hitherto marginalized segments of society should be conducive to enhancing the general wellbeing of society. Such an 'income redistributive' policy is based on the 'public interest' logic that siblings who inherit the wealth of their rich parents have shown no personal merit in building up these fortunes. Moreover, the poor can create for themselves and for the benefit of society at large 'considerable benefits' should public policies, guided by *principles of fairness*, provide them with the opportunity of quality education and training – along with employment at decent salaries/wages. To implement the foregoing policies, several thinkers have proposed action plans.[65]

The impact of the growing gap between rich and poor has been deemed a critical characteristic of an unjust society. Referring to the growing inequality in

American life, Michael J. Sandel argues that 'too great a gap between rich and poor undermines the solidarity that democratic citizenship requires…'. For a solution, he calls for a

> consequential investment in an infrastructure for civic renewal: public schools to which rich and poor alike would want to send their children; public transportation systems reliable enough to attract upscale commuters; and public health clinics, playgrounds, parks, recreation centres, libraries, and museums that would, ideally at least, draw people out of their gated communities and into the common spaces of a shared democratic citizenship.[66]

Inequalities are likely to exacerbate social tensions and conflicts – as episodes of hunger riots in some poor countries have shown, especially when these occur within high unemployment contexts. Indeed, jobseekers without work for more than one year 'run significant risks of demoralisation, loss of self-esteem and mental health problems'.[67]

Referring to *altruism*, one could mention personalities known for their philanthropic projects while simultaneously deriving large pecuniary benefits from polluting projects. This was notably the case of billionaire Stephan Schmidheiny (an erstwhile owner of Eternit whose asbestos factories in Italy were responsible for about 3,000 deaths). He, along with another billionaire partner Jean-Louis Marie Ghislaine De Cartier, were convicted as majority shareholders of Eternit Genova Co. (owner of asbestos factories in Italy), by an Italian court on 13 February 2012 to 16 years in jail (raised to 18 years for Schmidheiny, then aged 65, by an Italian appeals court on 3 June 2013, and dropped in the case on De Cartier who passed away on 21 May 2013 at the age of 92). The estimated package of penalties totalled some 200 million euro in punitive damages and compensation to victims and their families, public authorities, and Italian insurance entities.[68] They were charged for knowingly causing 'permanent health and environmental catastrophes', by allowing toxic asbestos dust from the production of roofing materials and pipes to circulate on the factory floor (asbestos fibres cause lung inflammation and cancer). Italy's Supreme Court overturned the 18-year prison sentence of Stephan Schmidheiny on 19 November 2014 – arguing that the statute of limitations had already expired in 1998.

In recent years, several researchers have sought to measure changes in the level of happiness for particular countries or communities. Most have endeavoured to build a Gross National Happiness [GNH] index. That index takes account of: standard of living (as conveyed by the average 'purchasing power' per capita); freedom (economic, political, and personal); equality (notably by reference to income, gender, ethnicity, and race); social relations (mutual respect, tolerance, trust, and solidarity); and justice (rule of law, respect for civil rights, and absence of corruption in governmental and business quarters).[69]

Factors that contribute to individuals' happiness or wellbeing are difficult to delineate or measure with scientific accuracy. Ambivalence of sentiments and thoughts can be perplexing: with (a) *positive factors* (such as perceptions of beauty of empathy), coexisting or alternating with (b) *negative ones* (such as pain, anxiety, or hatred) within the same individual. Indeed, personal feelings cannot be readily and objectively ascertained and measured (for example with respect to their intensity and/or duration). Moreover, individuals have complex and diverse perceptions of 'good life', since pleasures could encompass different variants between such extremes as: (1) the futile, withering, transient, ephemeral, or debilitating ones (that could hurt health and the capacity for enjoying life over the long term) on one hand, and (2) the deeply felt and enduring pleasures that are compatible with a healthy long life. Pleasure can be derived from material sources (for example food) or from immaterial ones (for example cultural activities). The *wise person* will be the one who exercises good judgement in refusing, for reasons of enlightened self-interest, to indulge in ephemeral pleasures that turn out to be harmful over the medium-long term.

Similarly to pleasure, sources of suffering are varied. They cover physical pain; destitution; grief; defeat; indignities (namely the gratuitous exploitation or abuse inflicted by others); handicaps; natural calamities; and other factors. If humans fail to attain their earnestly desired aspirations, anxiety and suffering could ensue. Some sturdy and resilient individuals would not be deterred by the stigma of earlier failures and may well resort to new approaches and/or exert additional efforts to overcome obstacles. Others are too frail to achieve desired objectives during their respective 'active' life-time horizon, and may well succumb to an obsessive fear of chronic failure, leading possibly to despair. Harsh geographical conditions or turbulent socio-political situations generally have a grave debilitating impact on individuals and their communities.

Disparate conditions and asymmetrical relations (economic and non-economic) have generally characterized humans across the globe and the ages. Uneven conditions among countries, communities, and individuals have always existed worldwide with reference to key factors such as: natural resources endowment; health and wealth; disposable or after-tax income; business opportunities; scientific-technological know-how; military power; good governance and justice; socio-economic stability; control of pollution and of pandemics; savvy leadership; quality of life; luck; and others.

Inequalities often result from the exploitation of certain people by those in commanding positions of power (e.g. through enslavement, forced child or adult labour, gender/cultural exclusions, and other ways of trapping defenceless people). Such exploitation continues to exist in various parts of the world.[70] Brazil's pig iron producers, for example, lure poor people into remote camps, forcing them to produce charcoal, working and living in appallingly precarious conditions. Ill-informed workers are often tricked by their employers to amass large debts for accommodation and work equipment that they are unable to reimburse. Such practices *chain with debt for life* these hapless workers to their ruthless employers.[71]

Another example of dire exploitation and suffering is that encountered by miners (including children as young as seven-years old) in the south of the

Democratic Republic of the Congo (Zaire) working in cobalt mines amid perilous conditions (DRC produces 50 per cent of world cobalt) in an unregulated market. Scores of miners die annually, and many suffer from long hours of work (up to 12 hours daily), and from the absence of equipment to protect them from lung or skin diseases.[72] Cobalt is primarily used in the manufacture of smart phones and electric cars by a few transnational companies that admit to their lack of monitoring their supply chains for compliance with avoiding 'human rights' abuses.

In Burkina Faso, children work in small-scale artisanal mining. Because of their small size and their agility, children (as young as six years old) are used to operate in cramped goldmines with narrow tunnels and shafts underground. Unable to defend their interests in an impoverished population, many of these children suffer from respiratory, hearing, sight, and muscular problems. They are exposed to mercury used in the process of extracting gold from its ore.[73]

Regarding disparities in wealth, one NGO estimated that in 2013 'almost half of the world's wealth is owned by just one per cent of the [world] population'.[74] The foregoing source argues that:

> Some economic inequality is essential to drive growth and progress, rewarding those with talent, hard earned skills, and the ambition to innovate and take entrepreneurial risks. However, the extreme levels of wealth concentration occurring today threaten to exclude hundreds of millions of people from realizing the benefits of their talents and hard work.

For a fairer and more prosperous world, Oxfam calls on appropriate global measures, notably a clamp down on tax evasion by companies and the institution of a living wage for all workers.[75] Oxfam confirmed in January 2016 that 'the richest 1% now have more wealth than the rest of the world combined … and that the richest individuals hide $7.6 trillion' in tax havens.[76]

Over the past century, the United States has been faced with a rising trend of inequality in income and wealth. In a richly documented study submitted to the Conference on Economic Opportunity and Inequality at the Federal Reserve Bank of Boston, the Chairperson of the U.S. Federal Reserve System queried 'whether this trend is compatible with values rooted in our nation's history, among them the high value Americans have traditionally placed on equality of opportunity'.[77]

Certain communities and governments continue in the twenty-first century to use or condone measures of discrimination, ostracism or exclusion – thereby fomenting all kinds of hatred. These measures are applied by devious parties who exploit meanly to their advantage such characteristics as ethnicity, gender, religion, age, residence, socio-cultural backgrounds, ideologies, nationalities, traditions, disability, wealth and income, or other markers. Often, certain segments of society – treated arbitrarily as pariahs or outcasts for perverse reasons – are further victimized by a variety of cruelties or injustices heaped on their dignity.[78]

Even peacekeeping UN missions, widely seen as striving for the public good of the deprived, can be a source of tragedy. This happened to Haiti whose population is among the poorest in the world. The country suffered from an epidemic of cholera that started in October 2010, after a devastating earthquake on 10 January 2010. In 2016, the UN administration admitted that the Nepalese contingent of peacekeepers were at the origin of the cholera outbreak, implying that it should compensate Haitian victims, estimated at 9,300 dead and a million infected by November 2016.[79] UN peacekeepers, whether from developed or developing countries, have also been responsible for violation of human rights (e.g. sexual exploitation and other abuses) in a few host countries.

Extreme deprivation has been the lot of a significant portion of humans; their rescue from their dire conditions requires resources which can be deemed relatively moderate compared with other expenditures (such as large military budgets, and/or sizeable spending on addictive drugs that cause considerable health damage to their users). Destitute communities are afflicted by a variety of chronic disadvantages or ills that include hunger, poor health, insalubrious housing, illiteracy, disasters provoked by the natural elements (e.g. harsh climatic conditions) or by humans (such as exclusion from decent work or from business opportunities). The vast majority of countries and people who are currently dependent on *aid* (in the form of charitable handouts) would prefer to have, instead, access to gainful work, business opportunities, and fair trade.

Destitution leads to higher levels of preventable problems: infant mortality, stunted bodies or minds, low resilience to diseases, shortened lives, ignorance due to absence of education and training, precarious employment, delinquency and crime, disintegration of family-cum-social relations, economic stagnation, and other ills.[80] Surmounting poverty is ethically desirable, as well as for reasons of efficiency and progress worldwide, as has been demonstrated empirically.[81]

Official definitions of poverty lines (in the U.S., this was $22,314 or less for an annual income of a family of four, and $11,139 for a single person in the first decade of the twenty-first century) are often used by the public authorities to assist the very poor below the foregoing thresholds. Moreover, controversy exists with respect to the composition and monetary definition of 'poverty'.[82] If markets become inefficient, leading to higher costs (for reasons of monopolistic practices, red tape, corruption, ignorance of consumers, adverse terms of trade, or other factors), the income of households would then buy a smaller basket of goods and services – assuming no change in quality – compared to with situation of efficient competition.

Care should be exercised in the appraisal of any single indicator by avoiding the lumping-up of heterogeneous groups and applying averages without any qualification. The fact that a given country has a relatively *higher income-inequality* does not necessarily mean that the people in that country are on average worse off, compared with a *lower income-inequality* country.[83]

'Widening differences' in disposable income need not invariably signal exploitation and injustice for the less fortunate. In periods of growth in economic activities, both high- and low-income groups become better off – although the disparity of incomes and of wealth could well increase – with rich people becoming richer at a faster pace than poor people. Edmund S. Phelps argues that

> heightened entrepreneurial activity indirectly lifts up *both* [*sic*] those already enjoying much of the good life and – up to a point, at any rate – disadvantaged workers too, taken as a group. The resulting dynamism, the stepped-up rate of commercially successful innovation, creates jobs in new activities and in so doing it draws the disadvantaged into better work and higher pay.[84]

Extreme inequality of income and wealth in a particular society could well indicate indifference or lack of concern by the opulent ruling class towards the destitute and the marginalized; it might undermine social cohesion leading to dysfunctions and political tensions. Thus, for societies that have a stronger aversion to *inequality*, a lower average disposable income per person and a low Gini coefficient could convey a 'better off' situation – compared with other societies with a higher average disposable income per person and a high Gini coefficient.[85]

Although poverty can be reduced in periods of growth, outrageous wealth-cum-income disparities among members of a given society can increase, with a potential adverse impact on social cohesion and political stability.[86] Indeed, 'narrowing of inequality helped support faster and more durable growth, apart from ethical, political, or broader considerations', a comprehensive empirical investigation found.[87] It is also reckoned that growing wealth and income inequalities could be harmful to efficiency, social stability and the natural environment.[88]

For the same average per capita figure in two comparable communities, the discerning analyst can reasonably argue that the lower the degree of income/wealth inequalities in a community, the higher the level of general wellbeing. Indeed, the *concentration of wealth* or *income* among the few will deny the low-income components of society resources they could use to enhance their capability to realize whatever they deem valuable for themselves. The binomial factors of (a) the *concentration* of wealth among the few and (b) the absence of a socially acceptable *re-distributive policy* in favour of those at the bottom of the social pyramid would weaken society's cohesiveness. The dissatisfaction of people left on the scrap heap could well be a source of social turmoil, especially if those in command have grabbed the state's wealth by improper means.[89]

Economic growth in contemporary societies has generally been associated with rising employment. The correlation between *GDP growth* and *job creation* has not been invariably high or significant for all countries at all times. Indeed, economic growth in several countries could have moderate or insignificant impact on employment. This is the case of countries' whose GDP growth could be fuelled by an increase in the export proceeds of their natural resources, without yielding a direct or indirect significant increase in employment. One could expect the governments of these countries to raise their employment in due course through such means as (i) infrastructure developments, and (ii) education and vocational training, health insurance and housing schemes, and (iii) fiscal-financial incentives offered to investors in labour-intensive activities, assuming the domestic economy has the requisite competitive conditions for such activities.[90]

Fallout of economic inequalities

Rising inequalities in wealth or income among members of a given community are likely to stoke up social strife and discord, criminality, ill-being, and overall instability. This was expressed by a leader of an emerging country, Chile, thus:

> In our opinion, there is no incompatibility between growth and a more equal distribution of wealth. Indeed, we are convinced there is a virtuous relationship between the two. International evidence shows that extreme inequality is not just unfair; it is also a potential source of social tension which can reduce the dynamism of an economy. Countries lose the main motor of growth – the capacity to innovate and to take risks – and populism arises.[91]

These words have proven premonitory; with the conservative government policies of President Sebastian Pinera who took office in early 2010 for four years after Ms. Michelle Bachelet's first mandate, an upsurge of demonstrations broke out late in August with popular demands for social justice. Indeed, with relatively high economic growth (estimated at 5.2 and 6.5 per cent in 2010 and 2011 respectively,[92] students and workers complained of rising inequalities in sharing the benefits of growth vis-à-vis other segments of society.

Students who initially triggered the protests wanted state financial support for quality education, and the trade unions wanted state funding for their pension schemes. Protests have since grown into a more general movement demanding business tax increases to pay for education, health, and pension schemes. Ms Bachelet, re-elected President of Chile on 15 December 2013 by 62 per cent of the voters, had promised to fund free and universal education through tax increases. Her opponent (the conservative billionaire Sebastian Pinera who governed as Chile's President from 2010 to 2014) won Chile's presidential election on 17 December 2017 with 54.6 per cent of the votes (effective 11 March 2018) against Bachelet's centre-left nominee Alejandro Guillier.

Ascertainment of the state of *poverty* in a community has also to be viewed from the perspective of potential *vulnerability* over a long multi-year time horizon. An individual, a household, or a community, that currently live above the poverty line, could encounter in a future period risks that lead them to succumb to poverty. These risks cover an array of events; they stretch from those largely due to nature's elements (earthquakes, tsunamis, flooding, hurricanes, tornados, droughts, dust storms, extreme rainfall, heat/cold waves, blizzards, blazes, volcanic eruptions, etc.) to those resulting from human activities, whether macroeconomic (e.g. financial-economic shocks, violent conflicts, barriers to trade, embargoes, etc.), industry-related (e.g. polluting activities, dangerous products, stressful activities), or household-related (accidents, health problems, loss of jobs, break-up of families, and others).

To a well-informed development scholar,

> ... poor people and poor countries are most vulnerable to risk. This is both because they do not have the savings, insurance, and other means to protect themselves from risks (for example by investing in flood defences, irrigation, or robust infrastructure), and because the poorest tend to be concentrated in the most risky places – such as slums without sanitation and on fragile agricultural lands which are vulnerable to flooding and valley floors and floodplains which are prone to flooding.[93]

Indeed, vulnerability is a potentially important source of trapping people into poverty, in the absence of safety nets mechanisms. Such mechanisms can include (i) personal safeguards or third-party guarantees, (ii) public authorities' welfare schemes, (iii) private civil society's collective solidarity programs to rescue the distressed, (iv) development of new opportunities to generate income by concerned parties to compensate for their eventual losses, and/or (v) the possibility of relocating outside disaster areas.[94]

A country's vulnerability can result from diverse situations. These include (a) volatility of earnings that are largely dependent on a single commodity, (b) sales that are heavily dependent on one single major trading partner whose demand is uncertain, (c) critical inputs that are provided mostly from one or very few fickle source(s), (d) export/import/transit routes that are unreliable and can be blocked by adverse geo-political decisions, or economic barriers to trade (as has been the case with a few land-locked countries), (e) national policies and practices that hamper productivity and value creation, (f) external rivals that are likely to chip away market shares by offering attractive substitutes, and/or (g) declining bargaining power of a trading country vis-à-vis partners.

Capital-intensive activities (e.g. those in extractive industries) are often owned or operated by large foreign transnational companies. They generally generate relatively limited direct employment in host countries. To reduce unemployment and boost value creation in the national economies, it pays host governments to redeploy the income or tax proceeds derived from these companies to various other sectors of the national economy. These cover building infrastructures (power, transportation, potable water supplies, sanitation, telecommunications, schools, etc.) that could attract other kinds of business activities. Most host governments have introduced regulations requiring foreign companies to hire and train national workers, to purchase supplies from local businesses, and to transfer technological and management know-how to domestic entities.[95]

The diminution or accretion of a country's wealth could be due to a variety of factors. Among factors that reduce a country's wealth, one could mention: unemployment; human rights abuses; excessive/sub-optimal depletion of non-renewable resources; accidents and pollution; congested traffic and or gridlocks of transport means; urban problems (such as squalid dwellings, overcrowding, and lack of recreational space, absence of sanitary infrastructures); ecological or biosphere degradation (through toxic emissions or debris affecting land, water, air and space); profligate waste generation neglecting safe recycling or re-use; dangerous activities or products (such as poorly protected underground mining; tailings of mercury to separate gold from ores; noxious effluents; unsafe sweatshops); and others. The accretion of wealth could be generated by controlling the foregoing negative factors through redesigning optimally habitat, economic activities, transport networks, and leisure-recreational facilities.

To reduce the level of poverty in any given society, civic society reformers have advocated 'affirmative action' plans to be underwritten by the public authorities. These plans call for special support in money or kind to the hitherto marginalized. They include: scholarships to facilitate their access to education and training, attractive work or business opportunities, medication, salubrious housing, and others. Such measures are vital to enhanced productivity, growth, and welfare. Remedial support and effective empowerment of the hitherto forgotten, excluded, neglected or disfavoured segments of society should enable the disadvantaged to develop their potential for work and value creation – ultimately benefiting society at large, besides them. A key challenge encountered by contemporary society is the perpetration of privileges and sinecures for the few in several countries.

Worldwide solidarity would require the abolition of all sorts of discrimination (national and transnational), and improvements in the conditions of society's underdogs – ideals seldom observed. Governmental agencies have often provided foreign aid through bilateral channels, *tied* mostly to donors' interests (economic, political, cultural, and others) mostly favouring friends, partners and/or allies among recipient countries. Multinational development entities, such as the World Bank or regional development banks or funds, are likely to be relatively less influenced by narrow political interests of their major contributors – compared with national development agencies that prioritize their countries' interests in allocating aid.[96]

Some authors believe that humans are generally inclined to share with other humans in situations of adversity.[97] Others argue that the behaviour of the run of the mill individuals, communities or governments falls short of such empathy. They argue that the powerful and cunning seek to have their interests and their laws prevail over others' legitimate rights.[98] The diversity, complexity and ambivalence of human nature allow for cruelty and compassion/empathy to coexist or alternate, with different intensities, among individual or communities. Some individuals could tame or neutralize inherent impulses to cruelty, while others are unable or unwilling to repress or control effectively such impulses.

All governments of the world agreed in 2000 on a programme to progress towards the implementation of the *Millennium Development Goals* (MDGs) – although such project was non-mandatory. The programme seeks a minimum threshold of wellbeing for all human beings. The selected goals are: the eradication of extreme poverty and hunger, generalization of universal primary education, promotion of gender equality, reduction of child mortality, improvement of maternal health, reduction of major diseases, sustaining the environment, and overall global development. The year of 2015 was set-up to attain the designated targets,[99] among which is notably that of halving the proportion of the world's poverty-stricken people between 1990 and 2015.

Level playing developmental policies should provide all members of society threshold conditions – notably in education, basic health care, salubrious housing, and non-discriminatory access to decent work at fair remuneration. This would allow individuals 'upward mobility' in society, thanks to personal merit – banning nepotism, cronyism, elitism, gender favouritism, or other discriminatory criteria. Individuals would then be rewarded in relation to their talents, hard work, exigencies of their responsibilities, and their effective contribution to wealth creation in the enterprise. Moreover, financial packages are not the sole concern of collaborators in a business; non-material factors (such as respect of dignity-cum-justice, and harmonious social relations) have a vital importance in sustaining the motivation of humans in contributing their best.

For those who are deprived of resources or opportunities, or those unable to help themselves, safety nets are required for their survival and for using their untapped potential. Indeed, in a society based on fairness, solidarity and social cohesion, it behoves public authorities (along with the support of civil society organizations) to offer support to blighted communities and those ranking on the lowest rungs of the wellbeing scale. This should hopefully provide them with the necessary requirements for a decent life (for food, education, healthcare, shelter, and/or decent work opportunities). Safety nets are generally funded primarily by mandatory state redistributive measures through progressive taxation and appropriate transfers to the poorest.[100] For the sake of effectiveness, such safety nets should be governed by the principles of equity, transparency, and accountability – underpinned by sanctions for misdeeds.

Nevertheless, one does encounter in periods of *budgetary austerity* regressive governmental measures in which the deployment of safety nets is considerably cut back or even sacrificed with individuals in acute need left on the scrap heap! The dismantling of 'survival' safety nets could be viewed as callous and could well ignite rioting among the poor, the unemployed (notably youth beleaguered by idleness), and other marginalized people. Private voluntary aid to the hungry, thirsty, injured, sick, or other disabled people are insufficient; they are often volatile and ad hoc, and bulge during periods of prosperity. Safety nets should therefore be underwritten by governmental levies collected from the more fortunate and income-producing segments of society. Governmental policies favouring wealth/income redistribution need to overcome staunch resistance from entrenched vested interests of well-off persons. Many of these persons are lacking in empathy and solidarity, as they would cling stubbornly and unjustifiably to their positions of power, wealth or privilege regardless.

Safety nets set up to alleviate the after effects of crises should be transitory, pending the introduction of necessary reforms geared at growth and stability.

Policymakers need to guard against the misguided use of safety nets. In particular, safety nets are counterproductive if they infantilize lackadaisical persons by offering 'too generous' conditions that encourage laziness and idleness. For example, some 'free riders' could shirk their responsibility of exercising their 'best effort' to seek work, and prefer to solicit their social insurance for unwarrantable health benefits – basking in the favours of a *nanny state*. For example, they could invoke a variety of innocuous handicaps certified by their accommodating doctors (such as back or knee aches), with no incentive to seek actively work or training – thus living for a long time as parasites on the revenues generated by the hard-working people. Disabilities vary considerably from the severe and painful to the benign; thresholds of disadvantages or woes differ among countries. The WHO considers that one in seven worldwide suffers from a certain disability.[101] Since 1992, The United Nations have set the third of December as the International Day of People with Disability, aimed at increasing global awareness of the rights of disabled persons, and the gains to be derived from their active integration in society.

Cultural-ethnic discriminations

To unlock opportunities requires the elimination of discrimination within countries and across countries worldwide. This means that individuals and segments of society – hitherto victimized by disenfranchisement, discrimination or abuse inflicted by ruling self-declared 'elites' – get empowered (with access to political rights, education, jobs, public services, property ownership, affordable financing, and other rights). Promoting balanced relations (within a community and among communities) should help in averting conflicts, stymieing aggressions, and sustaining peace. Nevertheless, individuals and groups in positions of privilege or power seldom *share willingly* a significant portion of their benefits with the poor – excepting the very few prompted by humane motives.

Entrenched societal discriminations can be illustrated by reference to the *caste system* that rigidly and harshly segregates society into several segments. Certain segments of society are denied their fundamental rights, rejected, or subjugated to 'elite' groups. Lower caste people have for long been inured to the trampling of their dignity, and to the degrading treatment they have suffered at the hands of upper castes who, with no opprobrium, ban them from partaking in social or religious activities. Lower-caste people have limited opportunities for decent work; they are forced to accept to toil in low-paid, arduous, unsafe, menial, and/or soiling activities (such as disposal of dead animals and manual cleaning of sewers). They accordingly live in utter misery along with their children, and are thus subject to high mortality rates. This situation could drive them into despair, suicide, or revolt.[102]

Scorned, humiliated, dehumanized, and exploited by the force of tradition – lower-caste people suffer from multiple indignities (disenfranchisement, ostracism, stigma, denigration, and/or confinement to ghetto-like insalubrious areas). Generally landless, they are snared by employers with a small loan, or crushed by usurers' terms (interest rates could well exceed 100 per cent p.a.). Their lenders are often local feudal lords who enslave them along with their siblings who inherit the debts of their parents; these debts are often contracted in periods of crisis, such as the loss of subsistence crops or family bereavement). Their children are also subjected to hard and hazardous work. They are, furthermore, deprived of regular access to nutrition, schooling, higher education, health care, decent shelter, and upward mobility for attractive jobs – compared with dominant groups.

Prejudice is at origin of the plight of lower castes in India – such as the Dalits and Harijans (the lowest caste, often called 'untouchables'), autochthonous people, and others. Lower castes – officially referred to as Scheduled Castes (SCs), Scheduled Tribes (STs), and Other Backward Classes (OBCs) – along with Muslim and Christian communities in India have suffered from social stigma and economic disadvantage vis-à-vis upper-caste Indians who claim hereditary superiority. They are denied social mobility by mores that have harshly confined them to menial, unclean, degrading and/or miserly paid occupations for centuries verging on enslavement (such as the Musahar or 'rat-catcher/eater caste' who toil in stone quarries and agricultural fields, or as rag pickers). They suffer from the opprobrium heaped on them by upper castes who refuse, by Hindu centennial tradition their entry to Hindu temples, any physical proximity in living or working quarters, the right to draw water from common wells or to share meals, and lack of equal work opportunities.[103]

Two eminent Indian scholars offered incisive insightful analyses on the state of inequalities in the world's most populous country with the universal suffrage. They conclude their evaluation in eloquent terms thus:

> All countries of the world have inequalities of various kinds. India, however, has a unique cocktail of lethal divisions and disparities. Few countries have to contend with such extreme inequalities in so many dimensions, including large economic inequalities as well as major disparities of caste, class and gender. Caste has a peculiar role in India that separates it out of the rest of the world. Many countries, to be sure, have had in the past (and to some extent even right now) caste-like institutions that place people in confined boxes. But India seems quite unique both in terms of the centrality of caste hierarchies and in terms of their continued hold in modern society (despite a great many pieces of legislation outlawing any practice of caste discrimination). And caste stratification often reinforces class inequality, giving it a resilience that is harder to conquer. Gender inequality, too, is exceptionally high in India, particularly in large parts of the northern and western regions, where the subjugation of women is fairly comprehensive. It is the mutual reinforcement of severe inequalities of different kinds that creates an extremely oppressive social system, where those at the bottom of these multiple layers of disadvantage live in conditions of extreme disempowerment.[104]

In recent years, marginalized people have been helped through 'affirmative actions', although these programs have proved of limited or questionable impact in eradicating exclusion. One could well cite in this respect various research studies. One such study argues that:

> Despite decades of preferential treatment in different forms, public life in India outside of politics is disproportionately dominated by upper castes. They continue to dominate public institutions, skilled professions, and the media, while the SCs, STs, OBCs, and Muslims are way behind the upper castes in all spheres of public life, and in higher and professional education specifically.[105]

India's alleviation of dire poverty is handicapped by multiple embedded obstacles to equality based on the caste system, race, religion, ethnicity, minorities' languages, inadequate literacy, peripheral regions, origins – among other factors.[106]

Since independence in 1948, the Indian Federal Authorities have introduced legislation that seeks to protect the hitherto battered and marginalized segments of society from abuses, and offer them opportunities to improve their lot – for example through banning child labour and mandating that children between the ages of 6 and 14 be in school (law enacted in 2010). These federal laws have been inadequately enforced by state authorities. UN agencies reported in 2013 that 28 million Indian children are still working in dismal conditions (exposed to harsh and hazardous conditions) to survive – with no access to education and health care.[107]

Other sources estimate that the total number of persons living in modern slavery in 2014 reached 35.8 million. India had the highest number (14.3 million), followed by China (3.2 million), Pakistan (2.1 million), Uzbekistan (1.2 million), and Russia (1.0 million); the foregoing countries accounted for 61 per cent of total enslaved humans. Percentage-wise, in relation to their populations, India ranked fifth after Mauritania, Uzbekistan, Haiti, and Qatar. Among 167 countries surveyed, China ranked 91st.[108] The foregoing index (broadly defined to include forced labour, human trafficking, and child brides) should help in disseminating information on the evolution of the state of modern slavery worldwide. Critics claim that figures published are based on shaky data.[109]

Some lawless countries, such as Libya in the period of 2011–2018, have allowed informal 'slave markets' to sprout; these 'markets' auction the services of captured young sub-Saharan African migrants forced or lured to leave their homelands. These migrants are generally clandestine and dream of work in a hospitable and prosperous Europe. Some of these migrants (estimated in 2017 to be between 700,000 and a million, out of a total Libyan population of 6.3 million) have been subject to kidnapping by human traffickers who exact ransoms. They are detained and forced to work for those who 'buy them' from the traffickers in 'slave markets' (for as little as $400) if they or their families are unable to pay the declared ransom. They are often subjected to torture or even death should they escape.[110]

In developed societies, one finds also separations among classes. Thus, working-class children, given the poverty of their parents, are trapped in environments that fail to offer them quality education, thus denying them the opportunity to development and progress similarly to the middle and upper classes. Other small indigenous groups, mostly living frugally in isolated areas may not deem their particular way of life necessarily unattractive, and some are keen to be left undisturbed by modernity.[111]

Gender discriminations

Despite human rights' proclamations (notably extolled by the UDHR), *gender* discrimination continues unabated in various regions of the globe. Indeed till today, mores blatantly deny girls/women rights equal to those of boys/men (in access to education, nutrition, or health care; access to jobs of responsibility and authority; remuneration packages; social rights such as driving or travelling unaccompanied by immediate male family members; political participation; parental authority and inheritance rights; etc.). Male misogynists invoke various pretexts – such as the need to respect traditions or religious beliefs, the women's primary responsibility for attending to rearing children, and other such considerations.

In several patriarchal misogynous communities, women are arbitrarily and forcefully relegated to a subordinated status under 'machismo ascendency' traditions. This has been the case in several austere obscurantist societies that ostracize women and girls from their fundamental human rights (confining them to procreation, rearing children and – in some societies – subjecting them to bodily mutilation, such as excision). Discriminatory legal frameworks and customary practices in several societies have condoned violence (such as maiming or 'honour' raped women victims who get killed by members of their own family!!!). According to United Nations sources, 'violence against women and girls is one of the most widespread, persistent and devastating human rights violations in our world today'.[112]

Gender inequality is conspicuous in certain regions of the world where the writ of patriarchal traditions is paramount. In Saudi Arabia, for example, women need the consent of a male guardian (father, husband, brother, or in the absence of the latter, the next closest male relative (called *wali*) to travel abroad for whatever purpose (for study, health treatment, work, etc.). Various indices seek to capture gender discrimination.[113] It is well documented that women have generally been at a disadvantage vis-à-vis men in most societies and across the ages. This has been evident with respect to various areas: education; health care; job opportunities, remuneration, and other economic, social and political rights. Such iniquitous discrimination is detrimental to society's wellbeing.[114]

The famous motto of the French Revolution's 'liberty, equality and fraternity' did not include women! No wonder, one can admire the political struggle of playwright and essayist Olympe de Gouges (1748–1793) who demanded that French women be given the same rights as French men in the Declaration of the Rights of Man and of the Citizen of 1789.[115] Her campaign was thwarted by men then at the helm of the French Revolution – despite the considerable sacrifices women had borne in toppling the absolute monarchical system. She was also a pioneer in France in favour of the abolition of slavery.[116] Her courageous defence of universal values, human equality, and freedom for all is deemed exemplary. Indeed, she espoused the cause of all humans that are unjustly excluded (for reasons of race, gender, out-of-wedlock birth, tyranny, etc). Her stand against capital punishment did not preclude her tragic ending as 'a martyr of her ideals', guillotined at the age of 45 during the French Revolution's Reign of Terror under Robespierre.

For a modern example of noble volition to brave gender injustices, one can refer to the case of the 15-year old Pakistani schoolgirl Malala Yousafzai who had started at the age of 11 with an anonymous diary, chronicling brutalities against women and girls in her country. She was shot in the head by a fanatical Pakistani Taliban on 9 October 2012 (the Taliban ideology opposes the education and employment of women). After successful surgery in the UK in February 2013, she has undertaken, at the risk of her life, to carry on her campaign for the right of all children including girls, to be granted a fair education, despite the opposition of the obscurantist fundamentalists. She was chosen by the European Parliament as the laureate of the Sakharov Prize for Freedom of Thought (with a prize of 50,000 euro) at a ceremony held on World Children's Day on 20 November 2013. In 2014, she was awarded the Nobel Peace Prize (making her the youngest Nobel Prize winner at the age of 17), jointly with Kailas Satyarthi, aged 60, the rescuer of tens of thousands of Indian children forced into slavery in hazardous industries. The prize rewarded them 'for their struggle against the suppression of children and young people and for the right of all children to education'.

Whenever possible, women have joined actively with men in their quest for socio-political reform. Emblematic women figures in the early 2010s protests included (a) Ms Asmaa Mahfouz who was awarded the Andrei Sakharov Prize for Freedom of Thought worth 50,000 euro by the European Parliament (joining Mr Alaa Abdul Fattah in Egypt who helped ignite the online call to freedom, starting 25 January 2011 culminating with the resignation of Hosni Mubarak on 11 February 2011 after some 30 years of his autocratic rule of Egypt); and (b) Ms Tawakul Karman in Yemen who was awarded the Andrei Sakharov Prize for Freedom of Thought, for the same cash prize, by the European Parliament. Named after Soviet physicist and dissident Andrei Sakharov, the award was offered 'for their contribution to historic changes in the Arab world and as a symbol for all those working for dignity, democracy and fundamental rights in the Arab world and beyond'.[117] Ms Tawakul Karman had also been awarded the 2011 Nobel Peace Prize (along with two Liberian women) 'for their non-violent struggle for the safety of women and for women's rights to full participation in peace-building work'. Despite their active involvement in movements of socio-political reforms, women continue to suffer from a lower status compared with men.[118]

To remedy the situation of relative marginalization of one half of humanity's population, namely women when compared to men, the United Nations General Assembly declared 11 October the *International Day of the Girl Child* (Resolution 66/170 of 19 December 2011). The foregoing date is set to remind all parties concerned (UN agencies, Member States, civil society organizations, and various other private stakeholders) of the need to foster gender equality. This would then require similar access to basic necessities as for boys. This includes: comparable quality education and training; health care and nutrition; protection from violence; protection from early forced marriages; protection from genital mutilation; opportunities for decent work; etc. Exclusion, exploitation, or discrimination encountered by women are at the very basis of their poverty compared with men. By striving for gender equality, several ills encountered by women compared with men could be mitigated or eliminated, thereby ushering in a more equitable and prosperous world for all human beings.

Life cycles and capabilities

Several scholars and researchers have resorted to the paradigm of 'life cycles' to interpret the changing capabilities of individuals, organizations or communities in order to improve or sustain their wellbeing. This paradigm considers that all humans, whether taken as separate individuals or as groups of individuals acting together within an entity or an organization, generally evolve through a broadly common pattern. Starting with infancy, the *process of progress* passes chronologically through four main stages. They are: first, rapid ascension; second, early blossom; third, full maturity; fourth, initial decline; and fifth, ultimate extinction. Understanding *individuals' capabilities*, the physical and the cognitive, over different phases of a life cycle has been resorted to by *Lifespan development Psychology*. Psychologists often divide the periods of the *life cycle* into eight phases: prenatal, infancy, early childhood, middle childhood, adolescence, early adulthood, middle adulthood, and late adulthood. Such divisions could help find optimal means to enhance wellbeing in each phase of the said cycle (see Exhibit 2.4).

Individuals

Several scholars have sought to identify major phases of a typical human's development, covering physical, cognitive, emotional, and social domains. A pattern of eight consecutive phases is often proposed. They are: the *prenatal, infancy and toddlerhood* stages (birth–2 years), *early childhood* (2–6 years), *middle childhood* (6–11 years), *adolescence* (11–18 years), *early adulthood* (18–40 years), *middle adulthood* (40–65 years), and *late adulthood* (65 years–death). The above-mentioned phases overlap, interact, and are influenced by multiple forces.[119]

Aspirations of an individual (in matters of wealth, power, health, education, achievements, long life, notoriety, etc.) may well exceed their effective capabilities to realize them within set time horizons – despite her/his earnest *volition*.

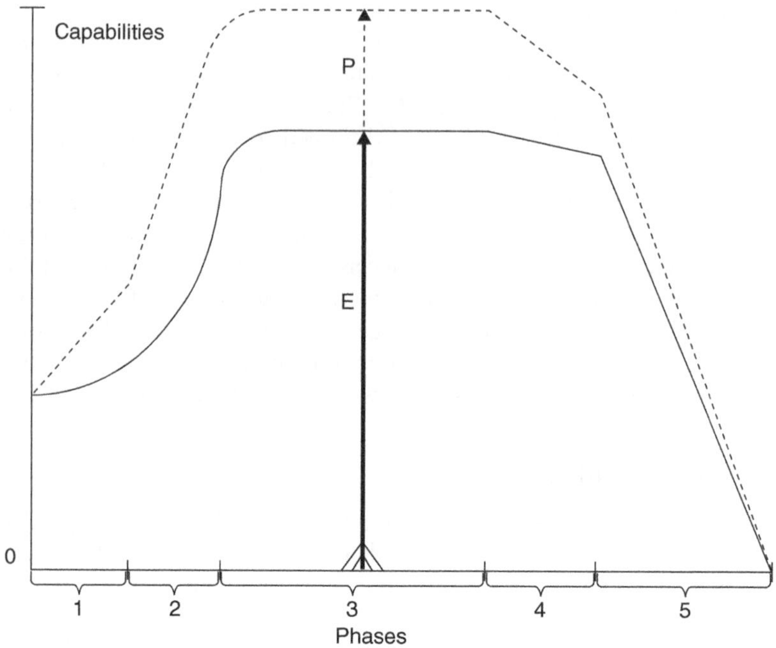

Exhibit 2.4 The life cycle of a representative individual: existing and potential capabilities.

Source: author.

Notes

E = *existing capabilities at a given point of time* ________

P = *potential capabilities that can be developed* – – – – – – – – –

Total capabilities (existing + potential) of an individual or an entity vary over the five main consecutive phases of a life cycle:

1 *Childhood*
2 *Youth*
3 *Early adulthood*
4 *Full maturity*
5 *Senior terminal stage*.

Gaps separating *aspirations* from *capabilities* for a given individual vary in importance over time, as the conditions of the person concerned change. Projects built on *aspirations* that exceed current-cum-prospective *capabilities* for an individual could prove unattainable and a source of frustration or anguish by the party concerned. Moreover, one should point out that an individual's specific aspirations could be different (divergent) from those of the bulk of her/his community.

Aspirations pertaining to individuals are multifarious in a world of complex and heterogeneous societies. Deliberately thought-out and earnestly desired aspirations should be distinguished from day-dreaming, chimera, illusions, phantasms, utopia, or Shangri-La.

Shared aspirations within a group are likely to be a strong force of cohesion. Diversity of backgrounds (whether based on ethnicity, religion, culture, education, geographic residence, or other factors) can also be a source for opening up vistas and opportunities for greater creativity and achievement. Such diversity need not be an insurmountable hurdle for reaching a 'social pact' based on *mutual acceptance of differences*, *constructive dialogue*, and *effective and honest cooperation* – guided by respect for basic human rights. Disparagement of *otherness* can be due to ignorance, prejudice, fear, lust for power, and other shady motives. The sharpening of attitudes of alterity within a community is likely to be counter-productive in so far as they could block potentially fruitful exchanges and cooperation, and could foster seeds of mistrust and discord.

The minimal threshold of a human being's aspiration to wellbeing is to have the capability of freeing oneself from life-threatening *destitution* and from *servitude*; these are among the worst calamities a human can encounter. Assuming that the obstacle of utter destitution is successfully overcome, a human being could then think and work for her/his other material, moral, social, and political 'wellbeing needs'. The goal of global wellbeing would remain vacuous 'lip service' unless all parties concerned are willing and able to mobilize their resources and commit to the realization of that purpose.

Individuals are well advised to concentrate on things they can do, and not to brood on things they cannot. Accordingly, unless the individuals concerned are willing and able to realize their highly desired aspirations, the whittling down of these aspirations becomes warranted to avoid the potentially negative effects of *over-reaching*. The larger the *aspirations-capabilities* gaps, the greater are the degrees of potential dissatisfaction resulting from unrealizable targets. *Aspirations-capabilities* gaps apply generally to an individual. They could also be used for a family, a business entity, a non-profit organization, or a community.

Capabilities can be enhanced by various approaches. Even the handicapped (for physical, mental, psychic or emotional reasons) could improve their lot thanks to appropriate techniques. The 'aspirations-capabilities' gap hypothesis was first probed by K. C. Calman.[120] Focusing on persons in the terminal phase of their life cycle, Calman's argument is that the wider the gap between (a) the health situation of a person (capabilities) and (b) that person's desired but unattainable health objectives (aspirations, the greater is the suffering – and vice versa. While Calman's *aspirations/capabilities* gap model is concerned with cancer patients in the final phase of their life, some analysts may apply it to any period of the life cycle – whether in periods of impairment, or in periods of fine health.

Given a propitious environment, and as individuals gain in capabilities (through the judicious use of their accumulated knowledge, skills, experiences, etc.) they could be motivated to raise the ceiling of their aspirations. Alternatively, they would have to moderate their current aspirations should their capacities decline. Indeed, persons with *aspirations – capabilities* gaps deemed excessive, and in the absence of the possibility of enhancing their capabilities, a tapering down of their 'too high' aspirations is recommended. This will help them to quench their potential dissatisfaction and reduce their frustration or suffering from likely failures. Realistic people with such high gaps would re-order or scale down the level of their aspirations, or space out their implementation over longer time horizons, as warranted by their personal and environmental conditions during their life cycle. When lucid and willing individuals consciously align their aspirations with their capabilities, they can reasonably reach a condition of equanimity. Nevertheless, some researchers doubt the capacity of certain persons – and in particular in the case of frightened or withdrawn patients – to assess objectively their current conditions and/or their future prospects.[121]

For some persons, dissatisfaction with current conditions can become a stimulus for creativity to change things for the better. This applies to persons with entrepreneurial sanguine temperaments and motivation. For other persons with (i) undeveloped or limited *capacities* (mental, psychic, and/or physical) to solve problems, (ii) absence of drive and ambition to face up to risks, or (iii) proclivity to inertia (for reasons of health, powerful rivals, contrarian forces, ostracism, and/or other factors), *aspirations* to develop their potential capabilities are likely to be constrained. To avoid distress, it is incumbent on the discerning individual to continuously evaluate lucidly and realistically her/his capacities (the actual and the potential) in relation to the pursuit of desired aspirations.

Broadly speaking, individuals can be conceptually split into two major categories:

The *first* category is that of *optimistic* or *sanguine* individuals undeterred by difficulties. They are propelled by a strong drive to overcome current constraints or obstacles in their impelling quest to attain ardently desired objectives. Optimistic predispositions (intellectual, emotional and physical) of individuals bent on realizing their projects are likely to energize them along with their cohort, despite adversities. They can be described as particularly resilient, capable of recovering easily from misfortunes or shocks.

The *second* category is that of *cautious* or *pusillanimous* individuals with a low appetite for risk-taking. Their permeating anxiety has a debilitating impact that deprives them of the willingness to overcome challenges. Unsuccessful 'wannabes' could suffer from despondency, defeatism, fatalism, possibly leading in extreme cases to utter despair that could terminate ultimately in their choosing to end their own life.

Persons belonging to the second category are likely to have a higher aversion for risk-taking, compared with those in the first category. They are fragile and unable to accomplish aspirations that turn out to be too ambitious, measured by reference to their effective capabilities. Haunted by the fear of possible failure in view of their currently perceived capabilities, these persons would then have to moderate ambitious objectives, lest they blunder. Compared with wholesome persons (i.e. those who are sound in body, mind, and ethics), humans suffering from handicaps need greater will and stamina to develop their constrained capacities to obtain things available to their peers.

During certain periods of their active life, some individuals are energized by the prospects of accomplishing novel or arduous tasks, and thrive on pursuing ambitious aspirations that would appear to the general public 'too exacting'. In such pursuits, these individuals have clear preferences for solving problems, risk-taking, and/or *joie de vivre* in their adventurous endeavours. Their behaviour is accordingly less deterred by uncertainty or the eventuality of failure to attain their objectives – compared with the bulk of their cohort. Should they fail, they are willing to bounce back and struggle again thanks to their resilience.

Creative persons with foresight, sanguine temperament and unflinching determination for achievement are present in all domains: business (e.g. green shoots entrepreneurs), sports and trying adventures (e.g. mountain climbing, and other sea, land, or space adventures), science and technology, artistic works, community development, socio-political activities, and many others. With optimism and courage, they seek relentlessly and incrementally to realize their ambitions. They could be frustrated by various mishaps, yet they will endure and will not fall into disenchantment. Bent on reaching their earnestly desired goals throughout a possibly difficult or chequered 'life span', the unfazed achievers would exhilarate in knocking over successive obstacles. That joy could well dwarf suffering sustained from setbacks during the ascension process. Then, any stress or disappointment resulting from the foregoing 'unsuccessful' efforts can be deemed 'productive' by the person concerned to the extent these efforts generate useful knowledge and sustain the resolve of the persons concerned to attain in the future their objectives. Moreover, an incremental process of achievements could gain momentum. Evidently, pioneers who brace themselves for new challenges resort to high physical, mental and emotional preparations.

Espousing gradualism in the implementation of aspirations often proves a judicious approach in so far as it avoids debilitating anxieties and suffering generated by the shocks of sizeable failures to attain in time targets that turn out too ambitious or illusory. As expressed by Confucius, the 1,000-mile journey starts with a first small step. Nevertheless, the journey towards progress could encounter relapses provoked by natural disasters or man-made catastrophes. Gradualism could provide the concerned individuals timely additional knowledge on their personal capabilities at facing up to challenges, instilling in them confidence and serenity to realize more demanding targets.

Fulfilling aspirations in one's field of predilection and staying on top of things, regardless, and for a long time, can be a source of stress and burnout. Some achievers at the zenith of their powers may even feel unbearable anguish regarding the possibility of their slipping down. This can be eloquently illustrated by the saga and tragic fate of Chef Bernard Loiseau, whose talent and laborious skills were honoured by the French Government. He reached the top (with the iconic three-star prize awarded by the famous *Michelin's Gastronomic Guide*) for his '*nouvelle cuisine*'. He was the first three-star restaurant to introduce his business into the stock exchange. With his enterprise heavily indebted, Loiseau was haunted by the eventuality of being retrograded (i.e. losing the Michelin's top rank). This drove him to the brink of despair, and ultimately driving him to commit suicide on 24 February 2003 at the age of 52.[122]

Groups' pressures on individuals to 'perform' continuously in an ever-stressing competitive environment could accordingly prove unbearable, leading to the degradation of life's quality for the persons concerned, who could be crushed and end their life. The above-mentioned stunning misfortune happened to another *Michelin three-star chef*, 44-year-old Benoît Violier, the responsible chef for the prestigious restaurant of the Hôtel de Ville de Crissier, near the city of Lausanne in Switzerland. He was also awarded by the French *La Liste* (a gastronomic guide) the top ranking among the world's leading restaurants in December 2015. Nevertheless, he committed suicide at his home on Sunday 31 January 2016, on the eve of the publication of the new *Michelin gastronomic listing*. Some sources had speculated that his fatal action could have resulted from his emotional reaction to the possibility of losing one star of his three-star top rank.

To measure changes for wellbeing, some analysts propose carefully designed questionnaires to serve as 'measuring rods'. Medical centres are increasingly resorting to such techniques. For example, pain measurement (varying on a scale of '0' to '10') is generally proposed to patients, assuming these patients possess a discerning analytical intellect and the capability to translate the flow and intensity of feelings into words or figures.[123] Other techniques resort to tiny sensors implanted into the body of patients; these sensors collect up-to-date data on changes in their physical health and warn them accordingly.[124]

Some medical researchers (psychiatrists and neurologists) have sought to estimate *current* feelings of *subjective wellbeing* or *satisfaction* that differ from *overall life satisfaction*. These researchers' computational model is based on the responses of a large number of people repeatedly asked to report their 'feelings as they go about their lives'. Happiness was construed as an emotional reactivity to recent monetary rewards.[125]

According to the above-mentioned study,

> ...the subjective well-being or happiness of individuals is an important metric for societies. Although happiness is influenced by life circumstances and population demographics such as wealth, we know little about how the cumulative influence of daily life events are aggregated into subjective feelings. Using computational modelling, we show that emotional reactivity in the form of momentary happiness in response to outcomes of a probabilistic reward task is explained not by current task earnings, but by the combined influence of recent reward expectations and prediction errors arising from those expectations. The robustness of this account was evident in a large-scale replication involving 18,420 participants. Using functional MRI [magnetic resonance imaging], we show that the very same influences account for task-dependent striatal activity in a manner akin to the influences underpinning changes in happiness.[126]

Comparisons of *pleasure* or *pain* among individuals are difficult to ascertain. Indeed, questions asked on pleasure or pain, and answers obtained could turn out to be equivocal – with skewed, inadequate, or inexpressible interpretations in current languages or measuring rods. When pain or pleasure is inexpressible for any person (who could be muddled, confused, and unable to communicate lucidly), it would be advisable to consider the inputs of reliable and knowledgeable persons (e.g. family members, friends, and/or professionals). In all circumstances, one should guard against potential errors or bias (conscious or unconscious) of these persons.

A few persons are able and willing to resort to mysticism, meditation, spiritualism or contemplation – thereby attaining serenity that could predispose them to overcome or abate suffering. As put by Arianna Huffington: 'One of the best – and most easily available – ways we can become healthier and happier is through mindfulness and meditation. Every element of wellbeing is enhanced by the practice of meditation.'[127]

Moreover, behaviours based on sobriety (as opposed to consumerism and profligacy that causes loss of resources, waste, and health problems) generally contribute to the perennial protection of life, nature, and wellbeing on planet Earth.[128] To attain comprehensive equanimity throughout one's life, the praxis of relative *moderation* in various domains becomes a commendable approach. Personal and group behaviours that favour *temperance* over the unbridled push for gluttony and satiation, power and domination, or hubristic glitz may well spare the persons concerned the risks of stress, anxiety, burnout, sleep deprivation, suspicion, fear, and other health problems.

Some thinkers have sought to explain why some destitute people (generally excluded and humiliated) adapt to their state of deprivation and indignity. Amartya Sen expressed this view thus:

> The utilitarian calculus based on happiness or desire-fulfilment can be deeply unfair to those who are persistently deprived, since our mental make-up and desires tend to adjust to circumstances, particularly in making life bearable in adverse situations. It is through 'coming to terms' with one's hopeless predicament that life is made somewhat bearable by the traditional underdogs, such as oppressed minorities in intolerant communities, sweated workers in exploitative industrial arrangements, precarious share-croppers living in a world of uncertainty, or subdued housewives in deeply sexist cultures. The hopelessly deprived people may lack the courage to desire any radical change and typically tend to adjust their desires and expectations to what little they see as feasible.[129] They train themselves to take pleasure in small mercies.[130]

Seldom would one find contemporary people voluntarily and continuously accepting to 'adapt to deprivation'. The hypothesis of Sen and his disciples that 'adaptive preferences' would make the *deprived* content with their predicament is subject to questioning. Indeed, it is unrealistic to assume that – in an increasingly interconnected and transparent world – the 'exploited and the destitute' lack the desire and/or the will to improve their lot (similarly to other well-provided humans). Their resentment and anger vis-à-vis those responsible for their destitution could well act as a spring-board (see the 'dynamics of emancipation' in Chapter 5 (p. 224)). To succeed, they need skills, lasting willpower, and some external transitory support.[131]

The destitute – trapped into ignorance, misery, and social injustice – can improve their lot once they learn that it is possible and legitimate for them to overcome prejudices and stereotypes held against them by ruling elites. It is unrealistic to assume that persons born and/or reared under bondage will accept their subjugated status and their destitution willingly throughout their life span (see Exhibit 2.5). Their strife for liberty, dignity and progress could, however, turn ineffectual for a while vis-à-vis those who concentrate power and wealth in their hands. Nevertheless, sacrifices of the down-trodden are likely to pay-off in due course – should they demonstrate sufficient resilience.[132] Nevertheless, despite the poor's willingness to improve their lot and the intervention of local or central governments to stimulate business activities in low-income regions through financial support, the *political clout* of the rich can prove a formidable handicap. Indeed, the *haves* will resist raising taxes at their expense.[133]

Exhibit 2.5 'Adapting to' vs 'breaking away from' destitution

In 1958, the International Bank for Reconstruction and Development (for short the World Bank) set up a team of 13 persons, at the request of the Libyan Government, in order to produce a comprehensive *plan for the development of the Libyan economy*. The country was then amongst the world's poorest, heavily dependent on foreign aid. This author's assignment was that of *Assistant* to the Mission's Chief, P. S. Narayan Prasad, with the duty of scouting for information (collecting factual data and soliciting interviews) needed for producing the World Bank's Report on *The Economic Development of Libya* (later published by the John Hopkins University Press in 1963).

In his fact-finding assignment, various situations attracted the attention of the author regarding the validity of the '*adaptive capacity*' paradigm. Instead of 'adapting' permanently to their poverty status, the author found that another paradigm could also explain the *emancipatory* behaviour of the poor. That behaviour can be explained by the stamina of '*breaking- away*' from poverty traps; it is illustrated hereafter by three contextualized episodes encountered by this author as member of the World Bank team for the development of Libya:

The first consisted of a visit to a 'literacy programme' class offered by UNICEF in the 'Sebha' oasis town of the Fezzan province in the south-west of Libya. The person in question, a Tubu[134] young adult, was introduced to the World Bank team by his UNICEF instructor. We learned that he was held in bondage by his master with the daily task of drawing water from a well. With courage and determination, he earned his freedom to enrol in the UNICEF literacy class. He looked puny, and his hands were badly scarred by the rope he had used during his bondage for lifting buckets of water. His skin was severely wrinkled by the harsh sun of the desert (reaching some 50 degrees Celsius during summer time and in the shade). The World Bank team was impressed by his personal saga and his commitment to prepare for the emancipation of his community, starting with an effective programme to *spread literacy and inculcate needed skills*.

The second concerned a meeting with a notable in El-Beida town of the Djabal al-Akhdar in the province of Cyrenaica of North-Eastern Libya. He had pitched a tent for his family in the garden of his house which was vacant. Some of the World Bank's team members commented that his use of a tent for residence might reflect his preference for the 'Arab Beduin' life-style, instead of living in a house equipped with modern functionalities! When I queried him, he took me inside the house to show me the crumbling ceiling. He just needed *access to financial services for vital repairs* that would allow him to house his family in safety in order to have a productive life. He told me this was the case with many members of his community who sought to extirpate themselves from chronic poverty.

The third event illustrated the need for *solidarity-cum-security*. The World Bank team was offered the chance to visit the Ghadames oasis in south-western Libya next to the Algerian frontier in order to meet a traders' caravan on its business trip across the Sahara Desert. We reached the oasis by private plane in a few hours flight from the capital city of Tripoli, while the Tuareg[135] business caravan had been patiently plodding together for several days across the vast and forbidding African Sahara desert to reach Ghadames, crossing several national frontiers. The World Bank team and the travelling tribesmen met to discuss developmental issues of primary concern to protecting their nomadic life and brave collectively the risks of their journeys across the forbidding vast Sahara Desert. To the pleasant surprise of the World Bank team, their symbolic hospitality was shown as the team was offered fresh milk, milked personally by the Tuareg chieftain of the caravan from his she-camel. The *precious liquid* (milk) was offered as a token of solidarity by the notable to be shared from the *same pot* by all those present at the meeting, each free to drink according to need his personal thirst from the common receptacle.

All the above-mentioned individuals (the Tubu liberated fellow, the Arab notable farmer, and the Tuareg chieftain) impressed the author in so far as they typify an epic behaviour – notably their unwillingness to '*adapt to destitution*'. They considered their current ordeals of poverty and insecurity surmountable, and were looking for developmental solutions to overcome these challenges. These solutions were based on: *acquisition of knowledge and skills*, *access to financial services*, and *solidarity-cum-security* – respectively. Fuelled by the hope of improving their wellbeing, the above-mentioned protagonists illustrate people's refusal to accept their current predicament of chronic poverty and insecurity.

Source: author

An individual's capability at promoting her/his wellbeing is determined by innate conditions (whether biological, psychic, intellectual or emotional) – as well as by social, economic, political, and environmental conditions. Individuals' *journey in life* is seldom rectilinear and stable in view of the complexity and brittleness of human nature that encounters multiple vagaries. That journey can be subject to unpredictable upheavals, and sinuous or chaotic tracks – different from the stylized, simplifying models. The said *journey* does not therefore exclude doubts or confusion, followed by anguish and tribulations arising from potential dangers. An individual's potential capabilities could be enhanced (i) through removal of obstacles for their access to opportunities, and/or (ii) through stimuli (e.g. public investments in favour of education and training, health services, safety nets, entitlements for distressful situations, etc.).

During a person's life cycle, the gap between her/his *effective capabilities* versus her/his *aspired capabilities* has been used as an indicator of patients' suffering. This was originally proposed by Dr K. C. Calman.[136] The suffering resulting from the above-mentioned gap can be alleviated through palliative measures.

When crushing pain becomes intolerable, that situation could force the person concerned to deliberately and consciously end her/his life. One vividly eloquent case, in modern times, is that of the South Korean Choi Yoon-hee, a 63-year-old 'happiness guru' who committed suicide (along with her 72-year-old husband). She is the author of about 20 books on happiness and hope, and an inspiring television star on these subjects. She apologized to her family, friends, readers and audiences for succumbing on 7 October 2010 to the fatal decision to end her life because she could not bear the excruciating pain of her two-year-long 'lung and heart diseases' any longer, according to a note she left. Her husband joined her in ending his life in unison, prompted by perfect empathy and love.[137]

To alleviate suffering and avoid ultimate despair, it is necessary to calibrate one's ambitious wishes in line with one's current capabilities. In failing health, such alleviation can be resorted to through *palliative* care – when *preventive* and/or *curative* medicines are ineffective. This would call for using pain-killers, psychotherapy, spiritual exercises, or other means that moderate suffering and/or shorten the period of inexorable degeneration. This would allow the person concerned to reach a 'comfort zone' with a reasonable level of equanimity in the terminal phase of life. For some individuals, systems of beliefs allay fears and moderate suffering; faith becomes then a fountainhead of fortitude, and possibly psychic or mental plenitude.

Philosophers and other thinkers have expressed their views on the subject of ageing since antiquity.[138] One could point to healthily ageing persons who enjoy a serene vision of existence, thereby making their life's terminal phase a lesser source of angst.[139]

The objective of aligning an individual's aspirations closely to her/his capabilities (physical/mental/psychic) is to help the person concerned to avoid angst due to failures resulting from unrealistic or illusory expectations. Thanks to the combination of 'discernment and will', the said alignment should help the individual concerned to tether within the limits of her/his strength and resources. This is realized by accepting and adjusting, if possible with serenity and fortitude, to her/his changing condition in the inescapable progressive tapering off in one's life's terminal phase.[140] It is temerarious to set-up a *vade-mecum* on this subject valid for all humans. Nevertheless, academic and research centres increasingly focus on remedying emotional turbulences through the therapeutic use of mindfulness.[141]

Groups, nations, states, and/or civilizations

Life cycles of organized communities, economic groups, or socio-political entities (e.g. dynasties, states, empires, civilizations, etc.) extend over longer periods than those for individuals. Their pattern of evolution starts with *infancy* and early growth, thereafter blossoming into *maturity* with an apex of achievements, before the *decline* in fortunes (for multiple reasons covering internal dissentions or external aggressions). Placid groups or civilizations eventually fail in their vigilance, languish, and get overrun, dismantled, or absorbed by other more dynamic, newcomer orders.

People in an organization hold together thanks to multiple factors. Notable among these is a conscience of belonging to one or more of the following categories: class (for example, the proletariat, professional elites, landowners, the military, political ideologies, or others), belief systems, shared cultures and/or traditions, common vision and purpose, and other factors that contribute to effective solidarity and social cohesion. Their *prosperity* can increase and consolidate in propitious times. It can wane when people succumb to despondency and fail to agree and respond collectively, energetically and creatively, to challenges.

Challenges could result from a variety of sources: internal dissensions (for ethnic or other reasons) among society's components; intolerable abuses by established regimes; moral turpitudes of rulers; the rise of powerful rivals; adverse environmental factors (for example earthquakes, droughts, depletion of resources); and other factors. These problems could brew and develop over the long term. The demise of states or civilizations – though difficult to forecast – has been analysed by several historians and social scientists. While particular societies tend to excel and prosper ahead of others over certain stretches of time, there is no assurance regarding these societies' capability to maintain indefinitely or for long the momentum of their initial drive for superior achievements.

Social and political groups' evolutionary process comprises – similarly to individuals – four main phases: (a) *infancy* of communities or cities starting with *dearth* or *poverty* (in the realms of material, intellectual, artistic or other fields), followed by (b) *development* and *growth*, culminating in (c) *maturity* with an apogee of *power*, *sophistication* and *prosperity*, and ending up in (d) *decline* and *decadence* resulting from profligacy, internal dissentions, external aggressions, or other factors that destroy material and non-material assets. Such decline in fortunes and ultimate demise of an erstwhile prosperous and/or powerful social group can be provoked by unresolved internal dissensions, or by external expansionary parties that succeed in imposing their writ.

Life cycles of states (national or supra-national) have been richly documented and interpreted by various authors.[142] The terminal phase of a socio-political group's cycle would generally wither, and get transformed, breakup, mutate, and/or dissolve within other group(s) – under the influence of endogenous or exogenous factors. As amply illustrated by archaeological and historical studies around the globe, several ancient communities have followed the above-presented pattern.

Several communities that started with low standards of living have become prosperous – thanks to the discovery and commercialization of their natural resources. This applies notably to Arab Gulf communities, whose populations had lived till the 1930s frugally from pearl fishing, trading dates for imported products, or grazing their livestock in oases. With the discovery and extraction of large oil riches, Gulf communities have become prosperous, with standards of living among the highest in the world. Their cities boast currently luxurious hotels and mansions, skyscrapers, entertainment facilities, vast shopping malls, marinas, and other modern facilities. It is incongruous, however, to have in these countries in the midst of the summer heat (with intolerable temperatures reaching 50 degrees Celsius in the shade) sport tournaments held in fully air-conditioned stadiums, golf courses abundantly watered by soft water (itself produced from energy-intensive desalination plants), or 'artificial snow' ski runs, etc.!

Upon the depletion of petroleum deposits or the loss of their commercial value, desert states solely dependent on the extraction of petroleum for their livelihood are likely to suffer. Lacking perennial sources of potable water, it will not be surprising that arid countries' habitat would fall into ruin overtaken by the surrounding hostile deserts, with urban agglomerations turning eventually into ghost towns. Their populations are likely to move to other more hospitable areas and/or dissolve into other more prosperous communities. What applies to oil-rich communities could also apply to other communities that have benefited – for a stretch of time – from their rich endowment in other natural resources. One can nevertheless point out to other desert cities (for example Las Vegas in Nevada – the United States) that have continued to thrive after the gold and silver 'rush' of the latter part of the nineteenth century. Desert cities could compensate for the absence of potable water locally by importing it or through the desalinization of sea water. This presumes that local people have opportunities for the development of other lucrative activities (e.g. gambling, entertainments, and tax-free entrepreneurial businesses) that appeal to business creators and a wide market of potential customers.

Ibn Khaldun (AD 1332–1395), often considered a pioneer in the disciplines of *political economy*, *sociology*, and *historiography*, examined the life cycle of states and civilizations. In his widely cited magnum opus 'al-Muqaddimah' (The Prolegomenon), he examined over long stretches of history the existence of a typical pattern for growth and decline in prosperity (applying to dynasties, states, civilizations, social organizations, and cities). He attributed a leading role to *asabiyyah* (defined as a highly *cohesive solidarity* based on a shared sense of belonging to a group, making individuals subordinate partially or totally their personal interests to those of the group). The political power derived from *asabiyyah* (originally based on the kernel of kinship and getting larger with the support of groups sharing the same cultural background, belief systems, and collective aspirations) can wane. The above-mentioned entities or polities could suffer over certain periods from lack of cohesiveness, resources and credible power; they would then become vulnerable to various internal or external forces that usher the phase of decay and disintegration.[143]

Four centuries before Adam Smith (1723–1790 – often referred to as the father of modern economics), Ibn Khaldun had expounded in his *Introduction to History* five fundamental factors of the growth process: demographic growth, technical progress, the search for individual profit, the principle of private property, and the soundness of political and legal institutions. According to Olivier de la Grandville:

> It is not surprising therefore that we owe to Arab civilization the first comprehensive description of the fundamental causes of growth. In his *Muqaddimah* (1377), the Arab historian Ibn Khaldun went even further and set himself to explain the causes of the rise and decline of civilizations ... Ibn Khaldun's contribution encompasses not only the description of the growth process, but also what needs to be done to set it in motion. His essay therefore is not only positive or descriptive; it is normative as well, and it shares that characteristic with Adam Smith's '*Inquiry into the Nature and the Causes of the Wealth of Nations*' that came four centuries later.[144] ... Ibn Khaldun has been a precursor of innumerable economic ideas that would be independently rediscovered only centuries later.[145]

Life cycles (of an individual, a business entity, a social group, a nation, a polity, or a civilization) do not necessarily progress smoothly. Their trajectories can indeed be impacted by unexpected events: *positively* (e.g. by exceptional prosperity due to booming exports), or *negatively* (e.g. by natural catastrophes or devastating wars).

'*Are humans capable of learning from past crises or disasters?*' Although historical events are seldom identical, the question merits continuous probing. To reflect on this subject, instructive cases are presented below (see Chapter 4) in the fields of (a) financial intermediation, (b) migration, (c) international trade, and (d) socio-economic development. These cases have affected the economies of the United States, Europe, and Africa; they shed light on methods used to fend off the common scourge of poverty-cum-vulnerability.

Notes

1 See, for example, Angus Deaton, *Income, Aging, Health and Wellbeing around the World: Evidence from the Gallup World Poll*, Princeton University and National Bureau of Economic Research, July 2007, 45p.
2 www.isr.umich.edu.
3 www.happyplanetindex.org.
4 See, for example, Sir Cary L. Cooper and Michael P. Leiter, eds, *The Routledge Companion to Wellbeing at Work*, Routledge, 2017, 387p.
5 See, for example, www.worldvaluessurvey.org.

6 See, for example, Valerie Möller, Denis Huschka, and Alex C. Michalos, eds, *Barometers of Quality of Life Around the Globe – How Are We Doing?*, Springer, 2008, 238p.

7 See, for example, Philip Moons, Werner Budts, and Sabina De Geest, 'Critique on the Conceptualisation of Quality Of Life: A Review and Evaluation of Different Conceptual Approaches', *International Journal of Nursing Studies*, vol. 43, 2006, pp. 891–901, Elsevier.

8 See Enrico Giovannini, Jon Hall, Adolfo Morrone, and Giulia Ranuzzi, *A Framework to Measure the Progress of Societies*, OECD Working Paper, September 2009, 23p. (www.oecd.org/progress/taxonomy).

9 Veena S. Raleigh and Catherine Foot, *Getting the Measure of Quality: Opportunities and Challenges*, The King's Fund, 2010, p. 23/32p.; www.kingsfund.org.uk.

10 See, for example, Fiona Nunan, *Understanding Poverty and the Environment – Analytical Frameworks and Approaches*, Routledge, 2015, p. 112/206p.; also UNEP World Conservation Monitoring Centre in Cambridge: nea@unep-wcmc.org.

11 Thomas Helbling, 'Externalities: Prices Do Not Capture All Costs', *Finance & Development*, 29 July 2017, 4p.

12 See, for example, Robert D. Klassen and Stephan Vachon, 'Greener Supply Chain Management', in Pratima Bansal and Andrew J. Hoffman, eds, *The Oxford Handbook of Business and the Natural Environment*, 2012, pp. 270–289.

13 Diane Coyle, *GDP – A Brief but Affectionate History*, Princeton University Press, 2014, p. 27/159p.

14 See his *Historical Statistics on World Population, GDP and Per Capita GDP 1–2008 AD*, available online via: www.GGDC.net/maddison; see also D. S. Prasada Rao and Bart van Ark, eds, *World Economic Performance – Past, Present and Future, Essays in Celebration of the Life and Work of Angus Maddison*, Edward Elgar, 2013, 432p.; the book's analyses review Maddison's pioneering works that have ushered in new vistas for economic development – for example Chapter 7 titled 'Making the International System Work for the Platinum Age', by Ross Garnaut, pp. 162–192; and Chapter 9 titled 'Explaining Success and Failure in Economic Development', by Adam Szirmai, pp. 227–267.

15 Walter Scheidel, *The Great Leveler: Inequality from the Stone Age to the Twenty-First Century*, Princeton University Press, 2017, p. 6/528p.

16 Erik Brynjolfsson and Andrew McAfee, *The Second Machine Age – Work, Progress, and Prosperity in a Time of Brilliant Technologies*, W. W. Norton & Company, 2014, p. 111/306p.; see also UNU-IHDP and UNEP, *Inclusive Wealth Report 2012, Measuring Progress toward Sustainability*, Report Director Anantha Duraiappah, Cambridge University Press, 2013, 336p.

17 See Marc Fleurbaey and Didier Blanchet, *Beyond GDP – Measuring Welfare and Assessing Sustainability*, Oxford University Press, 2013, 306p.; 'Measuring Economies – The Trouble with GDP', *The Economist*, 30 April 2016, pp. 21–24; Professor Sir Charles Bean, *Independent Review of UK Economic Statistics: Interim Report*, Crown copyright 2015, 93p.; and Exhibit 2.2.

18 For an analysis of issues of measurement of wealth accretion (or destruction) in a given economy over a given period of time, to be compared with a base period, see for example, (i) Diane Coyle, 'Rethinking GDP – It May Be Time to Devise a New Measure of Economic Welfare with Fewer Flaws', *Finance & Development*, March 2017, pp. 16–19, and (ii) the paper of Friedrich Scneider, 'Size and Measurement of the Informal Economy in 110 Countries around the World', Workshop of Australian National Tax Centre, Canberra, 17 July 2002, 50p.; and Tim Callen, 'Gross Domestic Product: An Economy's All', *Finance & Development*, 29 July 2017, 3p.

19 See Sarah C. White and Chloe Blackmore, eds, *Cultures of Wellbeing: Method, Place, Policy*, Palgrave Macmillan, 2016, 290p.

20 United Nations Development Programme, *Human Development Report 2013 – The Rise of the South: Human Progress in a Diverse World*, p. 56/204p.
21 The underlining of words is added by this author [Mikdashi] for emphasis.
22 Diane Coyle, *GDP – A Brief but Affectionate History*, Princeton University Press, 2014, pp. 14–15/159p.
23 See: The Committee for the Prize in Economic Sciences in Memory of Alfred Nobel, *Angus Deaton: Consumption, Poverty and Welfare*, The Royal Swedish Academy of Sciences, 12 October 2015, 34p.
24 See, for example, 'Measures of WELLBEING', *The Economist*, 25 February 2012, pp. 53–54; and John Harvey and Vicki Taylor, *Measuring Health and Wellbeing*, Sage, 2013, 140p.
25 See, for example, Bart Hobijn and Charles Steindel, 'Do Alternative Measures of GDP Affect its Interpretation?', *Current Issues in Economics and Finance*, Federal Reserve Bank of New York, November 2009, 7p.
26 See, for example, Darrell Huff, *How to Lie with Statistics*, Penguin Books, 1954, 124p.; also 'Performance Indicators – How to Lie with Indices', and 'Performance Indices – Ranking the Rankings', *The Economist*, 9 November 2014.
27 See Timothy M. Smeeding, 'Poverty Measurement', in David Brady and Linda M. Burton, eds, *The Oxford Handbook of the Social Science of Poverty*, Oxford University Press, 2016, pp. 21–46/915p.
28 See, for example, David Brady and Linda M. Burton, eds, *The Oxford Handbook of the Social Science of Poverty* , Oxford University Press, 2016, 915p.; also Roy J. Romanow, 'Promoting Progress: Making it Happen', *OECD World Forum on Measuring and Fostering the Progress of Societies*, Istanbul, 30 June 2007, 22p.
29 Communities stretch from small entities (e.g. family or clan) to larger ones (e.g. tribe, nation, or a conglomeration of nations). Members of a community bond together thanks to common key factors. Notable among these are: language and culture; history and traditions; basic interests; creeds and values; aspirations and goals; vision and mission; fighting off common enemies or dangers; and a durable willingness to live together in harmony and solidarity. The 'community bond' can be formalized through a social pact. That bond can loosen and become fragmented with the impact of rising socio-economic inequalities, divergent ideologies, polarization of ethnic-cultural differences, and/or racial antagonisms.
30 See, for example, OECD Health Policy Studies, *Value for Money in Health Spending*, 2010, 200p.; and Joseph Kutzin, Cheryl Cashin, and Lelitta Jakab, eds, European Observatory on Health Systems and Policies, *Implementing Health Financing Reform, Lessons from Countries in Transition*, World Health Organization, 2010, 411p.
31 See, for example, 'Farming in Ethiopia and Kenya – Qatnip', and 'Yemen – Qat Wrenching', *The Economist*, 21 January 2017 and 6 January 2018, p. 28 and p. 23 – respectively.
32 For measurement techniques, see for example: Ann Bowling, *Measuring Health – A Review of Quality of Life Measurement Scales*, 3rd ed., Open University Press, 2005, 211p.
33 *How's Life? 2013 – Measuring Well-Being*, OECD Publishing; also www.oecdbetterlifeindex.org; and Daniel J. Benjamin, Ori Heffetz, Miles S. Kimball, and Nichole Szembrot, *Beyond Happiness and Satisfaction: toward Wellbeing Indices Based on Stated Preference*, National Bureau of Economic Research, Working Paper 18374, 48p.
34 See, for example, Bengt Brülde, 'Happiness, Morality, and Politics', *Journal of Happiness Studies*, Springer, vol. 11, no. 5, 2010, pp. 567–582. *HLY and protection of the ecosystem* have been combined to measure the 'Happy Planet Index 2.0' (HPI, see: www.happyplanetindex.org); Robert Prescott-Allen, *The Wellbeing of Nations – A Country-by-Country Index of Quality of Life and the Environment*, Canada's International Development Research Centre, 2001, 342p.; also John Eyles and Allison

Williams, eds, *Sense of Place, Health and Quality of Life*, Ashgate, 2008, 221p.; and International Society for Quality-of-Life Studies: www.isqols.org.

35 See, for example, Roger Crisp, 'Wellbeing', in *Stanford Encyclopedia of Philosophy*, 6 September 2017; copyright Roger Crisp, roger.crisp@st-annes.oxford.ac.uk; see also 'Wellbeing', in Ted Honderich, ed., *The Oxford Companion to Philosophy*, 2nd ed., Oxford University Press, 2005, pp. 955–956.

36 See, for example, Sudhir Anand, Paul Segal, and Joseph E. Stiglitz, eds, *Debates on the Measurement of Global Poverty*, Oxford University Press, 2010, 446p.; also Sudhir Anand and Amartya K. Sen, 'Human Development Index: Methodology and Measurement', *Human Development Report Office*, New York, July 1994, 19p.

37 See, for example, Karen Sudmeir-Rieux, Manuella Fernandez, Ivanna M. Penna, Michel Jaoyedoff, and J. C. Gaillard, eds, *Identifying Emerging Issues in Disaster Risk Reduction, Migration, Climate Change and Sustainable Development – Shaping Debates and Policies*, Springer, 2017, 288p.; also the *World Congress on Risk 2015 in Singapore*, www.sra.org.

38 See Nick Bostrom, 'Existential Risk Prevention as Global Priority', *Global Policy*, vol. 4, no. 1, 2013, pp. 15–31; and Graciela Chichilnisky and Armon Rezai, eds, *The Economics of the Global Environment – Catastrophic Risks in Theory and Policy*, Springer, 2016, 649p.; see also *Centre for Study of Existential Risk* at: http://cser.org/.

39 'What America Has Learned from Its Largest-Ever Spill', *The Economist*, 18 April 2015, p. 39.

40 See, for example: Guy Hutton, Gerardo Sanchez, and Bettina Menne, *Climate Change and Health: A Tool to Estimate Health and Adaptation Costs*, World Health Organization – Regional Office for Europe, 2013, 45p.

41 Cour des comptes – French State Official Audit Agency, *The Costs of the Electronuclear Technology*, Paris, January 2012, 438p.; www.ccomptes.fr.

42 www.sortirdunucleaire.org.

43 See U.S. Nuclear Regulatory Commission, *Three Mile Island Accident*, Fact Sheet, Washington DC, 1994, 8p.

44 For documentation on nuclear power, see: www.nrc.gov.

45 Richard Hindmarsh and Rebecca Priestley, eds, *The Fukushima Effect – A New Geopolitical Terrain*, Routledge, p. 284/298p.

46 See, for example, Fiona Nunan, *Understanding Poverty and the Environment – Analytical Frameworks and Approaches*, Routledge, 2015, pp. 161–162/206.

47 See: www.pisa.oecd.org.

48 The World Bank, Roumeen Islam, and Gianni Zanini, *World Trade Indicators 2008 – Benchmarking Policy and Performance*, Washington DC, 2008, p. xxiii/125p.

49 Jose Guimon, Associate professor at the Department of Development Economics of Universidad Autonoma de Madrid, 'From Export Processing to Knowledge Processing: Upgrading the FDI Promotion Toolkit', *Columbia FDI Perspectives*, no. 186, 7 November 2016, 4p.

50 Inge Amundsen, 'Nigeria: Defying the Resource Curse', in Aled Williams and Philippe Le Billon, *Corruption, Natural Resources and Development – From Resource Curse to Political Ecology*, Edward Elgar, 2017, pp. 17–27/178p.

51 See UNEP, Report on Nigerian Oil, 7 August 2011; also Julia Ruth-Maria Wetzel, *Human Rights in Transnational Business – Translating Human Rights Obligations into Compliance Procedures*, Springer, 2016, 265p. (in particular Chapter 2 'Nigeria, Shell and the Ogoni People', 11–18p.); and 'Shell Accepts Liability for Two Oil Spills in Nigeria', 3 August 2011, in www.guardian.co.uk.

52 'Nigeria – Continued Gas Flaring Harms Both the Environment and the Economy', and 'Nigeria's Oil – Crude Politics', *The Economist*, 5 April 2008, p. 44, and 28 March 2015, p. 40 – respectively.

53 'Iraq – The Blighted City: The Shocking Decline of Iraq's Oil Capital', *The Economist*, 21 November 2015, p. 38.

54 See, for example, Paul R. Ehrlich, *The Human Bomb*, Sierra Club/Ballantine Books, 1968, 201p.
55 See Gary S. Becker, 'The Economic Way of Looking at Life', *Nobel Lecture*, December 1992, 21p.
56 'The Economics of the Coming Spaceship Earth', in H. Jarrett, ed., *Environmental Quality in a Growing Economy*, Baltimore/MD, Resources for the Future/John Hopkins University Press, 1966, pp. 3–14.
57 See D. H. Meadows *et al.*, *The Limits to Growth: A Report for the Club of Rome's Project on the Predicament of Mankind*, originally published in 1972 – later revised and updated; see also, Martin Mulligan, *An Introduction to Sustainability – Environmental, Social and Personal Perspectives*, Routledge, 2015, 309p.; Jeffrey D. Sachs, *Common Wealth: Economics for a Crowded Planet*, Penguin Press, 2008, 400p.; Edward B. Barbier, *Scarcity and Frontiers – How Economies Have Developed Through Natural Resource Exploitation*, Cambridge University Press, 2011, 748p.; Edgar Pisani, *Une politique mondiale pour nourrir le monde [A Global Policy to Feed the World]*, Springer, 2007, 150p.; and Anthony D. Barnosky and Elizabeth A. Hadly, *End Game – Tipping Point for Planet Earth*, William Collins, 2015, 264p.
58 See, for example, Julian Simon, *The Ultimate Resource I: People, Materials, and Environment*, 1996.
59 *Foreign aid* is recognized for its 'grant component' by the donor country that does not involve a quid pro quo on the part of the recipient country. The absence of such a quid pro quo can be due to a variety of motives. Among these motives, one could mention notably: altruism on the part of the donor country (e.g. the desire to alleviate conditions of extreme poverty in matters of health, nutrition, housing, education, etc.) or emergency situations (such as addressing famines and rescuing people following on natural or man-made disasters). Other motives may include political-military alliances, commercial pacts, and/or responding to donor countries' specific interests. *Foreign aid* can be offered directly by donor countries (bilaterally) or indirectly (via multilateral institutions) to the recipient country. It can take the form of convertible financial resources, or in-kind designated products (i.e. in the form of goods or services provided by the donor country). It can furthermore carry specific conditions to be honoured by the beneficiary (e.g. regarding the use to be made of aid).
60 See, for example, Sambit Bhattacharyya, 'The Historical Origins of Poverty in Developing Countries', in David Brady and Linda M. Burton, eds, *The Oxford Handbook of the Social Science of Poverty*, Oxford University Press, 2016, pp. 270–292/915p.; see also United Nations Development Programme, 'What is Poverty? – Concepts and MEASURES', *International Poverty Centre*, December 2006, 24p.
61 Regina S. Axelrod and Stacy D. VanDeveer, 'Introduction: Governing the Global Environment', in Regina S. Axelrod and Stacy D. VanDeveer, eds, *The Global Environment – Institutions, Law, and Policy*, 4th edition, Sage, 2015, p. 21/413p.
62 See Arnim Langer, Frances Stewart, and Rajesh Venugopal, eds, *Horizontal Inequalities and Post-Conflict Development*, Palgrave Macmillan, 2012, 346p.
63 Thomas Piketty, *Le Capital au XXIe siècle*, Seuil, September 2013, 976p.; also translated into English by Arthur Goldhammer, *Capital in the Twenty-First Century*, The Belknap Press of Harvard University Press, 2014, 696p.
64 Piketty op. cit., p. 27.
65 See, for example, Anthony Atkinson, *Inequality: What Can Be Done?*, Harvard University Press, 2015, 384p.
66 Michael J. Sandel, *Justice: What's the Right Thing to Do?*, Farrar, Straus and Giroux, 2009, pp. 266–267/308p.
67 Raymond Torres, Director, International Institute for Labour Studies, in: *World of Work Report 2010*, ILO, p. vii; see also UN Department of Economic & Social Affairs, *Report on the World Social Situation 2011: The Global Social Crisis*, UN

Department of Economic & Social Affairs, 113p.; and FAO, *The State of Food Insecurity in the World*, Rome, 2011, 50p.: www.fao.org.

68 See www.swissinfo.com, www.bloomberg.com, www.france24.com, and other news agencies.

69 See Karma Ura, Sabina Alkire, Tshoki Zangmo, and Karma Wangdi, *An Extensive Analysis of GNH Index*, The Centre for Bhutan Studies, May 2012, 213p.; accessible at: www.grossnationalhappiness.com/. For complementary documentation, see also Ruut Veenhoven Director of the 'World Database of Happiness' and founding Editor of the *Journal of Happiness Studies*, Erasmus University Rotterdam, The Netherlands: (1) 'Measures of Gross National Happiness', *OECD World Forum on Statistics, Knowledge and Policy*, 27–30 June 2007, 29p.; and (2) 'Can We Get Happier Than We Are?', in Ingrid Brdar, ed., *The Human Pursuit of Well-Being – A Cultural Approach*, Springer, 2011, pp. 3–14/271.

70 See, for example, The World Bank, *2013 World Development Report on Jobs*, 327p.

71 'A 21st Century Evil – Charcoal Slaves', *Al-Jazira*, 25 March 2012.

72 The research by two NGOs [namely Amnesty International and Afrewatch] was published on 19 January 2016, 88p.

73 Lydia van der Putten, Universiteit Leiden – KidsRights Report, *Minors not Miners – Hazardous Child Labour, with a Focus on Gold Mining in Burkina Faso*, April 2014, 21p.; www.kidsrights.org. The International Labour Organization (ILO) launched the World Day against Child Labour in 2002. It estimated in 2016 that 168 million children were still in child labour (the 105th ILO Conference).

74 Oxfam Briefing Paper, *Working for the Few: Political Capture and Economic*, 20 January 2014; see www.oxfam.org.

75 *Richest 1% to Own More Than Rest of World [by 2016], Oxfam Says*, 19 January 2015 www.bbc.com/news/business.

76 Oxfam Briefing Paper no. 210, *An Economy for the 1%*, 18 January 2016, 44p., written by Deborah Hardoon, Sophia Ayele, and Ricardo Fuentes-Nieva.

77 Janet L. Yellen, 'Perspectives on Inequality and Opportunity from the Survey of Consumer Finances', 17 October 2014.

78 See, for example, United Nations, *The Millennium Development Goals Report 2009*, New York, 57p.; The World Bank, *Conflict, Security, and Development, World Development Report 2011*, Washington DC; and UNDP, *Human Development Reports – Annual*.

79 Speech of UN Secretary General Ban Ki-moon on 2 December 2016 at the UN General Assembly.

80 See, for example, the reports of Save the Children charity: www.savethechildren.org.

81 See The World Bank, *World Development Report 2006: Equity and Development*, Washington DC, September 2005, 320p.

82 See Simon Maxwell, *Poverty Briefing – The Meaning and Measurement of Poverty*, Overseas Development Institute, 3 February 1999, 4p.

83 Using a statistical dispersion measure developed by the Italian statistician and sociologist Corrado Gini in 1912: A Gini coefficient of zero expresses perfect equality where all values are the same [for example, where everyone has an exactly equal income]; a Gini coefficient of one [100 on the percentile scale] expresses maximal inequality where only one person has all the income.

84 Edmund S. Phelps, *Macroeconomics for a Modern Economy*, Economics Nobel Prize Lecture, 8 December 2006, 26p.

85 See: International Institute for Labour Studies, *World of Work Report 2010, From One Crisis to the Next*, Geneva, ILO, 2010, 122p; also IMF, *Fiscal Monitor – Tackling Inequality*, October 2017, 114p.; OECD, *Economic Policy Reforms 2014 – Going for Growth*, Paris, 2014, 120p. www.oecd.org/growth/GoingForGrowth2014.

86 See, for example, G. William Domhoff, *Wealth, Income, and Power*, Department of Sociology, University of California at Santa Cruz, 19 September 2013, 21p.; www2.ucsc,edu/whorulesamerica/.

87 Jonathan D. Ostry, Andrew Berg, and Charalambos G. Tsangarides, *Redistribution, Inequality, and Growth*, IMF Staff Discussion Note, February 2014, p. 26/30p.

88 See, for example, Oxfam, *The Cost of Inequality: How Wealth and Income Extremes Hurt Us All*, 18 January 2013, ref.: 02/2012; Joseph Stiglitz, *The Price of Inequality: How Today's Divided Society Endangers Our Future*, Norton, 2012, 414p.; also 'Inequality – Unbottled Gini', *The Economist*, 22 January 2011, pp. 67–68.

89 See, for example, Tom Burgis, *The Looting Machine: Warlords, Tycoons, Smugglers and the Systematic Theft of Africa's Wealth*, PublicAffairs, 2015, 319p.

90 See, for example, 'Growth Strategies or Jobs Strategies', pp. 87–90, in World Bank, *World Development Report 2013: Jobs*, World Bank, 327p.; and International Labour Organization, *World Employment and Social Outlook: Trends*, 19 January 2016, 91p.; also: Perrine Toledano, Olle Östensson, and Kaitlin Y. Cordes, 'Parsing the Myth and Reality of Employment Creation through Resource Investments', *Columbia FDI Perspectives*, no. 213, 20 November 2017, 4p., The Columbia Center on Sustainable Investment.

91 An interview with the then President of Chile Michelle Bachelet, 'Promoting Growth and Social Progress', *The McKinsey Quarterly*, 2007 Special Edition, 'Shaping a New Agenda for Latin America', p. 36.

92 IMF Public Information Notice dated 24 August 2011.

93 Ian Goldin, *The Pursuit of Development – Economic Growth, Social Change, and Ideas*, Oxford University Press, 2016, p. 104/214p.

94 See, for example, Wim Naudé, Amelia Santos-Paulino, and Mark McGillivray, eds, *Vulnerability in Developing Countries*, United Nations University Press, 2009, pp. 2–4/321p.

95 See, for example, the United Nations Conference on Trade and Development – UNCTAD, *Guidance on Good Practices in Corporate Governance Disclosure*, New York and Geneva, 2006, 42p.; and UN Global Compact, *Corporate Governance – The Foundation for Corporate Citizenship and Sustainable Businesses*, 2009, 7p.; also: www.unglobalcompact.org and www.gcgf.org.

96 See, for example www.solidarites.org; also Z. Mikdashi, *OPEC States and Third World Solidarity*, The OPEC Fund for International Development, Vienna, December 1980, 25p.

97 See, for example, Jeremy Rifkin, *The Empathic Civilization*, Jeremy P. Tarcher Inc., 2010, 674p.

98 See, for example, Simon Baron-Cohen, *Zero Degrees of Empathy: A New Theory of Human Cruelty*, Allen Lane, 2011, 190p.

99 www.undp.org/mdg.

100 See, for example, Brian Keeley, *Income Inequality – The Gap between Rich and Poor*, OECD, 2015, 117p.

101 See 'Disability – Who Counts?', *The Economist*, 14 December 2013, p. 56.

102 See, for example, the books of the Dalit writer Harsh Mander in: www.penguinbooksindia.com [e.g. *Unheard Voices: Stories of Forgotten Lives*], and articles in *The Hindu – New Delhi*, [e.g. 'Barefoot, Imprisoned for Life', 9 January 2011]; also 'Forced Labour in India – Toil and Trouble: Where Slavery Persists in All But Name', 'India's Ungoverned Spaces', and 'Caste Prejudice in India – Unconscionable', *The Economist*, 3 November 2012, 1 June 2013, and 27 January 2018, p. 49, 49–50, and 44–45 – respectively.

103 See, for example, Sujatha Kidla, *Ants Among Elephants: An Untouchable Family and the Making of Modern India*, Farrar, Straus and Giroux, 2017, 320p.

104 Jean Drèze and Amartya Sen, *An Uncertain Glory – India and its Contradictions*, Allen Lane, 2013, p. 213/434p.

105 Zoya Hasan and Martha C. Nussbaum, eds, 'Introduction', in *Equalizing Access – Affirmative Action in Higher Education in India, United States, and South Africa*, Oxford University Press, 2012, pp. 8–9/273p.

106 See Sita Venkateswar and Sekhar Bandyopadhyay, eds, 'Introduction', in *Globalisation and the Challenges of Development in Contemporary India*, Springer, 2016, pp. 1–15/270p.; and 'India's Muslims – An Uncertain Community', *The Economist*, 29 October 2016, pp. 44–45.

107 See UNICEF and ILO Reports: www.unicef.org, www.ilo.org.

108 See *The Global Slavery Index 2014*, 135p. in: www.globalslaveryindex.org/report/.

109 See 'Performance Indices – Ranking the Rankings', *The Economist*, 8 November 2014, www.economist.com/node/21631039/print.

110 The UN International Organization for Migration, and international media sources: CNN, BBC, Reuters, etc. on 18 November 2017.

111 See: www.uncontactedtribes.org; and info@survivalinternational.org.

112 UN Secretariat statements on the occasion of 'International Day for the Elimination of Violence against Women', 25 November 2017.

113 See OECD Development Centre, *Social Institutions & Gender Index – 2014 Synthesis Report*, 68p.: www.genderindex.org; also Ricardo Hausmann, Laura D. Tyson, Yasmina Bekhouche, and Saadia Zahidi, *The Global Gender Gap Index 2013*, World Economic Forum, 388p.; see also the Gender Inequality index of the UNDP.

114 See, for example: 'The Gender Gap', *The Economist*, 7 October 2017, p. 13, 54–56, and 65–67; and Janet G. Stotsky, 'Gender and Its Relevance to Macroeconomic Policy: A Survey', *IMF Working Paper*, WP/06/233, October 2006, 68 p.; also 'Boosting Women's Status May Help Strengthen Economic Growth', *IMF Survey*, 29 January 2007, pp. 28–29.

115 See her Declaration of the Rights of Woman and the Female Citizen published in 1791; for an English translation, see *The French Revolution and Human Rights: A Brief Documentary*, translated, edited, and with an introduction by Lynn Hunt, Boston/New York Bedford/St. Martin's Press, 1996, pp. 124–129.

116 See her play on 'Slavery of the Negroes', written in 1784 and titled originally 'Zamore and Mirza', or 'The Happy Shipwreck'.

117 Press Service of European Parliament, *Focus*, 27 October 2011.

118 See, for example, Yasmin Jawad, 'A Gendered Perspective on the Arab Spring: Arab Women Caught Between Internal and External Conflicts', in Christopher K. Lamont, Jan Van Der Harst, and Frank Gaenssmantel, eds, *Non-Western Encounters with Democratization – Imagining Democracy after the Arab Spring*, Ashgate, 2015, pp. 85–101/241p.

119 See, for example, Laura E. Berk, *Development Through the Lifespan*, 7th edition, Pearson, 2018, pp. 8–11/673p., plus appendices; see also Tara L. Kuther, *Lifespan Development – Lives in Context*, Sage, 2017, 534p., plus appendices.

120 See his: 'Quality of Life in Cancer – A Hypothesis', *Journal of Medical Ethics*, vol. 10, 1984, pp. 124–127.

121 See Alan Cribb, 'Quality of Life – A Response to K. C. Calman', *Journal of Medical Ethics*, vol. 11, 1985, pp. 142–145.

122 Lutz Krusche, in Mémona Hintermann and Lutz Krusche, *Ils ont relevé la tête [They Raised Their Head]*, JC Lattés, 2010, pp. 231–254; also Wikipedia.

123 See, for example, www.againstpain.org; www.pain.ch; also: Institute of Medicine of the National Academies, *Relieving Pain in America*, The National Academies Press, Washington DC, 2011, 364p.

124 connectedhealth@partners.org; 'Frugal Health Care in America' and 'Saving Britain's Health Service', *The Economist*, 18 June 2011, pp. 71–72.

125 See: Robb B. Rutledge, Nikolina Skandalia, Peter Dayanc, and Raymond J. Dolan, *A Computational and Neural Model of Momentary Subjective Well-Being*, Wellcome Trust Centre for Neuroimaging, University College London, London WC1N 3BG, United Kingdom; Max Planck University College London Centre for Computational Psychiatry and Ageing Research, London WC1B 5EH, United Kingdom; and Gatsby Computational Neuroscience Unit, University College London, London WC1N 3AR,

United Kingdom – Edited by Wolfram Schultz, University of Cambridge, Cambridge, United Kingdom, and accepted by the Editorial Board 2 July, 2014.

126 See: www.pnas.org/content/early/2014/07/31/1407535111.

127 Arianna Huffington, *Thrive – The Third Metric to Redefining Success and Creating a Life of Well-Being, Wisdom, and Wonder*, Harmony Books, New York, 2014, p. 38/342p.

128 See, for example, Anne Chaté, *Bonheur tranquille – Vivre avec l'esprit de moderation [Tranquil Happiness – Living with the Spirit of Moderation]*, Payot, 2009, 188p.

129 *Adaptive capacity* can be defined as the ability of a social system or an ecological system to adapt/adjust to changing environments. A higher *adaptive capacity* improves *resilience to perturbations* (such as extreme climate variability) by moderating potential damages, taking advantage of opportunities or coping with the consequences of change (ref. Marcus Taylor, *The Political Ecology of Climate Change Adaptation – Livelihoods, Agrarian Change and the Conflicts of Development*, Routledge, 2015, p. 53/206p.

130 Amartya Sen, *The Idea of Justice*, Penguin Books, 2010, pp. 282–283/468p.

131 See Abhijit V. Banerjee and Esther Duflo, *Poor Economics: A Radical Rethinking of the Way to Fight Global Poverty*, PublicAffairs, 2014, 320p.; David A. Clark, *Adaptation, Poverty and Well-Being: Some Issues and Observations with Special Reference to the Capability Approach and Development Studies*, Global Poverty Research Group, and Economic & Social Research Council, September 2007, 32p. www.gprg.org/; and Thomas Wells, *Sen's Capability Approach*, Erasmus University Rotterdam, 25 April 2012, Internet Encyclopaedia of Philosophy: t.r.wells@dunelm.org.uk.

132 See, for example, Judith Rodin, *The Resilience Dividend – Managing Disruption, Avoiding Disaster, and Growing Stronger in an Unpredictable World*, Profile Books Ltd, 2015, 398p.

133 See, for example, 'A Taxing Problem – Reducing Inequality in a Globalized Economy', *The Economist*, 21 October 2017, p. 70.

134 Tubus are an African ethnic group who live in northern Chad, southern Libya, eastern Niger, and northwestern Sudan.

135 Tuaregs belong to an ethnic group who have inhabited North Africa's Saharan desert since immemorial times. They are traditional pastoral semi-nomadic people, believed to be descendants of the Berber autochthones of North Africa. They principally inhabit oases within a vast Sahara desert that stretches from Libya to Algeria, Niger, Mali, Burkina Faso, and northern Nigeria.

136 See his paper 'Quality of Life in Cancer Patients – An Hypothesis', *Journal of Medical Ethics*, vol. 10, 1984, pp. 124–127; see also Hans Neuenschwander, Eduardo Bruera, and Franco Cavalli, 'Matching the Clinical Function and Symptom Status with the Expectations of Patients with Advanced Cancer, Their Families, and Health Care Workers', *Support Care Cancer*, Springer-Verlag, vol. 4, 1997, pp. 252–256.

137 'Happiness Preachers Tragic End', *The Korea Times*, 8 October, 2010; 'South Korean Happiness Guru Commits Suicide', *AFP News Agency*, 8 October 2010; Danielle Demetriou in *Telegraph*, 11 October 2010 [www.telegraph.co.uk]; also: www.joogangdaily.joins.com; and www.news.com.au.

138 See Helen Small, *The Long Life*, Oxford University Press, 2007, 346p.; also Marc Agronin, *How We Age: A Doctor's Journey into the Heart of Growing Old*, Da Capo Press, 2011, 302p.

139 Carol Graham, *Happiness around the World: The Paradox of Happy Peasants and Miserable Millionaires*, Oxford University Press, 2009, pp. 47–51/249p.; also Stephanie Hatch *et al.*, 'A Life Course Approach to Well-Being', in John Haworth and Graham Hart, eds, *Well-Being – Individual, Community and Social Perspectives*, Palgrave Macmillan, 2012, pp. 191–209/298p.; and 'How to Have a Better Death', *The Economist*, 29 April 2017, pp. 9–10 and 45–48.

140 See *The Quality of Death – Ranking End-of-Life Care across the World*, A report from the Economist Intelligence Unit, Commissioned by Singapore philanthropic house LIEN Foundation, 2010, 36p.; also available at www.eiu.com/sponsor/lienfoundation/qualityofdeath.
141 See the Oxford Mindfulness Centre: http://oxfordmindfulness.org/.
142 For the breakdown and dismantling of the Roman empire, see, for example, Montesquieu [1689–1755], *Considerations on the Causes of the Greatness and Decadence of Romans*, 1734; and Edward Gibbon [1737–1794], *History of the Decline and Fall of the Roman Empire*, published in six large volumes between 1776 and 1788.
143 See Faruk Yalvaç, 'Ibn Khaldun's Historical Sociology and the Concept of Change in International Relations Theory', in Deina Abdelkader, Nassef Manabilang Adiong, and Raffaele Mauriello, eds, *Islam and International Relations – Contributions to Theory and Practice*, Palgrave Macmillan, 2016, pp. 77–103/232p.
144 Olivier de la Grandville, *Economic Growth – A Unified Approach*, 2nd edition, Cambridge University Press, 2017, p. 1/428p.
145 Grandville, op. cit., p. 393.

3 'Value pies'

Roles of governments, businesses, and markets

Public authorities and wellbeing

The term 'community' covers diverse entities with a variety of functions and kinds of authority – stretching from (i) villages, cities, subnational jurisdictions ... to (ii) national, regional, and supranational groups. The interests and strategies of major protagonists in a business community are diverse. *Communities* are also diverse in many respects (with respect to their origins, structures, functions, resources, and other characteristics). They comprise people who bond together thanks to one or more critical factors. Notable among these factors, one could mention the following: shared historical background and collective memory; shared basic interests, creeds, values, aspirations, visions, and missions; common economic and political interests; a single ethnic and cultural patrimony; comparable habitat or lifestyle; unity within a solid institutional framework (e.g. that of a national or multinational state) that solidly binds together people; a durable willingness to live together in harmony and solidarity, and/or other binding forces or factors.

Public interest stands for the community's *public good*, while *egocentric interest* focuses on benefits sought by individuals, partisan groups, or segments of the community, regardless of their possible negative impact on other members of society.

Using a variety of potent instruments or levers (fiscal, administrative, financial, or other instruments), governments can dissuade individuals or private groups or institutions from resorting to harmful or wasteful practices, and can incite them to adopt *prudent management* of resources for the good of current and future generations. To protect public interest globally, operators can be obligated to avoid and/or remedy any depredations they are responsible for (at both the national and trans-national levels). Global cooperation should be underpinned by credible scientific surveys, and should include careful continuous monitoring, verification, reporting, control, and enforcement measures – with appropriate incentives or sanctions as required.

Hereafter, key issues of developmental states are examined. They cover: (1) developmental states' objectives, (2) the arsenal of instruments available to governments, (3) the potency of fiscal-cum-regulatory regimes, and (4) core principles of governance. Thereafter, the basic interests and strategies of business stakeholders are evaluated by reference to the generation, expansion, and split of 'value pies'.

Developmental objectives

Multiple factors influence the growth of national economies, and selected policies contribute to accelerating that growth. In this respect, two major approaches are often observed, *state interventionist* and the laissez-faire – with several variants in between. Among these variants, an often recommended approach is that of *developmental states*. According to a UN source, *developmental states* are defined as those that seek to promote 'economic development by explicitly favouring certain sectors, commanding competent bureaucracies, placing robust competent public institutions at the centre of development strategies, clearly articulating social and economic goals, and deriving political legitimacy from their record in development'.[1]

Developmental states get strongly involved in fostering the establishment of new businesses in the domestic economy. This goal can be realized through notably either of the following two broad approaches:

i Creating and nurturing of domestic enterprises in promising sectors. Such a policy will be effective for a given period of time, i.e. until the said enterprises are able to stand up to foreign competitors. The latter's superior competitive bargaining power could derive from their control of: strategic commodities, key technologies and know-how, abundant and cheap inputs, privileged access to market outlets, economies of size, efficient management, talents, and/or other advantages. This 'infant industry' policy has been resorted to often through: (i) administrative or regulatory measures (e.g. by imposing tariff and non-tariff levies on imports, offering subsidies for exports, and/or privileging national preferences in governmental purchases), (ii) significant governmental participations in the capital or voting power of key corporations – thereby permitting them to influence these corporations' strategies and to improve their creditworthiness, and (iii) fiscal exemptions for budding national enterprises over their initial few years of operation. The foregoing measures and strategies are aimed at replacing imports with domestic substitutes, at spearheading the development of promising new products (goods, services, or technologies), and/or at keeping decision-making and jobs of promising industries within national jurisdictions. Such protectionism is meant to be transitory (running over a 'few' years), premised on the existence of a domestic potential (human and material) capable of producing the needed goods and services at competitive costs in open markets.

In reality, the 'infant industry' policy has been troubled by the state's wrong choices – for example the prioritization of sectors with little prospects for economic development. Other problems are those of inefficiencies, corruption, and monopolistic practices. This has been the case in several developing and developed countries. Governmental agencies, including the military establishment in some countries (e.g. Egypt, Pakistan, Indonesia, Brazil, Russia, China, and others), are owners of businesses covering finance, consumer goods, textiles, natural resources, various equipment, etc.[2] In protected markets, vested interests get entrenched, thus making it too difficult for the authorities to remove the privileges (originally granted as temporary) to the beneficiary companies later on. Protected companies generally suffer from lower quality, lesser productivity, lower innovativeness, and poorer performance – compared with companies operating in vibrant competitive markets. Governmental interventions in support of employment can be implemented through reductions in, or exoneration from, fiscal or social charges payable by firms – in addition to overt or covert subsidies. Such measures could prove unproductive when they are applied to dying industries. Protectionist measures are offered in support of infant industries. These are nascent industries that suffer from dis-economies of scale compared with well-established foreign competitors. Accordingly, they need to be protected for a limited period until they can attain similar economies of scale enjoyed by their foreign competitors.

Subsidies cover a wide array of measures: aimed at inputs /and or outputs, income, or other factors that affect business performance. They can be linked to exports, imports or domestic business activities.[3] The Global Subsidies Initiative (GSI) is one indicator for the assessment worldwide of the monetary value of subsidies that governments offer on various products and services.[4] It operates under the guidance of a constellation of eminent expert personalities representing developed and developing countries. Governmental and inter-governmental organizations (notably the EU, the OECD, the World Bank, and WTO) have also sponsored research to assess the impact of governmental actions, mostly focussed on competition and trade policies.[5]

ii Enticing footloose investors. Several countries seek to attract ***footloose investors*** (e.g. in commercial, industrial, real-estate, financial or other services sectors) looking for profitable economic sectors to develop in the cheapest, least-regulated jurisdictions. These investors are typically free to move about. Moreover, they are enticed by tax incentives or lavish subsidies, credit facilities, absence of bureaucracy, light regulatory frameworks, cheap inputs (manpower, energy, raw materials, etc.), protection against expropriation of investments, and ease of doing business generally. Footloose investments can freely and easily relocate across jurisdictions in response to changing conditions.

Economists generally recognize that foreign investments offer *potential benefits* to a host country. These benefits could include: capital inflows; access to advanced technology, managerial expertise, logistics and infrastructures; higher employment; higher wages/salaries; access to international markets; cheaper and better quality of goods and services, and other benefits. Such benefits should not be at the expense of environmental protection and waste avoidance, fair competition, good governance, and sustainable development. Increasing trans-nationality of enterprises operating in multiple markets contributes to the decoupling of these enterprises' performance from that of their country of origin.[6]

FDI has nevertheless been opposed by certain host governments, often arguing that strategic sectors (for example those of natural resources) could be 'lost' to foreign interests, or that indigenous producers could be driven to the brink of bankruptcy.[7] Some sources, however, question the validity of existing empirical research that attributes to all foreign direct investments positive growth effects on emerging or developing countries. Indeed, some foreign direct investments aim at skimming the best of natural resources in host countries (minerals, timber, etc.) over limited time horizons. Sustainable healthy growth should protect the environment (by avoiding wasteful depletion of scarce resources, pollution, desertification, or loss of biodiversity), assure long-term food security, and adequately husband natural resources.

Some host governments may entice 'newcomer/footloose businesses' by offering them exemptions from fiscal charges over long periods, and from regulatory requirements. Corrupt rulers may even condone a degree of waste, pollution or depredation of natural resources should this approach favour the creation and development of business activities. By such actions (or inactions) these governments could invoke the motive of reducing unemployment and/or accelerating economic growth despite the detrimental impact on the ecosystems (e.g. by hurting the quality of air, water, soil, and biodiversity). Other host governments, with the strong support of their people, are guided by the long-term public interest of protecting the environment through minimizing waste and pollution (for example through measures of recycling, re-usage or reprocessing of discarded materials, and banning practices that could injure indubitably Earth's quality of life).

iii Protectionism. Governmental support for national enterprises (especially the newly created ones) needs to be limited in time and scope in order to avoid jeopardizing their long-term competitiveness and their dynamics (in matters of innovation, employment, and growth). Indeed, such support could render the protected businesses feckless and/or less dynamic in open competitive markets. Moreover, protectionism may delay costly adjustments or reforms. Policies intended to prevent companies from downsizing due to redundancies, or from delocalizing from high-cost markets to lower-cost ones, are not sustainable over the long run. Indeed, in an open world economy, public authorities cannot force companies to keep their relatively onerous labour force without risking the demise of the companies concerned.

Unless judiciously managed, the delocalization of businesses (to other regions within the same country or beyond national jurisdictions where skills and other resources are available at lesser costs), the privatization of state enterprises (with the ensuing redundancies of superfluous employees), downsizing (by the spinoff of poorly performing non-core business units), and the subcontracting of selected functions to minimize costs – all could create social tension, and disrupt the life of employees and workers. The latter's psychological distress could lead to family problems, burnouts, and even suicidal actions. Indeed, grave personal problems might ensue when very high standards of performance are abruptly imposed on workers or personnel without appropriate training or coaching.

The above-mentioned psychological problems encountered by France-Telecom (renamed Orange at privatization in 2004) had led to 35 suicides among its personnel in 2008–2009. Some of its personnel suffered in the transition from a *state monopoly* (with the guarantee of jobs-for-life) to that of a *private enterprise* declaring job redundancies in a highly competitive market. Streamlining its personnel (by cancelling 22,000 posts and changing the activities of 10,000 persons between 2006 and 2008) along with subjecting its remaining employees to exacting standards of performance have proved unbearable to some employees. Management demands with respect to higher turnovers, cost savings, higher profit margins, improved quality of service, innovation, forced geographic re-location of personnel, retraining into new jobs, incitements to resign, and other measures were deemed by French tribunals to constitute institutional 'moral harassment' subject to prosecution.[8]

Assuming that work opportunities are temporarily limited, one can also imagine various solutions for *sharing jobs*. Management would then try to induce workers to voluntarily accept to reduce their work load and/or their pay in order to avoid dismissal. In this way, the pool of workers connected with the concerned enterprise is not likely to shrink. The partially employed workers can then be readily called upon to resume full-time work once the activities of their enterprise pick up. Indeed, management may want to maintain its relations with highly qualified or talented employees to avoid losing for good their strategic know-how, their vital expertise, and their web of contacts to competitors. The existence of an unemployment insurance scheme (governmentally or privately funded) can conceivably compensate some of the shortfalls in salaries sustained by the partially employed over the crisis period – hoping that period does not too last long.

Policy-makers need to evaluate objectively their approach towards *reviving economic activities*. They should guard against measures that incapacitate the dynamism of the business sector. Among ill-conceived policies, one could mention: an easy monetary policy that generates inflation; protectionism that thwarts international division of labour and comparative advantages; venal bloated bureaucracy that produces inefficiencies and stifles innovation of dynamic enterprises; abuses of power through cronyism, nepotism, corruption or patronage regardless of merit.

Instrumentalities

To valorize their creative potential, entrepreneurs need to operate in hospitable soundly regulated open markets that respect the principles of good governance. Evidently, to perform their wealth-creating activities, entrepreneurs should not be shackled by bureaucrats who delay or block actions for unjustified complicit-cum-venal egocentric interests. Understandably, the state and its agencies have to perform their 'gatekeepers' functions of: protecting consumers/users from monopolistic practices; controlling the quality of products; controlling and sanctioning fraud; assuring the safety and salubriousness of working conditions; barring pollution; and other public-interest responsibilities.

Good governance is an intrinsic part of development. As put by Armartya Sen,

> ...political liberties and democratic rights are among the 'constituent components' of development ... [along with economic growth that] tends to expand the size of public revenue, which can be used for social purposes, such as schooling, medical services and health care, and other facilities that directly enhance the lives and capabilities of people.[9]

One can refer to two broad models of democracy: (i) a *representative* democracy through an assembly of freely elected legislators who mirror the different currents of its citizens' aspirations, and is empowered to legislate and rule by popular mandate over a few years, to be followed by elections at regular intervals that allow for reversibility of ruling parties, or (ii) *direct* democracy through frequent votes by citizens that propose new laws, call for changes in existing laws, or endorse proposed new legislations (proposed by their elected assemblies of representatives, by a political party, or a group of activist citizens) to be approved by referendum. The latter form of democracy is more suited for small communities and straightforward issues. According to Sen, the effectiveness of 'democracy has to be judged not just by the institutions that formally exist but by the extent to which different voices from diverse sections of the people can actually be heard'.[10] Sen argues that the origins of democracy have multiple sources that are not confined to the 'Western societies'.

Democratic regimes that represent the will of the people's majority through free elections should offer guarantees for the protection of minorities' basic human rights. In societies with authentic democratic representation, basic covenants express the central wishes of a wide spectrum of nationals. This naturally calls for the separation of powers: the executive, the legislative, the judiciary, the regulatory, along with accepting the operation of independent free media (Exhibit 3.1). These regimes have generally avoided governmental *dirigisme* in favour of *market economy* models.

Priorities among a community's objectives need to be consensually reached, and means for their timely realization need to be deployed effectively. To illustrate, public authorities could well sacrifice the policy of *balanced budgets* (based on governmental expenditures aligned to receipts), and/or the policy of monetary rigour (premised on monetary growth commensurate with real GNP growth). They could thus resort to *deficit financing* and *monetary expansion* for a while, in order to stimulate business activities and consumer spending with a view to overcoming slumps.

Some democratic regimes provide citizens with the right to recall politicians (that is to disavow them before the end of their full mandated period) should these politicians fail to realize the programs they had promised, respond judiciously to the people's desiderata, or address effectively challenges as they arise. While majority rule in democracies through universal suffrage and the ballot box is generally advocated, this should be done in full respect of the legitimate rights of minorities, thereby enabling individuals from these minorities to stand for public office, represent their groups, and safeguard their basic human rights in all walks of life.

Exhibit 3.1 Institutions and instrumentalities in a vibrant modern economy

An open-ended list[11]

1 Socio-political institutions: based on popular wishes (i) expressed through universal secret ballots allowing for peaceful alternation of power among competing national political groups, and for (ii) clear separation of powers among *the legislative*, *the executive*, *the judiciary*, and *the regulatory* to allow for the operation of 'checks and balances'.

2 Sharing of authority/responsibility: Devolution of powers from the national to the regional and local levels – allowing for pluralism, and the representation and protection of minorities.

3 Security apparatus: under civilian control.

4 Judiciary: easily accessible, low-cost, fair, and independent from executive authorities.

5 Media: based on the truthful communication of facts and events, coupled with freedom of expression.

6 Civil service, regulatory authorities, and enforcement agencies: impartial, autonomous and accountable, effective in applying 'prudential and anti-criminal' laws and enforcing obligations via a system of incentives and sanctions.

7 Education, health care, social security, and culture: efficient, universally accessible, at moderate cost (no cost for the poor).

8 Infrastructure: should provide, at reasonable cost, the necessities (e.g. potable water, salubrious habitat, safe working conditions, energy, public transport, communications, etc.).

9 Macro-micro policies: guided criteria of efficiency, stability, non-discrimination, innovation, employment, and growth.

10 Protection of property rights: covering physical, financial, intellectual, and cultural assets and patrimonies.

11 Financial intermediation: wide, diverse, liquid and safe financial markets.

12 Fiscal and social charges: comparatively reasonable, and fairly shared among society's components.

13 Crisis management: early warning systems to fend off conflicts or crises; insurance and guarantee mechanisms, safety nets, welfare benefits for disaster risk compensation or poverty alleviation.

Source: author

The mission of regulators is to anticipate and contain malpractices or scams through effective controls, before crises fester and contaminate whole sectors of national economies, eventually spreading internationally. It may appear strange that within the same country, some regulatory agencies could have different standards of control. For example, U.S. state-chartered commercial banks can be supervised by *state* or *federal* regulators – the former proving relatively less rigorous or demanding. Such leniency could delay corrective actions and generate ballooning problems.[12]

Governmental intervention is justified in periods of crises: to contain and correct market malfunctioning, re-invigorate economic activity, and sanction abuses. The great challenge of public authorities is to know *when* to intervene, *what* instruments or mechanism to use, *how long* to be involved and/or *how much* resources to commit – while minimizing the adverse consequences of their actions on future developments. The foregoing policies require *wisdom* and *political will* – which are unfortunately not commonly available, as shown by historical events.[13]

Potency of fiscal-cum-regulatory regimes

In view of the significant weight of modern states' functions, fiscal receipts have become increasingly important for funding governmental activities. The state needs to finance its basic functions (such as defence and security, administration of justice, compliance with regulations, education-cum-research, crisis management, safety nets, health care, etc.). Fiscal revenues flow from a variety of impositions – targeting income, capital gain, wealth and property, consumption, production, sales, export/import trade, inputs, financial transactions, inheritance, social services, licences, and others. It is reckoned that taxation of *consumption* has a lesser negative impact on growth, compared with the taxation of *salaries* or *capital*; the latter taxes would slow down investment, employment, and innovation.

In an open competitive world economy, governmental support for nascent local enterprises could be resorted to over a fixed period of time. That support seeks to prop up promising *infant* industries that seek to replace imports with domestic substitutes. Such industries need nurturing for a while to be able to compete in due course (possibly after a few years of development) vis-à-vis well-established foreign groups.

State support is varied; it includes direct subsidies to firms (in money or in kind) or indirect subsidies (for example support to selected inputs, or to outputs by guaranteeing government-sponsored purchases at remunerative prices; funding at favourable terms; alleviation of fiscal burdens or tax breaks; business-friendly regulatory frameworks and efficient public administration; appropriate safety nets; encouraging partnering with foreign groups; opening up foreign markets through active diplomacy or by providing aid to recoup initial expenses in these markets; and other types of support. Such advantages to budding businesses are supposed to be limited in time, to be unwound after an initial period of fostering.

A tax break in favour of small business may look like favouritism, giving the impression of 'free riders'. Nevertheless, if the tax break boosts entrepreneurial activities, brings in more sales or export revenues and more employment (compared with other businesses), then – from society's overall wellbeing standpoint – that tax break can be deemed warranted. Indeed, the bulk of small entrepreneurial businesses may well need tax breaks (or other incentives, financial or in kind) to compensate for constraints they encounter (owing to diseconomies of small size, limited know-how, concentration of risks, etc.).

Governments also support overtly or covertly large enterprises, for example by fiscal measures, because they are already big employers and are susceptible to delocalize if they are not satisfied with their fiscal incentives.[14] The United States tolerates secrecy laws, and weak oversight (this is notably the case in its constituent member states Delaware, South Dakota, Nevada or Wyoming) and this is deemed part of the problem of tax evasion.[15] Other federal governments allow a certain degree of fiscal competition among constituent jurisdictions.[16]

The architecture of a vibrant democratic polity can be adapted to suit a variety of societies. In all circumstances, *sound regulatory frameworks* are needed. These should underpin good governance, efficient competitive markets, honest and transparent information, clear bankruptcy procedures that protect the interests of creditors and investors, anti-corruption/anti-criminal mechanisms, efficient and effective supervision, and fair dispensing of justice (with dissuasive sanctions for offenders).

Business groups that ignore in their activities the basic desiderata of society (e.g. with respect to honesty and transparency; quality of goods and services; fair treatment of customers, employees and other stakeholders; and respect of the environment) are bound over time to be adversely affected. This is likely to show up through: loss of trust by customers, stricter governmental regulations and sanctions, turmoil among employees, loss of access to funding, or other adversities. Firms have been urged by the authorities, public opinion pressure groups, and NGOs to adopt and implement guidelines for 'best practices' and 'codes of good behaviour'.[17] Several corporations have also publicized their 'nicely' drafted codes of conduct for public relations purposes – with no assurance of strict enforcement.

Besides official regulators, other parties can act as gatekeepers with the mission of protecting the 'public good' through the disclosure of irregularities and abuses. They include: reputed investigative media bent on the careful scrutiny of facts, assessors of businesses, credit rating agencies, certified fraud examiners, private detectives, credible whistle-blowers, NGOs that monitor compliance with the generally accepted principles of *business ethics*, and others. Their mission is to detect and deter fraud, with the view of promoting the integrity of professional activities (business, politics, social, etc.) in all walks of life.[18] Legislation in a few countries pledges to protect whistleblowers who disclose irregular covert practices (such as those pertaining to corruption, conflicts of interest, money laundering, tax dodging, fraudulent manipulation or falsification of data, and other wrongdoings).

Whistleblowers have received official recognition and protection after information on financial scandals.[19] The United Kingdom (the UK Financial Conduct Authority and the Bank of England Prudential Regulation Authority) and Switzerland (the Swiss Federal Government and its Swiss Postal system[20]) have recently offered job protection and/or financial compensation to whistleblowers. Nevertheless, media sources reckon that:

> Switzerland's treatment of whistleblowers remains shoddy – and unlike in most developed countries, risks getting worse. It offers no legal protections

at all to private-sector whistleblowers, and none are in sight. The penalties for breaching financial secrecy have increased since Mr Elmer [a Swiss whistleblower] was first arrested [19 January 2011]. A whistleblower who sells data now faces up to five years in prison. Switzerland is almost alone in refusing to help other countries if their financial-crime investigations rely on stolen data.[21]

Governance

'Corporate governance' evaluations and scores are prepared by financial analysts – such as Standard & Poor's which has developed a set of criteria and an appropriate methodology for that purpose since 1998. Its approach is applicable internationally, and is based on the OECD governance principles. These comprise transparency, accountability, fairness, sustainable development, anti-corruption, and others. The OECD's *Guidelines for Multinational Enterprises* (adhered to by the 34 OECD members and 8 non-OECD countries) was updated on 25 May 2011.[22] By respecting guidelines for corporate governance, a company can enhance over the long term its image and its performance to the advantage of all parties concerned. Tools have been developed and applied to assess and rank governance factors in many countries on a yearly basis. Among key factors included in this evaluation is the factor of *perceived corruption* conveyed by public polls.[23] Tools (e.g. the Baruch Index of Corporate Disclosure regarding political donations offered by corporations) could reveal the lobbying power of businesses.

Enterprises that abide by the norms of business ethics stand to gain over the long term in customer loyalty, and in performance. Past events have shown, however, that self-interest is generally deeply embedded in human nature. A few decision-makers continue to privilege their personal interests at the expense of other stakeholders. Although rules of honesty and prudence are likely to continue to be flouted, installing transparent systems of checks and balances, underpinned by effective sanctions-cum-incentives could reduce the occurrence of such misbehaviour. A sound and effective regulatory framework based on good governance and accountability becomes thus a 'vital national asset'.

Innovations of a blockbuster nature are not the only sources of success for modern enterprises. Innovations can involve small improvements in products. Instead of producing quality products with *longer life cycles* some businesses adopt 'programmed obsolescence' policies for their products over shorter time horizons in order to increase their sales' volumes and to raise their revenues.

In the comprehensive analysis of costs-benefits of business activities from the standpoint of society at large, public policies have to take full account of externalities – with the objective of minimizing the negative fallouts and maximizing the positive ones. On the negative side, one would include pollution and accidents of all sorts generated by business activities. These have to be evaluated by reference to the impact of 'collateral damages' on current and future generations. This is the function of the decision tool called 'health impact assessment' whose dual purposes are to (a) predict the consequences on health of particular actions, and (b) inform the concerned decision-makers.[24]

The United Nations Millennium Declaration (Resolution adopted by the General Assembly on 8 September 2001) has re-emphasized the fundamental objectives: peace, security and disarmament; development and poverty eradication; proper observance of human rights and good governance;[25] caring for the vulnerable; and protection of the biosphere.

Focusing on governments, one UN source has argued that:

> Good governance promotes equity, participation, pluralism, transparency, accountability and the rule of law, in a manner that is effective, efficient and enduring. In translating these principles into practice, we see the holding of fair and frequent elections, representative legislatures that make laws and provide oversight, and an independent judiciary to interpret those laws. The greatest threat to good governance comes from an environment of corruption, violence and poverty, all of which undermine transparency, security, participation and fundamental freedoms.[26]

Business people need to be reasonably assured that the rule of law and the use of honest practices free from racketeering are prevalent in the economy in which they are invited to invest and operate. Nevertheless, treachery and plunder have often been resorted to. Prompted by greed, many individuals and business groups have used their ingenuity to circumvent laws and regulations, by poaching public resources.[27]

By eliminating obstacles to business opportunities, the scope for creativity and growth is bound to expand. One needs to acknowledge that improved equality of chances does not necessarily lead to equality of socio-economic conditions. While recognizing that a world economy characterized by open and level-playing competitive markets is, over the long term, beneficial for the largest possible number of participants, there are bound to be losers in the interim who cannot adjust readily. This applies to inefficient businesses that cannot be turned around; they are consequently driven into bankruptcy with loss of jobs and wellbeing to local communities. It is accordingly advisable to prepare workers for greater flexibility – such as change of residence (with implied difficult decisions of disposing of family property and sacrificing community relations); or accepting new jobs (subject to being trained). Admittedly, training workers in new skills at an advanced age poses some challenges, especially when the jobs proposed are poorly attuned to the conditions or aspirations of workers that are laid off.

Domestic pressures often lead governments to espouse protectionist policies aimed at resisting the relocation of enterprises outside national territories – despite objective economic reasons for such relocation (in particular cost advantages). Protectionist policies applied across the board are likely to prove counterproductive and unsustainable over the long run. They will further provoke other governments to retaliate. Favouring 'national champions' in an economic union comprising several states is incompatible with the *raison d'être* of that union. For example, the European Union (EU) calls for equal competitive treatment in the production and free movement of goods, services, funds, enterprises, and people. Indeed, governmental intervention in favour of 'national champions' is at variance with a single level-playing field characterized by a convergence of economic-fiscal-monetary policies. To contend with the competition of other countries' global firms (e.g. those of the Untied States, China, Japan, etc.), the EU authorities could then favour the growth of EU enterprises within the EU's market and/or internationally.

The argument for nationally owned 'strategic' industries to be protected has generally been used to cover enterprises that have attained commanding heights in national economies. These enterprises belong (a) to technologically advanced sectors (underpinned by research that produce patents of significant value to society), and/or (b) security-sensitive industries. Their owners are precluded from selling them to foreign interests. In particular, foreign state-owned investor companies come under the close scrutiny of many host governments on the grounds that these foreign state-owned companies are subject to the political dictates of their countries of origin. The strategic industries' argument has been abusively stretched out by some host governments to include food processing, metallurgy, infrastructures, mineral resources, etc. – in order to accommodate entrenched vested interests (economic, socio-political, bureaucratic, and others).

Much of the success of a business group depends on its constituent stakeholders who adhere diligently to the group's goals and strategies, and who implement a 'balanced sharing' of responsibilities, benefits, and costs. Certain prerequisites are needed, starting with mutual understanding and trust to avoid conflicts or stalemates. Exchanges, discussions, debates, dialogues, and negotiations aimed at reaching judicious compromises among protagonists should then lead to trade-offs and eventual pacts that reconcile differences with workable positive settlements.

For an illustration, one can refer to the German socio-political pact regarding *business governance* which has been enshrined in the Co-Determination Act of 1976; the Act calls on companies with more than 2,000 salaried persons to include employees'/workers' representatives – on an equal basis – in their companies' supervisory board (*Aufsichtsrat*) with the mandatory proviso that the chairman of that board should represent the shareholders with a preponderant vote in case of a tie. The *Aufsichtsrat* appoints the management board (*Vorstand*) and functions as a controller of their activities. Called *Mitbestimmung* (literally co-determination), this approach has reduced tensions and confrontations between workers'/employees' representatives on one hand, and owners/management's representatives on the other hand. Other German companies that employ between 500 and 2,000 employees (the publicly held AG, partnerships limited by shares [KSaA], and limited liability companies GmbH) are governed by the One-Third Participation Act (*Drittelbeteiligungsgesetz*). Under the foregoing legal regime, *one-third* of the supervisory board must be employees, compared with *half* in the co-determination regime.

Through supervisory boards, employees and workers are informed and consulted on matters of concern to them. Although workers'/employees' representatives are generally in minority positions in the above-mentioned boards, they have the opportunity of concerting without delay with the shareholders' representative and avoiding the risks of costly *polarization*, *confrontations* or *deadlocks* in favour of *dialogue* and *compromise*. By involving employees and workers in the high organs of enterprises as is the case in the German model, the smooth running and the productivity of businesses have reportedly improved. This has contributed to reducing the levels of discontent and the frequency of strike actions; it has also contributed to improving workers'/employees' pay and/or job security. From an ethical standpoint, one researcher argues that 'Co-determination seems to be an obvious and non-paternal way of considering the interests of employees.'[28]

Besides co-determination, there are other factors that influence labour-management relations. Chief among these are traditions of dialogue in lieu of confrontation, and labour-market conditions. Accordingly, a labour market characterized by low unemployment will provide greater bargaining power to workers and their trade unions. This has happened in January–February 2018, when German industrial workers staged through their trade union I G Metall a strike that yielded, after a few days of confrontation, mutually satisfactory results. These consisted of salary hikes of about 4.3 per cent beginning April 2018, and other payments spread over 27 months, and the right to reduce their weekly hours of work from 35 to 28 to care for their children, elderly or sick relatives, and be able to return full time after two years.[29]

In other countries, owners or their representatives (namely senior executives) have the sole power over decision-making in running business entities. Even in France, where the labour movement has a relatively long history, French legislation lags behind the German legislation in the effective *inclusiveness* of workers'/employees' representatives in the consultative-cum-decision making process. To satisfy their claims (in salary increases, better working conditions, refusal to slim or delocalize employment, seeking higher redundancy benefits, etc.), workers and employees – spearheaded by trade unions' officials – resort often to sit-downs and public protests in their bargaining with employers' representatives. Occasionally, French workers or trade unionists manage to hold managers hostage and occupy company premises until they get satisfaction. This happened with the French tyres plant of Goodyear in 6–7 January 2014 at the end of a long simmering conflict. Violent clashes with the police in the foregoing conflict reportedly injured 19 officers in March 2013.[30] Other managers of French-based businesses had also been roughed up or held as temporary hostages by workers set on keeping their jobs and/or improving their severance pay (e.g. those belonging to Caterpillar Inc., 3M Co, Sony Corp., Air France, etc.) as per various press releases.

Besides public authorities and their agencies (covering such domains as the legislative, regulatory, executive, and judiciary functions), other parties could claim a stakeholder status as watchdogs for public interest. This applies notably to independent NGOs. Their mission is to monitor, analyse, report, and evaluate objectively the conduct or the performance of entities under their purview; they are supposed to alert the general public and the authorities concerned with misconducts – as judged by reference to fundamental values or best practices. By exercising their activities in an objective and impartial spirit, NGOs can then be considered legitimate gatekeepers that deserve to be trusted for their integrity, fairness, and sound judgement. NGOs (such as Transparency International) alert the general public to grave malfunctioning or abuses – such as the predation of stakeholders' wealth, booties, or the spoiling of ecosystems.

Partisan interests can be strongly supported by handsomely paid lobbyists in the pay of big companies or pressure groups. Lobbyists seek to obtain privileges for these groups such as tax breaks or trade advantages.[31]

Policies and practices of governments are generally subject to the sway of powerful partisan interests. It is not uncommon to find in this century political decision-making usurped by powerful groups who resort to self-serving practices. They include political and non-political pressure groups (whether at the global, regional, national, or local levels) who are able to mobilize important resources (in money, talents, or influence) to lobby successfully for important favours or privileges; these are obtained from venal politicians, legislators or bureaucrats – compromising notably safety, public health, human rights principles, and sound regulations. Elected members of legislative assemblies can themselves be lobbyists. This is the case of Swiss parliamentarians whose members are authorized to exercise professional activities (such as corporate board memberships) in addition to their parliamentary mandate. This could admittedly distort their 'public interest' mission, and skew their support for legislation that favour the partisan interests that remunerate them.[32]

Politicians have often been influenced by lobbyists who can dress up as 'neutral and impartial experts'. For an example, the media had widely reported on putative 'independent experts' who received from manufacturers of nuclear equipment, and/or operators of nuclear-power plants relatively attractive pay or grants linked to their 'vouching' for the safety and efficiency of nuclear power plants.[33] Venal legislators, politicians, or regulators get in hock to pressure groups that manipulate public opinion to serve their partisan interests. These groups flout the tenets of honesty and good governance to satisfy their egocentric interests.[34]

Some lobbyists are recruited by powerful parties with 'deep pockets', such as major corporations. The latter in the United States are not constrained in their funding of political campaigns to support election candidates – be they parliamentary or presidential candidates – according to the U.S. Supreme Court ruling of 20 January 2010, reversing a 20-year ban (that capped contributions to political action committees to $5,000 per person per year). The risk of a direct causal link between *size of wealth* on one hand, and *political power* on the other hand (with a possible adverse impact on democratic life) has been of particular concern to social activists seeking to promote democratic institutions.[35]

Privileged parties (who benefit from positions of power, social status at birth, nepotism, cronyism, inheritance, etc.) are likely to hold firmly to their current advantages at the expense of other segments of society – using various means at their command. They can influence lawmakers (sometimes by offering them or their family members, jobs or consultancies) who pass laws skewed in their favour. Developed countries with democratic systems of government are not immune from the foregoing problems, despite their proclaimed principles of espousing 'good governance' principles.[36] Partisan lobbying groups are able to poach senior staff from Congress and governmental agencies by offering them higher salary packages.

It is revealing to note that regulatory state agencies in developed countries – though ostensibly espousing 'anti-bribery' codes of ethics for strict enforcement by both governmental agencies and private parties – have not been constantly vigorous in enforcing these conventions, such as the OECD Convention on Combating Bribery of Foreign Public Officials in International Business Transactions, adopted on 21 November 1997.[37]

Among the large contracts which allegedly had cover-ups for forbidden practices in 2010, BAE Systems admitted to two criminal charges of corporate corruption, and agreed to pay $400 million and $50 million to governments in the United States and Britain respectively to end corruption probe.[38] Anti-corruption 'campaigners believe the UK is unwilling or unable to force its semi-independent territories in the Caribbean and the Channel Islands to adopt public registries of the true owners of companies and other entities. Those territories include some of the tax havens [e.g. the British Virgin Islands] most favoured by the corrupt' as stated by Tom Burgis on the eve of an anti-corruption summit in London.[39]

Gatekeepers

The architecture of a vibrant democratic polity using the building blocs of institutional regulatory frameworks can be adapted to suit different socio-economic conditions. In all circumstances, sound regulatory frameworks are needed to underpin good governance, efficient competitive markets, honest and transparent information, clear bankruptcy procedures that protect the interests of creditors and investors, anti-corruption/anti-criminal mechanisms, efficient and effective supervision, and fair dispensing of justice (with dissuasive sanctions for offenders). However, institutional and regulatory frameworks may not have the scope and depth of action for marshalling efficiently the behaviour of human parties to attain desirable goals.

Business groups that ignore in their activities the basic desiderata of society (e.g. with respect to honesty and transparency; quality of goods and services; fair treatment of customers, employees and other stakeholders; and respect of the environment) are bound over time to be adversely affected. This is likely to show up through: loss of trust by customers, stricter governmental regulations and sanctions, turmoil among employees, loss of access to funding, or other adversities. Firms have been urged by the authorities, public opinion pressure groups, and NGOs to adopt and implement guidelines for 'best practices' and 'codes of good behaviour'.[40] Several corporations have also publicized their *nicely* drafted codes of conduct for public relations purposes – with no assurance of strict enforcement.

Besides official regulators, other parties can act as gatekeepers with the mission of protecting the 'public good' through the disclosure of irregularities and abuses. They include: reputed investigative media bent on the careful scrutiny of facts, assessors of businesses, credit-rating agencies, certified fraud examiners, private detectives, credible whistle-blowers, NGOs that monitor compliance with the generally accepted principles of *business ethics*, and others. Their mission is to detect and deter fraud, with the view of promoting the integrity of professional activities (business, politics, social, etc.) in all walks of life.[41] Legislation in a few countries pledges to protect whistleblowers who disclose irregular covert practices (such as those pertaining to corruption, conflicts of interest, money laundering, tax dodging, fraudulent manipulation or falsification of data, and other wrongdoings).[42]

High economic growth is not a panacea for progress in wellbeing. Indeed, growth in certain economic sectors could generate *collateral damages* (e.g. in grave industrial accidents, pollution, and health problems) that could exceed in importance the 'growth benefits' accruing to society. Under these circumstances, it is in the national interest to moderate the 'high economic growth' in sectors that produce high negative collaterals that exceed benefits, in favour of sectors that produce *net benefits* for society. To stem the tide of major risks encountered by humanity (i.e. pollution and toxicity, radioactive materials, devastating industrial accidents, pandemics, exhaustion of natural resources, etc.), regulatory cooperation is needed at the local, regional, and/or global levels – especially since several sources of these risks are long-lasting, and capable of migrating easily across frontiers.

Regulatory frameworks have been established to address the abovementioned risks. This has been prominent in risks that can readily spread over wide areas beyond national territories. Institutions have been created to monitor and control such risks. Some of these institutions offer help to confine such risks to the territories of their occurrence, and possibly to eradicate them. For examples, one could mention transnational/global institutions in the following domains: climate, money laundering, tax evasion, pandemics, addiction, criminal/terrorist organizations, etc. In the field of peace and security, institutions have been set-up to ban weapons of mass destruction. This would include toxic/chemical gases, nuclear bombs, cluster bombs, napalm bombs, explosives, and others. Seldom are international organizations' regulations fully implemented. Indeed, several countries cling to their sovereign powers. Nevertheless, as the world is turning increasingly interconnected and interdependent, supranationality, though an arduous construction, is becoming a necessity in several domains such as the safety of consumer goods, health protection, security of energy sources, etc.

Multilateral specialized institutions are needed to carry out comprehensive honest *monitoring* and effective *compliance* with rules of safety and salubriousness on planet Earth, underpinned preferably by incentives, along with sanctions or penalties (in the administrative, fiscal, financial or other fields). Finally, all policies and programmes should converge towards the desirable stage of sustainable development originally defined as 'development which meets the needs of the present without compromising the ability of future generations to meet their own needs'.[43]

In the twenty-first century, a community or a country cannot live in isolation, cut-off from the rest of the world. The *ills* or the *prosperity* of a given community or country are unlikely to be fully contained permanently within political or geographical frontiers; these influences can spill over far into other regions, eventually affecting the whole of planet Earth. The spread of calamities can be illustrated by reference to grave food shortages, severe pollution, terrorist attacks, violent conflicts, cybercrime, pandemics, protracted economic-financial crises, and nature's destructive forces (e.g. earthquakes, volcanic eruptions, tsunamis, tornados, cyclones, torrential rain and floods, and other climatic upheavals).

Prosperous populations cannot live insulated from destitute populations surrounding them or living in their midst, by holding them back indefinitely with legal/administrative, or physical barriers, or by sheer force. Nevertheless, several countries continue to erect bastions of separation vis-à-vis certain other alien countries or groups – ostensibly to protect their security, prosperity, way of life, culture, ethnic purity, or other criteria.

One should not belittle the potential advantages of globalization (reducing barriers) that open up opportunities for worldwide progress over the long term in many wakes of life. This is likely to happen when *low-cost* countries (e.g. those enjoying valuable abundant and cheap inputs, or those who benefit from fiscal charges' reductions or exonerations) manage to attract businesses from *higher cost* countries. The latter countries need therefore to compensate the 'loss in national income and employment due to delocalization of their businesses to offshore business centres' with the creation of new innovative businesses in which they are able to command comparative advantages. Indeed, the creation of such new businesses require investments in know-how with relatively long gestation periods. The loss of jobs due to the delocalized businesses in the high-cost countries would produce negative fallout on social stability. The gain of the *low-cost country* would, in such circumstances, become a loss for the *high-cost country*.

In periods of economic restructuring, the unemployed (especially adults at an advanced age) encounter difficulties in retraining and redeploying from dying jobs into newer ones, or in moving their homes to less attractive locations (within the same country, or to foreign countries). Full-time long-established employees living in a particular geographical location and with enterprise-specific skills are particularly less amenable to adaptation – compared with younger employees. The latter are capable of occupational versatility, geographical mobility, willingness to adapt to new (possible alien) social environments, and to accept readily training for new opportunities.

Business stakeholders

Several parties – we call them the stakeholders – are interested in the development of a business. The concept of *stakeholder* in a firm can be broadly defined as 'a person or a group that affects, or is affected by, a corporation's decisions, policies, and operations'.[44] The stakeholders of a firm can be split into *primary* and *secondary*. The primary stakeholders are owners/investors, creditors, workers/employees, suppliers of inputs, customers, and other economic agents that engage in direct operations with the business that produce value for themselves. Secondary stakeholders do not deal directly with the firm but influence (or get influenced by) its activities; they comprise the general public, communities, NGOs, and the media. For example, the community can be impacted negatively (by the pollution generated by the firm's activities) or positively (by the recruitment of locals).

Among the definitions of *business performance*, one could distinguish between: (i) the *narrow* definition that focuses on return to one category of stakeholders, namely owners of invested capital, and (ii) the *comprehensive* definition which refers to the total net benefits derived by a wide spectrum of stakeholders interested in an enterprise. In the latter definition, 'stakeholders' of an enterprise comprise: owners (majority and minority); lenders-investors; executives and management; employees and workers; customers; suppliers; subcontractors; partners and suppliers; various intermediaries; public authorities (at the local, national, regional, and/or international levels); current and future generations; and other concerned parties. Stakeholders' performance should be viewed over the longer term, and should take account of changes in the quality of products. Thus a policy of linking *salaries* solely to employees' *output* should be avoided if it is a source of deterioration in the quality of products or services provided. Moreover, such a payroll policy could prove counter-productive in so far as it leads to grave health problems (e.g. through stress, burnouts, suicidal behaviours, or other collateral dehumanizing damages sustained by the concerned workers or employees) and the development of absenteeism.

Those who own businesses generally stress the objective of 'shareholder value' or return on invested capital. By comparison, managers and employees focus on their compensation-cum-retirement pension benefits, the advancement of their careers, and their tenure (i.e. stable employment). 'Proportionality' of benefits among stakeholders of an enterprise – though difficult to calibrate, attain and/or maintain – is a worthy objective to seek in order to strengthen the value-creation motivation of all parties concerned in the performance of the enterprise over the long term.

Succinctly put, a business leader's success in a competitive market is judged by her/his ability in *serving optimally customers* through the efficient organization and management of *human* and *material capital*. Thus, a CEO who contributes to raising returns of shareholders thanks to innovation and marketing skills without resorting to firing employees has greater merit compared with a CEO who raises returns of shareholders by resorting to massive firing of employees.

On the responsibilities of the CEOs of companies (whether belonging to the private or the public sector), Laurence D. Fink, the CEO of the world's biggest private investment group [managing over $6 trillion in investments worldwide in 2018], commented thus:

> We also see many governments failing to prepare for the future, on issues ranging from retirement and infrastructure to automation and worker retraining. As a result, society increasingly is turning to the private sector and asking that companies respond to broader societal challenges ... Companies must benefit all of their stakeholders, including shareholders, employees, customers, and the communities in which they operate ... Companies must ask themselves: What role do we play in the community? How are we managing our impact on the environment? Are we working to create a diverse workforce? Are we adapting to technological change? Are we providing the retraining and opportunities that our employees and our businesses will need to adjust to an increasingly automated world ...[45]

Modern organizational theory of strategic management has emphasized the positive role of 'balanced partaking' among *stakeholders*.[46]

> The conventional notion that the corporation should create wealth only for its shareowners is incorrect. The corporation should be redefined to emphasize its relationships with and responsibilities toward *all* [*sic*] stakeholders, both voluntary and involuntary ... The stakeholder model of the corporation fits in with broadly accepted normative and ethical considerations.[47]

With a fair sharing of benefits in the 'value pie' among stakeholders, the latter's cohesiveness, synergy and motivation are likely to be considerably enhanced.

The stakeholder approach takes into consideration *all* contributors to *value creation*. It is based on the assumptions of mutual benefits of these contributors operating within network relations. As well expressed by researchers in this field:

> Mutuality implies that the firm and stakeholders are contributing to value creation and are included in value distribution. Thereby, firms and stakeholders are seen as owners [*sic*] of their contributions. Mutuality induces superior forms of innovation, competition and the operation of firms and stakeholders, striving for solutions to complex problems, difficult issues or innovative products and services.[48]

Exhibit 3.2 lists the main categories of stakeholders that contribute to value creation in the firm, directly or indirectly. Their interests are generally *concordant* in one domain, namely their drive at creating value by their firm. They do nevertheless compete in the domain of splitting the value pie created collectively. To illustrate, shareholders have as primary interest 'return on their invested capital'. By comparison, buyers are keen to purchase at attractive price-quality mixes, and employees are primarily concerned about job security and salary enhancement. The fulfilment of foregoing concerns of buyers and employees could reduce margins and return on capital – other things remaining unaltered.

Members of each category of stakeholders mentioned in Exhibit 3.2 do not have strictly homogeneous interests. A detailed analysis would then require splitting each category into sub categories whose members share more closely common interests. Depending on the firm's activities, certain categories of stakeholders have a legitimate pre-eminent claim on the value pie created. Trailblazing innovators-developers are thus among those who deserve comparatively higher remuneration, in comparison with those entrusted with unskilled activities. Similarly, those risking their capital in start-ups at the initial *seed stage* (founders, angels, crowd funding of start-ups) do not expect any revenue for a few years. Their returns will come thereafter as their innovative ideas bear fruits and produce significant growth in revenues. Venture capitalists are indeed entitled to higher returns, compared with investors in *senior debt* or *bank* lenders.[49]

Relations among a modern society's stakeholders are asymmetrical – with those in command over resources wielding economical-cum-political clout.[50] Influential stakeholders in business corporations generally belong to top management, or those that represent large investors. Their decisions have usually a substantial impact over other stakeholders' interests, such as employees or workers. In establishing priorities among competing or rival claims, top executives are generally well placed to privilege their own personal interests at the expense of other stakeholders.

A few chief executive officers (CEOs) candidly admit that they are not the sole *engine* of performance in their group. One such successful CEO transferred the '*responsibility of change*' from his office to employees, 'creating a company that was, in many ways, self-run and self-governing ... increasing the speed and quality of innovation and decision-making in the value zone'. The CEO in question has realized that his talented employees are front runners in generating value for the enterprise.[51] Probing the sources of success, many analysts have privileged the factor of 'merit' – namely *talent* and *hard work* in things they can excel in. 'Meritocracy', however, has not been the sole 'pollinator' of success. One should add the factor of *luck* (or a combination of propitious circumstances) as a contributor to the success of an individual or an organization. Put differently, many highly talented and hardworking people never achieve success without an element of luck.[52]

Exhibit 3.2 Key interests and strategies of a firm's stakeholders

1 Entrepreneurial leaders are agents of change. They seek to create net value in their ventures through innovative products or efficient processes that are either (a) conceived and developed internally by their teams, or (b) acquired from third parties. Creators of businesses and their close collaborators/family members usually have a controlling stake in the seed capital of their start-ups. They also expect their qualified siblings to have a significant role in the management or control of family enterprises – unless they decide to sell their enterprise to a third party.

2 Shareholders/investors seek attractive returns on their capital. They expect honest, transparent and regular reporting and disclosure of substantive information on current and prospective developments of their investments. Many investors in large listed companies are represented by fund managers (pension funds, mutual funds, hedge funds, etc.) who may trade more or less actively their shares on stock exchanges.

3 Inventors and innovators expect to be handsomely rewarded for their creativity, in so far as that creativity boosts their firm's long-term profitability.

4 Customers in a competitive market are interested in the most attractive quality/price mix of products, after-sale services, security of supplies, and rapid responsiveness to changing needs.

5 Executives and managers are interested in attractive compensation packages: Successful managers are recognized for their efficiency in organizing and deploying resources with the objectives of controlling risks and enhancing *business performance* (measured by reference to growth of net profitability in competitive markets over the medium-longer term).

6 Employees and workers seek decent salaries and retirement benefits, along with stability of employment. They strive also for: reasonable and safe working conditions; health and security protection; training and promotion; equal treatment and open opportunities (i.e. without discrimination or bullying); reasonable daily hours of work and vacation periods to avoid stress or burnouts; adequate and timely information on the development of business activities; adequate sharing in the firm's productivity increases. Through unionization, workers and employees can enhance their collective bargaining power vis-à-vis employers on wages/salaries and working conditions.

7 Creditors/lenders and guarantors seek to protect their funding of enterprises, and to receive adequate risk-adjusted yields.

8 The board of directors' duties notably consists in evaluating the firms' performance in the light of its objectives. It examines the strategies and programs of senior executives and managers in realizing the firm's goals as set by its stakeholders and in particular its owners (majority and minority).

9 Other parties in the value chain cover suppliers of various inputs (e.g. raw materials and accessories), processing or manufacturing facilities, transport and storage, technology and know-how, financial intermediation, marketing and distribution, etc.). These parties seek to protect their interests (e.g. regarding sales, prompt settlement of bills, absence of graft, business-friendly relations, etc.). In globalizing markets, several parties are linked (directly and indirectly) to transnational firms whose 'value chain' spans multiple countries.

10 Civil society gatekeepers are generally independent non-governmental organizations (NGOs). As non-partisan think-tanks and/or monitors of irregularities, they are primarily concerned about protecting *public interest* through research and alert systems.
11 Local communities look generally for job opportunities, growth in economic and social activities, healthy and productive settings, and good governance.
12 Public authorities: their main activities cover the levy and collection of adequate tax proceeds to fund basic public functions. The latter comprise: security, justice, regulation, education and research, various infrastructures, safety nets (for health care, pension and/or unemployment payments, disaster relief, poverty alleviation, affirmative action towards disadvantaged persons or marginalized communities, etc.).
13 Specialized institutions offer regulatory oversight and/or ultimate support to certain businesses. This is the case with financial intermediaries which rely on central banks or other monetary authorities for liquidity in periods of severe credit crunch.

N.B.: Each of the above listed categories of stakeholders can be split into subcategories whose constituent members have more *closely aligned* or *shared interests*.

Source: author

Among the above-listed stakeholders, the group of creators-developers of new original businesses activities that appeal to markets expect high returns compared with other self-employed persons who replicate existing business models. Hereafter, we reflect on the expectations of three major categories of stakeholders: shareholders-investors, workers-employees, and executives-managers.

Investors in businesses

Shareholders/investors in businesses are a heterogeneous group. Some are traders in shares privileging the short term, and other investors who hold their shares for the long term. Short-term shareholders would not mind sacrificing jobs to reduce wage bills in order to increase their shares' financial returns and market value before selling them. Owners of businesses have their stake represented by ordinary shares. They are the first to bear eventual losses. Workers, fiscal authorities, lenders (whether represented by financial institutions or senior bond holders) are the last to bear losses. There are hybrid instruments which combine features of ownership and lending.

Besides business creators such as founding shareholders who provide the business prototype and the seed capital necessary for the launching of a business project, other potential contributors to the funding of a new business are: business angels; pension funds, life insurance funds, mutual funds; hedge funds; religious or ethically/socially responsible investors' funds; corporate gadflies; wealthy family trusts; university and other endowments; sovereign wealth funds; internet platforms, and others.[53]

Though sharing in common the objective of enhancing their returns on capital, the above-mentioned institutional shareholders/investors could differ with respect to many factors such as: time horizons for realizing their investment objectives, governance principles and rules, socio-ethical values, business strategies, activism in influencing management and in trading shares, and other matters. Dissatisfied shareholders would sell their shares, unless they have the clout to replace under-performing top management.

In the split of the value pie, some analysts admit the difficulty of rewarding *fairly* the various categories of stakeholders. They criticize the stakeholders' approach as being *imprecise* in guiding management. They consider that the shareholders' model is more realistic (with its *primary focus* on maximizing return to the firm's owners who provide risk capital and are the first to bear eventual losses). According to the above-mentioned analysts, management has the fiduciary duty of serving first and foremost owners' long-term interests, and that objective should rigorously guide management's strategies. Yet, not all shareholders are interested in the long term, such as hedge funds gadflies whose 'activist investors hold their stock for a very short period of time and may have the potential to reap profits based on short-term trading strategies that arbitrate corporate policies'.[54]

Business leaders and regulators may well favour giving more 'voting rights' to shares held over relatively long periods. Thus the Florange Act in France, adopted on 29 March 2014, provides for the automatic granting of double-voting rights to shares held in a registered form by the same shareholder for at least two years – unless two-thirds of shareholders have voted against this rule. These shares are known as 'loyalty shares'. The Act allows companies to opt out of this automatic granting of double voting rights and continue their governance rules based on their bylaws principle of 'one-share one-vote'.

Linking voting rights to the length of time shares are held by investors is based on the rationale that the longer the duration of holding the shares, the more attractive are the company's prospects for investments that require long gestation periods. Moreover, to entice founders (notably family firms) along with long-term investors to list their privately held company in stock markets to raise additional capital without losing control over their firms, regulations could privilege them with extra voting rights for their shares, compared with 'newcomers' or 'trading' shareholders. Non-voting shares (equivalent to 'income bonds') could also be offered to 'newcomer' investors.

Such *undemocratic* voting rights for shares would frustrate the actions of corporate raiders, and lower the market value of listed firms' shares. It would also discourage new investors. Nevertheless, these firms would then be protected from potential 'aggressive' takeovers, and their poorly performing management would not be dislodged by a majority of disgruntled investors (if the multiple-voting-rights shareholders support the said management). Companies with multiple classes of shares generally underperform over the long term and suffer from more stock price volatility, compared with those with voting power proportionate to capital at risk.[55]

Workers and employees

In the category of workers/employees, one could differentiate several sub-groups with *varying significance for the enterprise's capacity to generate value*. Depending on the nature of the enterprise and its competitive position, sub-categories comprise:

a Talented employees empowered with the requisite resources to be deployed in specific fields deemed strategic for sustaining the prosperity of the enterprise under consideration; and
b Unskilled or moderately-skilled workers.

Depending on the nature of the business, talents and skills could encompass any one of the following domains: marketing, research and innovation, logistics, planning and strategy, fiscal and accounting services, finance, engineering, manufacturing or industrial transformation, and other activities.[56]

Good business governance requires employers to provide safe and healthy working conditions for their workers and employees, and to remunerate them commensurately to their contribution in net value creation within the firm. In conformity with the strategy of the business leader Charles Koch, who is worth $40 billion, 'workers should be paid according to the value they add rather than their position in the hierarchy ... [In Koch Industries] workers are paid more than their bosses'.[57]

Nevertheless, certain employers (e.g. in Bangladesh's textile industry) have exploited notoriously their employees with miserly pay, unsafe working conditions, and long working hours that lead to accidents and health problems. The said employers seek to attract multinational firms through lower prices and the *dumping* of workers' legitimate rights, avoiding compliance with regulations of safety, often by bribing local officials.

Business leaders should guard against pushing to the extreme considerations of productivity, for example by transforming work into repetitive dehumanizing activities, or by basing their personnel's pay solely on the criterion of higher volumes of production or sale per unit of time. Excessively high exigencies set by management for their workers with blunt enforcement of rules are likely to prove counterproductive and could well lead to burn-outs, mental depression, and other health problems (possibly provoking suicidal attempts by persons concerned). In contrast, empathic leaders towards their workers would favour harmonious relations and a congenial environment within the enterprise, thereby leading to greater cohesion and cooperation among the personnel and more profitable results.[58]

To improve their returns, multinational companies have generally adopted the strategy of delocalizing from high-cost to low-cost countries (costs covering all inputs, taxation, fees, social charges, exacting multiple regulations, etc.). In an open world economy, domestic jobs in high 'wages/salaries' countries will then shrink, unless buyers are willing to pay higher prices for the products in question, prompted by so-called 'economic patriotism'. Simply put, these buyers would accept to purchase home-produced goods at prices higher than those obtaining for equivalent imported goods. Such 'patriotic' behaviour in favour of local jobs is, nevertheless, not likely to be predominant among consumers in market economies. Consumers are generally motivated by low prices – assuming other factors do not deteriorate, such as quality of products, after-sale services, or security of supplies.

Executives and managers

Conflicts of interest and imbalances in relations among stakeholders of a business entity can be illustrated by reference to the authority wielded by executives vis-à-vis other stakeholders. Chief executive officers (CEOs), thanks to their asymmetric superior power (vis-à-vis the atomized owners/investors in the company's capital) are able to obtain hefty compensation packages by influencing members of the compensation committee. Components of compensation cover salaries, current and deferred bonuses, pension and severance pay, housing, family insurances and other allowances, aircraft usage, car service, club memberships, benefits in-kind, and/or other perks. Some components of the executives' compensation package are unrelated to their performance.[59]

It is generally argued that compensation for executives should be commensurate with their effective contribution to the 'value pie', and to market conditions of supply-demand for such talents. Sound regulations effectively applied can limit rapacious or predatory practices in compensation packages of senior management (i.e. payments unrelated to their effective contribution in the creation of value for the enterprise). Top executives are likely to exploit their positions of power within corporations, as documented by some sources.[60] Other researchers have, disputed the evidence that U.S. executives are overpaid.[61]

Independent analysts estimate that the pay of some executives is 'excessive', equivalent to a rip-off of shareholders, consumers, workers, and/or tax payers. Such conduct is often condemned by public opinion and chided by responsible political leaders in various market economies.[62] Indeed, salary in private enterprises should be linked to clusters of factors. Important ones cover personal talents and skills (e.g. problem-solving aptitude), innovation, sound strategies, capacity to lead and endure, loyalty, rigour and discipline, vigilance, and solidarity.

Privileging *financial return* over the near term could well be made at the expense of *quality of products, service, efficiency, control of pollution*, or the *motivation of workers*. A streamlining strategy was the strategy adopted by the erstwhile CEO of Alcatel-Lucent Michel Combes, who resorted to the suppression of 10,000 jobs in the company worldwide over his two-year leadership. He deemed his severance bonus of 13.7 million euro well-deserved on the basis that he had revitalized the company before its sale to Nokia.[63] Public outrage was expressed by political parties, labour unions and the French government of the left, which was struggling to revive the economy and reduce unemployment. Under pressure from public opinion, the company's board decided on 10 September 2015 to reduce the severance pay of Combes to 7.9 million euro following recommendations from France's financial watchdog and the employers' federation. It said that the review had been made with the 'full agreement' of Combes.

For an eloquent example of excessive executive compensation, one could mention the case of CEO Daniel Vasella of Swiss-based Novartis who was offered late in February 2013 CHF72 million ($76 million) on retirement as a 'non-compete' payout, on top of an estimated CHF300 million he had already received in pay and bonuses during his 17 years as top executive. He had to forgo cashing in the sum after a wave of outraged popular criticism in Switzerland. Somewhat influenced by the foregoing practices, the Swiss voted into a constitutional law on 3 March 2013 a popular initiative (68 per cent in favour) that toughens rules of corporate governance on listed companies. These include requirements to have a binding approval at the annual general assembly of shareholders on the appointment of all boards of directors and on their compensation, as well as the compensation packages of senior managers' (salaries, bonuses, loans, retirement benefits, incentive and participation plans, etc.) of any corporate group whose shares are publicly listed. Severance payments, advance payments, and other extraordinary payments to the foregoing are to be prohibited, as well as additional payments by any affiliate belonging to the group.

Penalties for contravening the voted text are stiff. They could reach up to three years in jail or forfeiting up to six years' salary. Pension funds, as institutional shareholders of listed companies, will have to vote in full transparency in line with the interests of their pensioners. Board members are barred from personal contracts (such as consulting) with firms belonging to the same group, and they cannot claim severance packages.[64] The popular vote regarding senior management compensation was reached despite the $8.5 million spent by its opponents in publicity and lobbying against the above-mentioned popular initiative, according to the Swiss-German newspaper *Blick*.

To motivate executives to create value for their enterprise, their compensation package should be carefully calibrated by reference to their (i) effective contribution (net of risks) to the performance of the business entity over the long term, and (ii) abidance by the principles of good governance. Since effective contribution is likely to be exaggerated by the self-interested and auto-regulated executives, some civic personalities recommend using for a ceiling of top executives' compensation packages a multiple of the lowest salary paid to a full-time employee working in the same corporation. Nevertheless, no consensus has been reached in this domain. The CEO of Credit Suisse (the second-largest Swiss bank) Tidjane Thiam received in 2015 CHF20.3 million (one Swiss franc was then equivalent to one U.S. dollar). The above-mentioned CEO's pay was 363 times the lowest full-time salary at the bank, according to the Swiss news agency ATS on 20 June 2016. That CEO's remuneration (inclusive of bonuses) was considered 'excessive', illustrating the widening gap between top executives' salaries and lowest paid in the same enterprise covering 27 large Swiss enterprises.[65]

Other Swiss citizens have questioned the high salaries and bonuses in the banking sector. They cite UBS (the biggest Swiss bank) which paid CHF2.5 billion in bonuses to its staff in 2012, despite a CHF2.5 billion loss in that same year. The head of the UBS's investment bank, Andrea Orcel, received in 2012 CHF26 million as 'recruitment compensation', equivalent to 385 years of an average employee salary in the same year. The ballooning of CEO compensation packages is illustrated by the fact that the CEO of a major Swiss corporation earned in 1984 six times the average full-time salary paid to an employee in her/his enterprise; in 2011, the differential rose to 43 times.[66]

Another notable example of high executive compensation is the record $159 million pension entitlement in mid-2013 to John Hammergren, CEO of McKesson, a major American wholesaler of health-care supplies. It is a moot point whether such a pension is truly deserved or whether it is at the expense of other stakeholders – such as customers (seeking lower prices), employees (seeking better pay), shareholders (seeking improved returns), and/or other stakeholders.[67]

CEO compensation (salaries, pension benefits, severance pay, non-competition clauses, etc.) has often been linked to the market performance of the company's shares, although the executive in question need not be solely responsible for that performance. The highest 'salary pay' publicly known is that of Apple's CEO Tim Cook, who received in 2011 $378 million. It is also perplexing to see some executives receive hefty pay upon leaving their company, even though the company was near bankruptcy. This was the case of former CEO of American International Group (AIG), Martin Sullivan, who pocketed $47 million in 2009 'for severance as a reward for a job well done' as decided by AIG's board of directors – although AIG's sustained a staggering loss of $99 billion in 2008 and its share price had declined by 98 per cent under his leadership. The U.S. taxpayer had to bail out AIG with a loan of over $180 billion.[68]

Egocentric greedy executives (bent on satisfying primarily their sole personal interests) tend to cannibalize their stakeholders' legitimate rights. Other executives have shown they can behave with substantial concern for their stakeholders. Thus, the most senior managers of Europe's largest family of cooperatives, Mondragon (based in the Basque region of Spain), have agreed to limit their remuneration to less than eight times the lowest paid co-operative worker.[69] These socially motivated senior managers are content with reasonable compensation packages. They feel that they derive other 'immaterial benefits' in the form of personal ethical fulfilment that elicits general public recognition and praise. Practices of 'hypertrophied compensation packages' were chided by the leaders of the Group of Twenty representing the largest economies of the world.[70] Several countries and entities have sought to make compensation packages fit as closely as possible the true performance of persons concerned. We could refer to the speech of the Governor of the British central bank in which he stated (*italics* added by this book's author for emphasis):

> Here in the UK, the Bank of England has adopted a new code for banks prescribing deferred variable performance payments, introducing the *ability*

> *to reduce deferred bonuses when subsequent performance reveals them not to have been fully deserved, and paying bonuses in stock rather than cash.*
>
> The deferral of bonuses awarded today allows them to be reduced before they are paid if evidence emerges of employee misconduct, error, failure of risk management or unexpectedly poor financial performance by the individual, their team or company ... The Bank has just completed a consultation on a requirement for *variable remuneration to be clawed back after payment*.
>
> These provisions will apply not only to employees that are judged culpable directly, but also to others who could reasonably have been expected to identify and manage risks or misconduct but did not take steps to do so, and senior executives who could reasonably be deemed responsible by establishing the culture and strategy of the organization. *Where problems of performance or risk management are pervasive, bonuses should be adjusted for whole groups of employees.*[71]

Several governments have introduced various measures to control abuses in matters of executive payroll. These include: full and clear disclosure to stakeholders, binding shareholder votes on executives compensation packages (as per the U.S. Dodd-Frank act signed by President Obama on 21 July 2010), a cap of the salary component (e.g. an 'x' multiple of the lowest paid full-time salaried person, or a multiple of the mean salary), compensation packages to be inversely related to changes in corporate debt (as a means of protection against excessive indebtedness), long-term ownership of the company's stock, claw-back on compensation packages for under-performance extending over several years, compensation committees to be voted by shareholders, etc.[72]

Business organizations' features as stimuli of 'value creation'

Business models are protean. They are often initially designed by ingenious business creators. They become in due course accepted by the business community and get formalized in due course by legislation and governmental regulations. Business models have become more diverse and sophisticated over time and among countries – to accommodate evolving complex needs. Characteristics of business models are varied and are continuously evolving. They can be useful in motivating (or vice versa in constraining) stakeholders in the process of value creation. A few of these characteristics are illustrated and evaluated hereafter.

In the twenty-first century, business models can be classified by reference to a variety of criteria: *size* (from the micro to the mega companies); *legal status of ownership and management* (single owner or partnerships with managerial roles plus unlimited liabilities; publicly traded companies with limited liability of shareholders and no managerial role; state-owned or controlled firms; mixed private-governmental partnerships; private-equity firms; cooperatives owned by employees or users/consumers; limited vs unlimited liability of a few owners-partners); unlisted- or publicly listed companies; *geographical extension* (from local to regional and trans-national); extent of *diversification of activities* (covering specific services or goods vs conglomerates); *duration of business* (covering limited or unlimited periods); *performance*; and other criteria. New models of corporations and of financial instruments are continuously being introduced by the business community, subject to the approval of legislators-regulators.[73]

Public authorities may foster – through laws, regulations, or inducements – a variety of models for business creators to choose from. Depending on business leaders, some models could prove more conducive to value creation and the wellbeing of stakeholders. These models can be classified by reference to various criteria – such as job creation, value added, high exports or sales, innovative products, profitability, or other criteria. The prevalence of any one business model at any one period of time does not exclude the concomitant existence of other models operating in the same country. In estimating the performance of different business models, the analyst needs to be careful in choosing criteria for comparative evaluation. Indeed, components of success for one type of business organization in a given historical and socio-political environment may not be transposable to other times, regions, or cultures.

Governmental policies may favour the coexistence of a variety of business models in response to a variety of needs and contexts. These may comprise models aimed at (i) promoting and protecting 'national champions' and sometimes 'regional champions' as is the case with a few European Union's enterprises in certain economic sectors deemed of 'strategic' importance to *national* or *regional security*, (ii) organizing 'growth hubs' of competencies to promote cooperation in innovation (covering a wide spectrum of micro enterprises to medium and large enterprises) and to develop business affairs by taking advantage of physical proximity that facilitates interaction, networking, exchanges of technological know-how, synergy, and/or efficiency in sharing of certain functions, and (iii) facilitating the international expansion of business groups in making productive use of opportunities available transnationally through various frameworks – while complying with the rules of open fair trade [such as those set by the World Trade Organization, WTO].

The shareholder-owned 'public company' status came into existence in the mid-nineteenth century, with seven main characteristics which have been fine-tuned over time. *First*, it offers successful founding entrepreneurs the possibility of calling on the potentially large resources of financial markets – thereby allowing the company to buttress its original 'seed capital' with additional funding in line with available opportunities. *Second*, it provides the general public with investment opportunities, thereby enabling them to diversify their patrimonies. *Third*, it offers shareholders limited liability in so far as third-party claims can only be enforced on the assets of the firm (excluding the assets of the shareholders). *Fourth*, it gives the enterprise a legal personality that elongates its life beyond that of the human founders. *Fifth*, it 'locks in' the capital of the firm, thereby enabling it to implement long-term projects (disaffected shareholders have only the option of disposing of their shares in the market place). *Sixth*, it can call on competent professional management if the company's founders are not available for the day-to-day operations. *Seventh*, it is subject to stricter official regulation by comparison with privately held companies, in order to ensure honest periodic reporting on their activities and the prevention of abuses vis-à-vis investors, creditors and other stakeholders.

Management of limited-liability companies

Managers' interests are at variance with those of shareholders when they get compensation packages undeserved by reference to their effective performance. Shareholders, as 'principal', expect their 'agent' (namely top management) not to grab value creation at their expense. Violation of shareholders' rights by management has led the authorities to exercise tighter controls and increase sanctions on culprits. Family businesses do not encounter the foregoing problem of dichotomy (namely that of 'Family Owners v. Professional Managers') in so far as top management is run by family members. Nevertheless, family businesses have the disadvantage of blurred lines between what belongs to family members and what belongs to the firm. Moreover, family members get generally employed without due *scrutiny* and *evaluation* of their competencies (comparable with that of professional managers).

Burdensome regulations on companies whose shares are publicly traded can, however, entice their majority owners to transform them into becoming privately owned, often by accepting to be bought by *private equity funds*. The latter consist of clubs of a few large investors (individuals, families, or institutions). Privately owned companies are lightly regulated and generally benefit from lesser taxation – compared with corporations whose shares are publicly held and traded on stock exchanges.[74]

Inventiveness is not limited to technology. It applies equally to business organizations and strategies. Some business entities, for example, may choose strategies driven by thinning-out management and flattening the decision-making hierarchy. Their objectives are to alleviate the burdensome and costly hierarchies of management, and speed up the decision-making process. This is not only common among cooperatives whose select members are involved in the decision-making process of their enterprise, but it can also be found in privately owned companies.

For an example of a company that has empowered its employees, the Morning Star Company 'self-managing professionals' is an interesting case. The company's personnel are colleagues without titles. They initiate communication and coordination of their activities with fellow colleagues, customers, suppliers and other industry participants.[75] The above-mentioned company processes tomato production (25 per cent of California's production) with sales of approximately $350 million in 2011. The company has performed attractively, judged by double-digit returns on capital over several years, coupled with the satisfaction of collaborators and customers.[76] Nevertheless, such self-management does not fit all business enterprises.

Hereafter, a few features of business organizations are presented and evaluated by reference to their potential contribution to stakeholders.

Focus on core business

Several sizeable companies have espoused a model of vertical integration (that comprises all the activities needed starting with the production of primary goods and services and ending with the delivery of finished products to consumers). Others have chosen the strategy of focusing on core activities while sub-contracting significant portions of their non-core activities to independent competing companies. The company which concentrates on its core business exploits its superior expertise and/or monopolistic positions.

Sub-contracting within a national jurisdiction – called *outsourcing* – does not have a negative impact on national employment and economic activity. When work is shifted abroad – called *offshoring* – national employment would suffer. *Offshoring* is prompted by many favourable factors in foreign host countries (e.g. lower cost, better quality, lesser regulatory bureaucracy, lower fiscal charges, proximity of export markets, and other factors). This also has its risks for transnational companies, notably with respect to (a) loss of control over the governance of offshore sub-contractors, and (b) potential risks linked to natural catastrophes and/or political problems in host or transit countries. To alleviate the foregoing problems, transnational companies have adopted a strategy of wide diversification, with their procurements originating in several countries.

It could save on costs to have private consortia of firms (through jointly owned subsidiaries) in selected business activities, owing to the imperatives of required sizeable investments and diverse technological/managerial inputs needed. Such requirements are seldom available within a single company, except for the few giant groups. This applies notably to extractive industries, and infrastructure activities. This is the case with certain types of transport industries (for example, railways and highways, oil and gas pipelines, electric high-tension grids, community transport, air and space projects, to mention but a few) that justify a so-called *natural monopoly* consisting of a single sizeable operator to avoid the duplication of facilities and the squandering of resources.

A statutory single operator as mentioned above has to win its franchise competitively, and observe stipulated conditions (for example of *efficiency*, *quality*, and *innovation*). The public authorities' requirements imposed on a single operator need to be underpinned by incentives and/or sanctions, with effective controls and supervision by the regulatory authorities. The optimal situation is that which yields economies of size or scope (by avoiding the wasteful duplication of physical facilities and redundant operating costs), while concomitantly incentivizing operators by offering them an attractive share in the gains of efficiency – with the balance of such gains to be passed to consumers. Such a regulatory principle is easier to express than to apply. The subject has been treated by several contemporary economists, notably the Nobel Laureate in Economic Sciences Jean Tirole.[77]

Companies that have found it beneficial to concentrate on core activities can be illustrated by reference to airline manufacturers in the first quarter of the twenty-first century. Boeing outsourced 80 per cent of its planes' components. Airbus (which was producing internally 80 per cent of the value of its aircraft until 2007) decided on 28 February of that year to concentrate on *core* activities where its technological know-how is vital for its competitive edge and its long-term performance. Airbus has since that date divested its noncore activities to several subcontractors that offer the best mix of competitive price/quality and of delivery/servicing terms. Airbus management has furthermore decided (a) to concentrate its industrial activities on fewer sites in France, Germany, Spain, and the UK (with Toulouse finalizing the construction and assembly of the larger A350 and A380 aircraft, and Hamburg the medium-sized A320, and (b) to spin-off other activities to sub-contractors.[78]

Indeed, a sizeable firm – especially if it has a dominant market position (e.g. as a monopsonist or an oligopsonist[79]) – would reap additional benefits if it can stoke up competition among its numerous suppliers and sub-contractors. In view of its size, the said firm could incite its suppliers of inputs to deliver higher-quality goods or services, and/or offer better contractual terms (e.g. lower prices; secure or flexible delivery schedules; rapid accommodation of customers' changing needs; and/or offering after-sale services).

It is not uncommon to find a small or medium-sized enterprise (SME) – especially when it is a subcontractor – cautious of accepting a big order from a major firm, lest it becomes too dependent on that firm. Several small subcontractors have had to fold, once they have lost the business of a big customer, a fact confirmed by the industrial experiences of this author. The said subcontracting companies would normally be reluctant to allow their dependence on a major customer to exceed 25 or 30 per cent of their turnover, and would favour a range of 8 to 12 per cent. Indeed, an SME could well refuse a big order from a single firm if it has the opportunity of 'spreading broadly' its business activities among several buyers – other things remaining equal. Such a policy of spreading business risks among several buyers/suppliers – to the extent markets permit – contributes to reducing the volatility of returns and facilitates the obtaining of commercial credit for the subcontractors concerned.[80]

State, private, or mixed-ownership enterprises

Several countries have favoured the establishment of state companies in various sectors of their economies for reasons of ideology or strategy. These countries' regimes consider that they could put to good use their controlling interest in state companies to boost certain sectors, and prevent foreign ownership that could transfer business know-how and jobs to other jurisdictions. Despite their professing 'liberal ideologies' that favour private-sector ownership of business assets, some governments have built up over the years sizeable portfolios of stakes in selected business entities.[81]

For those who espouse the 'free markets' model, the principal role of the state should be that of *regulator*. It is accordingly not desirable to assign to state agencies the function of owning and operating commercial assets (real estate, agribusiness, minerals extraction, transport entities, financial intermediaries, manufacturing industries, commercial services, etc.) in competition with private enterprises. From the standpoint of efficiency and innovation, governments are well advised to promote the creation of private enterprises (in preference to bureaucratic state agencies), subject to ensuring that these enterprises comply with the laws and regulations of fair competition, transparency, and accountability.

Public authorities may have a propensity to overlook the failings of managers of state-owned enterprises (often political appointees) and may be inclined to shelter them from open market forces and the competition of more efficient privately-owned enterprises (whether national or foreign). Public funds could be used to maintain inefficient entities 'under perfusion' (by bailing out 'lame ducks') in lieu of using such resources more productively in social goods (such as security, law and order, justice, foreign relations, education and research, healthcare, safety nets, cultural activities, and others). The state is *more* effective in its role as regulator and *less* effective as an operator. In terms of performance in *mixed economies* (i.e. those that accommodate both state and private enterprises) available statistical studies on return on capital show superior results achieved by the private-sector companies compared with their state-owned peers.[82] One can, nevertheless, understand that security motives may drive some states to confine 'sensitive' sectors (for example, certain defence-related activities) to nationals under state control, assuming these agencies operate in conformity with the law and the criteria set up by the authorities, and are subject to appropriate oversight by democratically elected bodies.

State ownership and management of businesses is generally espoused for ideological reasons. State businesses often suffer from the ills of bureaucracy, political favouritism, and cronyism. By comparison, independent privately-owned business units operating in a freely competitive and transparent environment are likely to produce higher levels of performance – aided by their capabilities to *innovate*, to improve *efficiency*, enhance *resilience*, and show *adaptability to new conditions*.

In situations of 'natural monopoly' (e.g. connecting cities or agglomerations with an electrical grid, telecommunication networks, roads, hydroelectric dams, etc.), economic rationality calls for awarding a concession to a single operator. That operator can belong to the state or to the private sector. When an operator is chosen for reasons of efficiency, governmental regulators and law-enforcement agencies need to ensure that customers are not denied *access* to such public utilities' infrastructures, or are not subjected to *exploitative pricing*. Private-sector *excesses* can translate into monopolistic profits, and/or higher compensation packages reaped by the executives and management of the operating company at the expense of customers.[83]

Public-Private Partnerships (PPPs) can prove an attractive approach in funding and managing large and sophisticated public infrastructure projects when governments' finances are strained and governmental bureaucracies are lacking in competence and efficiency. Subject to a proper designing of infrastructure projects with a judicious distribution of risks and returns (through appropriate instruments or vehicles) that incentivize various partners, PPPs offer attractive opportunities for the growth of an economy by tapping the large resources of international capital markets.[84]

Some governments have favoured contracting public services to the private sector. These services could comprise construction of hospitals and health services, housing and educational facilities, school meals, sport and cultural complexes, penitentiaries, road building, servicing military bases, etc. Public authorities have assumed that private enterprises are more efficient and more rigorous in their management. They have been mistaken.

Other analysts have found that PPP is a superior approach to that of contracting public services to the private sector. Indeed, governmental partnership could insure that governmental socio-economic objectives blend harmoniously with legitimate private profits.[85] The success of one business model versus another (here subcontracting versus PPP) will depend on the quality of business leadership, the skills of management, and the rigours of controls. Employing some 43,000 worldwide, Carillion's business decisions proved disastrous, driving the company into bankruptcy. Its collapse in January 2018 owes largely to barely profitable contracts, uncontrolled cost over-runs, a spree of business acquisitions in unfamiliar industries, excessive bonuses to executives, heavy indebtedness and pension liabilities (jointly estimated at $2.8 billion), unwarranted distribution of dividends, and other loss-making practices.

Some researchers question the benefits host governments could derive from owning minority interests in an investment project operated by sophisticated majority investors who could resort to leonine manipulative practices to reduce the revenues that should accrue to these host governments. For example, foreign investors can finance the project with debt provided by their affiliates and bearing large deductible 'interest charges' that reduce taxable income accruable to host governments. Majority private shareholders could, furthermore, set transfer prices that minimize taxable income in host countries, by charging management fees, shipping fees, and/or marketing fees that reduce the declared taxable profits of the investee company. Foreign global corporations have some leeway in assigning a significant part of their profits to tax havens where they have little or no business, thereby 'optimizing' (i.e. reducing) their overall tax bill.

It is not uncommon that a majority shareholder can take important decisions before board meetings, while keeping their hosts in the dark. The latter often lack the know-how of transnational managers and/or are subject to venal influence. Finally, host governments in certain developing countries do not have access to honest and judicious advice at the time of negotiating deals, to take advantage of future possible changes in economic conditions such as a rise in commodity prices.[86]

A version of funding cooperation between the private and the public sectors is 'blended finance'. This type of financing is often used to fund developmental projects in which private capital is enticed to be involved when other financial contributions are offered by other sources at concessionary terms. These terms could consist of: lower interest rates than those prevailing in competitive markets, extendable maturities of loans, subordinated debt status of certain lenders, and various subsidies offered by developmental or philanthropic institutions. The private commercial sector funding component will then get returns that match market conditions. Such 'blending' is likely to attract private capital to targeted projects. These projects often belong to the categories of social development and environmental protection.[87]

Employee- or customer-owned enterprises

Some socially minded business leaders have set up cooperatives in which delegates from the body of employees or workers participate, along with professional management, in running businesses. Their participation is reckoned to boost their motivation to increase overall business benefits with positive results for all stakeholders. These cooperatives cover various business sectors. One notable historical example is that of Jean-Baptiste Godin (1817–1888) in France. Thanks to a patent registered in 1840, his foundry plants got off to a good start in the manufacture of cast iron heating stoves and enamelled bathtubs, and became soon after extremely profitable. Son of a locksmith, he wanted his workers (who numbered more than 2,000) to share in the enterprise's wealth creation, not only through wages, but also through their ownership of capital. He was inspired by thinkers such as Charles Fourier (1772–1837) and Claude Henri de Rouvroy de Saint-Simon (1760–1825), who advocated fraternal relations in organizing their secular society, where wellbeing is rationally attained through peace, equality, freedom of expression and belief, and the solidarity of business owners-managers with their workers in overcoming poverty and inequity.

Godin set-up the *Familistère de Guise* and invited his workers to own the foundry business (through the *Association cooperative du Capital et du Travail*). He introduced a fraternal 'life style' for his workers through the original construction next to the foundry in Guise of a community (named Familistère) with an original architecture for a housing compound named *Social Palace*; the latter boasted comfortable housing, a communal bath, laundry, shops, restaurants, theatres and other entertainment facilities, a swimming pool, a public library, a nursery, a school with obligatory free-of-charge education, etc.[88]

It is unrealistic to have workers/employees conform voluntarily for long to a pre-conceived habitat and uniform life-style imposed by their employers, even if it is a material improvement over their current situation. They may well consider conforming to such a format an unwelcome intrusion into their private sphere of life. After many ups and downs, the Godin foundry was sold to a major metallurgical firm *Le Creuset*. The cooperative association for the

Social Palace was dissolved in 1968 and apartments were sold to private owners who have become free to adapt their living quarters to suit their personal needs.

It is argued that ownership stakes by employees/workers (through share-ownership, share-option schemes, pension funds, profit-sharing plans, etc.) raises their motivation to enhance the productivity and performance of the concerned enterprises.[89]

Nevertheless, employee 'mandatory equity participation' in the enterprises for which they work has its drawbacks. It could (a) limit the scope for the further development of the business, when fresh capital is needed and employees are unable to provide it, and (b) raise the risks of employee dependence on the enterprise they work for. Another drawback of these enterprises is the propensity of workers/employees to 'protect' their jobs by non-economic strategies – such as blocking needed streamlining or downsizing, opposing delocalization of business activities to markets with cheaper inputs and/or with hospitable regulatory environments, opposing consolidation or mergers with other groups to improve their competitiveness, etc. Employees' ownership of their enterprises could well become unattractive if retiring employees are unable to sell their shares to existing or incoming employees or dispose of them in the open market at attractive prices.

Should, however, managers and employees clash regarding business strategies, the company is bound to suffer. Differences of interests could arise in a variety of areas, such as compensation packages, management strategies, establishment in other countries, changes in core activities, mergers or spin-offs, and others. In periods of recession, unless employees and management accept sacrifices (for example in cutting their pay, accepting longer working hours, or being put temporarily on a part-time basis), the company could be driven into bankruptcy.

The vulnerability of worker-owned enterprises can be illustrated by reference to worker-owned Fagor, Spain's largest appliance-maker with 5,600 workers. Fagor is a member company of the world's largest group of cooperatives, Mondragon, which employed about 80,000 people in 27 countries, with revenues of about 14 billion euro in 2012). Member entities of the Mondragon group had vetoed further financial support for the bailout of Fagor: the company could not survive, despite a 20 per cent cut in workers' salaries that had proved insufficient to restore its competitiveness, especially vis-à-vis Asian competitors.[90] Competitiveness of such enterprises is not solely affected by salaries (including social charges levied by public authorities); it can also be considerably impacted by the *risk of obsolescence* of its products. In 'turning around' an enterprise that is faced by the foregoing risk, management has to be continuously concerned about the satisfaction of consumers' changing needs and tastes (e.g. via quality/price, high value innovation, efficient service to customers, and other factors) that put it ahead of competitors.

Enterprises can be successfully set up as cooperatives, under the supervision of a board of trustees and run by professional management. They would then function similarly to profit-making enterprises, with surplus income ploughed into the business to improve productivity and cushion eventual reverses. In principle, they are keen to sell goods or services to their members at the lowest possible prices. This is the case of Switzerland's largest retailer *Migros Cooperatives*, founded in 1925 by Gottlieb Duttweiler (and which had about two million members in 2013). It owns about 20 food and beverage manufacturing plants, and several stores in neighbouring France and Germany. Its businesses include banking, oil, hotels, consumer goods, etc.[91]

Saving institutions known as *Raiffeisen* are another leading example in continental Europe of *financial cooperatives* owned by savers. Since the nineteenth century, they have offered their members financial facilities at reasonable terms (compared with usurers) spanning consumer loans, mortgages, investment products, and other financial facilities. Micro-credit institutions, of more recent creation and development, are also co-managed or monitored by delegates from their depositors.[92] Individuals and communities are evidently unequal in a variety of ways, and this situation is bound to affect their bargaining power and their benefits. Small businesses, with no access to commercial lenders, are often better served by financial intermediaries organized as cooperatives, compared with shareholder-owned sizeable banking corporations that cater preferably to sizeable firms. To sustain their activities, microfinance institutions need (i) to cover their full costs, (ii) generate profits that permit them to expand their activities, and (iii) adhere to a *stakeholders' business philosophy* driven by reasonable benefits for all parties concerned. Nevertheless, financial charges on small loans (interest + administrative costs) could reach excessive levels (possibly 20 per cent per year or more) unless properly contained by streamlined processes.

Whether owned by financial investors, workers or customers, enterprises have generally sought to favour their owners. Thus, the consumer-owned cooperatives tend to tilt towards the commercial practice of serving their customers through better quality/price products – while the investor-owned enterprises seek to enhance the gains of their shareholders.

Business hubs

A business hub represents a *cluster* of cooperating or competing entities of all sizes, usually operating within a delineated geographic district; its activities could focus on one or more sector(s) covering production, trade, finance, research and development, and others. A hub can have a local/regional, a national, or an international calling. Hubs could grow considerably within a favourable business-friendly socio-economic environment and an efficient regulatory framework. Synergy among cooperating parties can also favour the growth of business hubs. This in turn will help expand their access to inputs and to market outlets, and enhance their image. They are likely to become dynamic cities, similar to the iconic example of Silicon Valley in California.

Hubs can benefit from several factors. Among these are proximity to sizeable markets, availability of resources at reasonable cost, favourable financial terms, exemption or low fiscal charges, light regulatory requirements, and/or easy access to infrastructure facilities. Hubs generally attract a variety of businesses along with research-academic centres geared to industrial/technological innovations.

It is possible to have a hub-like industrial district belonging to a single company. This is the case of the world's biggest vertically integrated chemical company BASF, whose conglomerate covers oil and gas, petrochemicals, commodity chemicals, specialty chemicals, agrochemicals and biotechnology. The BASF *Verbund* (i.e. cluster of companies) is currently concentrated in a geographical district in Ludwigshafen in Germany, and comprises a constellation of some 250 factories. The latter manufacture about 8,000 inter-related products (the by-product of one process is used for further processing into other products to extract maximum value) at the same site, thereby enhancing the 'value chain' of the BASF cluster. Accordingly,

> what is left over from one process is used only a few hundred metres away to make something else … Compared with having, say, 70 separate factories some 100 km apart, BASF calculates its cluster enjoys annual savings of €300 million ($380m) in logistics, €150 million in energy and €50 million in infrastructure.

In 2015, BASF spent close to 2 billion euro on R&D out of 70.4 billion euro of sales revenues, with some 1,000 patents annually generated.[93]

According to BASF:

> Verbund is all about intelligent interlinking of production plants, energy flows and infrastructure. Also, know-how and customers are intelligently connected to each other. The Verbund system creates efficient value chains that extend from basic chemicals right through to high-value-added products such as coatings and crop protection agents. In addition, the by-products of one plant can be used as the starting materials of another. In this system, chemical processes consume less energy, produce higher product yields and conserve resources. In that manner, we save on raw materials and energy, minimize emissions, cut logistics costs and exploit synergies. These solutions enable BASF to sustain competitiveness in every world region while making our customers more successful.[94]

For reasons of logistics and efficiency, large diversified transnational companies may find it advantageous to set up their activities in a convenient geographical location. In so doing, they organize their production and services synergistically in order to attend optimally to their regional and/or international customers. Such a location would then become a business hub that is likely to attract other companies (competitors, sub-contractors, suppliers of inputs, financial services providers, research entities, etc.). These hubs have been set-up by U.S. *conglomerates* (e.g. GE), German technology groups (e.g. Siemens), the Japanese cross-shareholding *zaibatsus* (e.g. the Mitsubishi group), and the Korean *chaebols* (e.g. Samsung).

Contemporary business giants have expanded their activities thanks to 'information-technology platforms' they have developed for connecting people and businesses *globally* at relatively low cost. These platforms are aimed at mutually beneficial exchanges among participants in regulatory-friendly environments. Exchanges are instantaneous and cover a variety of needs. They include transactions in physical goods; advice in various domains; contacts facilitation among all kinds of talents, skills and businesses; and others.[95]

Business evaluation

Several tools are available to analysts for assessing the prospective attractiveness of a going concern or a business project. They include the commonly used tools of 'internal rate of return', the present value of 'net discounted cash flows', EBIT (earnings before interest and taxes), EBITAD (earnings before interest, taxes, amortization, and depreciation), and the SWOT (Strengths, Weaknesses, Opportunities, and Threats) approach illustrated in Exhibit 3.3.

SWOT seeks to map key factors (internal or external to the enterprise) that reflect the relative current and prospective attractiveness (namely costs/benefits) of a business project based in a given country or region and operating over a projected period of time in openly accessible markets. Besides the SWOT approach, one could use a 'multi-year business plan' (extending over three to ten years, depending on the nature of the business and its expected period of full fruition) using various techniques for the calculation of 'return on invested resources' such as the 'discounted cash flow' technique or its equivalent, the 'internal rate of return'.

The 'business plan' presents the objectives, priorities and timing for the implementation of the project. Carefully estimated information is needed, notably regarding: investments in human and material resources; organization and strategy; expected disbursement of funds and generation of revenues; and other key business data. Continuous pursuit of research for reliable data should serve to remedy lacunae, shortcomings and/or errors of a business plan in order to overcome hurdles as they arise. Continuous fine tuning of a business plan serves to improve business efficiency and performance, and to address successfully changes in competitive conditions and in the socio-political environment. Fast changes would then require nimbleness on the part of a business leader in addressing opportunities and overcoming challenges as they arise.

Some models of 'business evaluations' focus on specific categories of businesses. One such model evaluates the relative attractiveness of *start-ups*.[96] In the final analysis, and in the absence of a single accurate reading that aggregates all key factors in one single measure, the business judgement and the savvy of decision makers become very important in reaching an optimal evaluation.

Exhibit 3.3 Assessing the economic attractiveness of a business project: the 'SWOT' approach

An open-ended list of critical factors

A *Strengths*

1 Innovative know-how in R&D and niche position(s) for fine quality products.
2 State-of-the-art hardware and software.
3 Diversified business lines.
4 Efficient organization, good governance and honest management, marketing skills, and transparent reporting.
5 High employee motivation thanks to good working conditions.
6 Widely based loyal clients.
7 Fast reactivity to clients' orders and changing needs.
8 Easy access to funding and substantial free cash flows.
9 Resilient businesses capable of overcoming potential crises (e.g. through reducing non-essential manpower and wage bills in adversely impacted business lines).
10 Abundant availability of key inputs (such as raw materials, services, software and hardware, spare parts, etc.).
11 Attractive margins, return on invested capital, and other performance indicators.
12 Solid reputation for best practices in matters of: quality of products, after-sale services to customers, speedy deliveries, marketing skills, etc.
13 Potential synergy and economies of size in several functions between the investing company and the targeted project (e.g. in accounting and back-office functions, financial services, information systems, human resources, sales, purchases, insurance, etc.).

B *Weaknesses*

1 Inefficiencies, high costs, low margins, and poor customers' services.
2 Volatile markets and revenues.
3 Cyclical industries.
4 Limited outlets.
5 Problems affecting the supply chain of inputs (quality, security of flows, logistical dysfunctions, unreliable contractual terms, heavy dependence on a single supplier, etc.).
6 Risks originating from selected business' stakeholders, such as special favours to executives.
7 Limited talents or skills.
8 Redundancies, nepotism, or cronyism.
9 Financial difficulties
10 Organizational inefficiencies.

C *Opportunities*

1 Steady growth of demand and market share.
2 Introducing new or improved products in response to user/consumer potential needs.

3 Prospects for profitable diversification in new sectors.
4 Potential benefits from the introduction of new technologies or skills.
5 Gains in synergy and streamlining.
6 Easy access to finance.
7 Availability of inputs at reasonable terms.
8 Relatively attractive fiscal regimes.
9 Ease of doing business.
10 Agreeable environment (geographic, socio-political, cultural, academic, etc.) which appeals to talented persons.
11 Add-on acquisitions producing economies of size and/or market leadership.

D Threats

1 Low entry barriers for competitors.
2 Superior competitor advantages (in technology, product quality, attractive access to inputs, wide and efficient marketing networks, efficient infrastructures, etc.).
3 Growing scarcity and prices of obtained inputs.
4 Markets are easily cannibalized.
5 Volatility of markets.
6 Socio-political risks that affect customers, partners, suppliers, or subcontractors.
7 Relatively heavy fiscal and social charges.
8 Unstable domestic and/or regional socio-political conditions.
9 Inappropriate macro-economic policies.
10 Oppressive regimes that exclude potentially creative, talented people and eviscerate the national economy(ies).
11 Delinquent bureaucrats, regulators, and other officials.

The above is an open-ended listing of key factors of attractiveness or riskiness of a business project. Some of these factors could overlap or duplicate with others (whether positive or negative). In tabulating the totality of listed factors, care should be exercised in avoiding redundancies, and in assessing the relative weight (from one to 10) or ranking (e.g. top, high, above average, average, moderate, low, negligible) of each factor before arriving at a reasonable overall synthetic measure of attractiveness.

Source: author

In the absence of reliable market value for the business project under consideration, a surrogate approach can be used. It consists of quantifying each significant component of the SWOT categories (and ultimately synthesizing the values of the estimated categories – the positive and the negative); this is the *Delphi* method used in forecasting. The method assumes that group judgement is superior to individual judgement. The *Delphi* method consists of a process that relies on estimates offered by a selected number of independent experts in the field under consideration. The manager of the process, also called the facilitator, requests each expert to offer her/his written assessment of the SWOT project, and the reasons behind their assessment. Chosen experts do not meet, do not know who is involved in the process, and remain anonymous to each other. Anonymity serves to avoid the hegemony of any one expert, and/or problems arising from ego.

The facilitator will carry out perhaps five consecutive rounds of consultations. The results of the previous round are communicated to all the experts, giving each expert an opportunity to fine tune or revise her/his assessment in the light of information offered by their peers. After a few rounds, it is believed that results are likely to converge. The facilitator will then calculate the mean or median to be used as an appropriate overall valuation of the project's SWOT components.

For judging the attractiveness of a project, the above-mentioned *Delphi method* may not prove the sole pertinent approach. The business leader could rely on the recommendations of trusted colleagues or experts, or the rule of thumb. Often, a strategic decision (e.g. an acquisition, a spin-off, the commercialization of an innovation, entering into a new market, delocalization, diversification, vertical or horizontal integration, the shut-down of production plants, etc.) is founded on the personal judgement or acumen of the top person in charge.

To quote a practitioner-cum-scholar on *business strategy*:

> SWOT remains managements' most popular strategic tool in spite of the large number of 'more sophisticated' tools that have become available since its appearance in the 1950s ... Something happens and you have to do something about it. You look around. What resources are available? What are the opportunities and options? What else might happen? It is just common sense ... SWOT works when strategists trust their 'subjective' judgements about categorizing and estimating its components ... A SWOT analysis can be an exploration of a possible world rather than the present one to be left behind.[97]

Incentives for business development

Innovations (whether in new products or processes) with high growth potential (in sales, employment, or value-added) represent opportunities for their creators and their stakeholders. The state has an important role in stimulating such creative entrepreneurs. The latter generally start *small*, a situation which poses them significant challenges in periods of slumps or stuttering growth. In these periods, firms are wary of hiring, lest they get stuck with employees (a) for whom they have no work, and (b) who cannot be readily laid off without exorbitant compensation. Small firms in particular have relatively limited financial resources – compared with larger firms – to allow them to retain well-qualified workers during a temporary *slump*, pending an expected *recovery* in business activities.

Hurdles encountered by small-size business show-up notably in: (a) *diseconomies of scale* (higher unit costs in view of the relatively small 'sub-optimal' output), and (b) the inability of the small business owner-manager to focus single-handedly and competently on all the functions of his business. He needs to be relieved from certain tasks by recruiting collaborators with *specialized skills* (e.g. in the areas of product quality, marketing, administration, finance, technology, logistics, accounting and reporting, human resources, or others). Often, in view of the dearth of their financial resources to recruit and retain full-time the requisite talents, several of these activities in small enterprises are often handled by the owner-manager, with enduring difficulties.

Other interrelated challenges encountered by small enterprises are: (i) lack of product/geographical diversification, (iii) dependence on very few customers, (iii) *funding constraints* – compared with larger companies – in view of a relatively low equity cushion (to absorb possible losses, or to invest in expansion), (iv) inadequate *reporting procedures* (on functions, investments, lines of business, etc.) that hamper analysis for assessment, accountability, and controls, and (v) reluctance to recruit owing to concern over the eventuality of incurring large severance payments for the dismissal of redundant workers, should they be obliged to lay them off. Which of the above-mentioned disadvantages is the *Achilles heel* varies from one small company to another.[98]

The World Bank Group has built up a composite indicator of 'ease of doing business' by reference to *time* and *costs*. It uses ten major indicators: starting a business, dealing with licences, hiring and firing, registering property, getting credit, protecting investors, paying taxes, trading across borders, enforcing contracts, and closing a business. The World Bank has adopted a uniform methodology for the collection of reliable data on indices that allow international comparisons on a sound basis, and provide policy-makers with the opportunity of examining actions needed to improve the competitive position of their country.[99] The bank's worldwide ranking (currently covering 185 countries) would incite laggard governments to liberalize their procedures, on the understanding that such liberalization contribute to higher investment and the boosting of economic growth.

In some countries, honest but insolvent entrepreneurs are treated as fraudsters, and some could be forced to wait several years before re-starting a business. Certain jurisdictions (national or sub-national) ban them for life from senior executive positions in large companies.[100] Barring criminal charges, showing forbearance towards entrepreneurial individuals' past failures could open up possibilities for these persons to learn from past errors, improve their competencies, bounce back, and succeed in creating new performing businesses. Efficient regulations and business-friendly environments based on stable and predictable sound principles contribute to entrepreneurial dynamism. In several market economies, entrepreneurs are, however, stymied by various socio-administrative hurdles that hamstring their creativity – such as red tape (tedious, redundant, or duplicate procedures) of a stifling bureaucracy without the possibility of recourse to ombudspersons.

To bolster innovation and value creation, regulatory frameworks should allow entrepreneurial individuals to resort to new trials, despite earlier non-productive starts. Insolvency regimes should not treat honest insolvent entrepreneurs similarly to fraudsters.[101] It is reckoned that legislation providing small business borrowers with bankruptcy protection (for example through insurances or guarantees) would promote the entrepreneurial culture.[102]

The bulk of those registered as self-employed need not be entrepreneurial. Indeed, in the absence of steady jobs in periods of recession, many individuals would incorporate. Their motives could be varied, namely to reduce their taxes, obtain aid from public authorities, and/or protect their social standing (for example by calling themselves consultants, thus avoiding the stigma of being 'unemployed'). Dubbed 'necessity-driven entrepreneurs', these self-employed are driven into starting their business because they have no other work options. They are to be contrasted with 'opportunity-driven entrepreneurs' who choose to launch their business in view of their high expectations of value creation by their project.[103] Entrepreneurial enterprises that should be incentivized are those that have the potential of producing *superior* contributions over the longer term to society (in employment, national income, innovations, exports, environmental benefits, and others). They are the opportunity-driven entrepreneurs.

Among the pioneering studies in this field, the GEM (Global Entrepreneurship Monitor) reports have identified 'high-expectation entrepreneurial firms' (in existence for less than four years) that expect to achieve rapid growth in employment (i.e. to have at least 20 employees within five years). These firms are responsible for 80 per cent of newly created jobs, according to a survey covering some 70 countries worldwide.[104] One needs to take into consideration the net job creation of start-ups, after deducting the estimated job destruction caused by the same ventures.[105]

Notable among the barriers that impact small business in the world economy are those relating to (i) opacity of foreign markets (for example regarding business practices, competitors' advantages, or potential partners), (ii) lack of access to reliable distribution channels in foreign markets, (iii) the general reluctance of financial institutions to lend to 'untested' small enterprises, and (iv) various onerous regulatory hurdles (such as bureaucratic, superfluous rules regarding product safety). A refundable tax credit against 'expenses incurred' to enter foreign markets could moderate the adverse impact of the above-mentioned *barriers*.

Selective governmental stimuli in support of small export businesses are vitally needed by economies concerned with national objectives of reducing unemployment, promoting innovation, enhancing value-added activities, boosting exports, and sustaining growth. These stimuli would include: improving ready access to credit at reasonable terms; moderating burdensome reporting and administrative procedures; extending free professional advice on valorizing their products, reaching new customers, reporting and accounting; and/or obtaining temporary tax breaks or tax credits. Moreover, legislation that provides small business borrowers with bankruptcy protection (for example through insurances or guarantees) favours risk-taking, and generally promotes the entrepreneurial culture.[106] The foregoing measures have been resorted to by various governments in favour of start-ups.

The French government, for example, supports the most dynamic enterprises (whose annual growth in turnover exceeds 34 per cent) among independently owned or controlled small-medium size enterprises (SMEs): these employ between five and 250 salaried persons with a turnover of less than 50 million euro. These companies with dazzling growth potential are awarded the label of distinction '*gazelle*', and benefit from the seasoned advice of experienced business leaders and financiers.[107] Moreover, the French government agency OSEO provides financial support (direct funding or guarantees) at attractive terms to SME innovative companies.[108] Nevertheless, support measures have been constrained in periods of dearth of public funds, while social charges on firms have remained comparatively burdensome.

Indeed, in periods of recession (such as the 2008–2014 period) the number of corporations shrinks considerably. In particular, the SMEs, compared with larger companies, do particularly suffer. This is principally attributed to lesser volumes of sales, dearth of funding, as well as to excessive administrative burdens and social charges borne by the SMEs – given their relatively small size.[109]

Independent non-governmental and non-profit organizations can also help entrepreneurial projects with considerable growth potential. This is the case for the Startup America Partnership, which provides entrepreneurial budding companies valuable resources such as advice and mentorship; access to essential services at reduced costs; assistance in recruiting, training, and retaining talents; acquisition of new customers; introduction to *thought* leaders; attracting major corporations as potential partners or customers; and information on appropriate sources of funding. The above-mentioned NGO covers the United States, with an extensive network of grassroots and seasoned entrepreneurs, academics, independent local talents, executives of established large companies, and governmental agencies.[110] The multiplication of high-performance entrepreneurs should ultimately contribute to society's wellbeing.

Knowledge-intensive industries

Among the various drivers of growth, *human capital* is reckoned to be the most important factor over the long term. One inter-governmental think-tank defines it 'as the knowledge, skills, competencies and attributes embodied in individuals that facilitate the creation of personal, social and economic wellbeing'.[111] For a simple shortcut proxy indicator of human capital, analysts often use the per capita 'education and training' period of the population aged between 25 and 64 years. The upper limit of age (i.e. 64) takes into consideration the fact that human beings currently live longer in good health: they are thus able to absorb new know-how and skills, and remain productive over longer periods.

Education, as a key component of human capital, is crucial to enhancing capabilities and wellbeing. In modern societies, governmental policies underline the role of education, as expounded below:

> Inclusive education – broadly defined as the provision of good quality 'Education for All' in mainstream setting, and more narrowly as the provision of this type of education for persons with disabilities – has acquired increasing prominence in global development discourse in recent years. It has become a justification for, or even *the* [*sic*] justification for, many development initiatives in the field of education.[112]

Among the parties involved in hatching, developing and shoring-up entrepreneurial capabilities, institutions of 'learning, research, and training' have been gaining in importance over recent decades as eminent contributors to innovation, economic growth, and societal progress. Indeed, the world economy has witnessed an upward trend of knowledge-intensive business activities. Education, research, experience, and competencies – all represent the stock of *human capital* available within any economy. The higher the quality and the size of that stock of human capital in an economy and the more efficient is the deployment of that capital, the higher the level of innovations and business opportunities.[113]

Business leadership in the twenty-first century requires multiple talents that offer these decision-makers opportunities to valorize novel ideas in complex environments. Increasingly, universities offer programmes that address subjects from the perspective of several disciplines (e.g. in business, public administration, natural sciences, and technologies) to enable participants to accede to managerial positions in knowledge-intensive firms. For possible academia-industry approaches that nourish entrepreneurial talents, three complementary approaches deserve mentioning: (a) *practical learning* through courses designed and run by start-up creators, and experts in entrepreneurship-cum-management, (b) *internships* within dynamic enterprises that accept to train eligible select students, and (c) *industrial parks* set-up by higher centres of learning, public entities, professional associations, or enterprises.[114]

With respect to *internships*, programmes may well be based on the following process:

1 Qualified students from business, engineering, physical sciences, and other disciplines spend a few weeks of work with an entrepreneurial business, offering help as requested by the entrepreneur, and assimilating 'practices and experiences' they are exposed to.
2 They operate under the dual guidance and supervision of their professor and the host entrepreneur (or one of her/his associates).
3 By the end of their sojourn in the enterprise, they prepare a report on their activities (certain confidential details can be omitted or made available solely to a designated direct supervisor, to protect proprietary information).
4 They receive academic credit for time spent productively within the enterprise, and are graded by the faculty member, after consulting with the entrepreneur or his associate.
5 Host enterprises are proposed by individual students, faculty, student associations, professional groups, or others.

6 No remuneration is expected by students. Eventual contributions by host enterprises go to a fund to defray the expenses of the 'practical learning' programme of students (for transport, meals, accessories, and others).
7 The possibility of teaming-up between two or more students hailing from different backgrounds is likely to be productive in terms of novel ideas, and deserves to be countenanced.

Beyond their traditional mission of teaching and research, several academic institutions have also developed, for students and graduates aspiring to become entrepreneurs, *industrial parks* or *incubators* that foster the development of *start-up* companies. Facilities provided by *industrial parks* consist of premises, laboratories, educational programs, and computing centres that could be made available at reasonable terms to these graduates intent on creating and developing their businesses. Graduates – as potentially budding entrepreneurs – would then benefit not only from the technical and back-office facilities available to them at favourable terms, but they could also call on the expert advice of faculty members and researchers. Should these start-up companies take off, the academic institution is likely to derive some positive fallout (notably in income and reputation). Owners of a start-up company would normally, after an agreed period, leave the incubator park, to allow for a fresh group of aspiring entrepreneurs from among the new graduates to move in. *Industrial parks*, set up by higher centres of learning and research, have proved their utility for students and alumni endowed with entrepreneurial talent and spirit, and committed to valorize their innovations (see Exhibit 3.4).

Exhibit 3.4 'Knowledge-intensive' businesses fostered by universities

Selected features

1 University-based industrial parks are business incubators that offer valuable contributions for start-ups, micros and SMEs (notably via direct access to expert faculty and experienced professionals; training and advice; introductions; infrastructure such as laboratories or computing centres), and privileged contacts and interviews with outsiders (investors, lawyers, accountants, potential clients, and other relevant professionals – often graduates or alumni of the sponsoring universities). Hosted grass roots entrepreneurs are generally not burdened by excessive fees or inroads into their gains. Pursuit of knowledge, considered in all its varied dimensions and components, should lead to the cross-pollination of ideas, thereby opening up opportunities for all parties concerned.
2 If constrained by limited funding, higher centres of learning and research can pool their resources in order to build reasonably well-equipped and efficient industrial parks that enjoy a 'critical mass'. By sharing investments and know-how, these centres allow budding entrepreneurs to benefit from better facilities in order to ferment their creative ideas – eventually to facilitate the blooming of entrepreneurial entities in an auspicious environment. It could

prove quite productive for such cooperation to focus on a cluster of related innovations in one or a couple of selected industrial sectors. This strategy could eventually lead to the creation of poles of technological-business excellence.

3 Seasoned entrepreneurs and academics, sitting as a jury panel, could collectively separate the *wheat* from the *chaff* among numerous candidates seeking to join the industrial park as potential entrepreneurs. Carefully prepared multi-year business plans (possibly extending up to ten years for certain proposed projects), should be fully documented in order to prove their relative attractiveness.

4 Access to finance at reasonable terms is a major hurdle for innovative entrepreneurs. With limited personal resources, entrepreneurs generally call, to begin with, on a coterie of family and friends, followed by 'business-angel' networks and venture capitalists. Industrial parks can facilitate entrepreneurs' access to funding their projects. Evidently, not all countries have sufficient sources of funding. Moreover, certain entrepreneurs shun third-party investors with equal voting rights per share, since they want to keep exclusive control over their projects.

Source: author

A university-sponsored investment fund could countenance taking minority interests in selected 'knowledge-based start-up projects' in the expectation of deriving benefits from their sale at their maturity in later years. The said fund could act as a facilitator that attracts new business creators and investors. For examples, one could mention the Cambridge Science Park and the business incubator St John's Innovation Centre in Cambridge, and the Oxford Centre for Entrepreneurship & Innovation's Venture Club: www.sbs.ox.ac.uk; also: www.isis-innovation.com. Similarly to other academic-sponsored entrepreneurship institutions, the Entrepreneurship Centre for Entrepreneurial Learning at the University of Cambridge *Judge Business School* seeks to empower aspiring entrepreneurs via the development of appropriate leadership talents, managerial skills, and the creation and fostering of early-stage ventures.[115]

Transforming the structure of an economy from heavy dependence on the export of unprocessed raw materials with *low* value in favour of transformed *higher* value-added products is generally considered beneficial to employment and growth in income. The foregoing requires the observation of several preconditions over the long term, chief among which are: (a) attracting students, researchers, and trainees to scientific-technological fields that could generate inventions and innovations in various human endeavours, (b) incentive systems that stoke personal motivation (for example through appropriate working conditions and pay), and (c) doing away with burdensome bureaucratic regulations that shackle investors, innovators, and business creators.

Regarding time horizons for hosting innovators and entrepreneurs to allow them to fructify their projects, industrial parks could entice budding start-ups not to linger unduly (for example by fixing time limits of, say, five years), from a very early stage blueprint, followed by a prototype that opens into a fully fledged sustainable viable business project. Nevertheless, flexibility may be called for, depending on the nature of individual projects.

In wrapping up on the contribution of academia to entrepreneurship, one could cogently argue that higher centres of learning and research could be well advised to host *industrial parks* to provide their entrepreneurially minded students or alumni with the appropriate know-how and contacts. These students have then the opportunity to familiarize themselves with the nature, potential utility and limitations of various business *models*, *methods* or *tools* relevant to their projected enterprises. One can also argue that academia offers an attractive environment to debate business issues – such as risks, management techniques, ethics, and good governance (through workshops, seminars, conferences, peer exchanges, etc.). It can thus impress on business participants the advantages of abiding by standards of best practices.[116]

This chapter has analysed the role of governmental policies, business strategies, and knowledge centres in economic development. To fructify, entrepreneurial talents need the contributions of many other stakeholders, as expressed below:

> For economic development to occur it is not enough for entrepreneurs to start new firms; some of those firms must grow over time. Although entrepreneurs launch new ventures, the types of people who are able and willing to engage in this activity may be ill-suited to manage a complex learning organization. The innovation process requires the integration into the organization of professional, technical and administrative personnel who are willing to stay and build companies that they did not found and which they do not own. Policies that place too much stress on entrepreneurship as the key to economic development can undermine the collective and cumulative process of organizational learning required for innovation to occur.[117]

Notes

1 United Nations Development Programme, *Human Development Report 2013 – The Rise of the South: Human Progress in a Diverse World*, p. 57/204p.
2 See, for example 'Cronies and Capitols – Businesspeople Have Become Too Influential in GOVERNMENT', *The Economist*, 10 August 2013, p. 52.
3 See, for example, Roumeen Islam and Gianni Zanini, *World Trade Indicators 2008: Benchmarking Policy and Performance*, World Bank, Washington D.C., 2008, 121p.
4 See www.globalsubsidies.org.
5 See, for example, Jens Hoj, *Competition Law and Policy Indicators for the OECD Countries*, OECD Economics Department, Working Paper No. 568, 8 August 2007, 39p.
6 See, for example, UNCTAD, *World Investment Report 2005*, pp. 13–22; 'Companies' and Countries' Prosperity – Decoupled', *The Economist*, 25 February 2006, pp. 67–68; and John Kline, 'Evaluate Sustainable FDI to Promote Sustainable Development', *Columbia FDI Perspectives*, no. 82, 5 November 2012.

7 See, for example, Karl Sauvant, 'A Backlash against Foreign Direct Investment?', in: *World Investment Prospects to 2010 – Boom or Backlash*, The Economist Intelligence Unit and The Columbia Program on International Investment, 2006, pp. 71–77.
8 AFP and other media: 6 January 2015.
9 Amartya Sen, *The Idea of Justice*, Penguin Books, 2010, 346–347/468p.
10 Ibid., p. xiii.
11 For a historical assessment of the role of institutions in economic development, one could refer to Ha-Joon Chang, *Kicking Away the Ladder – Development Strategy in Historical Perspective*, Anthem Press, 2002, 187p., and in particular Chapter 3 'Institutions and Economic Development: "Good Governance" in Historical Perspective', pp. 69–123.
12 See Sumit Agarwal, David Lucca, Amit Seru, and Francesco Trebbi, 'Inconsistent Regulators: Evidence from Banking', *Journal of Economic Literature*, January 2012.
13 See, for example, Charles Collyns, 'The Crisis through the Lens of History', *Finance & Development*, International Monetary Fund, December 2008, pp. 18–20.
14 See, for example, David Cay Johnston, *The Fine Print: How Big Companies Use 'Plain English' to Rob You Blind*, New York, September 2012; and U.S. Senate Permanent Subcommittee on Investigations, *Hearing to Examine Billions of Dollars in U.S. Tax Avoidance by Multinational Corporations*, 20 September 2012.
15 'Financial Transparency – The Biggest Loophole of All', *The Economist*, 20 February 2016, pp. 49–50.
16 See, for example, Dietmar Braun, Christian Ruiz-Palmero, and Johanna Schnabel, eds, *Consolidation Policies in Federal States – Conflicts and solutions*, Routledge, 2017, 319p.
17 See, for example, *Business for Social Responsibility* which advises hundreds of member firms: www.bsr.org.
18 See also Andrew Crane and Dirk Matten, eds, *New Directions in Business Ethics – Managing Business Ethics*, vol. IV, Sage Library in Business and Management, 2012, 406p.; see also www.fraud-magazine.com.
19 See, for example, Paul Moore, *Crash Bank Wallop: The Memoirs of the HBOS Whistleblower*, New Wilberforce Media, 2015.
20 See: www.poste-courage.ch.
21 'The Whistleblower's Story', *The Economist*, 23 December 2017, pp. 64–66.
22 See: John Evans, 'Responsible Business Conduct: Re-Shaping Global Business', *Columbia FDI Perspectives*, no. 50, 7 November 2011.
23 See the independent non-governmental organization Transparency International: www.transparency.org.
24 See John Kemm ed., *Health Impact Assessment – Past Achievement, Current Understanding, and Future Progress*, Oxford University Press, 2013, p. 3/311p.; see also Rob Gray and Irene M. Herremans, 'Sustainability and Social Responsibility Reporting and the Emergence of the External Social Audits: The Struggle for Accountability?', in Pratima Bansal and Andrew J. Hoffman, eds, *The Oxford Handbook of Business and the Natural Environment*, Oxford University Press, 2012, pp. 405–424.
25 *Governance* generally refers to the body of laws, rules, norms, guidelines, regulations, codes, techniques, and/or understandings that are applicable to a community or a constituent party thereof (such as an organization, a business, a market, a network, a socio-political group, etc.) or other entities, be they governmental and non-governmental, formal or informal.
26 www.un.org/en/globalissues/governance/index.shtml.
27 See, for example, World Bank Group, *World Development Report 2017, Governance and the Law*, pp. 278–281/281p.; also Moisés Naim, *Illicit – How Smugglers, Traffickers, and Copycats Are Hijacking the Global Economy*, Doubleday Publishing, 2005, 253p.; also 'Reputation Management', *The Economist*, 12 March 2011, pp. 63–64.

28 See: Heiner Michel, *Co-determination in Germany: The Recent Debate*, Johan Wolfgang Goethe-Universität, March 2007, p. 22/25p.
29 Reuters and other media.
30 Bloomberg, 'Goodyear French Managers Held Hostage: Freed with Police Aid' press release, 10 January 2014; and 'A Two-Year Suspended Sentence of Goodyear's Previous Employees', *Le Monde*, 11 January 2017.
31 See, for example: C. B. Bhattacharya, Sankar Sen, and Daniel Korschun, *Leveraging Corporate Responsibility – The Stakeholder Route to Maximizing Business and Social Value*, Cambridge University Press, November 2011, 340p.; Dorothea Baur, *NGOs as Legitimate Partners of Corporations – A Political Conceptualization*, Springer, 2011, 204p.; George F. DeMartino, *The Economist's Oath – On the Need for and Content of Professional Economic Ethics*, Oxford University Press, December 2010, 272p.; and George Kassinis, 'The Value of Managing Stakeholders', in Pratima Bansal and Andrew J. Hoffman, eds, *Business and the Natural Environment*, Oxford University Press, 2012, pp. 83–100/698p.
32 See Willy Boder, 'The Independence of Parliament Is Questioned', *Le Temps*, Geneva, 8 May 2014, pp. 1 and 8.
33 See for example, 'Nuclear Industry Gave Millions [Japanese Yen] in Grants to Japan's Safety Experts', www.power-eng.com/news/2012/11/04/; also www.channelnewsasia.com/; and www.power-eng.com.
34 See, for example, R. I. Tricker, 'The Evolution of Corporate Governance', pp. 39–61, in Thomas Clarke and Douglas Branson, eds,: *The Sage Handbook of Corporate Governance*, Sage, 2012, 657p.
35 See, for example, Jane Mayer, *Dark Money – The Hidden History of the Billionaires Behind the Rise of the Radical Right*, Doubleday, 2016, pp. 227–230/450p.
36 See, for example, 'Corporate Lobbying – The Chamber of Secrets', and 'Lobbying – A Year in the Swamp', *The Economist*, 21 April 2012 and 13 January 2018, pp. 63–65 and pp. 35–36 – respectively; see also *LegiStorm LLC* which researches information on Members of Congress and congressional staff; and *Public Citizen*, a consumer rights advocacy group and think tank based in Washington, D.C., United States.
37 See *OECD Foreign Bribery Report – An Analysis of the Crime of Bribery of Foreign Public Officials*, OECD Publishing, 2014, 45p.; http://dx.doi.org/10.1787/978926 4226616-en.
38 See 'BAE Systems Handed £286m Criminal Fines in UK and US', and 'BEA to Pay $450 Million to End Corruption Probe': *BBC News* and *CNN.com* respectively, 5 February 2010; also 'Bribery Abroad – A Tale of Two Laws', *The Economist*, 17 September 2011, p. 60.
39 See article 'Actions Speak Louder Than Transparency in Corruption Crusade', *Financial Times*, 11 May 2016, p. 2.
40 See, for example, *Business for Social Responsibility* which advises hundreds of member firms: www.bsr.org.
41 See also Andrew Crane and Dirk Matten, eds, *New Directions in Business Ethics – Managing Business Ethics*, vol. IV, Sage Library in Business and Management, 2012, 406p.; see also www.fraud-magazine.com.
42 Whistleblowers have received official recognition and protection after information on scandals (see, for example, Paul Moore, *Crash Bank Wallop: The Memoirs of the HBOS Whistleblower*, New Wilberforce Media, 2015) have hit the media. The United Kingdom (the UK Financial Conduct Authority and the Bank of England Prudential Regulation Authority) and Switzerland (the Swiss Federal Government and its Swiss Postal system, see: www.poste-courage.ch) have recently offered job protection and/or financial compensation to whistleblowers.
43 World Commission on Environment and Development, *Our Common Future*, 1987, p. 43 [known as the Brundtland report]; also John Drexhage and Deborah Murphy, *Sustainable Development: From Brundtland to Rio 2012*, International Institute for

Sustainable Development, New York, 26p.; and Dieter Birnbacher and May Thorseth, eds, *The Politics of Sustainability – Philosophical Perspectives*, Routledge, 2015, 236p.

44 Anne T. Lawrence and James Weber, *Business and Society – Stakeholders, Ethics, Public Policy*, 14th edition, McGraw-Hill International Edition, 2014, p. 551.

45 Larry D. Fink's Annual Letter to CEOS, *A Sense of Purpose*, Blackrock, 15 January 2018.

46 See R. E. Freeman, *Strategic Management: A Stakeholder Approach*, Pitman, Boston, 1984; also R. Edward Freeman and John McVea, 'A Stakeholder Approach to Strategic Management', in *Handbook of Strategic Management*, Blackwell-Wiley, June 2005; and Sybille Sachs and Edwin Rühli, *Stakeholders Matter – A New Paradigm for Strategy in Society*, Cambridge University Press, 2011, 278p.

47 James E. Post, Lee E. Preston, and Sybille Sachs, *Redefining the Corporation, Stakeholder Management and Organizational Wealth*, Stanford University Press, 2002, pp. 32–33/376p.

48 Sybille Sachs and Edwin Rühli, *Stakeholders Matter – A New Paradigm for Strategy in Society*, Cambridge University Press, 2011, p. 198/278p.

49 See Orçun Kaya, *Start-Ups and Their Financing in Europe – Out of the Woods with Capital Markets Union*, Deutsche Bank Research, Frankfurt am Main, 29 September 2016, 14p.

50 See, for example, G. William Domhoff, *Wealth, Income, and Power*, Department of Sociology, University of California at Santa Cruz, 19 September 2013, 21p.; www2.ucsc,edu/whorulesamerica/.

51 Vineet Nayar, *Employees First, Customers Second – Turning Conventional Management Upside Down*, Harvard Business Press, 2011, 23p.; V. Nayar offers his views in his capacity as Vice Chairman and CEO of the $3.9 billion HCL Technologies Limited, leading a team of 83,076 professionals in 26 countries; also www.heltech.com.

52 See, for example, Robert H. Frank, *Success and Luck: Good Fortune and the Myth of Meritocracy*, Princeton University Press, 208p.

53 See, for example, James R. Copland, *Proxy Monitor Report*, Winter 2013, Manhattan Institute, New York, 11p.; and The CityUK, *Sovereign Wealth Funds*, March 2013, 8p.: www.thecityuk.com.

54 See Andrew Ross Sorkin, 'Democracy for Investors Has Its Limits', *New York Times – Global Edition*, 27 February 2013, p. 19 – quoting Leo E. Strine Jr., the chief judge of the Delaware Court of Chancery in an essay of the American Bar Association.

55 See, for example, Investor Responsibility Research Center Institute, *Controlled Companies in the Standard & Poor's 1500: A Ten Year Performance and Risk Review*, October 2012, 22p.; also 'Shareholder Rights – Out of Control', and 'Control Freaks', *The Economist*, 20 September 2014, pp. 67–69, and 25 November 2017, p. 66 – respectively). An example is the founder of Facebook Mark Zuckerberg, who has 14 per cent of the economic rights of the said company, while his class of shares has 51 per cent of the votes.

56 See, for example, Beth Jenkins and Lorin Fries, *PROJECT NURTURE: Partnering for Business Opportunity and Development Impact*, Harvard Kennedy School – Corporate Social Responsibility Initiative, 2012, 48p.

57 *The Economist*, 10 December 2016, p. 60; see also www.charleskochinstitute.org/.

58 See 'Global Economic Crisis Linked to Suicide Rise', *BBC News Health*, 18 September 2013 – citing World Health Organization documents.

59 See Weija Li and Steven Young [Lancaster University Management School], *An Analysis of CEO Pay Arrangements and Value Creation for FTSE-350 Companies*, CFA Society – United Kingdom; and the High Pay Centre, 4 January 2017, Stephan.Stern@highpaycentre.org.

60 See, for example, Jeff Madrick, *Age of Greed: The Triumph of Finance and the Decline of America, 1970 to the Present*, Knopf, 2011, 464p.

61 See, for example, Steven N. Kaplan, *Executive Compensation and Corporate Governance in the U.S.: Perceptions, Facts and Challenges*, University of Chicago Booth School of Business, 2012, 48p.
62 See, for example, Philip Stephens, 'Cameron Belatedly Signs Up to the Occupy Movement', *Financial Times*, 10 January 2012, p. 9; and Patrick Jenkins, 'Negligible Link between CEO Pay and Investor Value Boosts Case for Shake-Up', *Financial Times*, 28 December 2016, p. 11.
63 AFP and other media, 1 September 2015.
64 www.swissinfo.ch; 'Corporate Governance – Shareholders at the GATE', and 'Executive Pay – Fixing the Fat Cats', *The Economist*, 9 March 2013, pp. 57–58; and Bär & Karrer Briefing, March 2013, 5p.: www.baerkarrer.ch.
65 See Adrian Wüthrich, president of an independent organization 'Travail Suisse' that examines the evolution of salaries: www.travailsuisse.ch.
66 See Swiss Confederation, *Popular Vote of 24 November 2013*, pp. 3–13.
67 See 'McKesson CEO Entitled to Record $159M PENSION', *Modern Healthcare*, citing Associated Press, 26 June 2013; and 'Does John Hammergren Deserve to be the Latest Face of Executive Excess?', *The Economist*, 6 July 2013, p. 54.
68 See Michael Dorff, *Indispensable and Other Myths: Why the CEO Pay Experiment Failed and How to Fix It*, University of California Press, 2014, pp. 1–2/313p.
69 See: 'Mondragron – Trouble in Workers' Paradise', *The Economist*, 9 November 2013, p. 69.
70 See Financial Stability Board, *FSB Principles for Sound Compensation Practices*, 25 September 2009, 5p.; also other documents at: www.financialstabilityboard.org.
71 Speech given by Mark Carney, Governor of the Bank of England, at the Conference on Inclusive Capitalism, London 27 May 2014, 13p., www.bankofengland.co.uk/publications/Pages/speeches/default.aspx.
72 See, for example, Joseph J. Martocchio, *Strategic Compensation – A Human Resource Management Approach*, Pearson, 2017, pp. 252–279/404p.; and David Chandler and William B. Werther, Jr., *Strategic Corporate Social Responsibility – Stakeholders, Globalisation, and Sustainable Value Creation*, 3rd edition, Sage, 2014, pp. 272–284/617p.; also 'Executive Pay – Neither Rigged Nor Fair', *The Economist*, 25 June 2016, 16–18p.
73 See, for example, 'Rival Versions of Capitalism – The Endangered Public Company', and 'Schumpeter', *The Economist* – respectively 19 May 2012, pp. 14 and 25–27, and 1 October 2016, p. 60.
74 Privately held business entities have analysed by this author in an earlier book titled: *Progress-Driven Entrepreneurs, Private Equity Finance and Regulatory Issues*, Palgrave Macmillan, 2010, p. 195.
75 See: www.morningstarco.com.
76 See: Gary Hamel, 'First, Let's Fire All the Managers', *Harvard Business Review*, December 2011, pp. 48–60.
77 See The Royal Swedish Academy of Sciences, *Jean Tirole: Market Power and Regulation*, 13 October 2014, 52p.
78 Louis Gallois, CEO of EADS, parent company of Airbus, at his press conference of 28 February 2007: see also www.airbus.com.
79 A 'monopsonist' is a single buyer of a commodity in a given market. An 'oligopsonist' is one of a few major buyers of that commodity in the said market.
80 See, for example, Hélène Koch, 'La hantise des dependences – Dynatec' [The Obsessive Angst of Dependence – Dynatec], *PME Magazine*, Geneva, March 2007, pp. 50–51.
81 See, for example, 'Briefing State-Owned Assets', and 'The State as Shareholder', *The Economist*, 11 January 2014 and 28 June 2014, pp. 17–20 and 56, respectively.
82 See, for example, 'State-Owned Enterprises – Fixing China Inc', *The Economist*, 30 August 2014, pp. 45–46.

83 See, for example, the article of the head of research of the Italian Competition Authority Alberto Heimler, 'Local Public Services: Competition, Regulation and Competitive Tendering', in *Review of Economic Conditions in Italy*, no. 3, September–December, 2007, UniCredit Group, Rome, pp. 371–390.
84 See, for example, Torsten Ehlers, *Understanding the Challenges for Infrastructure Finance*, BIS Working Papers, No. 454, August 2014, 23p.; also The CityUK, *Infrastructure 2014 – Trends, Demands and Challenges*, 30p.: www.thecityuk.com/.
85 See, for example, 'The Collapse of Carillion – Cleaned Out', *The Economist*, 20 January 2018, pp. 33–34; and Herpreet Kaur Grewal and Martin Read, 'Lessons to Learn from Carillion', *FM World*, 5 February 2018.
86 See Louis T. Wells, Herbert F. Johnson Professor of International Management, Emeritus, Harvard Business School, 'Government-Held Equity in Foreign Investment Projects: Good for Host Countries?', *Vale Columbia Center on Sustainable International Investment*, 3 February 2014, no. 114.
87 See, for example, Richard Samans and Erik Solheim, *Blended Finance: A Primer for Development Finance and Philanthropic Funders*, OECD/World Economic Forum, 2015, 27p., and other documents.
88 See accueil@familistere.com, the official Website, in French and English.
89 See, for example, Joseph R. Blazi, Richard B. Freeman, and Douglas L. Kruse, *The Citizen's Share – Putting Ownership Back into Democracy*, Yale University Press, November 2013, 304p.; and Robert Oakeshott, *The Case for Workers' Co-Ops*, 2nd edition, Macmillan, 1990; 1st edition 1978.
90 See: 'Mondragron – Trouble in Workers' Paradise', *The Economist*, 9 November 2013, p. 69; and Andrew Bibby, 'Receivers Called in at Mondragon Co-Operative', *Guardian*, 14 November 2013.
91 www.migros.ch.
92 See Zuhayr Mikdashi, *Progress-Driven Entrepreneurs, Private Equity Finance and Regulatory Issues*, Palgrave, 2010, pp. 11–16/211p.
93 *The Economist*, 4 November 2006, pp. 77–78; and 17 September 2016, p. 60.
94 www.basf.com/.
95 See Adrian Wooldridge, 'A Special Report on the World's Most Powerful Companies', *The Economist*, 17 September 2016, 16p.
96 See: Alex Osterwalder, Yves Pigneur, Alan Smith, Tim Clark, and Patrick van der Pijl: www.BusinessModelGeneration.com.
97 J.-C. Spender, *Business Strategy – Managing Uncertainty, Opportunity, & Enterprise*, Oxford University Press, 2014, pp. 50–51/314p.
98 See Adrian Beecroft, *Report on Employment Law*, United Kingdom Department for Innovation and Skills, 24 October 2011, 16p.; see: www.bis.gov.uk.
99 See: The World Bank, *A Better Investment Climate for Every One*, World Development Report 2005, Washington DC, September 2004, 271; also www.worldbank.org; also The World Bank, *Doing Business 2013, Smarter Regulations for Small and Medium-Size Enterprises*, 10th edition, 282p.: www.doingbusiness.org.
100 See, for example, 'European Entrepreneurs', *The Economist*, 28 July 2012, pp. 17–19.
101 See, for example, European Commission, *A Second Chance for Entrepreneurs, Prevention of Bankruptcy, Simplification of Bankruptcy Procedures and Support for a Fresh Start*, Final Report of the Expert Group, January 2011, 13p.
102 See, for example, the publications of the inter-governmental think-tank the OECD on this subject.
103 See José Ernesto Amorós and Niels Bosma, *Global Entrepreneurship Monitor 2013 Global Report – Fifteen Years of Assessing Entrepreneurship Across the Globe*, Babson, Universidad del Desarrollo and Universiti Tun Abdul Razak, 2014, p. 11/103p.
104 See Erkko Autio, *2005 Report on High-Expectation Entrepreneurship*, GEM, 52p.
105 See, for example, Tim Kane, *The Importance of Startups in Job Creation and Job Destruction*, Kauffman Foundation of Entrepreneurship, July 2010, 8p.; www.kauffman.org.

106 See, for example, the publications of the OECD on this subject.
107 www.pme.gouv.fr/gazelles.
108 www.oseo.fr.
109 See, for example, Stefan Vetter and Jennifer Köhler, *Business Demographics and Dynamics in Europe – Trends in the Composition of the Company Landscape*, Deutsche Bank Research, 14 April 2014, 12p.; and European Commission, *Action Plan: The European Agenda for Entrepreneurship*, and *Minimizing Regulatory Burden for SMEs* – respectively 11 February 2004, 20p. and 23 November 2011, 14p.; also OECD, *SMEs, Entrepreneurship and Innovation*, June 2010, 212p.
110 See www.s.co.
111 Ref. Brian Keeley, *Human Capital – How What You Know Shapes Your Life*, OECD, 2007, p. 29/147p.
112 See Guy Le Fanu, 'Reconceptualising Inclusive Education in International Development', in Leon Tikly and Angeline M. Barett, eds, *Education Quality and Social Justice in the Global South – Challenges for Policy, Practice and Research*, Routledge, 2013, p. 41/220p.
113 See, for example, Soumitra Dutta, ed., *The Global Innovation Index 2012 – Stronger Innovation Linkages for Global Growth*, INSEAD, and World Intellectual Property Organization, 440p.
114 See: http://startuptraining.ch/program/business-concept/.
115 For contacts: http//www.cfel.jbs.cam.ac.uk/ and ec@jbs.cam.ac.uk.
116 See, for example, David Molian, 'Entrepreneurial Value Creation: Are European Business Schools Playing Their Full Part?', *European Foundation for Management Development*, Conference hosted by Maastricht University School of Business and Economics, 5–6 March 2012, 16p.
117 William Lazonick, 'Innovative Enterprise and Economic Development', in Wim Naudé, ed., *Entrepreneurship and Economic Development*, Palgrave Macmillan, 2011, p. 32 and pp. 18–33/373p.

4 Case studies

Four case studies presented in this chapter illustrate challenges of crises encountered by individuals, businesses, and governments in their endeavour to *alleviate poverty*, *reduce vulnerability*, and *improve resilience*.

First, the U.S. financial crisis of 2007 – and more specifically U.S. subprime housing mortgages – had among its main causes the drive on the part of public authorities and of financial intermediaries to fund the 'housing needs' of lower-income individuals, generally by discarding prudential rules of solvency, financial discipline and credit-worthiness.

Second, the sizeable movement of able-bodied poor or distressed people (notably from Africa, Latin America, and the Middle East) who head for northern countries has had an important driving force in the desire to have a decent and secure life in the countries of destination – dubbed 'citadels of prosperity' owing to their restrictive migration policies.

Third, referring to trade in cotton, West African and other developing countries have been disadvantaged by the U.S. agricultural subsidies to its own domestic cotton producers, tilting international trade advantages in favour of the U.S.

And finally *fourth*, the pauperization and depopulation of villages in West Africa has been moderated, thanks to the commitment of devoted European-African philanthropists and social entrepreneurs.

The empirical illustrations offered below examine policies, strategies, and practices aimed at solving *diverse problems of poverty*. The solutions presented by governments, businesses, philanthropists, or entrepreneurs have had mixed results. These four cases have *one major common concern* of central importance to a major theme of this book – namely the drive for 'poverty alleviation'. Although *poverty* in each case may arise from differing reasons and in markedly different contexts (geographical, economic, cultural, etc.), successes in handling it depends essentially on the *quality of leadership* – a key running theme throughout this book. Our illustrations are connected in so far as they should help the reader better delimit and comprehend the quintessence of *the poverty problem* which has been faced perennially by humankind.

The U.S. subprime crisis of 2007 and its global fallout

The efficient deployment of financial and human resources is vital to the prosperity of communities at all levels: local, national, and transnational. This chapter seeks: *first* to identify the principal dysfunctions of financial intermediaries during the decade starting in 2006–2007, and to evaluate the approaches to overcome the related financial crisis; *second* to examine level-playing field behaviours in international trade (with a focus on cotton); and *third* probe the role of social entrepreneurship in revitalizing slumbering regional or national economies.

In our evaluation of past events and in the search for solutions, one has to admit with humility that it is easier to be wise *after* mishaps than *during* a crisis. Nevertheless, people often have short and selective memories of what happened. Indeed, newer generations may not fully comprehend circumstances of the past, and may fail to put themselves in the environment and conditions of their counterparts in the past. Other people may recognize that there are lessons to be learned and warnings to be heeded from past disasters. By studying the causes of these disasters, they believe that they are able and willing to avoid future tragedies similar to those encountered in the past.

Banks are at the centre of financial flows and investment transactions; their stakeholders are legitimately concerned about protecting their interests. Major stakeholders in financial intermediation (along with their key selected interests) are listed below:

1. Lenders: need to ascertain the creditworthiness of their clients and seek attractive margins and fees.
2. Depositors and savers: seek the safety and relative accessibility/liquidity of their funds.
3. Shareholders-investors: expect adequate returns, and the solidity of their bank.
4. Borrowers: expect reasonable financial charges and adequate lending terms.
5. Other bank customers: demand transparent and honest disclosure of yields/risks of financial transactions.
6. Executives and managers: seek attractive compensation packages.
7. Employees: seek reasonable salaries; job training and security; healthy and stimulating work environment.
8. Board of directors: are responsible for protection of stakeholders' rights and interests; oversight of risks; compliance with laws and regulations; net value creation over the long term.
9. Central bankers, financial regulators, and financial stability boards: are responsible for tuning money supply and liquidity to favour growth and stability in the economy; control of money laundering; honest and transparent reporting; abidance by prudential standards of capital adequacy, liquidity, solvency, and risk management.
10. The financially excluded (estimated at 2.5 billion worldwide in 2017) do not have access to the financial system owing to their poverty.

11 Public authorities' oversight: protection of public interest (municipalities, cities, regions, sub-national and national jurisdictions) – with respect to fiscal matters, the environment, employment, good governance, business ethics; and other domains.

The first case study of this chapter focuses on the decade-long residential-property crisis in the United States. U.S. property prices started tumbling in the summer of 2006, and the property boom finally exploded on 15 September 2008 with Lehman Brothers (then the fourth-largest investment bank in the United States) declaring bankruptcy. That collapse produced a chain reaction of losses, spreading to European financial groups in particular. The burst of the property boom had forced various *monetary* and *fiscal* authorities to intervene in support of ailing financial intermediaries. Rescue measures included central banks' drastic cuts in interest rates, the flooding of national economies with liquidity, the injection of equity capital into several institutions at the brink of bankruptcy, and other measures.[1]

Notable among the causes of the U.S. subprime mortgages crash and its-decade-long duration are *greed* and *misconduct*. They explain the (a) unsound risk-management practices (especially on the part of lenders), (b) home buyers' unrealistic assumption of continued appreciation in the price of their properties, (c) underestimation of risks by rating agencies, (d) the deliberate circumventing of prudential rules by the chain of intermediaries that offered high loan-to-property value reaching 95 per cent, and (e) the failure of oversight by the regulatory authorities in their exercise of timely vigilance to detect and correct malfunctioning of financial intermediaries, and to sanction misconduct and fraudulent operations.

The responsibility of bankers in the mortgage crisis is manifest. As put by a well-documented research study,

> Home prices peaked in mid- to late 2006 [declining shortly thereafter by about 30 per cent in major markets]. Nevertheless, the mortgage market continued to attract investors. Many financial firms increased their risk taking … In good times, at least, subprime mortgages were more profitable to originate and hold than prime mortgages, and some firms decided to take more risk, not less, in an attempt to garner the increased yield. Many firms dealt increasingly in mortgages based on no or low documentation of borrower characteristics. Some mortgages allowed borrowers to state their income or otherwise failed to establish whether a borrower was a good credit risk or not [*sic*]. This kind of imprudence invited fraud and abuse once unscrupulous people learned which lenders failed to verify such statements.[2]

U.S. housing mortgages for low-income risky borrowers

The U.S. subprime mortgage bubble gathered momentum in the early 2000s as cheap housing credit was readily made available to potential home owners. Home buyers were enticed to buy housing mortgages in the expectation that the rising trend of property prices would be sustainable and that they could finance indefinitely their mortgages at moderate interest rates. However, house prices started falling in the summer of 2006 with a massive tide of U.S. home owners' defaults leading to the meltdown of that sector's assets in the United States and beyond.

In an environment of permissive regulations and lax controls, brokers and mortgage companies – prompted by short-term profits – had been aggressively peddling housing loans to borrowers seeking home ownership, generally without the requisite screening rigour for ascertaining their creditworthiness. Financial intermediaries had then fanned the above-mentioned 'real estate bubble' by disregarding the earning power of their borrowers and by lending to them on the basis of an expected rise in properties' prices. Reductions in mortgage underwriting standards were reportedly encouraged by the public authorities since 2004 – to favour low-income or minority borrowers in their search for home ownership.[3]

Bank financing of low-income or minority borrowers who lack creditworthiness is likely to become a source of damage for municipalities and other local authorities. Mortgages, with high debt to property value and high interest charges, when unpaid, have blighted cities with foreclosures. This could eventually lead to substandard housing, segregation, loss of property tax revenues by the authorities, and disbursement of public aid to distressed borrowers. The foregoing argumentation was used by the City of Miami vis-à-vis Bank of America and Wells Fargo in November 2016. It alleges that 'loans to minority borrowers were more than five times as likely to result in foreclosures than loans to white borrowers'.[4]

Shenanigans and reckless techniques were used by a few rogue market players to entice insidiously some borrowers – including those with poor credit records. Home buyers were often ill-informed and ill-advised on their mortgage contract terms. With the connivance of mortgage agents, lenders had loosened credit quality standards to allow borrowers to exaggerate the value of their mortgaged property and/or their capacity to service properly their debts.

Mortgage companies and other lenders did not keep these housing loans on their books. Indeed, the said lenders – in lieu of being content with interest margins on their lending portfolios – sought *fee generation* derived from such operations as: originating, packaging, securitizing and selling mortgage-backed securities to institutional investors. Indeed, shortly after their origination, a significant portion of the mortgages were collected in special purpose vehicles (SVPs) for use as collateral for bonds sold to a worldwide circle of institutional investors. Through disintermediation, the originators of loans shifted the risks of debtors to third-party investors in assets-backed securities. Investment bankers that sell these securities have occasionally used sophisticated models of 'financial engineering'; these models could well hide high risks incomprehensible to unsuspecting investors.

Through a chain-reaction process, the U.S. 'subprime mortgages' crisis has had ripple effects, continuing worldwide till 2017. The paroxysm for the deepening and spreading of the sub-prime financial crisis was aggravated by Lehman Brothers' default, after the refusal of the U.S. government to bail it out on the weekend of 13–14 September 2008; that long-established investment banking institution closed its business the following Monday, bringing in its wake the demise of several other financial intermediaries.

Financial rating agencies (an oligopoly of three U.S.-based private corporations – namely Standard & Poor, Moody's Investors Service, and Fitch) have also been widely blamed for contributing to financial crises in recent years, in so far as they underestimated real risks of their 'client issuers' who paid them the fees for rating services.[5] The three rating agencies had not removed the 'investment grade' of Lehman Brothers' securities until the morning of its default (!). Despite their failings, the three agencies continue to dominate in the U.S. market and internationally as the 'nationally recognized statistical rating organizations'.[6]

Oblivious to 'prudence lessons' that past banking/financial crises should have provided, a wide spectrum of financial intermediaries in the United States and internationally had by 2008 heavily speculated in the aforementioned asset-backed securities based on 'subprime mortgages' that fraudulently under-priced borrowers' risks (borrowers and lenders colluding in the process). Moreover, regulatory authorities have not been vigilant in their oversight. They should have enforced the compliance of banks with prudential rules (for example by requiring banks to moderate their risk-taking, and raising their capacity to absorb shocks through the constitution of substantial buffers of *liquidity* and *equity*).

Losses severely hit financial intermediaries in the United States, Europe, and beyond. The biggest originator of *subprime-mortgage loans* was Countrywide Financial (acquired by Bank of America in 2008), and the largest buyers of subprime backed securities were the two U.S. government-sponsored housing-finance giants, Freddie Mac and Fannie Mae. Since their goal has been to promote home ownership, the above-mentioned two financial intermediaries had lighter regulatory requirements compared with banks (in particular with reference to equity requirements and taxation levels), thereby reducing their cost of raising funds in financial markets owing to their status as government-sponsored enterprises. The two institutions had massively bought mortgage loans from banks, in order to securitize and sell them to pension institutions and mutual funds.

Other impacted parties comprised large groups in the United States – such as Citigroup, Bank of America, Merrill Lynch (bought out by Bank of America in September 2008), Morgan Stanley, and JP Morgan Chase (which acquired in March 2008 the near-collapsing Bear Stearns).

The first European bank to admit the 'junk quality' of its investments in U.S. subprime mortgages was BNP Paribas in a press release on 9 August 2007. It informed its customers that it was closing its three investment funds in U.S. mortgage securities. The news created a panic that spread rapidly among Western banks, destroying their trust in interbank lending, and leading to the 'haemorrhaging' of money from their institutions. The British bank Northern Rock was among the first victims.[7]

Among affected European banks were UBS, Deutsche Bank, Société Générale, Crédit Agricole, Credit Suisse, HSBC, RBS, and several other financial intermediaries belonging to the private or the governmental sectors. With reference to government-owned financial vehicles, one could mention the case of state-owned German banks (notably the federally owned KfW which should have focused on its mission of financing small and mid-sized businesses, and the Landesbanken, owned by the federated regional states and local authorities) – all run by political appointees lacking financial savvy. The bailing out of these banks for their U.S. subprime-junk toxic securities invested prior to 2008 had cost the German Treasury billions of euro by February 2008.[8]

Although the foregoing financial institutions should have had access to sophisticated risk management techniques, few of their managers have been wise enough to dodge 'toxic' structured products concocted by so-called 'rocket scientists'. Past events have raised doubts regarding the capability of financial institutions' management (along with their customers) to fully understand and evaluate the *value-at-risk* of these products, and to fathom their evolution under changing circumstances. Wisdom would call for guarding against temptations for reckless personal enrichment that could turn dangerously into excessive greed, leading to dereliction of duty, the plundering of other stakeholders, and threatening the viability of enterprises.

Lawsuits against financial intermediaries have been launched by (a) private injured parties (investors and banks) who bought from other financial intermediaries mortgage-based securities on the basis that they were of investment-grade quality, as well by (b) the authorities who accused these intermediaries of flouting regulations. Among U.S. regulators, one could mention notably the U.S. Federal Housing Agency (FHFA) which oversees Freddie Mac and Fannie Mae. It has been demanding refunds of scores of billions of dollars from major U.S. and European banks for subprime-mortgage loans sold to Freddie Mac and Fannie Mae using false information about borrowers and properties (lawsuits filed in September 2011).

Floating interest rates on mortgages, starting purposefully low to attract borrowers, with 'no down payment', and offering them high ratios of loan-to-property values and debt-to-income, have been a source of trouble for borrowers. Thus, the relatively low lending interest rates of the early 2000s in the United States were set originally to entice potential prospective homeowners to borrow excessively (with little concern for their capacity to reimburse) thereby transgressing the fundamentals of financial prudence. The starting interest rates were generally followed in 24 to 36 months by steep increases (upward interest rates resets could reach 3 per cent per annum) with penalties imposed on borrowers for early payment or refinancing. Such practices by fee-driven brokers, aggressively pushing clients towards home ownership, were resorted to with little concern to forewarn these clients on the risks, or for the observance of conventional prudential principles regarding their capacity to reimburse.[9]

Major players comprise politicians, regulators, mortgage brokers, property appraisers, lenders, deluded or culpable home-owners, rating agencies, auditing firms, government-sponsored financial enterprises, investment bankers, packagers of asset-backed securities, and investors in a far too permissive environment of opportunism and greed with no regard to principles and consequences (see Exhibit 4.1). Some of the foregoing players lacked critical judgement based on sound ethical principles, and a few were deemed to have resorted to collusion (for example in underestimating the risks at client firms in order to keep their business relations).[10]

The U.S. sued culprit banks and obtained damages for massive fraud (such as falsely certifying to the Housing and Urban Development Department that they had properly assessed the default risk of borrowers, so qualifying their loans for governmental insurance). Various studies have pin-pointed the responsibilities of each group in the debacle of U.S. and international financial intermediation in that period, with the general consensus of informed researchers attributing the crisis mostly to the above-mentioned protagonists' failures in rigour, judgement, or business ethics.[11]

Exhibit 4.1 Dysfunctional incidents in contemporary finance

Selected illustrations

1 Lenders, brokers, borrowers, rating agencies, investment bankers, hedge funds, and other financial intermediaries underestimated risks (inadvertently or purposely); their collective behaviour generated financial bubbles that burst into crises (refer, for an example, to the 'Subprime crisis' of 2007–2008 and its aftermath).

2 A few bank managers have resorted to deceit. For example, they concocted and traded in opaque 'synthetic' or 'structured' financial products (e.g. complex derivatives). These were 'dubbed' toxic in view of their very high risks assumed unknowingly by banks' customers who were tricked into buying them in expectation of glowing benefits.

3 Some financial operators have swindled and ripped off their customers who were duped with dud assets or irrecoverable investments (e.g. Bernie Madoff's Ponzi scheme fraud which was estimated by prosecutors to have reached $64.8 billion; he was sentenced on 29 June 2009 to 150 years in prison and the restitution of $17 billion).

4 A few bankers have had 'conflicts of interest' with their customers and have used privileged insider information for illicit gain to the detriment of these customers.

5 Certain banking institutions have actively solicited the hosting of doubtful customers (e.g. tax dodgers, money launderers, price fixers, and other rogue operators), and have conducted unauthorized operations (e.g. rigging interest rates such as LIBOR, the London Interbank Offered Rate, or exchange rates).

6 Senior management has failed to set up reliable control systems, and/or to supervise effectively the activities of their subordinates, with the consequence that their institutions incurred huge losses (e.g. in the case of Jérôme Kerviel, France's most notorious rogue trader who worked for Société Générale; he was jailed for five years in 2012 after an appeal court faulted him for a loss of 4.9 billion euro on unauthorized transactions).

7 Certain top executives have sought and obtained excessive compensation packages (i.e. incommensurate with their responsibilities or their performance) driven by greed and predation factors.

8 Venal politicians and regulators have pressured bankers to obtain for themselves and/or for their partisans gains or advantages to which they are not entitled.

Sources: the author has made use of documents cited in this book. For a synoptic presentation, see 'The Sins of Financiers', by Michael Black, former Director of the American Stock Exchange,in: *Oxford Today*, Trinity Term 2014, pp. 42–44

Systemic risks in a global context

In their gatekeeping responsibilities, governmental failings in matters of prudential *policies* and *regulations* can hurt other countries whose economies are reasonably well-managed. In globally and readily interconnected financial markets, decisive coordinated actions among economically important countries become necessary in order to avert, arrest, or moderate 'crisis contagion'. Such contagion could show-up in domino-like bank runs, exchange rate volatility, and amplified fluctuations in the value of financial assets – all exacerbated by 'herd-like behaviour' of individuals and institutions. The disruption of the financial system will impact adversely the real economy.

When, in a globalizing context, a crisis begins to grip the financial system of a given country owing to the default of a centrally important financial institution, a chain reaction of insolvencies and/or illiquidity could impact *partner countries*. Public authorities of the countries concerned need to use without delay effective measures that mitigate or solve collectively the problems at hand. The effectiveness and credibility of these measures hinges on reaching a consensus among governments in the said afflicted economies, in order to generate widespread confidence among the general public, business entities, and other market operators.

The closer the intertwinement among financial sectors and national economies, the higher would be the need for speedy coordinated actions worldwide. The European Union has tackled the 'contagion issue' through the harmonization of member countries' deposit guarantee schemes: a general minimum coverage of 20,000 euro, a single supervision structure, unified resolution procedures, and a common resolution fund.[12] It has also set-up in 2010 the European Systemic Risk Board within the European Central Bank to oversee, monitor, prevent, or mitigate conditions susceptible to produce systemic risk, and to ensure the efficient and secure functioning of member countries' financial systems.

Analysts have trouble finding explanations for crises. This owes notably to the multiple, intertwined known and unknown factors involved. It is thus difficult to gauge their importance, estimate their prospective evolution, and devise effective means for their control. The effectiveness of remedial actions in producing desirable results could prove uncertain or limited – owing, for example, to being 'too little too late'. With ominous indicators of a looming crisis, regulators, and bankers should act without procrastination – cooperating *inter alia* through multilateral financial organizations (such as the IMF and the BIS) in an interdependent world economy.[13]

Large highly leveraged financial intermediaries with sub-standard assets and unstable resources can generate volatility in exchange rates, interest rates, assets prices, yields, etc. – with potentially grave consequences. Among the latter, one could mention the drying-up of liquidity, depositor/investor panics, and business failures – all leading to the aggravation of unemployment. Among transnational financial risks, one could mention *systemic risk* resulting essentially from the high degree of interconnectedness of financial markets and institutions in the contemporary global economy. This shows up in the rapid domino-like chain reactions leading to the contagious transmission of shocks or problems originating in one market, one asset class, or one sizeable institution. The impact will be then felt by other markets or institutions in closely intertwined and interdependent economies and financial sectors. Privately held financial resources managed by commercial intermediaries dwarf those of official institutions (for example those of monetary authorities or sovereign investment funds). Nevertheless, it is difficult to predict the timing of serious difficulties that could arise with a big financial intermediary that are likely to produce a systemic risk requiring the intervention of public authorities.[14]

Globalization with the unimpeded flow of capital allows for the boom-bust rollercoaster to spread rapidly across markets.[15] Interconnected countries become more readily susceptible to economic-financial booms and bubbles, downturns and crashes, exchange-rate or commodity-price volatility. With respect to the latter, paper transactions (in benchmarked oil, minerals, and/or agricultural products) have grown substantially to become several times more sizeable than transactions in physical commodities, allowing financial intermediaries to speculate on the evolution of their prices with large positions (covering 'term' buying or selling, derivatives, or structured products) – without converting their positions into physical commodities. Such operations are deemed more lucrative by some bankers, compared with the traditional functions of lending to businesses or consumers.

The negative fallout from crises can be moderated through safety nets when authorities have the necessary resources and the determination to enforce them.[16] Within the public sector's tools of interventions aimed at re-floating banks and other financial intermediaries (through injecting capital resources and/or liquidity), one could refer to bail-outs and bail-ins, presented below.

Authorities' rescues and sequels

Some public authorities in market economies have espoused dogmatically the hypothesis that there is always a rapid natural adjustment, should any malfunctioning occur. This hypothesis has proved unrealistic in many situations. Governments have had to intervene, often belatedly, after crises have gathered unstoppable momentum. Interventions have been in funding troubled financial intermediaries, tightening sanctions for risk-control failures, creating equity and liquidity cushions, raising the frequency of monitoring and inspections (announced and unannounced), and other measures.

To fend-off and/or contain financial crises in a highly interdependent and readily connected world, coordinated actions among the authorities of major financial centres becomes necessary. Nevertheless, the missions and means of financial-monetary authorities could differ. For example, the European Central Bank (ECB) has for its primary mission to work for price-cum-financial stability (i.e. the absence of inflation or deflation in the eurozone). By comparison, the U.S. Federal Reserve Board (Fed) has two major goals: ensuring relative price stability, and promoting growth-cum-employment. Regarding means, the Fed can transact in governmental securities to influence the volume of money supply, while the ECB is formally barred from trading in member governments' securities. One needs to mention that the principal country in the eurozone, Germany, is 'terrorized' by the eventual danger of hyperinflation, similar to that it had suffered in the wake of the First World War.

A mix of policies and levers may have to be used to stabilize financial markets, and/or to boost economic growth. Among mechanisms available to the monetary authorities, one could mention deposit insurance, governmental funding or guarantees provided to the productive sector, central banks' easy credit policy, effective enforcement of prudential regulatory measures, and others. They could help moderate the contagious spread of crises or their prolongation – depending on the circumstances of the countries concerned. For the sake of effectiveness, coordination must be as comprehensive as possible among major financial centres in order to (a) avoid potential loopholes in regulations (regarding monitoring, reporting, supervision, control of risks, authorized business practices, fiscal matters, and others), and (b) generate the needed level of *confidence* among economic actors in order to rekindle economic growth.

To carry out productively their mission, regulatory agencies need relevant, detailed and reliable information, as well as appropriate tools to control system-wide risks. Unfortunately, lacunas in information are often encountered.[17] Moreover, the quality of regulatory institutions has been questioned by outsiders and insiders.[18]

The regulatory corpus comprises incentives-cum-prescriptions aimed at encouraging financial groups to adopt strategies for appropriate pricing and effective control of risks, and for shoring up sufficiently their capital base and their liquidity. Compliance calls for effective oversight/inspection by regulators who can impose timely, biting sanctions on those who violate laws, or infringe prescribed rules of prudence (using 'alert systems' for the prompt detection of problems and for their control). These sanctions could in drastic cases lead to (a) the closure of delinquent or failing institutions before their problems balloon and infect the financial system, and (b) penal measures against incriminated parties.

Bail-outs and too-big-to-fail

Circumstances may oblige a government of a market economy to bail out certain enterprises whose bankruptcy could become calamitous for the national economy, insofar as their demise could bring down concomitantly a multitude of interconnected enterprises dependent for their survival on the failed enterprises. This is likely to be the case of big-employer industries (for example the auto industry in the United States) or sizeable financial institutions, whose difficulties could hurt financial markets and the real economies of several countries.

Should the equity capital of a sizeable financial intermediary (bank, insurance company, hedge fund, financial conglomerate, etc.) be wiped out, and in the absence of new private shareholders, *public interest* may well justify reconstituting the capital of such a 'lame duck' with taxpayers' money until it recovers – hopefully within a short period of a few months. Public authorities' motivation for such help in a 'market economy' could well be to avoid a gridlock in financial markets. Among major governmental bail-outs for key participants in the subprime crisis was the world's biggest insurer, AIG, which had insured $2.5 trillion of bonds backed by mortgages invested by banks and others financial intermediaries. The insurer would have collapsed without the $182 billion of taxpayers' money, repaid in 2013 with $25 billion of profit for the taxpayer.[19]

The *shoring up* of heavily de-capitalized *sizeable financial institutions* is considered susceptible to generate systemic risk (notably among those referred to as *too-big-to-fail*). These institutions' recovery is deemed essential to the smooth functioning of national economies and avoiding international gridlocks. Their acquisition (partially or totally) by governmental agencies for a transitional period (until their full recovery) would then become necessary, subject to the installation of a new, competent and honest management.

Often, governmental support has favoured bailing out large financial institutions whose demise could be catastrophic for the national economy, insofar as their failure could grip the whole financial system and plunge the economy into a severe depression. Such 'bailing out' policy, usually referred to as 'too-big-to-fail' – does not encourage responsible rigorous behaviour on the part of management – as recognized by researchers, policy makers, and/or operators. Mastodon financial institutions in need of rescue could require sizeable resources beyond the capacity of a single country to provide. To avoid the spread of losses to other interconnected financial markets, an orderly downsizing of the defaulting financial institution whose activities span several jurisdictions would require rapid cooperation among various public authorities concerned and their governmental agencies.

Large banks' expectations that they could be rescued by the public authorities in periods of difficulties represent a source of moral hazard (i.e. an invitation to reckless management). Moreover, the implicit commitment by governments to bail them out offers them the opportunity of raising funds in financial markets at lower rates, compared with their smaller-size competitors who do not benefit from any such commitment. New proposals regarding the resolution of insolvent big banks have been agreed to by regulators of major financial centres (among other regulations aimed at strengthening the foundations of banking activities to be implemented by 2019, and referred to as Basle III – see the section on 'bail-ins' below). Savvy observers consider that a relatively high equity buffer, say close to a quarter of their risk-weighted assets, could protect large banks against potential crises.[20]

Bail-ins

Managers of sizeable financial institutions are generally tempted to assume higher risks, because they consider that governments will come to their rescue, with taxpayers' money, owing to their *systemic* importance in the economy. To expunge the moral hazard of bail-out and to strengthen discipline among bank managers, several measures are needed. Besides requiring the bank's existing shareholders to bear fully losses, other lenders to the bank will be made liable to 'assign' a portion of their funding to reconstitute the bank's capital. The bail-in 'rescue regime' calls therefore on the defaulting bank's owners to be in the first line of bearing losses of their troubled bank. Specifically, this regime expects the investors in an insolvent bank – primarily shareholders, holders of mezzanine instruments, subordinated debt, or junior bonds – to bear fully losses sustained by the troubled bank. Senior bondholders and large depositors are next in line as contributors in refinancing the bank and become thus the new shareholders. They are expected to shore-up the capital and liquidity of the bank before it is driven into total bankruptcy; they would then receive shares in the re-floated bank in consideration for their funding. Experts recommend excluding sight deposits with an original maturity of seven days from bail-in contributions.[21]

The above-mentioned funders of an insolvent bank contribute to the bank's total 'loss absorbing capacity'. Investors in the bank's bonds and large depositors (whose fixed deposits are not insured beyond a limited amount that applies to small deposits) are considered capable of evaluating their bank with respect to risks; their involvement in the eventual rescue of insolvent banks should accordingly incite them to be vigilant in monitoring and guiding management towards prudence. It is conceivable that major shareholders who have chosen management could be expected to recapitalize their insolvent bank to absorb a portion of the losses and contribute thus to its re-floating – subject to the reorganization of the bank under a competent new management. The foregoing measures would allow systemically important big banks to wind-up in an orderly manner without paralyzing the financial system and/or calling on the tax-payer to cover the potentially huge losses of a large defaulting bank.

Bail-in measures allow for the re-floating of a troubled bank after its rehabilitation, without recourse to state funding. *Bail-in* is defined

> as a statutory power of a resolution authority to restructure the liabilities of a distressed financial institution by writing down its unsecured debt

> and/or converting it into equity. The statutory bail-in power is intended to achieve a prompt recapitalization and restructuring of the distressed institution.[22]

The *bail-in* approach is intended to replace advantageously, from the standpoint of a national economy, the *bail-out* approach. This was judiciously expressed thus:

> Several factors have driven the consensus away from using taxpayer money to resolve banking problems. The first is that most EU countries feel they have exhausted their fiscal space, and that protecting their banks would not be their greatest priority. Moral hazard is the second factor leading to a change in paradigm. Public sector support will be seen as a 'bail out' of the banks which in turn implies that the private sector does not incur the costs of its own actions and may therefore not be deterred from undertaking such actions again.[23]

Regulatory authorities can be empowered to require large depositors to convert a portion of their deposits into equity or subordinated debt, and/or to write down a portion of their deposit by sharing in the losses of their banks as happened with the 2013 Cyprus banking/financial crisis. Big depositors are those with deposits above the insured 100,000 euro in the case of Cyprus and other Euro countries. The above-mentioned requirement encourages these big depositors to choose with discernment the banks they want to patronize, and to monitor carefully their activities with respect to prudential criteria. The legal obligation of sizeable depositors to absorb a portion of the bank's losses, should equity and subordinated debt of the affected bank prove insufficient, is premised on the assumption that these big depositors have the means (in material and human resources) and the interest in ascertaining and monitoring the quality of the bank's management. Small depositors (who constitute the majority of depositors) have, by comparison, a lower capability and limited resources to allocate to their investigation of banks, compared with large depositors. The foregoing requirement of obligating large funders of banks to bear eventually some of the losses would spare taxpayers from getting involved; such an arrangement can be readily implemented over a week-end, according to informed professionals.[24]

Small depositors Insurance schemes are generally readily implemented without delay, in order to avoid runs on dodgy banks. Such rapid implementation would quench depositors' panic and stop contagion to other financial institutions – nationally and internationally. The above-mentioned enforcement will preempt the chaotic withdrawal of funds, hoarding and/or the transfer of withdrawn funds to 'safer' vehicles, instruments, currencies, commodities, or other assets. Analysts and policy makers often recommend that guarantees should primarily apply to small depositors below a certain threshold (often calculated as a multiple [5 to 10] of per capita income).

As defined by a major European bank,

> The bail-in mechanism has three intended objectives: *First*, banks' investors rather than the general public are supposed to bear the costs of bank failures. The costs will not disappear, but will be reallocated. With a smaller number of people bearing the costs, the individual contribution is considerably higher than in the case of a tax-funded bailout. This provides an incentive for investors to monitor the entities they invest in more carefully. Of course this requires either professional investors or, in the case of retail investors, particularly high standards of investment advice from banks and asset managers when they distribute these products. *Second*, banks are no longer to rely on implicit government guarantees. Critics often claim that systemically important institutions and their investors can expect bail-outs in the event of financial distress as these banks are labelled 'too big to fail'. In that case, both parties would have an incentive to either take more risks on their books or monitor their investments less stringently as they would expect public funds to cover any shortfall in an emergency. This also implies lower funding costs for those banks. Of course, this argument only holds under the assumption that higher risks tend to lead to higher profits. Free market in death? *Third*, contagion effects for other financial institutions or the broader market are to be limited. With the bail-in tool, a quick recapitalisation may become possible as there is an *ex ante* ranking order of eligible liabilities. Graver consequences such as an immediate business shutdown or fire sale of assets may not be necessary.[25]

Liquidity arrangements

A bank's excessive maturity mismatch between its sources of funds (that happen to be in *short-term liabilities*) and its uses of funds (that are mostly transformed into *long-term assets*) hurts the bank's liquidity buffer. Faced with market illiquidity, banks with a relatively small liquidity buffer may be obliged to resort to a 'forced sale' of some of their assets at low prices, in order to honour their commitments vis-à-vis funders who seek to withdraw their sight claims. Such a forced sale of assets could adversely impact by contagion the value of other banks' assets.

Central banks, as lenders of last resort and creators of fiduciary money, can provide without undue delay ample liquidity over more or less long periods to a large spectrum of financial firms (and possibly non-financial firms) at easy terms. In the absence of market liquidity at moderate interest-rate levels, banks can therefore solicit from the central bank funds (i) using their private sector eligible assets as collateral, or (ii) by selling government securities they hold in their portfolio. Central banks' monetary stimulus can, furthermore, be boosted by enlarging the categories of banks' assets eligible as collateral for central bank financing with the objective of providing additional liquidity to markets.

The monetary authorities have two primary concerns: (1) to revive slumping national economies and (2) to protect financial stability. To achieve the first objective, the monetary authorities have to enable financial intermediaries to overcome credit crunches, and to allow them to fund their eligible customers (enterprises, investors, and consumers) at reasonable terms. The monetary authorities could also induce commercial banks to lend their excessive 'dormant' liquidities deposited with the central bank – either by (a) offering *state guarantees* (on inter-bank lending and/or on new loans to the private sector), or by (b) charging negative interest rates on hoarded liquidities. To achieve the second objective in periods of inflationary pressures or building-up booms, the central bank needs to tighten credit supply.

For example, banks that are likely to be affected adversely by a possible liquidity crunch could be authorized to change readily their legal organization to enable them to tap liquidity from the wide public of savers. For example, a U.S. investment bank (that deals traditionally with corporate finance) can be authorized to own deposit-taking banks that are capable of accessing the large retail market.

Authorities could encourage *acquisitions of troubled banks* by solvent financial groups that could rationalize, streamline and reduce costs (through eliminating redundancies and/or creating synergies). For that purpose, authorities could offer certain incentives (such as financing at favourable terms, fiscal rebates, exemption from anti-trust legislation, or other incentives), to facilitate the acquisition. Insolvent financial institutions beyond rehabilitation could then be allowed to go through the bankruptcy track – while guarding against an adverse systemic impact on the financial sector.

Divestment *of non-performing assets* of troubled financial institutions (i.e. the 'bad' banks) leaving the healthy part (the 'good' banks) to be bought-up by new investors with a new competent management. *Dud* assets will be fully provisioned and treated as losses – to be covered primarily by erstwhile shareholders. Under-performing assets could be 'parked' in state-sponsored or state-supported special-purpose vehicles for their future orderly sale at a propitious time, hopefully at above distressed price levels, once the financial tempest has subsided or passed away.

Besides the above-mentioned approaches to strengthen banking operations, the long-term prosperity of the financial and real sectors of an economy is based on sound profitability. Indeed, the first line of defence of a private business is its capacity to generate profits over the long term. Banks' profitability is largely generated from three sources: (a) *interest margins* (the difference between the average interest rate on loans and the average interest on customers' deposits and other third parties' funds), (b) various *fees* derived from financial operations and advisory services, and (c) income from investments of the bank's proprietary capital. Earnings serve not only to reward owners; they are also needed as capital reserves to be ploughed back into the bank to strengthen the equity buffer and enhance the bank's resiliency.

Capital buffer

Banks' *countercyclical capital buffer* policy in any given country contributes to improving the resilience of the banking system in the country concerned, thereby promoting overall financial stability. That policy helps to curb potential bubbles – such as those in the real-estate sector. These bubbles are fanned by a high growth of bank lending, measured notably by the ratios of: (i) *total credit* to *GDP*, (ii) *house prices* to *household disposable income*, (iii) *commercial property prices* to *total debt*, and (iv) *wholesale funding of credit institutions* to *total funding*. A rise in the foregoing four indicators has ushered periods of financial instability.

The 'countercyclical capital buffer' policy applies to a country's whole banking system. It seeks (a) to constrain excessive credit growth by requiring additional capital on bank lending during periods of relatively high growth of the national economy, and (b) to reduce the exigencies of capital requirements on loans during *periods of 'economic downturn* and *large bank losses'* in order to mitigate the impact of procyclical potential *tighter credit* during these periods. The 'countercyclical capital buffer rate' will not be reduced to accommodate the loss problems encountered by an individual bank.[26]

Programmes of support to financial intermediaries and markets have been substantial during the financial crisis that blew up late in 2007. In the United States, an agency of the U.S. Congress estimated in 2013 that support programmes (mostly in emergency credit, liquidity programmes, debt guarantees, deposit guarantees, and capital purchase of troubled major financial institutions) peaked at over 6 trillion dollars in the crisis period, excluding support by state and local governments. At the depth of the crisis recession in June 2009, U.S. annual real GDP reportedly fell by 5 per cent to $12.7 trillion. Federal financial support was made available mostly through the Federal Reserve System, the Federal Deposit Insurance Corporation, and the Treasury.[27]

The challenge encountered by public authorities in periods of economic downturns (with the retrenchment of investors, high levels of unemployment, and social gloom) is to implement without delay credible policies conducive to instilling an environment of confidence among economic actors to weather crises and re-launch growth in investment and consumption. The authorities concerned may need to explore different avenues, calibrated to the circumstances of the crisis at hand. These would include a mix of measures aimed at controlling *fiscal deficits* (especially by reducing governmental borrowing for non-productive expenditures) and *stimulating business development*. This would call for (a) reducing red tape, fiscal charges and other hurdles, and (b) incentivizing innovation that addresses vital needs, employment, and business creation. Such business development would in due course boost tax revenues, and reduce budget deficits and public debt burdens. The balancing of state budgets does not necessarily clobber business and strangle growth so long as public spending privileges *productive* investments at the expense of bureaucratic expenditures.

Economic revival in the Unites States after the Great Depression in the late 1930s was not due to monetary policy (low interest and easy credit, or the bailing out of banks), but rather to *governmental spending that 're-invented' the structure of the economy*. Governmental spending on procurements soared and transformed the U.S. South from a rural economy into a manufacturing one producing military supplies needed to wage the Second World War. Similarly, the U.S. economy's exit from the 2007–2013 economic doldrums is likely to materialize should the U.S. government privilege 'productive' investments – as opposed to increases in consumption through raising salaries or pensions. Investments are deemed productive if they are meant for education and training in skills, research and development, new technologies (e.g. information systems, and cleaner-efficient-sustainable energy), and infrastructures (such as power plants and grids, means of transport, and communication facilities).

One should acknowledge that the foregoing governmental investments have multi-year gestation periods, before they come to full fruition in boosting growth.[28] With a low propensity to spend (on investment and consumption) during a slump by the private sector, those favouring the Keynesian approach recommend the re-kindling of the economy by '*propping up demand*' through increased governmental spending (e.g. in education, research, infrastructures, health, safety nets, and the like). Forecasting the 'economic growth' impact of governmental policies, one should admit, is a complex exercise, subject to much uncertainty.

Governmental interventions encounter staunch opposition from the libertarians whose intellectual heroes are the Austrian Friedrich Hayek and Ludvig von Mises. Both firmly denounce state intervention (such as increased governmental spending or the tightening of regulations) as a false cure to economic crises. They worry about the misallocation of resources by governments – possibly leading to redundant highways, bridges, ports, airports, ghost cities, etc. Although it produces inequalities, anti-Keynesian economists argue that the capitalist model of open markets that are 'free' from governmental intervention is a superior producer of prosperity, compared with alternatives.

Economics does not have ready fully fledged solutions. Among queries often raised in periods of recession/stagnation are the following: Should the policy of balanced budgets be invariably observed? Alternatively, could budgetary deficits be tolerated over limited periods of time, in the expectation of ramping up growth that produces budgetary surpluses that could compensate for past deficits? To some parties, this dichotomy could be reconciled by changing the composition of governmental expenditures. The latter would then prioritize productive investments (in needed infrastructure, research, education, and incentives to businesses susceptible to generate readily high levels of employment) in preference to other expenditures (e.g. on bureaucracy).

Structural reforms (financial, fiscal, regulatory, etc.) that reduce bureaucratic burdens and instil *confidence* among economic agents are then called for: to encourage innovative entrepreneurs, and to entice companies to invest, banks to lend, and households to spend. Finding valid solutions by designing appropriate tools, calibrating them, and using the required mix of such tools to boost and generalize confidence in an economy or group of economies are challenges which could elude policy-makers over more or less long periods – as events of the past have amply demonstrated. In such eventuality, society may have to brace for absorbing the painful shocks of crises.

Nevertheless, fine-tuned regulatory prescriptions could protect the stability of the financial system. Notable among these measures is the creation of a countercyclical *capital buffer for banks*: (a) to be built-up during periods of upturns in the economy (thereby curbing high credit growth that shows up when credit rises faster than GDP), and (b) to be drawn on during periods of downturn to cover eventual losses and/or provide credit to alleviate an eventual credit-supply squeeze in economic downturns, as recommended by the Basel Committee on Banking and Supervision (referred to as Basel III, to be fully implemented by 2019). The above-mentioned countercyclical 'capital buffer' serves the dual purpose of (a) bolstering banks' resilience in periods of downturn, and (b) mitigating excessive increases in assets prices and/or credit growth.

'Crisis management' calls for in-depth objective diagnosis of existing problems, prior to designing optimal solutions. Unfortunately, available data may be incomplete, inaccurate, or misinterpreted to allow for effective remedies. Countries' circumstances and the international/regional contexts may be so different (e.g. with respect to currency rates, interest rates, or wage levels, etc.) that the impact of policy-measures could turn uncertain.[29]

Moreover, a *too easy* monetary policy (often characterized by very low interest rates coupled with the easy access of commercial banks to borrowing from central banks) can have its drawbacks. By flooding financial intermediaries with liquidity, such an easy monetary policy could induce bankers to neglect prudence and foresight by tempting them to lend to some borrowers who do not meet rigorously criteria of credit worthiness. Moreover, credit institutions could well under-price their own borrower risks, or may well fail to exercise the needed follow-up controls on the performance of their borrowers. It is also possible to find situations of shrinking financial resources available for lending or investment when financial intermediaries' management adopts excessively cautious attitudes, investors are too risk-averse to invest, and/or consumers are tight-fisted – all worrying about future uncertainties.

The monetary authorities in the United States and other financial markets tried over 2007–2015 to alleviate the credit crunch problems (characterized by banks' hoarding liquidity and drastically contracting of inter-bank lending, or their credit exposures to business and consumers) fearing an economic recession. The risk of a protracted sluggishness in the national economy and its adverse impact on employment and social stability has been deemed more important than the potential inflationary risk that hurts savers, pensioners, and fixed income earners.[30]

Nevertheless, rescuing the economy cannot rely exclusively on monetary policy. Excessive public debt issued by the monetary authorities can stunt the national economy for a long time.[31] Besides using monetary policy to overcome crises, complementary reforms are needed. These comprise structural measures (e.g. the sale of state-owned firms or state participations in business firms in the hope of rendering them more efficient and innovative, and privileging governmental investments in needed physical infrastructures, public support for quality education-cum-research, health care, etc.), incentivizing business creation and development (e.g. by shifting tax burdens from productive investments to consumption), investment in human resources (training in productivity and efficiency improvements), reducing business charges on jobs or downsizing to enhance their competitiveness, etc. Some of the foregoing measures require lengthy periods and significant commitment of resources before starting to bear fruit.

The U.S. subprime mortgage crisis of 2006–2007 and its trans-national propagation has been probed and commented on by a variety of authors; each analysis has emphasized selected factors. The *U.S. Financial Crisis Inquiry Commission* has revealed numerous causes for the inception and uncontrolled burst of the crisis. These include (a) excessive borrowing and risk-taking by households, (b) breakdowns in corporate governance of financial intermediaries, (c) breaches in accountability and ethics regarding 'duff' assets, (d) widespread failures in financial regulation to rein in excesses, and (e) policy makers' inadequate understanding of the crisis' parameters, and their inability to devise and implement effective means for surmounting such a crisis. The commissioners of this exhaustive investigation could not, however, reach a consensus on the hierarchy of the crisis' principal causes.[32]

In periods of crises characterized by the malfunctioning of the private sector or market inefficiencies, judicious governmental intervention (using appropriate instruments and means) and timely actions (by avoiding procrastination) would become necessary in order to prevent the worsening of the crisis and to facilitate exit with the least possible costs. A trajectory of healthy economic recovery calls for understanding the gestation and the evolution of crises, along with devising and using optimal instruments to control them. Tools generally involve a mix of stimuli and regulations which have to be attuned to the unfolding conditions and particularities of each crisis. Empirical research needs therefore to be continuously developed, re-interpreted and re-appraised, with respect to (i) the authenticity and comprehensiveness of collected data, (ii) the soundness and relevance of methods and models used, and (iii) the utility *of results* for policymakers, practitioners, researchers, and others.

In addressing a crisis challenge, no ready-made neat or single solution is available, and muddling through should not be excluded. Evidently, crises (financial and others) do not recur in identical manners – with respect to causes, symptoms, or impacts.[33] Moreover, regulators may not be fully abreast of the latest developments in markets and products (including new sophisticated financial products or derivatives) and of means of ascertaining and controlling their risks. For one keen observer of financial markets, 'the task of ensuring financial stability is far too big to rest on the shoulders of monetary policy alone, or even a combination of monetary and prudential policies'.[34]

Market discipline and regulations

Opening up markets generally contributes to competition and growth, assuming the parties concerned have level and balanced relations. This applies to cross-border deployment of financial resources that seek business opportunities (with higher returns or lesser costs) internationally, with potential benefits accruing to investors, capital-short enterprises, and other parties. Costs can be reduced thanks to higher efficiency, greater liquidity, diversification and moderation of risks, and promotion of financial innovation.[35] Moreover, open financial markets can prompt participants (namely shareholders, debt holders, depositors, and other holders of financial instruments) to be disciplined in their activities, assuming general *transparency*. The latter term refers to market participants' disclosure and monitoring of reliable and pertinent information that can be used by market participants. Thus, *excessive risk-taking* induces financiers to demand higher risk premiums or alternatively to reduce the amount of funding they provide to firms and other entities.[36]

Causes of economic crises are multifarious. A crisis may start in an economic sector in a given market, and spread to contaminate other branches of an economy and other countries. The complex and intricately connected crises of the decade following 2007 (which originated in an environment of permissiveness, greed, and abuse in the U.S. sub-prime mortgage sector) are an illustration. Transnational contamination through a domino effect spread of non-performing assets among financial intermediaries has thus affected many countries. A highly leveraged global financial system with unstable resources can produce volatility (in exchange rates, interest rates, assets prices, yields, etc.) and can consequently carry potentially grave risks for financial intermediaries. Several governments have had to rescue some of their defaulting financial institutions through massive public funding leading to partial participations in the capital of these institutions, or total nationalizations. In so doing, governments incurred excessive budgetary deficits and ballooning public debts they failed to honour.

Governmental foreign debts contracted vis-à-vis foreign creditor governments are renegotiated when the debtor government encounters re-imbursement difficulties. Collective solutions are proposed by creditor governments within an informal grouping referred to as the *Paris Club* that convenes, since 1956, under the chairmanship of a senior official of the French Ministry of Finance. To avoid the default of the debtor country and its exclusion from international financial markets, debt alleviation is resorted to. This covers multiple measures: a reduction of financial charges, a prolongation of the re-imbursement periods, a conversion of part of the debt into investments or aid, the export of goods by the debtor country at improved terms of trade, securitizing public debt and buying it back at depreciated market prices, etc.

Governments that are members of monetary unions should guard against flouting the usual norms of prudence by incurring excessive budgetary deficits financed by international borrowing. This happened in the eurozone, when a government's capacity to service foreign debt charges had proved impossible to honour without the support of foreign lenders. That support could come through fresh funding, extension of reimbursement periods, conversion of debt into investments, refinancing the debt with lower financial charges, and eventually partial debt forgiveness. Debt relief was particularly resorted to by foreign lenders to Greece over the 2010–2015 period. Successive Greek governments' forbearance for tax dodgers and the spendthrift habits of certain segments of society have led to excessive indebtedness as measured by reference to GDP, and these situations were often obscured by improper official reporting. The rescue by their euro partners (largely through debt rescheduling over longer maturity periods, along with partial debt forgiveness) and the IMF (through 'conditional' lending) has prevented Greece from defaulting and exiting the eurozone.

To avoid the flouting by any member country of the rules of a monetary union, analysts have recommended the establishment of a single 'economic government'. The perennial stability of a single currency zone cannot be realized unless member governments relinquish their sovereign powers in the economic field to a central authority. That supra-national authority will then be responsible for implementing *policies of convergence* aimed at establishing a level playing field. That convergence would cover budgetary matters; wages and salaries, pensions and unemployment benefits; executive compensations; personal and corporate taxation or incentives (to businesses, investors, and consumers); regulation and monitoring of markets; and other measures.

Corporate codes of conduct complement laws and mandatory regulations. These codes' recommendations encourage best practices over and above the official prescriptions. They have not prevented, nevertheless, the breakout of business scandals in the form of corruption and fraud, despite public outrage at earlier scandals. This was the case of a few major international banks that rigged (a) their declared interest rates for the London Interbank Offered Rate (LIBOR) till 2012[37] and the U.S. dollar/euro exchange rates of a $500 billion-a-day market. UBS and Barclays, for example, had to pay $1.4 billion and $300 million. The LIBOR (used to price financial contracts of various time horizons and in various international currencies) was set daily at 11:00 a.m. by the British Bankers' Association (which included incriminated banks) on the basis of estimates submitted by a dozen banks on their costs of borrowing. Financial transactions involving faked costs of borrowing or lending have covered notably mortgages, bonds, consumer loans, and interest-rate swaps (the volume of which in 2012 was estimated to exceed 300 trillion U.S. dollars). Since these events, regulators in major financial sectors imposed heavy fines on mortgage malpractices, manipulative trading, and tax evasion amounting to over $60 billion in 2012–2015. They have also assumed stricter oversight to avoid banks' violations of laws and honest trading.[38]

After the above-mentioned scandals, the regulatory authorities have tightened their prescriptions in matters of: *transparency* (for example with respect to risks relating to financial products offered to customers (depositors, investors, borrowers, or lenders), *honesty of reporting*, *comprehensive consolidation* (for example by refraining from the concealing of material components, such as losses, liabilities or litigations), *simplicity of presentation* so as to allow comprehension by the lay public, and adequate *sanctions* to deter malpractices.

All banks should be solid with respect to norms of: robust capital cushions, immediate access to liquidity, and risk assessment of exposure, as well as other matters. Supervisors should devote sufficient resources to control sizeable institutions, since the impact of their failure is bound to hurt the proper functioning of national economies (i.e. proportionately more than compared with smaller banks). Banks – no matter what size – should not be promised, explicitly or tacitly, a bail-out. Owners and investors in these banks will have to bear the full brunt of their foolhardy risk-taking (through loss of their capital, downsizing and dismantling, and other measures). Such mandatory sanctions will induce shareholders to choose a competent management that refrains from excessively risky operations and to build up their cushions of both *equity-subordinated debt* and of *liquidity*. To foster prudence-cum-return, bank management compensation packages (and in particular the bonus component) should be *dissociated* from short-term profits. Bonuses should be capped (the European Parliament has proposed the equivalent of one year of salary) and should be granted for long-term performance, with claw-back clauses should performance fall below set benchmarks applicable over multi-year time horizons. This will dissuade bankers from the temptation of making risky bets. It will also encourage performing executives/employees to stay longer, to realize the full bonus benefits they are entitled to.

Penalties

The U.S. Justice Department and other state agencies obtained a $1.375 billion settlement from S&P for defrauding investors in the period that led to the blow-up of the mortgage boom in 2007–2008. S&P was accused of issuing

> inflated ratings that misrepresented the securities' true credit risks. Other allegations assert that S&P falsely represented that its ratings were objective, independent and uninfluenced by S&P business relationships with the investment banks that issued the securities … Half of the $1.375 trillion – i.e. $687.5 billion – constitutes a penalty to be paid to the federal government and is the largest penalty of its type ever paid by a rating agency. The remaining $687.5 million will be divided among the 19 states and the District of Columbia.[39]

The Securities and Exchange Commission (SEC) charged Standard & Poor's with a series of federal law violations involving fraudulent misconduct in its ratings of certain commercial mortgage-backed securities. S&P agreed to pay SEC more than $58 million to settle the SEC's charges, plus $19 million to the New York Attorney General Office and $7 million to the Massachusetts Attorney General's office.[40] Several quarters have called on public authorities to expand the number of providers of financial ratings (with the possibility of creating governmental rating agencies), and requiring all rating agencies to abide by rigorous transparency standards (especially in revealing to the general public the methodologies they use).

Regulatory gaps, non-compliance with rules, and 'forbearance' of officials towards big economically-cum-politically powerful institutions have undermined the integrity of the financial system. Many culprit bankers had obtained immunity from criminal accountability. This was the case of the British-based international bank HSBC which agreed late in 2012 to pay in fines $1.9 billion to the U.S. regulatory authorities against obtaining immunity from criminal prosecution. U.S. regulators had feared that by invalidating HSBC's U.S. banking licence, they could have cost the national economy thousands of jobs, with the possibility of 'contagion' risks reaching several other financial centres and disrupting economic recovery.[41] By 2014, the largest fine imposed on an international bank was $2.8 billion on Credit Suisse, 'the largest monetary penalty of any criminal tax case on record, for helping U.S. clients evade taxes'.[42] Other penalties in 2014 had reached higher figures: $9 billion for BNP (for violating U.S. laws on dollar transactions with Iran, Sudan, and Cuba); $13 billion for JP Morgan (for U.S. subprime mortgages' irregularities); $16–17 billion for Bank of America (for claims related to the sale of subprime mortgage-backed securities that defaulted, and various other financial frauds leading up to and during the financial crisis).[43]

A more effective deterrent to misconduct than fines would be the withdrawal of bank franchises and judiciary prosecution of responsible individuals. Some regulators deem these banks are not only *too-big-to-fail*, but also *too-big-for-trial*. Their misconduct has not been sanctioned by closing them or prosecuting their senior management. Such closure has been recommended by a former director of global compliance at Citigroup and a former head of litigation at Salomon Brothers:

> I know firsthand the power of a regulator to put a financial institution out of business. I also know that the effective regulation of the marketplace requires that a prosecutor have these kinds of powers in his arsenal. Otherwise, regulation becomes simply another factor in calculating risk and is taken into account in pricing. Without the ability to impose the 'death penalty' on financial institutions, banking regulators … would be ineffective and bad bankers would become emboldened.[44]

Lessons

History is replete with episodes of crises and egregious conduct – of a more or less severe nature. One would expect that previous financial crises and failures would have alerted decision-makers to beware of outlandish risks that have had pernicious effects on society. Indeed, a decade prior to the blow-up of the subprime mortgage bubble in the United States in 2007–2008 with the crash in property prices, was the implosion of the large U.S. hedge fund Long Term Capital Management (LTCM) in 1998. LTCM was then the world's biggest hedge fund, run by a constellation of experienced and seasoned practitioners, Nobel Laureates in Economics, and distinguished professors at leading academic institutions. To avoid a global financial crisis, the New York Federal Reserve Bank had then engineered a rescue mechanism funded by LTCM's major international creditor banks, and facilitated its implementation. Many newcomers tend to forget or minimize the importance of past problems or crises; these persons believe they can do better than their failed predecessors.[45]

Crisis-resolution in financial intermediaries calls for appropriate and timely actions by public authorities (combining the judicious use of fiscal, monetary, regulatory, judicial, and other tools). Regulators need the requisite instruments and adequate resources to perform their responsibilities vis-à-vis economic agents (investors, lenders, depositors, borrowers, and the general public). Cooperation – through national, regional, and international institutions (such as the IMF, the World Bank, and the BIS) – would then become imperative when crises risk extending beyond national frontiers.[46]

A few economists have candidly admitted that learning from past events is subject to controversy. Olivier Blanchard (previously chief economist at the IMF and a renowned academic) argues that:

> ... there is agreement that macroprudential policies have to become part of the toolkit. But there is a great deal of uncertainty about the type of tools, given the changing shape of the financial system. In the monetary policy area, Blanchard agrees that many lessons have been learned. But there is no clear agreement on some of the key issues, such as the right size of central bank balance sheets or the type of instruments. And on fiscal policy, confusion remains about what constitutes safe levels of debt.[47]

Several years after the 2007–2008 financial crisis, the economic recovery in 2017 remained sluggish with relatively high levels of unemployment. For the sake of sustainable quality growth that averts crises and promotes the spread of social wellbeing, three areas of research and training deserve careful probing; they are succinctly presented below:

First: know-how for value creation

A principal mission of business education, one could reasonably argue, is to provide useful know-how that enhances the skills and competencies of participants (students, researchers, executives, personnel, middle and senior management, civil servants responsible for oversight of the business sector, and others) with a view to optimizing value creation for society's overall benefit.

In the field of business studies, management increasingly seeks programmes with a threefold thrust, namely: (a) teaching the latest in methodologies and techniques susceptible of rendering business activities more efficient and innovative, producing accretion in value, (b) raising the awareness of benefits obtainable over the medium/longer term by good governance, combined with respect for universal principles of ethics and fairness, and (c) enlivening participants' dormant or latent potentials through participatory sessions in which entrepreneurs and talented executives share their experiences with participants.

Some major multinational companies have set up their own internal business educational and training programmes, tailor-made to their specific needs. Such programmes enable the concerned enterprises to transmit, in an organized, continuous manner, the experiences of their talented management and experts for the benefit of the younger recruits to help them in capitalizing on the company's wealth of know-how. By developing managerial/entrepreneurial/technical competencies among a larger segment of the active population, training centres – whether they are independent or affiliated to business groups – are likely to expand the supply of potential managers/business leaders, and reduce the monopolistic benefits reaped by the few currently at the helm of enterprises. The moot point remains: 'How best to hatch out, nurture, and effectively diffuse entrepreneurial creativity and other skills?'

A properly incentivized environment encourages value creation, assuming judicious risk-taking. Knowledge and experience are likely to contribute to the success of a harbinger entrepreneur who can increase the efficiency of her/his actions by recruiting trusted qualified collaborators in various specialized functions (accounting, financial-economic analyses, planning, marketing, etc.). Otherwise, her/his innovative creative ideas could fail to bear the expected fruits. Examples of autodidact entrepreneurs exist. They have had the merit of innovating (in cutting-edge technologies, and/or novel business organizations or strategies) through their own personal efforts, studying in public libraries and without access to formal university education.[48]

Second: optimizing regulatory frameworks

Many researchers have acknowledged that the pursuit of personal gain is a high-intensity motivation in business. The fundamental challenge, however, is to guard against the pitfalls of excessive personal gain, leading to the slippery slope of unconstrained greed, foolhardy risks, short-termism, dishonest practices, and/or predation. The foregoing would undermine the motivation of various stakeholders for value creation. Lucre-motivated behaviours have often been studded with (a) negligence or impropriety, and (b) ingeniousness in circumventing rules.

Failure to observe transparency, accountability or honesty of transactions leads to self-serving practices that boomerang on parties concerned, eventually leading to disastrous results. This was the case of several financial intermediaries colluding among themselves to gain unwarranted profits. To avert such opportunistic manipulations, the variable portion of compensation packages (namely stock options or bonuses) available to executives and managers should be delivered on retirement or after a number of years of service, to encourage genuine value creation over the longer term.

Sound regulations generally seek to avert crises, and to protect against the malfunctioning of economies. Such regulations should be based on the collective proven wisdom of society, continuously enriched by experience of past failures and successes. Codes of prudence and deontological conduct complement laws and mandatory regulations, with recommendations encouraging *best practices*. Following on the breakout of business-financial scandals in past and recent years – characterized by excesses, corruption, or fraud – public authorities in several markets continue to enact additional prescriptions enforceable by the full authority of the regulatory-judicial system. A system of 'moderate' official regulations that privileges self-control, private initiative, and innovation, is to be contrasted with cumbersome and exacting official regulations with heavy bureaucratic machineries. Business decision-makers that abide by prudent risk management are likely to weather downturns or crises more effectively, compared with their profligate competitors. Anti-corruption and compliance research could benefit from the works of the global intergovernmental International Anti-Corruption Academy[49] and the Stolen Asset Recovery Initiative of the UN and the World Bank.

Third: formulation and implementation of business ethics

A community has better opportunities to thrive when the governance of its institutions is underpinned by universal ethical values. The fight against crime should be relentless for the perpetual welfare of any community. Wayward individuals and groups have been ingenious in devising multiple ways to circumvent ethical considerations by abusing others' legitimate rights. Civic leaders, thinkers, and ordinary citizens have to be continuously on the alert to identify existent and potential violations of human rights, using the UDHR as a cursor to guide human ethical behaviours in various domains.

The thorough study of human history does not show that the observance of ethical values has strengthened over time. Indeed, any eventual progress in this field is not *irreversible*. It behoves all humans, as individuals or communities, to continue without respite their exploration for means susceptible to (a) tame aggressive instincts of destruction and death by malevolent parties, (b) eliminate possible sources of peril that are liable to befall humanity, (c) avoid reversion to previous disastrous conditions, and (d) to transmit to future generations the valuable experiences of the past.

Progress in the ethical domains has not paralleled advances in the exact sciences or in technology. For an illustration, while humanity's advances in mathematics continue to build up on the achievements of earlier mathematicians, progress in ethical and socio-political values (e.g. those extolling *freedom*, *equality*, and *fraternity*) established by a community cannot be taken for granted as definitive. Indeed, the application of these values can be easily reversed by newcomers. In tandem with the spreading of knowledge and culture, one should recommend to all those concerned to seek the relentless inculcation and spreading of core *universal ethical values* (especially in relation to the application of UDHR's values).

Universal ethical principles consensually reached and solidly buttressed by enforceable legislation, national and supra-national, should be justice-driven. They should be guided by good governance at various levels – that of governments, business, civil society, and other stakeholders. This domain remains a top priority in our twenty-first century world, in so far as humans continue to be subject to multiple devastating conflicts. A cross-disciplinary approach, thoroughly studied and built up, may help in reaching a workable global code of conduct under the aegis of the UN University. This comprises an international community of scholars who are guided by the principles of the Charter of the United Nations; it is well positioned to research comprehensively on means capable of serving worldwide the core concerns of the UDHR. Under the aegis of the UN University, research on the implementation of global ethical behaviour needs to be pursued with the objective of protecting life and furthering harmony on planet Earth.[50]

In principle, past crises can offer stakeholders guidance for the formulation and implementation of judicious future policies or strategies, and the avoidance of potential traps. Nevertheless, some decision-makers are unlikely to heed warnings. Fuelled by hubris or greed, these persons believe they can do better than their predecessors in managing efficiently challenges as they arise. Others tend to overreach themselves by taking on challenges they know little about. Finally, some people tend to relax their vigilance by forgetting or overlooking past calamities or by minimizing their impact.

Escaping from their homeland's miseries and lured by 'citadels of prosperity'

A significant portion of the world population lives in desperate conditions – economically, socially, and/or politically. These conditions can be attributed to a variety of factors which comprise bad governance, natural calamities, socio-political turmoil, mismanagement, etc. Some countries have abundant natural wealth, yet their populations live in fear for their security and for their livelihood since they are subject to the vampire-like tyranny of rulers who usurp power, extort their people, and eviscerate national economies for their personal interests and those of their underlings. In the forlorn hope of a safe haven or an illusory El Dorado, many left their homes in search of sanctuaries and/or jobs. From the beginning, migration has been fraught with many dangers, with many risking their lives. In their exodus, thousands have perished annually, abandoned by unscrupulous traffickers to perish in deserts or jungles, even *forced* to drown at sea, or left to die (by hunger, thirst, diseases, criminal acts, and other fatal treacheries).

Natural disasters (such as droughts, floods, volcanic eruptions, earthquakes, tsunamis, etc.) or human tragedies (wars, genocides, enslavement, etc.) force hapless humans into exile, in search of safer environments away from their homeland's persecution, violence, injustice, or denial of other human rights. Many flee their homelands because they are denied by despotic regimes the freedom to benefit from domestic opportunities to create and prosper. The exodus of populations is not confined to unskilled or semi-skilled labour; it has extended also to 'brain drains' of highly skilled, knowledgeable, and/or entrepreneurial persons seeking more attractive opportunities in foreign lands.[51]

Relatively prosperous countries have generally been coveted by outsiders living in utter destitution with no (or limited) prospects for a better life. To protect their prosperity from envious outsiders, prosperous communities try to stop external intruders by erecting barriers. These barriers have evolved over the ages taking a variety of forms: physical walls with their control towers, water separations, man-made dunes, barbed/electrified wires, mined fields, missile systems, military fortresses and guards – besides natural barriers (seas and rivers, deserts, mountains, jungles, etc.). This was the case of India which walled off Bangladesh with a fence estimated in 2018 of some 3,300 km. That barrier has about the same length as the one to be completed by the U.S. Administration on its Mexican border aimed at stopping the movement of unauthorized migrants and/or illegal trade (notably narcotics) flowing from Latin America. Thousands of migrants manage to cross natural or man-made barriers – at the risk of their life. Most are *bona fide* persons seeking work opportunities and a better life in countries of destination. A few carry on with unauthorized trades (such as insidious drugs) at the risk of their life, occasionally operating with the hand-in-glove complicity of corrupt officials.

Physical barriers continue to be erected between several countries worldwide – generally invoking security. This is notably the case in the Middle East region where the most sophisticated techniques have been used to set up these barriers. Among the lengthiest and more recent of these walls of separation are those separating Israel from the Palestinian territories, and those separating Saudi Arabia from Iraq and Yemen. The primary reason for both cases is that of security.[52]

In periods of economic slumps and high domestic unemployment, a community's tolerance towards foreigners falls. Despite lip-service proclamations in favour of human rights, host governments tighten the noose on unauthorized 'economic migrants' seeking employment opportunities (to be distinguished from persons seeking political asylum owing to life-threatening human rights' abuses by rulers, repressive totalitarian regimes, and/or violent conflicts in their homelands). Illegal economic migrants of all hues are generally viewed by some prosperous host countries as besiegers of their 'citadels of prosperity'. This explains why several such countries have sought to bolster their defences against undesired economic migrants and lock them out by fencing their frontiers against the flow of such migrants. These countries have often held unwelcome migrants in detention centres before forcing them to return to where they came from.

Legally unauthorized migrants may be *ethically* in need (e.g. trying to escape from the persecution or distress in their country of origin). Migrants – especially those with no legal authorizations – could become stateless, living in limbo for indeterminate periods in countries of passage or destination. They are likely to be exploited by brutal traffickers in 'human distress' (e.g. by being subjected to long hours of toil in trying conditions with miserly pay and absence of social or health protection). They often live in squalid and overcrowded quarters lacking sanitation, running water, electricity, and air conditioning (when temperatures reach in summer 50 degrees Celsius in the shade).

Harrowing stories of ill-treatment have been reported by survivors and independent witnesses. They refer to deliberate forced drowning by [African] people smugglers who feared arrest;[53] suffocated lifeless bodies of men, women and children; shipmasters failing to rescue passengers of flimsy dinghies in distress; mass graves of migrants, and other dismal stories.[54] In its 2017 annual report, the UNHCR estimated the forcefully displaced at 65.6 million worldwide at the end of 2016.

Migrants pay for their journeys with their meagre savings or those of their families. They are often swindled and abused by modern slavery traffickers. *Illegal migrants* have been denied entry at border controls, or left stranded with no shelter, nutrition, or health care. If detained by police, they are often rebuked, reviled, kept lingering in detention centres, denied justice, tortured, and eventually coerced into returning back to where they came from (occasionally handcuffed and/or escorted by agents of deporting governments). Illegal migrants often live in shantytowns in foreign countries with the fear of being arrested, imprisoned, and eventually deported (whether by the authorities of the countries of *origin*, *transit* or *destination*). The abuses and injustices they bear are often not eligible for redress, given their status of clandestine migrants. These migrants have suffered considerably from xenophobia, and are subject to the anti-foreigner violence in which a few are reportedly killed.[55]

Unauthorized migrants are socially ostracized in host countries. They are brazenly subject to racism, discrimination or exploitation by unscrupulous employers in the 'underground' or 'black' markets (working with little respite in unsafe jobs), or left at the mercy of criminal networks (in the trade of prostitution or illicit drugs). They are denied salubrious dwellings, medical care, schooling for their children, and other basic protections for their families (should the latter be able to join them).

Even authorized migrants from various poor regions are often unaware of their legitimate rights and have been denied the usual protection or social benefits available to residents (such as access to decent housing, schooling for their children, social security, and the like). Employers' ill-treatment of migrant workers in certain host countries was reported by various researchers, NGOs, the media, social activists, and others. Hardships cover: changes in terms of employment, delays in providing work, unsafe working conditions, absence of decent housing (with no air conditioning in hot environments, filthy sanitation, costly food or water, etc.) the covering up of accidents or deaths, non-payment of wages, passports withheld, excessive fees charged by intermediaries, debt burdens at usurious rates, forced labour, sexual exploitation, physical abuse, etc.[56]

Employers in certain countries, as sponsors of foreign workers, routinely retain the passports of 'legal' workers till the termination of their contractual period (e.g. the *kafala* practice in the GCC countries). They could delay the timely payment of their salaries, deny them the right of bringing their families, and/or prevent them from leaving the host country or changing jobs.[57] The foregoing situation has been common in a number of wealthy countries, where drawing on foreign cheap labour has become akin to 'voluntary servitude' in so far as migrant workers know about these conditions before committing to work there.

Besides migration to foreign lands, there are internal migration drawing mostly on cheap labour from the marginalized rural areas of the same country; these internal migrants seek a better life in their migration to urban prosperous areas. They nevertheless suffer from discrimination and exploitation. As reported by *The Economist* writing on the hardships encountered by Chinese internal migrants:

> Newcomers live on building sites, or in windowless rooms in the basements of apartment blocks ... Beijing-born residents often treat the outsiders with scorn, blaming them for much of the city's crime and its pockets of squalor ... Migrants routinely suffer from dangerous work conditions, the withholding of wages, and state-imposed barriers in their access to housing, education and health care.[58]

Europe's economic powerhouse, Germany, has taken a positive stand in favour of immigration, subject to the integration of refugees in German society (requiring proper reception, housing, health care, subsistence benefits, schooling, and training) as expressed by a research team of the country's leading bank:

> Due to the low birth rate, which has persisted for more than 40 years now, and in the light of the approaching retirement of baby boomers in a few years, Germany faces the prospect of an increasing labour shortage and economic stagnation in the long term. Immigration could counter these trends if the refugees are integrated successfully. The costs of integration should therefore be seen as an investment in Germany's future.[59]

Judging by the exodus of African youth heading for Europe, despite all the risks they are encountering, one could be inclined to become pessimistic about the prospects for prosperity of the African continent. In that process, the skilled and the unskilled in developing countries look at Europe (and other rich countries, such as the oil monarchies of the Gulf) as lands of opportunity. They are willing to endure many sacrifices to reach their perceived El Dorados! The risk of death in deserts, at sea and at border crossings has not deterred them.

For insightful analysts, poor Africans and other marginalized people can prosper in their own countries with dignity, similarly to citizens of developed countries, if they are provided with their basic needs and the opportunities of enhancing their capabilities. Subject to good governance, they have high potential for economic, social, and cultural development. In this chapter we adduce two illustrations on African development, the *first* in the domain of trade in an agricultural commodity (namely cotton), and the *second* in the domain of social entrepreneurship in West Africa.

To combat measures of discrimination or abuse inflicted on migrant workers and their families, the United Nations General Assembly adopted in 1990 the *International Convention on the Protection of the Rights of all Migrant Workers and Members of Their Families* (A/RES/45/158). To contain the spread of hostility against migrants (often irrationally based on bigotry for alleged differences owing to race, culture, gender, faked information, or other prejudices), the UN General Assembly voted on 4 December 2000 for the creation of the *International Migrants Day* (A/RES/55/93) – to be celebrated by all member states annually on 18 December. The said celebration is designated to promote the protection of refugees and migrants, along with their families. The global objective of suppressing or moderating irrational discrimination vis-à-vis migrants and their siblings remains an arduous task worldwide.

World Trade distortions and the case of U.S. cotton subsidies

Level-playing economic relations can open business opportunities that contribute to higher standards of living and improved quality of life. Nevertheless, important distortions in international trade continue to exist for multiple reasons. These distortions can result from the operation of private or governmental cartels (with arrangements that are tacit or explicit, overt or covert) whose members seek to dominate a particular market; these cartels collude in price fixing, splitting markets, controlling quality and after-sale services. Their success depends on (i) the absence of threats from newcomers or potential substitutes, (ii) the absence of cheating among cartel members, and (iii) the enforcement of appropriate sanctions on culprits.

Governments can distort free trade when they intervene to boost their domestic enterprises at the expense of non-nationals via various measures. These measures comprise tariff and non-tariff barriers, subsidies,[60] tax breaks favouring domestic companies, governmental non-competitive exclusive purchases at preferential terms from national enterprises, etc.[61]

Bilateral or regional trade agreements (with preferences offered to member countries) can create trade diversion in the pattern of international trade (not related to factors of competitiveness) with welfare-reducing effects for trading partners.[62]

Repeated, prolonged delays in concluding negotiations or breakdowns in international economic cooperation are often due to entrenched dogmatic positions of protagonists who are influenced by partisan opportunistic interests. This was the case the *Doha Round's* negotiations (named after the Qatari capital where discussions started in 2001) that did not come to a successful conclusion by the originally set target date of 2011. As a means of boosting global economic growth and wellbeing, these negotiations had aimed at expanding multilateral trade (for agricultural goods, manufactured products, and services) by cutting subsidies in favour of national enterprises and by eliminating trade barriers on imports.

Poor countries are generally faced with skewed conditions of trade eloquently expressed thus:

> Behind the free market rhetoric and emphasis on the virtues of level playing fields, the hard fact is that some of the world's poorest farmers are being forced into a competition not with northern farmers, but with industrial country finance ministries. Comparative access to subsidies, not comparative advantage, remains the key to understanding agricultural trade.[63]

Indeed, several researchers have examined the distorting impact of subsidies on competition worldwide.[64]

Overt or covert barriers to fair trade hurt economies that cannot produce and export the goods or services they are competitively best positioned for. The adverse impact of such barriers on employment and prosperity can be dramatic. Pascal Lamy (previously European Commissioner for Trade) acknowledged, from his vantage position when he was Director-General the World Trade Organization (WTO), that the legacy of discriminations of past colonial/imperial systems had yet to be fully overcome. Referring to skewed trade relations favouring developed sizeable economies at the expense of the least developed countries, he has cogently argued that conditions obtaining in 2006 contain predatory practices 'as if economic decolonization had had to wait 50 years after political decolonization'.[65] He stated that 'Our [WTO] core business is to produce trade opportunities through multilateral trade opening and the building of multilateral rules to ensure a level playing field.'[66]

The legacy of the colonial past in South Africa can be illustrated by reference to the fact that:

> A cornerstone of colonial rule and subsequently of apartheid … was a land act passed in 1913 that prevented black people from buying land outside native reserves that made up just 13 per cent of the country. More than two decades after the end of apartheid, the country's white minority still owns [in 2015] most of the land.[67]

Native reserves were set up on less productive lands by the colonial authorities favouring white settlers. Apartheid policies remain current in other parts of the world at the behest of occupying or despotic powers as we write.

The implementation of the *level playing-field* objective implies multilateral open markets and parity of treatment. In reality, governments and groups flex their dissymmetrical bargaining power to obtain advantages. The Leviathan states (often prodded by their major business groups with trans-national interests) tend to exercise their 'market and arm-twisting' powers (thanks, inter alia, to their superior know-how, wealth, and industrial-military resources) in various international organizations or forums – such as the WTO, the World Bank, the IMF, or others. As candidly and eloquently put by Peter Mandelson in his erstwhile capacity as the EU Trade Commissioner:

> Through the WTO and our trade policy we [the European Union] have the means to defend a vision of globalization that does have rules; that does require everyone to compete by the same rule book. And what, uniquely, the combined weight of the European Union gives us is the strength both to shape that rule book and enforce it.[68]

This omits to mention the need for 'fair trade' principles vis-à-vis small developing nations.

Besides hegemonic states, leaders of large business groups command clout in so far as they control large institutions with vast resources (human, material, financial and otherwise). This can be illustrated by reference to financial institutions operating internationally. Several studies have estimated the extent of concentration of control over the world economy by a few leading transnational corporations, for short TNCs.[69] Such control has important implications for policy making. Indeed, a concentration of corporate ownership in a particular economic sector is likely to jeopardize market competition. Moreover, sizeable linkages among financial institutions worldwide are likely to accentuate systemic risks and global financial fragility.

Cotton subsidies

International trade is seldom guided by the trumpeted principles of fairness. This is illustrated hereafter by reference to the use of subsidies in the agricultural field. Referring to the cotton trade, several researchers have analysed the impact of U.S. cotton subsidies (disbursed through countercyclical payments, marketing loans, direct payments, and other programmes – see Exhibit 4.2). These subsidies boost U.S. production, thereby lowering the world price of cotton and consequently hurting millions of poor cotton producers. African countries are amongst those most affected – notably Benin, Burkina Faso, Chad, and Mali; all these countries suffer from endemic famine and under-nutrition, high child mortality, inadequate education, high unemployment, and other socio-economic ills.

The elimination of direct U.S. cotton subsidies would raise the world price for cotton, increase West African countries' income for about one million cotton-producing households, and enable them to meet adequately their food requirements.[70]

The comparative advantages of U.S. cotton producers in international markets are not limited to their domestic subsidies. Indeed, U.S. cotton growers are not subject to hurdles encountered by their African counterparts. These hurdles comprise: low efficiency of domestic ginning and other processing facilities; low yields of cotton seeds; deficient training, research, and extension services; inadequate control of diseases; shortage in financial services; bureaucracies; absence of appropriate infrastructures (for power, irrigation, road transport, storage or shipping); poor intelligence and communication to access and use profitably markets for inputs or outputs; and other problems.[71]

Subsidy policies resorted to by richer countries in favour of their nationals stunt the development of poor countries, as illustrated above. By benefiting from *fair* treatment, the poor can raise their capacity to earn and spend their income according to their own priorities, thereby improving their standards of living (through better nutrition, health care, education, jobs, housing, and in other ways). This will help them to reduce or eliminate their dependence on hand-to-mouth aid and charity for survival. Eventually, they will be able to start the process of kindling their dormant creativity, assuming proper environmental conditions.[72]

The United States is not the sole country that subsidizes its cotton producers. Several other countries, developed and developing, have similar policies in favour of their domestic producers, though they are not as egregious. China, for example, stimulates the growth of domestic cotton production by offering premium prices to its farmers on assigned quotas, loans at preferential interest rates, and advance payments to cotton producers before planting.[73]

A World Bank study concurs that 'After years of diplomatic efforts and legal procedures to obtain the elimination of rich countries' cotton subsidies, policy prospects for African cotton producers remain bleak' with 'billions of dollars of subsidies ... offered to a few thousand wealthy farmers to the detriment of the poorest countries in the world'.[74]

Exhibit 4.2 Skewed commodity trade: cotton

Swiftly after the Doha trade negotiations began, four cotton-growing, poverty-stricken countries in West Africa became the embodiment of international trade and economic injustice. With an average GDP per capita of $637, and among the least developed countries on earth, Benin, Burkina Faso, Chad and Mali (known as the Cotton-4 or C-4) rely on cotton more than any other commodity for their export revenues. These countries produce cotton more cheaply than anywhere else – a competitive advantage that logically should place the C-4 in a prime position to benefit from the world's ever-increasing desire for cotton products. But a wall of subsidies deployed mainly by four trading power blocks has fatally undermined the C-4's ability to trade their way out of poverty. The Great Cotton Stitch-Up reveals that in the nine years since the Doha Development Round was launched, $47bn has been doled out by the United States, the European Union, China and India to its cotton growers. Over 51 per cent of that $47bn has gone directly to U.S. farmers. Figures from the United States Department of Agriculture (USDA) reveal one farm in California has received more than $24m in subsidies over the past 14 years. It is American growers, the world's biggest cotton exporters, and Europeans to a lesser extent, who enjoy the benefits of 'white gold', so creating a global price dampening effect. Even today, despite a recent cotton price spike, cotton has lost more than half of its value compared with 1975 once the price is adjusted for inflation. For the Cotton-4, it is a situation that spells economic ruination. With no subsidies to bail them out, Cotton-4 farmers struggle against insuperable odds to compete. And a lack of revenue means C-4 governments cannot afford to build roads, ports and other infrastructure to catalyse a garment industry that would employ millions of people and create greater value in a desperately underdeveloped sector.[75]

Improving the competitive advantage of poor countries vis-à-vis rich ones should serve their development, progress, and wellbeing. The governments and the business groups operating in the said poor countries may be well advised to improve their governance, to control rapacious bureaucracy, and implement policies that favour transforming raw commodities (here raw cotton) into finished products (e.g. textiles and garments) with higher added value.[76] This will improve the poor countries' terms of trade[77] by raising their *export prices*, assuming their *import prices* do not rise by as much.

One can appropriately conclude by quoting the following judgement of a seasoned expert: 'It is hypocritical to preach the advantages of free trade and free markets and then erect obstacles in precisely those markets in which developing countries have a comparative advantage.'[78]

Revitalizing abandoned villages and social entrepreneurship

The case under study examines the edifying role of an exemplary bi-cultural couple (Babacar Mbow and Pascale Blanchard) who have worked hard in rejuvenating a stunted community in the Sahel region of West Africa, through the creation of a local business hub centred on a cluster of villages around Ndem (some 120 km north-east of Senegal's capital city). We highlight hereafter (i) key characteristics (economic, social, cultural, and spiritual) of their *visionary leadership*, (ii) their concrete contributions in making their *setting* more hospitable, (iii) their *ethos of toil and solidarity*, and (iv) their *business strategies* for socio-economic development.

The above-mentioned couple dedicated the better part of their adult lives to the noble objective of reversing the exodus of African population from the impoverished Ndem region. Their life story illustrates the praiseworthy role of social entrepreneurship in trying to remedy situations of vulnerability. Moving against the general migratory flows from poor to richer countries, the Babacar/Pascale case illustrates the process of stemming the risky exodus (with travel fatalities due to unsafe routes and traffickers' abuses) from a languishing, destitute region. They tried and managed to rekindle economic activity in hitherto deserted villages.

This is the story of a charismatic and compassionate couple, Babacar and his wife Pascale, who offer role models and a source of inspiration to many entrepreneurs. Their ambition, underpinned by ethical values, has consisted since 1984 of reviving a cluster of distressed communities in the African Sahel (namely the Ndem region of Senegal). With unwavering determination they have sacrificed the erstwhile comfort, tranquillity, and personal careers they have had in the capital city of a developed country (namely Paris in France) in order to bring hope and prosperity to people they care for who have suffered from drought and poverty over many years.

During his youth in the 1950s, Babacar had militated for social reforms in his country of Senegal. He was imprisoned several times with his comrades by the then French colonial authorities, before leaving to study in France. The Mbow couple were living comfortably in one of the world's most attractive metropolis, namely Paris, until 1984 when Babacar was spurred by a vision calling him to revitalize the drought-stricken native village of his forefathers, Ndem.

Babacar's devoutness has led him to offer spiritual guidance for the Ndem community through a school (known by the name of *daara*). As an adherent of the mystical Mourides' brotherhood, his teachings extol values of industriousness, self-reliance, solidarity, tolerance, mutual respect, and social harmony within religious-cultural diversity in an environment of peaceful relations. The brotherhood exhorts its members to *conscientious work*, and elevates it to the acme standing of *piety* – in so far as *toil* protects the community from the indignity of begging and living on alms.[79]

Specifically, Babacar and Pascale had to address several fundamental existential questions with crucial implications for themselves, their family, and their collaborators, chief among which are the following:

- Should they carry on with their life of relative comfort in Paris, or should they respond to the arduous challenge of rejuvenating a community in grave misfortune?
- Could their bi-cultural couple (they had then one child) immerse fully within the local African community?
- Were they able to bear a life of hard toil and austerity for long in their intended new 'home' with its harsh geographical-physical environment of an arid bush-land? Could they have a decent livelihood in Ndem, along with those who would join their project in due course?
- Does Pascale's family support her bold decision to leave her motherland and her French-Western culture, to depart and live in an African traditional society?
- Could they successfully remedy the problems that have forced young people to migrate from Africa to Europe (e.g. for reasons of absence of business opportunities, conflicts, exclusion, etc.)?

It took unfailing optimism and courage to leave Paris for Senegal, at a time when thousands of African people were fleeing their countries and heading north (notably to Western Europe) – lured by the possibility of decent work and a better quality life! The couple's bold move south to the Sahel region in West Africa was prompted by their lofty values, namely (a) their refusal to accept the presumed fatality of permanent poverty in sub-Saharan Africa, and the many indignities it brings in its wake, and (b) their firm conviction that a decent living can be honestly earned in that region through commitment, toil, entrepreneurship, innovation, and solidarity. Their goal of starting a new and meaningful life has proved an attainable challenge.

Socio-economic projects

The Mbow couple have proved to be an inspiration. Their venture has been emulated by enthused villagers who committed to build for Ndem and its region a reputation for quality artisanal hand-made cotton clothes, in addition to household wares, for sale in Africa and to boutiques in Europe and North America. Babacar founded the Association of Ndem Villages ANV in 1985 (comprising 15 villages) and became its president [his wife has become the Associate President of AVN]. In 2006, the ANV, with 4,600 members, changed its status from that of a cooperative to that of a non-governmental organization (NGO), in order to promote investments for the benefit of all community members. A levy on the artisans' profits has been used to build the community's infrastructures.

The villagers' initial wares have centred on weaving and knitting of the yarn in quality cloth-making, notably of multi-coloured patched garments inspired by African traditions of pluralism and spiritualism. Original fashion designs produced by local artists have appealed to African and non-African tastes. In due course, villagers' activities expanded to cover a variety of crafts and trades, such as fashion garments, embroideries, leather works, furniture, and other house wares. They use African cotton, natural dyeing, and other ecological materials from the region. The Ndem's cluster of business activities even expanded over the years to satisfy local needs for vegetables and cereals produced with techniques suitable for an arid climate (such as drip irrigation). All these activities have increased the economic autonomy and wealth of the local community. Ndem and its surrounding villages have thus revived to become an 'oasis of relative prosperity' – thanks to the leadership of the Mbow/Blanchard couple whose values and strategies have won over the adherence of villagers bent on vanquishing endemic destitution and painful exodus.

The inventiveness of local talents has been fostered in Ndem through the creation of a business hub called Maam Samba that comprises diverse handicraft workshops, facilities of storage, an exposition gallery, a sales office, and a coordination-cum-logistics unit. Achievements have included projects that have led to the revitalization of the local economy, ensuring its sustainability and its resilience. The said projects have been successfully launched, essentially thanks to the collegial solidarity of the community, under the impetus of the Mbow/Blanchard couple, supported by NGOs and developmental agencies. The main revitalization projects are listed in Exhibit 4.3.

Exhibit 4.3 Revitalizing abandoned African villages

The Ndem region in Senegal

1. Handicrafts centre that offers locally-made artisanal products covering: textiles; furniture; leather; natural dyeing; weaving; original artistic native designs; use of local bio-cotton; jewel-making; pottery; basketwork; gourds; and other goods).
2. Health: an infirmary and a maternity hospital catering for the region's population; a medical insurance scheme; transport of patients.
3. Education: a child day-care centre, an elementary school, and a secondary school; building up a library; a cafeteria offering lunch catering for school children from distant villages.

4 Soft water: drilling for underground drinkable water; central water storage; a distribution network for 15 villages; and pools that can recover rain water.
5 Agricultural diversification (besides the traditional cultivation of peanuts) compatible with the local ecology: parsimonious use of 'water dripping' techniques for agriculture; experimental citrus fruits plantation; cultivation of aloes besides peanuts as part of agricultural diversification; regeneration of the soil with compost.
6 Salubrious environment: nursery of plants; re-forestation; setting up domestic refuse incinerators; waste recycling.
7 Ecological sources of energy: extensive wide use of solar energy; bio-energy (using the discarded shells of locally produced peanuts, mixed with clay); peanut production accounts for around 40 per cent of cultivated land in Senegal.
8 Micro finance: launching a cooperative for financial services to serve savers, investors, and borrowers.
9 Telecommunication: connection with regional and national networks.
10 Electric distribution: permanently integrated within the national grid.

Despite the general spirit of solidarity, certain functions have failed to perform up to expectations. This applies notably to (i) the micro-credit cooperative (set up in 2006) and its failure to recuperate overdue loans, contracted by a few members; (ii) the failure of the Ndem cluster of villages to pay their pre-agreed token contributions for the purchase of an ambulance; (iii) the fickle commitment of some villagers to carry out voluntary communal works on a shared plot of land (whose sales should have benefited the whole community) since most villagers have been privileging their private activities to feed their families in need; (iv) delays in the accreditation by the Senegalese authorities of local schools that could help youngsters to stay and work in the region; and (v) the negative impact of the world post-2008 economic crisis on the sales of handicrafts, thereby leading to an exodus of artisans from the Ndem region.

The foregoing challenges have not deterred the Mbows and members of their *daara* to maintain their commitment to the mission of serving their community.

Ethos of toil and solidarity

Laudably, the Parisian Pascale has had to make a bigger leap than her Senegalese husband Babacar in countenancing a life in an African community eviscerated of its young people, with most families fleeing from misery! Pascale Blanchard enthusiastically accepted the mores and traditions of her adoptive community, and has changed her name to Sokna Aïssa Cissé. Her courage and stamina are epitomized by her determination to lift the people of Ndem from their destitution, in tandem with her husband, notwithstanding the harsh climate of the Sahel region (compared to France, her homeland of origin).

The Mbow/Blanchard couple began their new life in Senegal in 1984, by constructing a hut for their family (two adults with one child; they eventually had six children) on a plot of bush-land offered by the villagers who welcomed them as trusted guides to rejuvenate their withering community. They won back community members who had emigrated (to the capital city Dakar of Senegal or to foreign lands for their livelihood). The Mbow couple have 'rolled up their sleeves', leading by example, and created in 1985 the Association of Villagers from Ndem (AVN) with the aim of re-inventing a new Ndem as an *original* economic hub. Despite the vicissitudes of their new African residence, they established a profitable textile business. At the creation of their venture, Pascale provided her know-how and her capital (starting initially with her personal sewing machine that she brought from France). The marketing support of Pascale's mother was very valuable through a boutique outlet in the heart of Paris (Le Marais), selling articles and wares produced by the couple and their fellow villagers.[80] Their sales expanded internationally through Artisans du Monde, Oxfam, Fair Trade Platform, and other venues.

Influenced by the Mouride Sufi Muslim brotherhood, their steadfast work ethos has elevated their *community work* to a 'spiritual quest'. The mix of devoutness with business is an original approach to development.[81] Were it not for the visionary and courageous will of the Mbow couple, Ndem and its surrounding villages could have turned into ruined 'ghost towns', implacably exposed to the advancing desert as was the case with many other communities that had temporarily thrived in various parts of the world and subsequently lost their mainstay livelihood.

Other significant factors of success are (1) the couple's active and unrelenting personal commitment to the venture they launched, from conception till full realization and growth, (2) the genuine concern about the equitable treatment of stakeholders, (3) a dedicated group of like-minded enthusiastic collaborators ready to pitch in with their best efforts, (4) the reliance on competitiveness derived from local materials, skills, artists' ingenuity that blends tradition with modernity, and custom-made wares to appeal to a variety of tastes, and markets, and (5) support by a few aid-motivated NGOs.

Social entrepreneurs' performance should be measured by reference to the positive return in wellbeing to their stakeholders and their community. The above-mentioned couple's success owes much to its unity of purpose guided by ideals of *benevolence, human rights, tolerance, honest toil,* and *solidarity*. Their activities have generated multiple business opportunities. For an illustration in the textile industry, the value chain starts with local cotton farming and covers intermediate activities (spinning, twisting into yarn, weaving, and knitting into fabric, bleaching, dying, and printing of fashions) for ultimate sale to customers in the national economy or beyond. Such business developments have enabled people in the Ndem community to exit poverty traps, sparing them the hopelessness and humiliation of begging for aid or risking their life through the dangerous vagaries of emigration, often at the mercy of criminal traffickers who exploit human distress.[82]

The above-mentioned case studies illustrate prototypes of crises. Past crises could prompt parties concerned to create more adapted mechanisms and tools to foresee, monitor, prevent, moderate, contain, and/or resolve crises.[83] Admitting that past crises could offer lessons, the open question remains: 'Are future developments likely to replicate past events, and are upcoming generations able or willing to learn from past experiences?' To answer the foregoing, in-depth wide-ranging objective analyses could help in understanding the ins and outs of past crises and their relevance to present or future conditions.

The future for many remains a source of uncertainty and angst. Interpretation of events are influenced by personal ideologies or values. Historians could thus espouse certain analytical approaches and privilege certain information (consciously or unconsciously) at the expense of 'complex truth'. They could very well resort to debatable hypotheses (in the absence of comprehensive reliable information) or to a selection of facts in order to construct their account of past events. Each historian's version of an event is likely to be influenced by her/his own personal values and their socio-political environments. Thus violent actions by nationals against an occupying power could be considered legitimate by *freedom fighters*, while *occupiers* would dub them actions of *terror*.

Notes

1 See 'Housing in America – Nightmare on Main Street', and 'Briefing Housing in America', *The Economist*, 20 August 2016, p. 10 and pp. 15–17 – respectively.

2 Thomas H. Stanton, 'Risk Management and Decision Making: Lessons from the Financial Crisis for Federal Managers', in Thomas H. Stanton and Douglas W. Webster, eds, *Managing Risk and Performance – A Guide for Government Decision Makers*, Wiley, 2014, p. 251/308p.

3 See, for example, Charles W. Calomiris, 'The Mortgage Crisis: Some inside Views', *Wall Street Journal*, 27 October 2012.

4 Cornell University Law School, Legal Information Institute's Supreme Court Bulletin, 8 November 2016.

5 See, for example, U.S. Senate Permanent Subcommittee on Investigations, *Hearings on Rating Agencies*, Washington DC, April 2010.

6 See 'Rating Agencies – Undue Credit', *The Economist*, 30 May 2015, pp. 65–66.

7 Alister Darling, UK Chancellor of the Exchequer during the early period of the crisis, interviewed by the BBC, 9 August 2017.

8 See, for example, Wolfgang Reuter, 'Worst Financial Crisis? German State-Owned Banks on Verge of Collapse', *Spiegel Online*, 20 February 2008: www.spiegel.de; also KfW Bankegruppe, Frankfurt, Press Release, 22 September 2008.

9 See, for example, Statement of Sheila C. Bair, Chairman, Federal Deposit Insurance Corporation on 'Strengthening the Economy: Foreclosure Prevention and Neighbourhood Preservation' before the *Committee on Banking, Housing and Urban Affairs – U.S. Senate*, 31 January 2008, 6p.; also Claudio Borio, 'The Financial Cycle and Macroeconomics: What Have We Learnt?', *Bank for International Settlement*, BIS Working Paper No. 395, Basle, December 2012, 32p.; and Stephen G. Cecchetti, Ingo Fender, and Patrick McGuire, 'Toward a Global Risk Map', *Bank for International Settlement*, Basle, May 2010, 23p.

10 See: 'Reforming the Audit Profession: The Cost of COSINESS', *The Economist*, 5 April 2014, pp. 66–67.

11 See, for example, United States Government Accountability Office, Report to Congressional Requesters, *Financial Regulatory Reform – Financial Crisis Losses and Potential Impacts of the Dodd-Frank Act*, January 2013, 93p.; Robert W. Kolb, *The Financial Crisis of Our Time*, Oxford University Press, 2011, 400p.; and Timothy Geithner, *Stress Test: Reflexions on Financial Crises*, Random House Business Books, 2014, 580p.
12 See, for example, Patricia Wruuck, 'Deposit Guarantee Reform in Europe: A Systemic Perspective', *Deutsche Bank Research*, 19 December 2014, 20p.
13 See: Z. Mikdashi, *Regulating the Financial Sector in the Era of Globalization*, Palgrave, 2003, 275p.; also Luc Laeven and Fabian Valancia, 'Systemic Banking Crises: A New Database', *IMF Working Paper*, September 2008, 78p.
14 See, for example, Philip R. Lane, 'Financial Globalisation and the Crisis', *BIS Working Paper No. 397*, December 2012, 34p.; also IMF, *Global Financial Stability Report – Containing Systemic Risks and Restoring Financial Soundness*, Washington DC, April 2008, 192p.; Franklin Allen and Elena Carletti, 'Financial System: Shock Absorber or Amplifier?' and 'Comments of Yung Chul Park', in *BIS Working Papers No. 257*, Monetary and Economic Department, July 2008, 18p.; Eugenio Cerutti, Stijn Claessens, and Patrick McGuire, 'Systemic Risks in Global Banking: What Can Available Data Tell Us and What More Data Are Needed?', *BIS Working Papers No. 376*, Monetary and Economic Department, April 2012, 22p.
15 See, for example: United Nations Conference on Trade and Development, *The Global Economic Crisis: Systemic Failures and Multilateral Remedies*, New York and Geneva, 2009, 80p.; also Mathias Drehmann, 'Systemic Importance: Some Simple Indicators', *BIS Quarterly Review*, Bank for International Settlements, Basel, March 2011, pp. 25–35.
16 See, for example, Peter Starke, Alexandra Kaasch, and Franca van Hooren, *The Welfare State as Crisis Manager – Explaining the Diversity of Policy Responses to Economic Crisis*, Palgrave Macmillan, 2013, 240p.
17 See, for example, Ingo Fender and Patrick McGuire, 'Bank Structure, Funding Risk and the Transmission of Shocks across Countries: Concepts and MEASUREMENT', *BIS Quarterly Review*, September 2010, pp. 63–79; and Federal Reserve Bank of New York, *Central Bank Liquidity Tools and Perspectives on Regulatory Reform, Special Issue*, August 2010, 131p.
18 See, for example, veteran economist Peter Doyle's Resignation Letter, addressed to Mr. Shaalan, Dean of the IMF Executive Board, 18 June 2012, and published by Reuters and other media.
19 'AIG's Pilot Charts Post-Crisis Path', *Financial Times*, 21 July 2014, pp. 12 and 18; and U.S. Congressional Hearings.
20 See, for example, Neel Kashkari, President and CEO of Federal Reserve Bank of Minneapolis, speech on the 'The Minneapolis Plan to End Too Big to Fail', 16 November 2016, 8p.
21 See, for example, Andrew Gracie – Executive Director, Resolution, Bank of England, 'Making Resolution Work in Europe and Beyond – The Case for Gone Concern Loss Absorbing Capacity', Speech, 17 July 2014. 10p.
22 Jianping Zhou, Virginia Rutledge, Wouter Bossu, Marc Dobler, Nadege Jassaud, and Michael Moore, 'Resolving Systemically Important Financial Institutions: Mandatory Recapitalization of Financial Institutions Using "Bail-ins"', pp. 433/433–456 – quotation from an article in the book: Charles Enoch, Luc Everaert, Thierry Tressel, and Jianping Zhou, eds, *From Fragmentation to Financial Integration in Europe*, International Monetary Fund, 2014, 512p.; see also Lucy Chennells and Venetia Wingfield, 'Bank Failure and Bail-In: An Introduction', *Bank of England Quarterly Bulletin*, Q3, 2015, pp. 228–241.
23 Charles Enoch, Luc Everaert, Thierry Tressel, and Jamping Zhou, 'Securing a Safer Financial System in Europe', p. 6/1–35p.; article from the above-mentioned collective book.

24 See Paul Melaschenko and Noel Reynolds, 'A Template for Recapitalizing Too-Big-To-Fail Banks', *BIS Quarterly Review*, June 2013, pp. 25–39.
25 EU Monitor, Deutsche Bank Research, 29 April, 2016, pp. 4–5.
26 See, for example, 'Criteria for an Appropriate Countercyclical Capital Buffer', *Monetary Policy Report with Financial Stability Assessment*, Norges Bank, Oslo 2017, p. 56; also Adair Turner, *Between Debt and the Devil – Money, Credit, and Fixing Global Finance*, Princeton University Press, 2016, 302p.
27 *Financial Regulatory Reform*, op. cit., pp. 12 and 30–32.
28 See, for example, Joseph E. Stiglitz, 'A Banking System is Supposed to Serve Society, Not the Other Way Around', *Vanity Fair*, 23 December 2011; also in: www.commondreams.org.
29 See, for example, Roberto Perotti, *The 'Austerity Myth': Gain Without Pain?*, BIS Working Paper No. 362, Bank for International Settlements, Monetary and Economic Department, 24 June 2011, 63p.
30 See, for example, Board of Governors of the Federal Reserve System: Chairman Ben S. Bernanke, *Fostering Sustainable Homeownership*, at the National Community Reinvestment Coalition Annual Meeting, Washington D.C., 14 March 2008, 5p.; and Governor Randall S. Kroszner, *'Loan Modifications and Foreclosure Prevention'*, Testimony before the Committee on Financial Services' hearings, U.S. House of Representatives, 6 December 2007, 4p.
31 See, for example, Athanasios Orphanides, *Is Monetary Policy Overburdened?*, BIS Working Papers, December 2013, 37p.
32 *The Financial Crisis Inquiry Report*, Final Report of the National Commission on the Causes of the Financial and Economic Crisis in the United States, January 2011, 632p.; also available at: www.FCIC.gov.
33 See, for example, Richhild Moessner and William A. Allen, *Banking Crises and the International Monetary System in the Great Depression and Now*, BIS, December 2010, 38p.; and Oxford Economics, *Balancing Growth and Stability in EU Financial Reform*, May 2011, 28p.
34 Claudio Borio, *Monetary Policy and Financial Stability: What Role in Prevention and Recovery?*, BIS Working Papers No. 440, January 2014, p. 18/23p.
35 See, for example, Garry J. Schinasi, *Safeguarding Financial Stability – Theory and Practice*, International Monetary Fund, Washington DC, 2006, pp. 35–42.
36 See, for example, Patrick Calver and Jennifer Owladi, 'Pillar 3 Disclosures: Looking Back and Looking Forward', *Bank of England Quarterly Bulletin*, Q3, 2017 pp. 190–202.
37 See: Anthony Salz, *An Independent Review of Barclays' Business Practice*, April 2013, 236p.
38 See *The Wall Street Journal*, 20 May 2015, and other media.
39 U.S. Department of Justice – Office of the Attorney General, Press Release of 3 February 2015.
40 www.sec.gov/news/pressrelease/2015-10.html.
41 See, for example, Matt Taibbi, 'Gangster Bankers: Too Big to Jail – How HSBC Hooked Up with Drug Traffickers and Terrorists, and Got Away With It', *Rolling Stone*, 28 February 2013.
42 See 'Conviction Casts a Pall over Credit Suisse', *Financial Times*, 21 May 2014, pp. 8 and 15; also US Senate – Permanent Subcommittee on Investigations, chaired by Carl Levin, *Offshore Tax Evasion: The Effort to Collect Unpaid Taxes*, 26 February 2014, 176p.
43 It is reported that the total costs of the financial crisis for Bank of America over 2010 till early 2016 had reached $194 billion (*The Economist*, 23 April 2016, p. 57).
44 Harold Levy in *The Economist*, 19 July 2014, p. 14.
45 For other cases of financial crises, see: Charles P. Kindleberger and Robert Z. Aliber, *Manias, Panics and Crashes – A History of Financial Crises*, 6th edition, Palgrave

Macmillan, 2011, 356p.; and Jihad Dagher, *Regulatory Cycles: Revisiting the Political Economy of Financial Crises*, IMF Working Paper, January 2018, 88p.

46 See, for example, Ilias Pnevmonidis, *Cross-Border Bank Resolution: Old demons, Current Progress, Future Challenges*, Schulthess, 2015, 486p.

47 Olivier Blanchard and Rafael Portillo, 'A Road Map to "Progress and Confusion"', in Olivier Blanchard, Raghuram Rajan, Kenneth Rogoff, and Lawrence H. Summers, eds, *Progress and Confusion – The State of Macroeconomic Policy*, IMF/The MIT Press, 2016, p. 14/304p..

48 See, for example, the case of the self-taught scientist Stanford Ovshinsky in: Zuhayr Mikdashi, *Progress-Driven Entrepreneurs, Private Equity Finance and Regulatory Issues*, Palgrave 2010, pp. 11–16.

49 See: www.iaca-US/.

50 See, for example, Daniel Moellendorf and Heather Widdows, eds, *The Routledge Handbook of Global Ethics*, Routledge, 2015, 501p.; Charles Sampforde, Spencer Zifcak, and Derya Aydin Okur, eds, *Rethinking International Law and Justice*,Ashgate, 2014, 344p.; and Stephen Sterling, Larch Maxey, and Heather Luna, eds, *The Sustainable University – Progress and Prospects*, Routledge, 2014, 332p.

51 See, for example: Ian Goldin, Geoffrey Cameron, and Meera Balarajan, *Exceptional People – How Migration Shaped Our World and Will Define Our Future*, Princeton University Press, 2011, 371p.

52 See, for example, the analyses of Hasni Abidi, Director, the Study and Research Centre on the Arab World and the Mediterranean – Geneva, 'Saudi Arabia Is Barricading', *L'HEBDO*, Lausanne, pp. 36–37.

53 See, for example, 'Scores of Teenage Migrants Were "Deliberately Drowned" by Smugglers off the Coast of Yemen', *International Organization for Migration*, 9 August 2017, cited by the BBC.

54 See, for example, UN High Commission for Refugees, 'Mediterranean Takes Record as Most Deadly Stretch of Water for Refugees and Migrants in 2011', *Brief Notes*, 31 January 2012, in: www.unhcr.org; also documents by the Geneva-based *International Organization for Migration* [IOM], that is dedicated to promoting humane and orderly migration.

55 See, for example, 'African Migration – To the Land of Good Hope', *The Economist*, 5 March 2016, pp. 30–32.

56 See, for example, Quinn Kepes, *et al.*, *Labor Brokerage and Trafficking of Nepali Migrant Workers*, Verité, 2014, 108p.; www.verite.org.

57 See, for example, Amnesty International Report, *The Dark Side of Migration: Spotlight on Qatar's Construction Sector Ahead of the World Cup*, 18 November 2013 – www.amnesty.org/en/news/qatar.

58 Ref. 'Internal Migration – A Sorry Tale', *The Economist*, 13 May 2017, p. 46.

59 David Folkerts-Landau, Barbara Böttcher, and Stephan Schneider, *Influx of Refugees: An Opportunjity for Germany*, Deutsche Bank Research, 13 November 2015, 22p.

60 A regular publication on 'ranking' subsidies is provided by: *Global Subsidies Initiative*: www.globalsubsidies.org.

61 'Procurement Spending – Rigging the Bids', *The Economist*, 19 November 2016, pp. 25–26.

62 See, for example, Patrizia Tumbarello, 'Unravelling Asia's "Noodle Bowl" of Trade Pacts', *IMF Survey*, 18 June 2007, pp. 150–151.

63 United Nations Development Programme, *Human Development Report 2005*, published by UNDP – New York, and by Oxford University Press, 2005, 372p.; by Kevin Watkins – the lead author and the Director of the UNDP's Human Development Report Office.

64 See, for example, Myrto Kalouptsidi, *Detection and Impact of Industrial Subsidies: The Case of World Shipbuilding*, Department of Economics, Princeton University, May 2014, 48p.

65 Pascal Lamy, *Statement before the European Parliament Committee on International Trade in Brussels*, 17 October 2006.
66 *Aid for Trade Can Turn Possibility into Reality, Lamy Tells 'Global Review'*, WTO, Geneva, 20 November 2007.
67 'Land Ownership – I Had a Farm in Africa', *The Economist*, 28 February 2015, pp. 32–34.
68 His speech 'Can Globalisation Be a Level Playing Field', was pronounced at the MEDEF [The French Business Leaders Association] Summer University on 30 August 2007 – Document Ref: SP07-177EN; bold characters are added by this author for emphasis.
69 See, for example, Stefania Vitali, James B. Glattfelder, and Stefano Battiston, *The Network of Global Corporate Control*, Swiss Federal Institute of Technology, Zurich, 19 September 2011, 36p.
70 Julian M. Alston, Daniel A. Sumner, and Henrich Brunke (both Professors in the Department of Agriculture and Resource Economics at the University of California, Davis), *Impact of Reductions in US Cotton Subsidies on West African Cotton Producers*, Oxfam America, 2007, 35p.: www.oxfamamerica.org.
71 See, for example, Charles Amo Yartey, 'Burkina Faso's Cotton Crisis', *IMF Survey*, March 2008, p. 40.
72 For arguments for and against subsidies in the Fair Trade debate, see: Malgorzata Kurjanska and Mathias Risse, 'Fairness in Trade II: Export Subsidies and the Fair Trade Movement', *Politics, Philosophy & Economics* 2008, pp. 29–56, published by Sage on behalf of the Institute of Political Economy, http://ppe.sagepub.com/cgi/content/abstract/7/1/29.
73 Data from International Cotton Advisory Committee, and UNCTAD – see: http://unctad.org/.
74 Claire Delpeuch, *African Cotton Markets at Crossroads – Will the Price Spike Turn into a New Kick-Start?*, The World Bank, October 2011, 26p.
75 Source: Fair Trade Foundation, *The Great Cotton Stitch-up*, London, November 2010, 40p. (p. 5 of the Report). For additional information, see the World Trade Organization (WTO) compliance panel, in a 188-page final decision on U.S. cotton subsidies, delivered on 18 December 2007, 'Dispute Settlement 267: United States – Subsidies on Upland Cotton': www.wto.org. The WTO ruled that U.S. cotton subsidies harmed the cotton producers of Brazil, and West and Central African States – notably Burkina Faso, Chad, Mali, and Togo. The cotton sector in these African countries accounts for 5 to 9 per cent of GDP, between 35 and 40 per cent of export revenues, and employs 20 million persons. Additional information is available at: www.oxfam.org.uk, www.fairtrade.org.uk, www.wto.org, and www.hdr.undp.org.
76 See, for example, 'A Cotton Boll's Journey – From Shrub to Shirt to Shelf', *The Economist*, 6 May 2017, pp. 25–26.
77 A country's *terms of trade* measures changes in a country's export prices in relation to its import prices. It is expressed by the following ratio: [Index of Export Prices/Index of Import Prices] x 100.
78 Statement of Nicholas Stern, World Bank Chief Economist and Senior Vice President, World Bank – cited by *Africa Recovery*, vol. 17, no. 1, May 2003, p. 18; available at: www.africarecovery.org; email: Africa_recovery@un.org; also World Bank Press Release No: 2003/280/S in which Nicholas Stern estimated U.S. cotton subsidies, mostly accruing to a 'relatively small number of comparatively affluent farmers and corporations' in 2002 at $3.9 billion, three times U.S. foreign aid to Africa.
79 See: Tim Judah, *Senegal's Mourides: Islam's Mystical Entrepreneurs*, BBC News, 4 August 2011; and Laura Cochrane, *Weaving through Islam in Senegal*, Carolina Academic Press, 2013, 168p.
80 See also: www.ndem.org/; www.ongndem.com; and Rose Skelton, *Senegal Clothes Maker Gives Faithful Jobs and Hope*, Reuters and BBC News, 20 June 2006.

81 See also http://en.wikipedia.org/wiki/Mouride.

82 I presented selected aspects of the Ndem entrepreneurial community at the 2012 American University in Cairo *Research Conference on Entrepreneurship*. For other sources see: 'Ndem: A Senegalese NGO at the Service of its Community' (www.ekit-info.org/journal/ndem); also [PDF] 'Bienvenue à Ndem!' – www.WordPress.com/.

83 For an example of an NGO working in this domain, see the *International Crisis Group*: www.crisisgroup.org.

5 Evolving wellbeing

Reflections on selected signposts

This chapter offers succinct reflections on a few historical signposts regarding this book's central themes. Issues discussed cover principally a retrospective on selected past events or situations that have affected wellbeing. Our reflections cover such vital issues as freedom versus servitude; socio-political emancipation; the role of global cooperation guided by the common good; and science's links to ethical values. In interpreting human behaviour, one needs to be extremely cautious in avoiding anachronisms, in ascertaining the truthfulness of information, and in situating events in their proper historical perspective.

Overcoming subjugation

Contexts of life on planet Earth across time have changed considerably. Comparing social conditions of past human groups, some researchers in anthropology and/or archaeology have generally concluded that early human Neolithic communities (i.e. 10,000 years before our current era) had been living in relatively more peaceful environments, compared with the past 3,000 years. Indeed, land with its resources was available in abundance for Neolithic people, and there was little pressure for rivalry, given the plentiful bounties of nature and the relatively small number of humans living then. The Research Director of the National Centre for Scientific Research (CNRS), Department of Prehistory at the National Museum of Natural History (Paris) concluded: 'As shown by archaeological data, compassion and mutual help [*sic*] more than rivalry and aggression, had probably been key factors in the successful evolution of our species.'[1] Human cooperation vis-à-vis the adversities of the natural elements appears plausible in the early times of recorded history. The absence of lethal rivalries among human groups in these periods can be partially explained by the existence of vast territories with abundant resources capable of satisfying the then existing population.

Post-Neolithic human communities have resorted to war for a variety of reasons. Arbitrary wanton causes for wars exist and include innate impulses for predatory behaviours. Such behaviours would include the grabbing of other peoples' goods and property – seeking economic and geopolitical advantages.

These advantages consist inter alia of controlling strategic vital scarce resources, conquest and colonization of foreign lands, decimation of specific communities, and other brutal actions that are antonymic to human rights. Seldom is war prompted by 'true compassion' or 'just causes'. *Just causes* for foreign military intervention against a sovereign state are based on ethical criteria. They cover the following situations: (i) *protection of civilians* against brutal regimes (e.g. those that commit genocides vis-à-vis certain segments of their populations), (ii) *pre-emptive self-defence* vis-à-vis expected attacks, (iii) containment of *rogue* or *failed states* in which terrorists operate, and/or (iv) the *punishment of past offenders* whose crimes have gone scot-free or remained uncorrected.[2]

Progress in the living conditions of humans is an unending process of construction, and/or re-construction following the demise of old orders. Indeed, the quest for enhancing *wellbeing* across the ages and among diverse societies has been a central feature of evolving humanity. Since early recorded civilizations (circa 2100 BC), humans have sought long life, youthfulness, and vibrant health as conveyed by the epic poem of Gilgamesh.[3] Nevertheless, progress in wellbeing has often been confronted with contrarian, wayward, or destructive forces – endogenous or exogenous.

Among ancient civilizations that were first in addressing the phenomenon of *wellbeing* as evidenced by written documents, one could refer to pharaonic Egypt. Ptahhotep (circa 2414–2375 BCE) condensed on papyrus in his '*Maxims*' the wisdom of his ancestor sages with respect to *wellbeing*. He highlighted the role of dialogue, kindness, tolerance, generosity, empathy, and justice for a happy and harmonious life.[4] His moral principles were adopted by the *Instruction of Amenemope* (circa 1100 BCE). Addressing the upcoming young generation, Amenemope extolled moral values as essential prerequisites for a happy life. Drawing on the wise traditions of Ancient Egyptian sages, he underlined the need for honesty, moderation, humility, philanthropy, and solidarity towards the distressed. He admonished his disciples to avoid greed, cheating, and corruption.[5]

A few scholars of Ancient Mesopotamian civilizations consider the Code of Hammurabi (1772 BC), the sixth Babylonian King, to contain important bases of a fair society endeavouring to promote the wellbeing of its people. Hammurabi was revered by his subjects for his wisdom. In the epilogue of his Code, he stated:

> Let a wronged man who has a court case come to the statue of me as King of Justice and let the words of my inscribed stele be read out to him. Let him hear my precious words. Let my stele make his court case clear to him. Let him see his verdict, and set his mind at ease saying: 'Hammurabi … brought about well-being for the people forever and made the land have just ways'[6]

Comparing Ancient Greek wisdom to that of Babylonia, De Mieroop concluded that:

> Hammurabi thus expressed the idea that justice and wisdom are closely related many centuries before Plato stated it in his *Republic*. Plato's

> philosopher-king ruled in just ways because he had the wisdom to do so. Hammurabi claimed the same: he had the knowledge to 'direct the land along the course of truth and the correct way of life'. Importantly, the [Hammurabi] laws were not god-given but human creations.[7]

Nevertheless, the Code of Hammurabi had permitted debtors to sell their wives and children into temporary slavery, lasting a maximum of three years. Moreover, vanquished communities in ancient times were routinely enslaved as part of the victors' spoils of war. Poverty also compelled some people to submit to *debt bondage*. Not all slaves were treated similarly; some were abused to the extreme by subjecting them to cruel hard work.[8] Other enslaved humans fared apparently 'better' (see Exhibit 5.1).

In the ladder of atrocities, slavery ranks among the worst of calamities humans can possibly encounter. *Servitude* is antonymous to a *free dignified life*; it could hardly be endured except by supine individuals or social groups that are shackled by tyrannical forces. The acquiescence of humans to the domination of a tyrant has been strongly condemned by Étienne de La Boétie (1530–1563) in his *Discourse of Voluntary Servitude*.[9] He appealed to individuals and communities ruled by despots and their ilk to overcome break the shackles of servitude by defending their *fundamental* and *inalienable* rights to freedom, security, and justice. In his harangue:

> [The tyrant's power] is nothing more than the power that you confer upon him to destroy you. Where has he acquired enough eyes to spy upon you, if you do not provide them yourselves? How can he have so many arms to beat you with, if he does not borrow them from you? The feet that trample down your cities, where does he get them if they are not your own? How does he have any power over you except through you? How would he dare assail you if he had no cooperation from you? … Resolve to serve no more, and you are at once freed. I do not ask that you place hands upon the tyrant to topple him over, but simply that you support him no longer; then you will behold him, like a great Colossus whose pedestal has been pulled away, fall of his own weight and break in pieces.

Nevertheless, a few thinkers in the 'Age of Enlightenment' had condoned enslavement, racism, colonialism, men's ascendency over women, and other inequities. For example, French political thinker Alexis de Tocqueville, 1805–1859, author of *Democracy in America*, had openly supported the conquest and colonization of Algeria and the ethnocentric separation of European settlers from indigenous populations (the latter treated as subjects of a second zone). Brilliant minds of the seventeenth and eighteenth centuries have claimed the civilizational superiority of the 'white man' over the 'coloured' – in matters of achievements (in science, arts, culture, management, etc.). This was the case of David Hume (1711–1776), Voltaire (1694–1778), Immanuel Kant (1724–1804), and many other thinkers of that era. Some eminent thinkers are not immune from prejudices often prevalent in their periods. This applies to Kant whose ethical values are generally considered laudable, with some exceptions. In particular, he considers that other races are inferior to European, that husbands should rule over wives, and that women should be excluded from voting for so-called 'natural' reasons.[10]

Luminaries since ancient times have been concerned with wellbeing. These include Greek classical philosophers (such as Socrates, 469–399 BC; Plato, 429–347 BC; Aristotle, 384–322 BC; and Epicurus 341–270 BC), and Asian political thinkers or moralists (such as Confucius 551–479 BC; and Mozi 460–390 BC). Many thinkers in early civilizations reflected on society's key existential issues, such as 'just' government, social order, good conduct, ethical norms, and human rights.[11]

Regarding changes in the core meaning of a concept, one could refer to ancient Greek philosophers' interpretation of *happiness*, by comparison with modern thinkers. Reflecting on this subject, one contemporary thinker concluded:

> It is well known that happiness (*eudaimonia, eu zën*) and virtue were the central notions of ancient ethics. The question can be raised, however, whether the ancient notion of *eudaimonia* is the same as the modern notion of happiness. Isn't it misleading, it may be asked, or even quite wrong, to talk about happiness in relation to the ancients? The Greek term would be more accurately translated as 'human flourishing', 'having a good life' or 'well-being' maybe but definitely not by 'happiness'. Indeed many translators and scholars of ancient philosophy avoid the words 'happiness' and 'happy' as a rendering of the Greek terms *eudaimonia* and *eudaimön*.[12]

For another scholar, the Greek concept of *Eudaimonia* is:

> Literally 'having a good spirit', i.e. the state of having an objectively desirable life … This objective character distinguishes it from the modern concept of happiness, i.e. of a subjectively satisfactory life. Much ancient theory concerns the question of what constitutes the good life, e.g. whether virtue is sufficient for it, as Socrates and the Stoics held, or whether external goods such as good fortune are also necessary, as Aristotle maintained.[13]

Currently, Buddhist societies attribute to the term *happiness* the capacity of an individual's to attain self-control over one's passions or one's desires for material possessions; this is often achieved by resorting to exercises of meditation, along with compassionate actions vis-à-vis the afflicted or distressed.[14]

Ancient civilizations were not devoid of cruelty. Victorious armies generally resorted to the enslavement of women, children, and non-combatant men of vanquished opponents. Victors' enslavement of the vanquished was legitimized by political leaders and thinkers of ancient Greece, Rome, Mesopotamia, and the Levant who considered slaves as chattels that could be sold as merchandise (along with their siblings) and eventually bequeathed.[15]

Fundamental human rights (in the modern sense of the term) have seldom been rigorously observed in human history. For example, the 'iconic' ancient Athenian democracy (with an elected assembly combining executive and judiciary authority) excluded women, resident foreigners, and slaves (!) from participation. The said assembly had condemned Socrates to the death penalty in 399 BC, ostensibly on the grounds of so-called crimes of *impiety* and of *corruption* of minds (resulting from his free 'critical' thinking). No wonder Socrates' disciple, Plato, who attended the said flawed trial, was deeply disillusioned by a 'democracy' whose laws and majoritarian decisions were reached or influenced by an 'ignorant' and/or 'intolerant' majority. In lieu of a participatory democracy, Plato had advocated in his 'Republic' the ideal of ruling the *city state* exclusively by an elitist *assembly of learned persons*, namely the philosopher-kings who are recognized for their sense of justice, their wisdom, and their moral rectitude.[16]

Servitude has seldom been voluntarily sought. It was and still is imposed by brutal coercion on distraught people. Slave traders in the fifteenth till the twentieth centuries targeted innocent, peaceful, and hapless people – often chosen from certain ethnic backgrounds. Several indigenous rulers of countries from where ordinary people were kidnapped had been bribed in order to authorize or condone with impunity the enslavement of their subjects. Some 60 million individuals (men, women and children) were abducted and sold (with the active collaboration of local African chieftains) and shipped into bondage from Africa to the Western Hemisphere starting with 1492 (with the first permanent trading post built by the Portuguese at Elmina, currently a port in the state of Ghana in West Africa), and going well into the second half of the nineteenth century.

The Caribbean Community (Caricom, comprising 14 ex-British colonies) along with Haiti and Surinam are suing in court the British, French, and Dutch governments for reparations regarding the alleged genocide of autochthonous peoples and the enslavement of their ancestors forcefully brought from Africa. The UN Convention on the Prevention and Punishment of the Crime of Genocide (adopted by the UN General Assembly on 9 December 1948) defines genocide as 'any of the following acts committed with intent to destroy, in whole or in part, a national, ethnical, racial or religious group' (Article II).

Speaking at the United Nations General Assembly on 27 September 2013, the Prime Minister of Saint Vincent and the Grenadines Ralph E. Gonsalves asked:

> ... for reparations for native genocide [of the Callinago, the Garifuna, the Amerindian] and African slavery from the successor states of the European countries which committed organised state-sponsored native genocide and African enslavement ... The European nations which engaged in conquest, settlement, genocide, and slavery in our Caribbean must provide the reparatory resources required to repair the contemporary legacy of their historic wrongs.[17]

Besides the British, French, and Dutch governments, Spanish and Portuguese Conquistadors invaded and colonized the Americas from the late fifteenth century till the late seventeenth century. They devastated the established socio-political orders and dominated indigenous communities through superior military power. European conquerors resorted to coercive means to convert autochthonous peoples to their religion, and mercilessly subjugated them into a status akin to slavery; the natives who fell prey to invaders were then considered savages or barbarians despite their rich millenary civilizations.[18]

Upon their conquest of foreign territories, powerful states have arbitrarily imposed their authority, subjugated colonized people to an inferior legal status, and forcefully converted indigenous vanquished populations to the invaders' creeds. Moreover, invaders dispossessed autochthonous people of their lands and looted their wealth or heritages. Many invading nations have claimed their superiority (mental, moral, technological, etc.) and bestowed upon themselves the *right to civilize* other people called *savages*.

Among enslaved Caribbean nations, Haiti was the first black nation in history to win its independence under Jean-Pierre Boyer who overthrew the French imperial colonial power (defeating Napoleon's military expedition in January 1804). In another French-ruled Caribbean island, Guadeloupe, enslaved mulattos and Africans who had rebelled against the colonial French authorities were crushed in 1802 by Napoleon who reinstated the *slavery* regime; that regime was kept effective throughout French territories till 1848.

It is worth noting that, to have its independence recognized subject to the imminent threat of a new invasion by the French state bent on regaining sovereignty over its former colony, Haiti had to accede in 1825 to the diktat of the French monarch Charles X. The said monarch had sent an armada of 14 war vessels to blockade Haitian ports, should the Haitian state refuse to pay an exorbitant ransom of 150 million gold francs, ostensibly as 'compensation' to colonial French slaveholders. The above-mentioned ransom was exacted along with commercial privileges granted to French traders. The foregoing ransom was beyond the capacity of an enslaved destitute country that had won its freedom and independence after a bloody war against its colonial power; the said sum was ostensibly *reduced* in 1838 to 90 million gold francs, or the equivalent of 17 billion euro in 2015.

Judged by universal ethical standards, it is odd to have the hitherto enslaved victims compensate the colonial victimizers! For several historians and social scientists, such penalizing payment has been a major factor, among others, for blighting the Haitian economy and society for several generations and until today. One should add that the 'freed' slaves, their siblings-descendants, or their communities, were left without compensation for having endured in the past excruciating suffering (when traded as chattels along with their children, and coerced to toil for free for the benefit of their 'masters') – while their erstwhile 'masters' were compensated for their so-called loss of their 'slave property'!

The 'slavery wound' has remained vividly open for Haitians who were generally not content with a *moral apology* by their previous masters. Most Haitians still demand financial reparations from the French state, as reported by various media on the eve of the French President François Hollande's 'state visit' to Haiti on 12 May 1015. The French president, however, considered then that the French state owes Haiti only a 'moral debt' – in contra-distinction with a 'pecuniary debt'.[19]

To be likened to property (see, for example, the *Code Noir*, an edict by the French King Louis the XIVth) has proved to be a summum of *immoral treatment*, consciously and remorselessly accepted by some learned people of enslaving European nations. Indeed, in ancient, as well as in modern times including the period of 'Enlightenment' in Europe, a few of the brightest intellectuals have failed to condemn slavery. In the chain of responsibilities for the enslavement process, several parties were involved: foreign colonial governments; autochthonous rulers who betrayed their people; raiders and traffickers in human beings; foreign importers, transporters and employers of slaves; financiers; and other intermediaries.[20]

It is to the credit of Ibn Khaldun that he was among the very first thinkers to reprove in unequivocal terms the practice of slavery, which he deemed: 'One of the greatest injustices and one which contributes most to the destruction of civilization'. As conveyed by Olivier de la Grandville,

> Ibn Khaldun (1332–1395 A.D.) analyses in detail the principle of private property, not only from a legal but also from an economic point of view. In particular, he gives three examples, or situations, in which the principle is violated, with dramatic consequences for society: first, slavery, which was unequivocally condemned by Ibn Khaldun – to the best of our knowledge, he was the first writer to ever do so [*sic*]. Also the principle of private property is violated by the constitution of private or state monopolies, as well as by excessive taxation (p. 396).[21]

It was not until the second half of the twentieth century that slavery's practices were explicitly and formally banned worldwide in accordance with the Universal Declaration of Human Rights (UDHR). The corpus of basic 'universal human rights' today underlines each individual's inalienable fundamental right to freedom, security, belief, and justice – without exclusion or discrimination. Nevertheless, occult or disguised forms of slavery, along with other forms of abuses still remain alive in treacherous forms in several countries until today; they are based on ethnic, religious, gender, colour, social class, personal characteristics, or other prejudices in areas where the UDHR writ's does not run. The International Labour Organization (ILO) conservatively estimates that '20.9 million people are victims of forced labour globally, trapped in jobs into which they were coerced or deceived and which they cannot leave', owing to excruciating debt burdens they were tricked into.[22]

On matters of apologies for historic crimes and material reparations payable for them, some thinkers argue that:

> ...people in the present generation should not – in fact cannot – apologize for wrongs committed by previous generations. To apologize for an injustice is, after all, to take some responsibility for it. You can't apologize for something you didn't do. So, how can you apologize for something that was done before you were born?[23]

The foregoing argument of refusing apologies can be contested if the current generation is benefiting from the spoils obtained by culprit past generations. Descendants of persons known for their reprehensible actions could well consider themselves victims if they are called upon to offer reparations for the misdeeds of distant ancestors. Nevertheless, payments could justifiably be made by prosperous 'successor states' of the colonial era to an *atonement-cum-solidarity fund* (to be managed by a United Nations agency).

Several scholars and writers have documented episodes of dramatic exploitation of man by man that continue into the twenty-first century. In parallel, compassion and help have been offered by nobly motivated individuals. An oppressed community tends to sympathize with other oppressed ones, as happened between Native Americans pushed into the confinements of reservations and enslaved Afro-Americans in the United States.[24]

Official manuals of history, when written by authors belonging to the conquering victorious nations, have often been dodgy – in so far as they have been expurgated by watering down or omitting episodes of excruciating suffering or injustices inflicted by victors on the vanquished victims. Victors' spurious manuals would provide scant evidence of the heroic resistance of native populations, often dismissing information on *what* happened and *why*. Conquerors get ostentatiously glorified, while defeated peoples' rights get occulted or dismissed.

The Australian Aborigines are another example of a native population which has been almost decimated by the English colonizers. When Captain Cook arrived in 1770, they were 100 per cent of the total inhabitants (then about 300,000). Today, their descendants represent about 2 per cent of the Australian population (around 700,000). The Aborigines are Australia's indigenous people who were first to inhabit that continent for over 25,000 years, as proven by Carbon 14 on paintings left on rocks before the arrival of European settlers.[25] In the first decade of the twenty-first century, Australian officials apologized to the descendants of indigenous Australians for past abuses (such as denying them various civic rights, including ownership rights over their ancestral lands). On 13 February 2008, the federal government of Australia, led by Prime Minister Kevin Rudd, issued a formal apology to the indigenous Australians over the 'stolen generation' (also known as 'stolen children'). These were the children of Aborigines who were forcefully removed from their families by the Australian Federal and State agencies or by missionaries in order to 'civilize' and Christianize them. The forced removals occurred in the period between approximately 1869 and 1969, although in some places, Aboriginal children were still being taken until the 1970s.

One can also refer to other examples of exclusion or oppression of autochthonous populations – for example in North America.[26] European nations espoused the *Doctrine of Discovery* in the fifteenth century; that doctrine justifies their taking possession of, and their colonizing lands that they *found*, even if conquered lands were long inhabited and used by native peoples such as the Amerindians. Indigenous 'First Nations' suffered from marginalization, discrimination, abuse, and epidemics brought by new settlers.[27] The Canadian Prime Minister Justin Trudeau offered on 24 November 2017 a formal national apology to aboriginal children not already included in an earlier apology (that of 2008). Aboriginal children (a total of some 150,000 over some 100 years) were forcefully separated from their parents to be educated in accordance with the rules of state-run Canadian schools. More than 3,000 died at these schools and others suffered from physical, emotional, and sexual abuse.[28]

> The *Doctrine of Discovery* has been institutionalized in law and policy, on national and international levels, and lies at the root of the violations of indigenous peoples' human rights, both individual and collective. This has resulted in State claims to and the mass appropriation of the lands, territories and resources of indigenous peoples. Both the Doctrine of Discovery and a holistic structure that we term the Framework of Dominance have resulted in centuries of virtually unlimited resource extraction from the traditional territories of indigenous people. This, in turn, has resulted in the dispossession and impoverishment of indigenous peoples, and the host of problems that they face today on a daily basis … The Doctrine of Discovery continues to be treated as valid by the United States Government.[29]

Past crimes, especially the monstrous abominable ones such as slavery and genocides, should not be occulted. These crimes need to be properly documented by neutral, specialized international agencies. Atonement or reparation could alleviate the suffering of victims or those directly linked to them. Nevertheless, contemporaries of these horrific crimes who were unaware or incapable of countering these atrocities – along with the descendants of criminal forebears – cannot be held directly responsible for such crimes. Nevertheless, siblings with high ethical values may have the courage to condemn perpetrators of past criminal actions (including those committed by their parents or ancestors), and to make amends. It is interesting to note that in some circumstances, slaves became authoritarian masters (see Exhibit 5.1).

Exhibit 5.1 Mamluks: enfranchised slaves who became absolute monarchs

The word *mamluk* signifies in the Arabic language 'owned'. Around the age of 13, *ghulams* (boys or lads in Arabic) were abducted from their families or 'purchased' in slave markets. The mamluks were non-Arab mercenaries trained to serve Arab rulers, beginning with the Abbasid caliphate in Baghdad in the ninth century.

Many were Turkic (originating in central Asia) or Circassian (from the Caucasus); others had Georgian or Armenian origins. They formed a warrior caste of cavalry soldiers loyal to their masters, and lived separate from the local populations in garrisons. They were intensively trained as soldiers to serve in the armies of sultans or warlords, and were manumitted upon converting to Islam during their training. Their social status was superior to freeborn Moslems, and a few Mamluks managed to become eminent absolute rulers.

The reputation of *mamluks* owes to several remarkable feats. These included: (i) wresting power from the Ayyubi ruler of Egypt (namely sultan Al-Salih) in 1250, (ii) defeating the Mongol invaders in 1260 in the battle of Ayn Jalut located in contemporary Syria, (iii) ousting the Crusader kingdoms of Outremer in the Levant by 1291, and (iv) protecting the holy places in the Arabian peninsula from invaders. During their rule, craftsmanship, architecture, and research and innovation flourished in several disciplines.

Mamluk sultans ruled Egypt and Syria from 1250 and until 1517; in the last mentioned year, the Ottomans led by Sultan Selim I captured Cairo (thanks to the superior power of his infantry-men manned by another slave corps, namely the *janissaries*). Nevertheless, despite their inner bloody rivalries and other adversities, the Mamluk caste continued to form an important part of Egyptian Islamic society till the nineteenth century and assumed state responsibilities under Ottoman sovereignty. They even served for a while in Bonaparte's military expedition in Egypt in 1798. Their power was ended in 1811 when Muhammad Ali (an ethnic Albanian governor of Egypt appointed by the Ottomans) massacred several hundred Mamluk noblemen that he had invited to Cairo's Citadel for a faked celebration.[30]

Gaps between ideals and realities

Not all towering thinkers or leaders (whether in the political, economic, philosophical, literary, or other realms) who have extolled noble ethical values have conducted their own lives in conformity with their professed principles. There is often a dichotomy between the purport of their intellectual works and their actual conduct in life. Indeed, eminent thinkers and politicians have seldom been exemplary role models for society, and a few have had shocking behaviours or deeds as judged by their own ideals.

Among the pantheon of philosophers, moralists, educators or other illustrious and widely admired thinkers, many had abjectly failed to abide by their trumpeted principles, as shown by their deviant personal behaviours (candidly confessed, or deftly occulted) during their lifetime. It is thus possible to find luminous thinkers-philosophers who praise eloquently *exemplary values* in their writings while actually falling short of these values in their own actual behaviour. While paying lip service to compassion, empathy, or philanthropy, they could in fact behave *meanly* in contradistinction with their proclaimed system of values.

This hiatus between *theories* or *moral postures* on one hand, and the *actual behaviour* or *practice* on the other hand happened in several cases. For an example, we cite the prevarication of Jean-Jacques Rousseau (1712–1778, author of treatises extolling virtuous values, such as the treatise on educating children, titled '*Emile*, or *On Education*', 1762). He is recognized as a leading philosopher and moralist in the century of Enlightenment (namely the eighteenth century), whose philosophy is based on man's *innate goodness*. While it is normally incumbent upon parents to raise their children properly, Rousseau failed to show paternal *compassion* or *empathy* to his five newborn children. Indeed, he incongruously orphaned them callously at their birth by abandoning them remorselessly to foundling hospitals where survival rates were then dismally estimated at about 10 per cent. The children's ultimate fates are not known.[31]

Rousseau is generally admired by many thinkers for his 'noble' ideas. Professor Martha C. Nussbaum, for example, writes:

> Indeed, the only classical social contract thinker who devotes sustained attention to the malleability of the moral sentiments, their susceptibility to cultivation through education, is Rousseau, whose Emile attributes much current injustice to a perverse sentimental education and then proposes an education, based upon compassion [*sic*], that would support social justice. The fourth book of Emile is an immensely fertile starting point for further reflection on this problem ...[32]

Among the ancient Greek thinkers, Socrates' stature is iconic in so far as his personal behaviour is guided by a search for truth through the dialectical method (that opposes contradictory ideas to resolve their conflict). In order to defend his principles with integrity and courage, he accepted the Athenian assembly's death sentence dictated by an ignorant, uncouth group of elected deciders. They had accused him falsely of infecting the minds of youth. In modern times, Peter Singer – along with a cohort of other similar-minded thinkers – have had behaviours and actions that are faithfully inspired by their philosophies of ethics based on *effective altruism*. Singer defines the latter term as 'a philosophy and social movement which applies evidence and reason to working out the most effective ways to improve the world'.[33]

Other thinkers have belittled the role of ethical considerations in human conduct; they have been primarily concerned with pragmatic approaches and less with ideology. This is the case in the Renaissance of Niccolò Machiavelli (1469–1527), who is considered by several scholars as the father of modern political theory. His works analysed political power (i.e. the capacity of prevailing effectively on others). The ruling Prince could gain power through multiple means: cunning, ruse, duplicity, trickery, demagogy, hoaxes, flatteries, deceit, guile, or other similar techniques. Duplicitous charismatic politicians could topple tyrants to usurp later power for themselves. Impostors could resort to various practices to grab control of the state apparatus, and then tighten their grip on society. Enthusiastic but naive citizens fall prey to the cunning of these politicians, and are unwittingly swayed by the deceit of such imposters' rhetoric. Citizens eventually become subservient subjects used as sycophantic pawns at the mercy of rulers who have usurped power. These rulers are not loath to betray their people by hypocritical promises, in order to attain their objectives.

Machiavelli's views benefited from his personal experience in political affairs as a high official of the Florentine Republic (1498–1512, before the Medici's rulers recovered power) and his erudition in state affairs. His seminal book *The Prince* (completed in 1513 although formally published posthumously in 1531) reveals the critical role of a monarch's monopoly over coercive power and the use of unscrupulous methods to usurp power and passing it down to chosen successors. Other thinkers advocated *ethical goodness* to legitimize a long and peaceful reign over a country. Notable among these thinkers is Desiderius Erasmus (1466–1536) who exhorted rulers to be guided by the principles of justice, benevolence, honour, and sincerity.[34] His argument is that a prince cannot maintain for long his rule based on unjust practices, blatant inequality, and other abuses underpinned by violence. Such a prince needs therefore to be advised by an assembly of savvy sages.

In his subsequent works, in particular *The Discourses* (completed by 1519 and also published posthumously in 1531), Machiavelli examined the merits of a republic that allows for differences in views, debate, and the ultimate choice of optimal means for attaining effectively objectives that benefit citizens. In Machiavelli's words, should people in a republic depart from the law-abiding 'right path', they can be convinced to return. He said:

> for an uncontrolled and tumultuous people can be spoken to by a good man and easily led back into a good way. But no one can speak to a wicked prince, and the only remedy is steel ... To cure the malady of people words are enough.[35]

Demagogues (and those in cahoots), have often made sham claims, pretending that they impersonate their people's 'providential protectors', keen on assuring their prosperity in freedom, democracy, and justice. They dissimulate their true intentions and dupe their trusting people to wrest eventually absolute power.

That an absolute ruler could prove 'benevolent' is a mockery of historic reality. Indeed, absolute power corrupts and facilitates all kinds of abuses. Such a ruler may artfully trick his people by resorting to pawns, bribing selected influential persons with wealth that belongs to the whole community or nation, in order to cow his subjects into submission – hoping to control their minds, emotions, and behaviour. Often, subjugated communities do not wield the needed clout to defend their legitimate interests, since they are shackled by potentates who monopolize key levers of coercive power. In grabbing power and maintaining their sway, autocratic rulers have invoked diverse pretexts: protection of national sovereignty vis-à-vis foreign powers, speeding up domestic development, spreading social justice, and others. Their abusive use of power has generally fomented civil unrest.

Utility, rationalism, and wellbeing

In his theory of normative ethics, Jeremy Bentham introduced the 'principle of utility' for the evaluation of human behaviour by reference to *pleasure* and *pain* felt by the individual. His theory of ethics and government is founded on psychological *hedonism* (the doctrine of seeking for oneself as much pleasure out of life as possible) to be distinguished from *eudemonism* (the doctrine that right actions are conducive to happiness). Bentham advocates the greatest good for the greatest number (i.e. the maximization of society's total satisfaction level or the sum of utilities of all persons in a society). In this aphorism, there is implicit recognition that some innocent persons could suffer or lose their life in the process of protecting or furthering the happiness of the 'greatest number' in the community under consideration. In Bentham's words:

> By utility is meant that property in any object, whereby it tends to produce benefit, advantage, pleasure, good, or happiness (all this in the present case comes to the same thing), or (what comes again to the same thing) to prevent the happening of mischief, pain, evil, or unhappiness to the party whose interest is considered: if that party be the community in general, then the happiness of the community: if a particular individual, then the happiness of that individual.[36]

In the calculus of 'maximization of pleasure' and 'minimization of pain' over one's life, utilitarian thinkers posited that (a) pleasure/pain can be objectively and cardinally measured by reference to certain criteria: intensity, duration, certainty, proximity, fecundity, purity, and the number of persons to whom it extends, and (b) that units of pleasure, utility, and/or pain can be standardized to allow comparisons across periods and individuals.[37] The validity of the foregoing assumptions has been, nevertheless, questioned by many scholars. Moreover, pleasure could be inextricably intertwined with pain. Finally, the boundaries of the community whose 'pleasure maximization' is sought is not accurately defined; in particular it is not clear whether resident foreigners are included in the term 'community'.

Even the concept of pleasure is not clear. Would malevolent pleasure be included: that derived by torturers, sadists, predators, misanthropists, *schadenfreude*, etc.? Can fleeting pleasures be identified, measured, or compared to other feelings, the vital and the trivial? Are human pleasures generated from cruelty towards animals (e.g. in bullfighting, bearbaiting, dog-fighting, cock-fighting, etc.) acceptable? Unlike Jeremy Bentham, J. S. Mill 'believes it is possible to distinguish higher and lower pleasures – to assess the quality not just the quantity or intensity of our desires'.[38]

J. S. Mill's principle of *utility* is based on self-interest-cum-rational behaviour. Accordingly, Mill's typical person seeks an optimal use of her/his resources, guided by the maximization of *convenience* and *joy*. His *utilitarianism* offers, according to one authoritative scholar, 'a humane and progressive doctrine, which in practice brought to an end many injustices based on conservative orthodoxy'.[39] Mill's moral philosophy, while seeking the greatest happiness for the largest possible number of individuals, questions Bentham's doctrine that self-interest has precedence over the general interest. He considers that others' welfare does contribute to one's own welfare. *Pleasure* maximization for the group should be compatible with *universal ethical values* (i.e. not to be realized at the expense of wanton sacrifice in the legitimate rights of others).

Utilitarian thinkers have used the postulate of 'rational economic man' as a tool of analysis of human behaviour. J. S. Mill broadened his interpretation to acknowledge the crucial role of social and cultural institutions in *wellbeing*, and the need to examine human comportment from different angles. Referring to the principle of the *economic man's rational behaviour*, he stated that it was adopted not because 'any political economist was ever so absurd as to suppose that mankind is really constituted, but because this is the mode in which science must necessarily proceed'.[40]

One should query whether the postulates often used by economists (such as 'rational' humans, perfect and transparent knowledge, universal motives of maximizing utility or benefits) are invariably helpful in explaining the behaviour of consumers, investors, managers, employees, and other individuals or groups. Indeed, given the complex make-up of humans (with unwieldy emotions and unpredictable reactions) in a world with so many imponderables or unknowns, sole reliance on an omnipresent *rationality* is not a realistic assumption for understanding human behaviour. Empirical research in cognitive sciences has revealed the significance of emotional, impulsive, and other a-rational forces in human behaviour whether individually- or group-driven.[41] Herd-like behaviours of the masses are typically arational, and could lead to a rollercoaster pattern of exuberance alternating with gloom.

Humans, as individuals or groups, have not always been guided by the so-called 'rational hypotheses' (such as efficient markets, maximization of utility, coherent behaviour, absence of gridlocks, etc.), often used by classical or neo-classical economists. Modern economists have come to interpret the behaviour of humans on other premises than those of *strict rationality* in the *maximization of personal gain*. The breakthrough research of the 1992 Nobel laureate in Economics Gary Becker has interpreted human behaviour differently from the traditional 'rational behaviour' that seeks to maximize productivity and benefits. He widened the 'welfare' preferences of individuals to include ethical factors (such as altruism, loyalty, or philanthropy), non-moral factors (such as drug addiction or indifference to distress) or anti-moral factors (such as cruelty). His analyses have thus taken into consideration *prejudice* and *discrimination* vis-à-vis particular groups, as so-called 'welfare' factors in the 'rational behaviour' of certain decision makers – despite the discriminators' potential loss of real income.[42]

Other economists have praised self-interest as an effective 'fuel of growth', while contending that philanthropy and love are scarce resources that are subject to 'rapid depletion'. Among these economists are Kenneth Arrow,

Dennis H. Robertson, and Lawrence Summers. Contesting their views, one scholar argues that:

> Altruism, generosity, solidarity, and civic spirit are not like commodities that are depleted with use. They are more like muscles that develop and grow stronger with exercise. One of the defects of a market-driven society is that it lets these virtues languish. To renew our public life we need to exercise them more strenuously.[43]

In commercial transactions, buyers could implement the above-mentioned 'discriminatory preferences' through such electronic applications as 'BuyPartisan': by using a phone to scan a product's barcode, one can quickly see the political contributions of each company's CEO, Board of Directors, political action committees and employees to the two major political parties in the United States. *BuyPartisan* empowers consumers with awareness of the companies' contributions to political parties, and this could influence the spending pattern of these consumers. *BuyPartisan* allows you to find out whether 'what you are buying' matches your personal socio-political affiliations or opinions.

Some thinkers believe that living conditions are susceptible to continual improvements thanks to rationalism and progress in science. This was eloquently expounded in the 'Age of Enlightenment' (that refers to the period of creative ferment of knowledge in Europe in the eighteenth century) by the Marquis de Condorcet (1743–1794). Condorcet strived for a free, democratic and secular world. He was the precursor of 'positivism' in the social sciences, besides being a mathematician and a statesman.[44] He considered that the historiography of civilizations shows an incessant advancement in science and technology, at the service of universal human rights, global justice, and comprehensive wellbeing. Others deem Condorcet's views utopian and incongruous if judged by the tragic series of horrors perpetrated by some humans who have used advances in sciences and technology for purposes of mass destruction of life and property on planet Earth. Advances in science and technology are neutral; their applications, however, can be put to *beneficial* use in furthering the wellbeing of humans, or alternatively to *catastrophic* use in harming humans and nature.

Though he firmly believed and constantly served the ideals of the French Revolution [namely, liberty (with socio-political rights for all), equality (uniform application of rights/responsibilities, and the fair-cum-impartial administration of justice), and fraternity (concord and solidarity among all members of the community)], Condorcet's life ended prematurely and brutally in prison without a fair trial and as a victim of the 'Reign of Terror' under Maximilien Robespierre (1758–1794). The latter, in his fight against the oppression of the French monarchy, turned into an oppressor upon his assumption of power within the first French Republic.

Other thinkers on the opposite side of Condorcet's philosophical/ethical spectrum of thought doubt the validity of the hypothesis that 'rationalism' and 'science' are sufficient prerequisites for enhancing general wellbeing. As expounded optimistically by a contemporary social scientist:

> ... The PPIs [Positive Psychology Interventions] offer effective ways we can improve our happiness by changing the way we think about events and the goals we choose to pursue. Rethinking social policies regarding taxes, social welfare systems, family and work balance, and so on, offers the opportunity to improve the happiness of our society as a whole. Perhaps most exciting, these suggestions for improving both individual and society-wide happiness are based on sound scientific evidence.[45]

'Science', however, is not the sole prerequisite for improving happiness or wellbeing. 'Fundamental universal values' are its vital complementary prerequisite.

Indeed, humans are capable of a variety of contradictory sentiments and behaviours, stretching from the noblest and finest to the most abominable and cruel ones. Conscience and science need to progress jointly, if global wellbeing is to be enhanced durably, and the horrors of conflicts are to be avoided on planet Earth. With the potential dangers of obliteration resulting from the use of existing military arsenals, non-rational humans in command of such power and lacking in ethical values can provoke abominable tragedies. As expressed by the French thinker, François Rabelais (1495–1553) in his major treatise Gargantua (1534), 'science without conscience can ruin the soul', thereby emphasizing the bedrock importance of noble universal values as a fundamental driving force in the expansion of knowledge.

Condorcet, furthermore, advocated and strongly supported gender political equality. He sought open generalized access to education for the benefit of all members of society; other thinkers such as François Marie Charles Fourier [1772–1837] followed his pioneering call.[46] Condorcet became an active member of the Society of the Friends of the Blacks (established in 1788), and militated in favour of the definitive abolition of legislation authorizing slavery (which was belatedly abrogated in his country France in 1848). His stand of criminalizing slavery is particularly praiseworthy, especially when we realize that many of his contemporaries (intellectuals and policy-makers) had justified this iniquitous institution.

Among paradigmatic individuals in the realms of belief systems, philosophy, morality, and the like,

> ... only Socrates taught that 'there is no greater evil one can suffer than to hate reasonable discourse'. And only Socrates demanded of his followers that they jettison traditional certainties and strive toward a rational unity of word and deed ... Serene in his willingness to sacrifice himself, he will give up living in order to prove his unswerving commitment to his transcendental project, his unending search for wisdom.[47]

Artists' rendering of wellbeing

Artists (from the plastic, audio, visual, and other fields) and literary authors hailing from a variety of backgrounds have shed revealing lights on human aspirations and failings. Without passing any personal judgement on the quality of the artists' works, the following offer differing views on the human condition.

In search of wellbeing

The *Walking Man* bronze sculpture of Alberto Giacometti (1960) – given the figure's profile and gait – could convey a variety of interpretations to its beholders. Not knowing what is down the road, the sculpture can be viewed as a human odyssey in search of the path that leads to enhanced wellbeing. It could convey a man's potential trials and tribulations, perplexity or worrisome feelings while attempting to find a promising path within unchartered territories. It could also stand for a solitary man's quest for self-reliance in his life's journey, in the absence of prescience, to discover new environments and horizons. He could establish relations with other creatures, and explore new opportunities. The *Walking Man* advances either with blissful expectation or with anxious apprehension of life's contingencies. Exploring trails for a 'good life', the *Walking Man* plods forward in an uncertain enyironment. Unfolding events could offer him the sought-after rewards or bonanzas. Alternatively, a dark future could make him tumble into dangerous surprises!

Enthusiastic competitive performances

For an artistic representation of a cohort of athletes who ambition to attain lofty peaks, one could refer to a bronze sculpture *L'Elan* by Nag Arnoldi (1994). Its stylized exhilarated athletes, each drawn from the world's five continents, strive for accomplishment, carrying aloft the Olympic emblem with resoluteness, and confidence (guided by The Olympic motto *Citius, Altius, & Fortius* – the Latin for 'Faster, Higher, and Stronger'). The sculpture's current position meaningfully faces up to Europe's highest mountain (the 4,808 metre-high Mont Blanc in the Alps, from a plinth at the edge of Lake Leman in Lausanne – Switzerland), with its athletes eager to reach the highest summits. The scrutinizing observer could also imagine the fragility of the athletes' joint endeavours, should anyone encounter an unexpected accident that could cripple their collective aspirations. Organizers or sponsors of sportive events could induce their national or club athletes to 'out-perform' by using doping drugs or stimulants – regardless of adverse impact on their health and pleasure. Such a drive to *artificial performance* could make some athletes, and their sporting institutions neglect the necessary pillar of *ethics*, as evidenced by reported cheating in drug-taking instances resorted to by acquiescing competing individuals motivated by misplaced hubris, faked fame, and/or lucre.

Cooperation and solidarity

Several other artists have addressed felicitous conviviality and cooperation among humans of diverse backgrounds. This is the case of a painting showing a congenial exuberant cohort of children of all hues and backgrounds, holding up *Planet Earth*. Prompted by solidarity, exuding optimism, and imbued with collectively shared ideals of striving for the 'common good', these children face up to the vast firmament studded with innumerable bright stars while lovingly and protectively lifting up their healthy and wonderful planet.[48]

Fatal rivalries

In contra-distinction with the aforementioned 'optimistic' works of art, others have depicted aspects of human behaviour that produce disastrous conflicts – leading ineluctably to excruciating suffering and obliteration. Francisco Goya (1746–1828), a Spanish leading Master painter has illustrated the hideous side of human nature. Among his masterpieces is that of two egocentric pugnacious *brutish titans* spurred by irrational mortal hate, fighting a duel with bludgeons over a territory of moving sands. Their strife would eventually lead them to mutual obliteration by their getting bogged down and sinking together, gulped up by the supreme force of hostile Nature. Such an imagined dramatic scene of brutal conflict and death is a source of reflection on life's multiple vulnerabilities. Indeed, our planet is subject to destructive forces caused by human follies and/or by hostile environment.

Fear and destruction

Many museums and exhibitions in various parts of the world are hosts to artistic works that depict atrocious punishment, suffering, and retribution dispensed to innocent people.[49] Several works illustrate human agonies or angst in their severest manifestations. This is for example the case of *The Scream*, the famous 1893 painting of Norwegian Edvard Munch [1863–1944] showing a terrified human figure with an dramatic expression of pain, torment and anguish. Other artistic works convey certain dreadful aspects of human atrocities, such as Picasso's [1881–1975] allegory of *Guernica*, the martyr city in the Basque region that was horribly ravaged in 1937 by the Nazi Air force at the demand of General Franco. Aggressive behaviours could be contained by collective wills guided by universal human rights.

Power, partaking, battered countries, and emancipation

In several countries, entrenched autocratic regimes led by ensconced potentates have ruled as absolute monarchs or self-designated providential leaders protected by a fearsome security apparatus, praetorian guards, and/or a hegemonic single party system. By privileging egotistic interests at the expense of public interest, rulers have often suppressed ruthlessly aspirations for an open society and respect for basic human rights. Underpinned by colluding coteries and pernicious parasitic acolytes after the gravy train, a few of these autocrats have ruled through turpitude, cunning, coercion, torture, corruption, and other improper practices.

Popular protests against authoritarian, dysfunctional, rogue or discriminatory regimes have been driven by multiple forces. Among these, one could mention the peoples' desire to satisfy their basic aspirations for work, freedom, dignity, social justice and a decent life. The up-and-coming young generations have been influenced by their cohorts in democracies that espouse pluralism where people can express their diverse opinions freely and peacefully. Without any sense of compassion or guilt, and impervious to criticism for their violation of international laws and human rights standards, authoritarian regimes repress dissenters. Indeed, unable to buy off their opponents, a few rulers have quelled their citizens' demonstrations by bloody indiscriminate crackdowns through their brutal security-military apparatus or through affiliated spooks, mercenaries, or thugs.

Given the strong zeitgeist of a community, authoritarian regimes are deeply contested by people who strive to protect their fundamental rights. Rulers who cultivate their personality cult and scupper the legitimate rights of their people would eventually be toppled by nationals willing to brave the despots' oppression in their strife for their legitimate fundamental civil rights as citizens (and not as disenfranchised subjects). The risks of torture, targeted killing or 'forced disappearance' at the hands of security forces, secret intelligence agents, and militia-cum-Mafiosi in the pay of autocratic rulers have not deterred courageous demonstrators aspiring to establish a free and just participatory democracy.

Across human history, ensconced potentates have ruled as self-designated providential leaders. Underpinned by a political party or relying on a colluding coterie of pernicious parasitic acolytes after the gravy train, a few autocrats have managed to rule by cunning, coercion, torture, graft, and other improper practices – thinking that their rule can make them prevail in the long term over societies they had hoped to mould into docility. Indeed, authoritarianism is not a pre-condition for the stability of political regimes, as historical events have shown. The flame of freedom is likely to continue to animate many humans, despite considerable sacrifices. It is premised on the hope that their struggle would lead to a better life for themselves, their children, and future generations.

In deeply entrenched autocratic regimes, people's capability to introduce genuine democratic reforms through remonstrances or peaceful demonstrations cannot be crowned with success, except at the cost of substantial sacrifices on the part of demonstrators. A schematic presentation of major phases of a *positive scenario* that produces improvements in socio-political and economic institutions of an oppressed people is proposed in Exhibit 5.2. A *negative scenario* could prevail, however, when protestors are no match for the established authoritarian order. This has been the case of several countries in recent years, especially when the existing regimes have the support of foreign powers or when protesters are divided. In such a *negative scenario*, a power stalemate could ensue, gradually sucking the country concerned into the maelstrom of a protracted civil strife. Such an eventuality could lead to the chaotic situation of a 'failed' or 'rogue' state ruled by vampire-like warlords or mobsters, with foreign self-interested intruders entering the fray.

Exhibit 5.2 A scenario of evolving emancipation

1 CRITICAL PHASE – HUMILIATIONS AT THE HANDS OF AN OPPRESSIVE MONOLITHIC REGIME BECOME INTOLERABLE TO ITS PEOPLE: Overcoming their apathy, their seething anger and intense revulsion against rulers' multiple abuses explodes. This happens initially via peaceful demonstrations that gather momentum, leading up to a pivotal period of generalized successful popular defiance vis-à-vis the established order.

2 PROTESTERS' ASPIRATIONS FOR A 'BETTER LIFE' TRIGGER THEIR QUESTS TO: recover their dignity, human rights, and freedom in a democratic regime. The latter calls for accountability, pluralism; power sharing; social justice; equal opportunities; decent work; cultural tolerance; solidarity; etc.).

3 AUSPICIOUS CONTEXTS: external and internal conditions offer propitious environments and favourable opportunities for growing success of popular demonstrations aiming at 'regime change', and for the gradual consolidation of protesters' progress.

4 EXPANDING CAPABILITIES OF THE CONTESTING POPULATION: repression of peaceful demonstrations by established autocratic regimes encounters solid opposition by a united front of a fearless population, unfazed by the authorities' brutal clamping down. Demonstrators manage to resist, to gain in clout, and to avoid fragmentation and inner fighting that allow insidious forces to enter the fray.

5 RATCHING-UP ACHIEVEMENTS: the steadfast countering and dismantling of authoritative rulers' repressive apparatuses should boost the morale of protesters, and energize their resolve. Successful introduction of, and apprenticeship in, democratic institutions and practices guided by sound principles of governance in various domains (namely the legislative, executive, judiciary, regulatory, media, civil society, etc.) take hold incrementally.

5 RESILIENCE: The process of emancipation from tyranny and subjugation is seldom linear and uni-directional. Should there be stalling or setbacks in political reforms, protesters should have the grit and capability to repair the damage inflicted on them, and recover and adjust to new situations as they develop. Maintaining tenacious solidarity among protesters strengthens their resolve not to cave in.

6 ESTABLISHING A NEW 'PARTICIPATIVE' ORDER: The new regime is based on (a) a collective vision of desirable goals to be consensually reached over agreed future time horizons, and (b) the firm rooting of democratic institutions that accept pluralism, protect minorities, and uphold socio-political equity at the service of the public good.

Source: author

Tyrannical rulers are often kleptocratic. They prey on their people and impose their diktat on hapless victims with impunity. They eviscerate national economies for their sole selfish benefit and that of their family, clan or clique. Stolen assets are thus siphoned off to opaque offshore jurisdictions. They carry out their misdeeds while often impervious to the sufferings of the majority of their people.[50]

People are bound to feel revulsion vis-à-vis rulers who monopolize power and self-appropriate privileges at the expense of the rank and file. Resentment of such usurpation of power and riches by one person, family or clique is bound to build up, fomenting in due course civil unrest that culminates eventually in revolutionary upheavals, fuelled by people's legitimate aspirations for a dignified life consisting of decent work, justice and freedom. Uprisings have often followed peaceful demonstrations, often repressed violently by authoritarian regimes. Indeed, protesters were detained or abducted, held incommunicado in secret locations, locked up without trial, tortured, and eventually liquidated (often without the knowledge of families and friends).

Human beings may well slumber into subjugation for a while and accept rulers' diktats owing to their ignorance, apathy, resignation, and/or abnegation. The oppressed people may not be fully aware of, or enticed by, the potential felicity of freedom. By denying them civil and political rights, impostors deprive them of the opportunity of advancing their lot. They could ghettoize or forcefully exile certain communities. To break out from their socio-political subjugation, and to win their socio-political freedom and equality of chances, such communities would have to struggle and incur sacrifices – sometimes for a long time – before casting off their chains.

Historians have examined communities that have suffered from various types of regimes that stripped them of their civic rights. This has been the case of the Government of Bhutan that has trumpeted its policy of promoting people's 'happiness' through four means: good governance and democratization, stable and equitable socioeconomic development, protection of the environment and the ecosystem, and the preservation and promotion of national culture. Bhutan's substantial Nepalese minority has not benefited from such 'happiness policy'. In the name of Bhutan's cultural unity, the long-settled ethnic Nepalese minority has been (i) harassed into adopting the majority's dress codes, (ii) denied the teaching of their language, (iii) barred from college education, and (iv) excluded from obtaining business licences or employment in governmental jobs. Their protests, which started in the 1980s, eventually led the Bhutan authorities to force over 100,000 persons into exile (nearly one-fifth of Bhutan's total population) in the early 1990s.

Bhutan's discriminatory policies against its Nepalese minority (culminating in pogroms) have been considered callous and chauvinistic. Bhutan's ethnocentrism, by downgrading the Nepalese culture (especially the language, traditions, and Hindi religion) sought the assimilation into the Bhutanese culture, and was at variance with the universal values of tolerance, fair treatment, and the pursuit of happiness for all.[51]

Similarly, the Rohingya people, a Moslem minority in northern Myanmar (Burma) in the province of Rakhine, have been described as one of the most persecuted people in modern times – blatantly subjected to ethnic cleansing. Some 680,000 had to flee in the latter months of 2017, mostly into neighbouring Bangladesh, after their homes were burned, their properties were destroyed, and members of their families killed. Their survival in Myanmar had been put at risk with pogroms conducted by the Burmese army and radical Buddhists.[52]

Bigotry has not been limited to developing countries. Several rich democratic countries have persistently discriminated against certain minorities or immigrant populations and their descendants. Discrimination has covered employment, living conditions, health, education, civic engagement, and other areas.[53]

Exclusions, discriminations or chronic abuses of various types continue to exist in the twenty-first century – with several regimes refusing pluralism or multi-party systems. Discriminations exist in various domains, notably with reference to access to: (a) political rights (universal and equal suffrage, fair justice, real equality vis-à-vis the rule of law, etc.), and (b) economic rights (in property, work, or business opportunities). These obstacles undermine the entrepreneurial spirit, constrain employment, and decelerate socio-economic development. The poor are among the first to be hurt.[54]

Extolling one's 'unique' cultural superiority, at the expense of other cultures, is a source of tension that could eventually lead to confrontation and violence. Indeed, narrow-minded egotistic interests could lead in extreme cases to exploitation of other humans, predation, wealth destruction, lethal violence, and genocides (based on race, ideology, or religion). If humans recognize that they have composite hybrid cultures, then they are likely to become more tolerant vis-à-vis other cultures.[55] Protection of dignity, socio-political inclusiveness, and fair dispensing of justice constitute the mainspring of wellbeing. The participation of hitherto forsaken communities in their country's affairs is likely to promote security and stability, avoid radicalization, and contribute to the process of enhancing general welfare.

Popular uprisings that have the stamina and capacity to topple firmly entrenched autocratic rulers do not necessarily produce immediately democratic and stable regimes. A long period of initiation and of trial-and-error is needed to build up resilient, sturdy and transparent institutions acceptable to society-at-large (generally based on tolerance, pluralism, human rights protection, and alternation of political power in response to universal popular suffrage). It takes vigilance, luck, and time for democratic institutions to grow solid roots.

Risks of failed uprisings, and possible setbacks (with opportunistic parties re-establishing yokes of servitude) could occur. In periods of social turmoil, despots and their agents could manipulate popular movements through various techniques. These include misinformation, splitting protesters into antagonistic militant groups (based, for example, on ideologies, clans, tribes, sects, or ethnicity), or corrupting people with hand-outs from public money (!). Positions of influence or privilege could also be offered to those who declare allegiance to despotic rulers. The latter can pay infiltrators to spread malicious rumours and stir up hatred among their opponents – in order to weaken or smother fledgling democratic movements. Waiting in the wings or lurking below the surface with the aim of destroying in the bud freshly established democratic institutions, impostors may well appeal to credulous trusting populations, hypocritically pretending to be their saviours.

Lasting progressive reforms need time (years or decades) to take roots among the population, and to consolidate. Hijacking freedom-seeking revolutions is common. One could illustrate such a phenomenon by reference to the French Revolution of 1789–1799. In that historic episode, Napoleon Bonaparte (1769–1821) schemed by outmanoeuvring republicans and resorting to a putsch to establish his monolithic rule over 1799–1814. In particular, he usurped in 1799 the powerful post of First Consul within the triumvirate of the First Republic. Later in 1804, he dissolved the Republic and imposed himself as Emperor of France and its dominions with hereditary rights for his descendants. His sole writ remained undisputed till his ultimate military defeat in 1814 by a coalition of major European powers, and the re-installation of the monarchy in France. This was followed by other regimes until the current Fifth French Republic.

Democratic systems are protean. Examples exist of countries that have struggled over long years or decades to emerge from totalitarian regimes and become workable democracies. The birth, build up, nurturing and entrenchment of democratic institutions calls, furthermore, for propitious regional-cum-international environments. Protesters in various periods of history have often failed because of lack of stamina, or resilience to bear indefinitely 'sufferings' inflicted by *rulers with absolute power*. The latter would incarcerate, deport, torture, and ultimately 'liquidate' their opponents, while helpless victims wait for the moment of nemesis.

Although liberty- and dignity-driven revolutions could be achieved after tremendous suffering and destructions inflicted on civilians by those at the helm of arbitrary tyrannical regimes, heroic people seeking freedom would bear these sacrifices for the ultimate benefit of their children and society. Nevertheless, one could not exclude the 'hijacking of freedom-seeking revolutions' by sneaking despots disguised as democrats aided and abetted (militarily and/or economically) by regional or international hegemonic powers.

Democratic regimes allow for orderly changes, in response to popular wishes. British political leader Sir Winston Churchill (1874–1965), commented thus:

> Many forms of Government have been tried, and will be tried in this world of sin and woe. No one pretends that democracy is perfect or all-wise. Indeed, it has been said that democracy is the worst form of government except all those other forms that have been tried from time to time.[56]

Peter J. Katzenstein commented that:

> It was Churchill the racist who supported and participated in campaigns of ethnic cleansing and the establishment of detention camps in British colonies. And it was Churchill who hated Ghandi and Hitler equally, a fact that may explain his callousness during the great 1943 famine in Bengal – which was caused largely by Britain's mismanagement then under Churchill's leadership [the starvation of about 3 million humans despite the availability of stored cereals at that time in that region]. This was Churchill's first face. His second was the fearless and eloquent leader of Britain and the West, the man who helped greatly in defeating Hitler and the Nazis.[57] As to why people did not listen to Churchill's warnings about Hitler in the late 1930s, 'the short answer is that he'd used exactly the same language about Ghandi in the early 1930s'.[58]

One needs to admit that a few governments belonging to well-established democratic regimes have resorted to questionable policies and practices in seeking to subjugate other peoples and control their lands. Indeed, certain countries featuring 'democratic' principles in their constitutions, have paradoxically countenanced and propped-up foreign *puppet* 'despotic regimes' in other countries (including those resorting to torture and other cruelties) prompted by diverse motives (e.g. the control over foreign vital resources in client states, geo-strategic ascendancy over potential rivals, or other socio-political reasons). Moreover, leading world democracies are not totally immune from abusive practices, such as torture and/or capital punishment.[59] These democracies' agencies responsible for torture had hoped to obtain valuable information about their enemies through discredited coercive interrogation techniques that are condemned by international law. Their torture techniques had proved ineffective, and had failed to protect universal human rights in accordance with international treaties they have already committed to respect.

Nations have often placed their self-interest and gains before human rights – as their alliances and arms sales have historically shown. For diverse reasons (notably to serve their national interests), states governed at home by representative democratic regimes could cynically simultaneously protect disreputable underlings, including minion rulers that violate their people's basic human rights. Under the cloak of politico-military alliances, they can sell these client regimes arms (often used to repress nationals or other targeted peoples). These despots and their auxiliaries become then pliant agents, readily subject to the manipulation of hegemonic 'protector' states: for example, their rulers willingly accept to become captive markets for civilian or military products. On behalf of their 'patron states', they could even accept to 'sub-contract' conflicts vis-à-vis other countries.

Autocrats or dictators in developing countries had reportedly privileged companies and nationals of countries that support them. These dictators had also dispensed substantial 'secret gifts' in money or kind to leaders of countries that support them. This odd relationship had notably existed between France and its ex-colonies in sub-Saharan Africa – showing also episodes of African leaders misappropriating state wealth to buy for themselves private properties located in France.[60]

The essence of power rests in the capability of those in command to obtain their sought-after objectives. Wielders of *power* can exercise it in a variety of forms. Two main categories of power are distinguishable: the *soft* and the *hard*. The former relies on non-coercive levers, such as moral suasion, intellectual dialogue, cultural affinities and/or diplomacy, while the latter refers to coercion buttressed by credible material threats that could inflict harm on opponents (e.g. via physical-technological-economic forces).

Power has not been solely used for legitimate defence; it has also been used to dominate other peoples. In the early part of the twenty-first century, the United States is generally considered to be the leading world power. This is largely due to hefty military spending (some 40 per cent of global cumulated military expenditures), superior military technology compared with its rivals, and the deployment of several military bases worldwide. Moreover, the United States is the foremost seller of arms. Power cannot be solely linked to the physical size of military expenditures in hardware, technology, strategy, etc. The U.S. defence budget for fiscal year 2018 [1 October 2017 through 30 September 2018] was slated to reach $824.6 billion under the Donald Trump Administration.[61] States also resort to 'intelligence' in exercising their influence vis-à-vis counterparties (through enticements, threats, secret subversive operations, fake news, etc.) seeking to reach effectively and efficiently their desired goals before the ultimate use of force.

Policing other countries has costs and benefits. Among the major costs, one could mention resources taken from investments in the national civilian economy for use in the military sector, in addition to loss of life or health problems encountered by the civilian and military populations in periods of conflicts. Benefits can be evaluated from the standpoint of economic advantages wrested from vassal client states and geopolitical ascendency over potential rivals. The pecking order by reference to power is bound to change as new dynamic nations emerge and get ahead of waning ones.[62] Generally speaking, the wider the diffusion of power globally, the lesser is the scope for any one party to meddle into others' affairs. Nevertheless, such a diffusion may not be sustainable over the long term – as historical events have shown.

Some scholars and policy advisers have argued in favour of *concerted nonpolarity* among a group of major countries as conducive to 'encouraging a greater degree of global integration [that] will help promote stability. Establishing a core group of governments and others committed to cooperative multilateralism would be a great step forward.'[63]

Nevertheless, there is a risk that such a core group of major powers could turn into an exclusive oligarchy or condominium of a few major states that agree to divide the world into spheres of influence among themselves in order to exercise their hegemonic power over weaker states, guided by their self-serving interests. Moreover, the webs of interests and issues among polities are multiple and diverse. Some are considered universal (such as *human rights values*) while others are punctual (such as *commercial deals*). Finally, power relations are dynamic, susceptible to significant change over more or less long periods.

In a dynamic world, the relative weights of groups change, thereby creating new equilibria in power relations among countries. The current *mighty* with imperial designs could wane in future periods, and the hitherto *weak* could strengthen over more or less strong stretches of time – propitious conditions permitting. Excluded, oppressed or relegated people can rebel against *imposed orders* by the behemoth, and struggle successfully to assert their aspirations for freedom, dignity, and justice – obviously accepting the necessary sacrifices to realize their goals (see Exhibit 5.2 on emancipation).

Since 1945, there have been five permanent members of the 15-member states of the UN Security Council (namely the United States, Russia, China, France, and the United Kingdom) with veto power that have been used regardless of the ethical considerations of debated issues.[64]

Small states get easily buffeted by bigger ones who use their superior power to advance their interests. Often, such small states suffer from the overbearing intrusive policies of foreign predator regimes. Military and non-military ententes or alliances among a few powerful countries can create stability for a stretch of time. Nevertheless, such ententes could veer into the slippery path of tutelage by a club of a few powerful states with international or regional influence. These big and powerful states could then exploit the smaller and weaker ones, battering them as and when they deem it desirable (see Exhibit 5.3).

Exhibit 5.3 Key characteristics of battered states: the case of Lebanon

This has been the case of tiny Lebanon [10,400 km^2] that obtained its independence from the ruling French authorities on 1 January 1944. Lebanon's political life has been battered by overwhelming forces of aggression – local, regional or international.

Lebanon's diverse religious communities comprising Christians (largely Maronite Catholic, followed by Orthodox) and Moslems (mostly Shi'a and Sunni of equal importance, followed by Druze and Alawite) have impacted its political system, with parliamentary seats and governmental posts allocated on the basis of confession rather than on competence or political ideologies.[65] Besides the influence of confessionalism, political power in Lebanon has been largely under the control of a few hereditary feudal families or of oligarchs whose clout has been based on their clans and/or the patronage of influential regional or international foreign powers which support them.

Nevertheless, it is comforting and inspiring to note that Arab societies, similar to other societies, have found persons recognized for their rectitude and their commitment to the public good.

The temptation of corruption is not limited to resource-rich countries controlled by authoritarian rulers. It is also to be found in poor countries. One could cite Salim al-Hoss[66] who lamented the absence of good governance undermined by the ills of sectarianism and corruption that frays the social fabric to the detriment of the 'public good'.

Quoting Salim al-Hoss:

> In my country Lebanon we suffer from rampant sectarianism or confessionalism. It turned out that there is indeed a starkly close affinity between sectarianism and corruption. In one sense the fanaticism connected with sectarianism tends to dim and blur one's perception of social values and virtues, and to obstruct one's vision of truth and justice. In another sense it also too often serves as a bulwark for corruption, precluding the prosecution of sectarian leaderships for corruption-related perpetrations, as any charges are effectively portrayed as assaults against the sectarian community of the culprit.[67]

The Lebanese civil war of 1975–1990 was followed by other bloody conflicts in about half of the Arab League's member states that number 22. Few Arab regimes could avoid political turmoil by a timely adoption of some socio-political reforms. Multiple causes have been responsible for the turmoil: extremist interpretations of religion, sectarianism, clanship, ethnicity, ideologies, absolute monarchies, or totalitarian presidencies-for-life. Political control by the few has constrained the development of an entrepreneurial, competitive, transparent, and vibrant private sector in Arab societies.[68]

Lebanon (whose total resident citizens population is estimated at around four million in 2018) hosts some 400,000 to 500,000 Palestinian registered refugees.[69] These refugees continue to live, since 1948, along with their siblings, in delimited crowded and insalubrious camps. They have been denied the right to work, to own property, and to live outside designated camps. Belatedly in August 2010, the Lebanese Parliament accorded them a limited right of work in certain activities, though they remained excluded from work in the public-services sector and several professions such as the medical, legal or engineering where Lebanese nationality is a compulsory prerequisite.[70] Some Lebanese fear that Palestinians' permanent residency in Lebanon could upset the existing confessional balance and/or could thwart the return of Palestinians to their homeland Palestine. The fate of Palestinian refugees in other countries of the Near East also leaves much to be desired.

Somewhat comparable to Palestinians are Syrian refugees who have fled their country's civil war over the period 2011–2016; they numbered over 4 million surviving in neighbouring countries, in addition to about 6.5 million internally displaced. Compared with the national population of the host country, Lebanon is first on the list of countries hosting refugees (hosting about a quarter of its own population) followed by Jordan.[71] Moreover, Lebanon has become gravely impoverished after its own civil war (1975–1990). After the cessation of hostilities, it has been burdened by one of the world's highest public debt-to-GNP ratios. Since mid-2014, it has had a fractious government, a vacant presidency for two-and-a-half years (till November 2016), and an impotent parliament whose legitimate period of representation of four years had already expired and been thrice self-renewed without elections!

Lebanon has the world's highest level of refugees per head of population: Palestinian and Syrian refugees (mostly of the Sunni confession) make up about one quarter of the Lebanese population in 2016. Refugees suffer from hunger, unemployment, poorly paid jobs, homelessness, absence of schooling, child labour to support their families, child marriage, and xenophobia (largely fanned by the fact that these refugees' basic requirements cannot be underwritten by a country already struggling to protect its own poor). Syrian refugees have become a burden on the 'absorptive capacity' of the Lebanese society faced with a stagnant economy bedevilled by corruption. Even the UN agencies, such as the World Food Programme, are short of resources to fund the basic nutritional requirements of Syrian refugees.[72]

The economic, social, and political precariousness of Lebanon in the 2010s has been highlighted by several studies, suggesting that they could undo the country. Among the perils, the following are underlined: the break-down of infrastructures for sanitation, electricity, potable water, and rubbish landfill sites; the burgeoning of governmental debt; the absence of a legitimate parliament for several months; overdue vacancies of public jobs; the absence of a state budget; lack of reliable official statistics; vulnerability of banks and the national currency; generalized corruption; dysfunctional governmental services; etc.[73]

Another erstwhile Prime Minister of Lebanon has succinctly expressed people's deep aspiration to accomplish the triad of 'freedom, justice, and work' in these terms:

> Experience has shown us that dictatorships are not a sustainable guarantor of peace for minorities. Instead, only the emergence of a democratic and modern civil state, where all individuals are treated equally, regardless of religion or ethnic grouping, can bring lasting peace and stability. Furthermore, democracy and majority rule should not be used as an excuse to marginalize a minority … The political challenges we face as Arabs should not mask the many economic challenges awaiting us around the corner. The most pressing risk is the high unemployment especially among the youth.[74]

Note

Factors that have battered Lebanon's economic, political and social life are underlined by this author [Mikdashi], for emphasis.

Source: author

Notes

1 Marylène Patou-Mathis, 'No, Humans Did Not Always Make War', article originally published in French in: *Le Monde Diplomatique*, July 2015, pp. 20–21.

2 See, for example, Andrew Heywood, *Global Politics*, 2nd edition, Macmillan, 2014, pp. 246–269/590p.

3 See: N. K. Sandars, *The Epic of Gilgamesh*, Penguin Classics, revised edition, September 1987, 128p.

4 See Fredrik Hagen, *An Ancient Egyptian Literary Text in Context – The Instruction of Ptahhotep*, 2012, Peeters Publishers & Department of Oriental Studies, Leuven, Belgium, 313p.

5 See Harold C. Washington, *Wealth and Poverty in the Instruction of Amenemope and the Hebrew Proverbs*, The Society of Biblical Literature, Scholars Press – Atlanta, Georgia, 1994, 242p.; see also Hana Samadi Naaman, 'Histoire de la sagesse et des

sources du proverbe arabe', in *Les Proverbes de ma mère: Proverbes du Liban & leurs equivalents dans les langues du monde [The Proverbs of my Mother: Proverbs of Lebanon & Their Equivalents in the Languages of the World]*, Guethner, 2014, 667p.

6 Marc Van De Mieroop, *Philosophy before the Greeks – The Pursuit of Truth in Ancient Babylonia*, Princeton University Press, 2016, p. 174/297p.

7 Op. cit., p. 175.

8 See, for example, Hugh Thomas, *The Slave Trade: The Story of the Atlantic Slave Trade: 1440–1870*, Simon & Schuster, 3 February 1999, 912p.; Edward Baptist, *The Half Has Never Been Told: Slavery and the Making of American Capitalism*, Basic Books, 2014, 498p.; and Martin Meredith, *The Fortunes of Africa: A 5'000-Year History of Wealth, Greed, and Endeavour*, PublicAffairs, 2014, 784p.

9 Etienne de la Boétie, *Discourse on Voluntary Servitude*, original written in 1549, later translated by Harry Kurz, Black Rose Book, London.

10 Rauscher, Frederick, 'Kant's Social and Political Philosophy', *The Stanford Encyclopedia of Philosophy*, Summer 2012 Edition, Edward N. Zalta (ed.), URL: http://plato.stanford.edu/archives/sum2012/entries/kant-social-political/.

11 See, for example, Antony Black, *A World History of Ancient Political Thought*, Oxford University Press, 2009, 260p.

12 Eyjólfur K. Emilson, 'On Happiness and Time', in Oyvind Rabbas, Eyjolfur K. Emilson, Hallvard Fossheim, and Miira Tuominen, eds, *The Quest for the Good Life – Ancient Philosophers on Happiness*, Oxford University Press, 2015, p. 222/307p.

13 Professor C. C. W. Taylor, in: Ted Honderich, ed., *The Oxford Companion to Philosophy*, Oxford University Press, 2005, p. 271/1056p.

14 See, for example, Michael Pennock and Karma Ura, 'Gross National Happiness as a Framework for Health Impact Assessment', *Environmental Impact Assessment Review*, Elsevier, vol. 31, issue 1, January 2011, pp. 61–65; also Jeffrey D. Sachs, 'Restoring Virtue Ethics in the Quest for Happiness', in John Helliwell, Richard Layard, and Jeffrey Sachs, eds, *World Happiness Report 2013*, New York, UN Sustainable Development Solutions Network, www.unsdsn.org.

With respect to lofty spiritual values closely linked to wellbeing, a caveat expressed by a historian deserves our full attention. He said 'Christian crusaders, Islamist militants, or the leaders of 'freedom-loving nations', all justify what they see as necessary violence in the name of a higher good. Buddhist rulers and monks have been no exception. So, historically, Buddhism has been no more a religion of peace than Christianity' (source: Dr Alan Strathern – Associate Professor of Modern History, Oxford University, 'Why Are Buddhist Monks Attacking Muslims?', *BBC News Magazine*, 1 May 2013.

15 See, for example, Victor Caston and Silke-Maria Weineck, eds, *Our Ancient Wars – Rethinking War through the Classics*, University of Michigan Press, 2016, 289p.; also UNESCO, *Struggles against Slavery – International Year to Commemorate the Struggle against Slavery and Its Abolition*, 2004, 34p. www.unesco.org; and *Brief History of Slavery in the Occident*: www.herodote.net.

16 See, for example, David Keyt and Fred D. Miller, Jr., eds, *Freedom, Reason, and the Polis: Essays in Greek Political Philosophy*, Cambridge University Press, 2007, 316p.

17 http://gadebate.un.org/68/saint-vincent-andgrenadines.

18 See, for example, Michael Wood, *The Story of the Conquistadors*, BBC – History, 29 March 2011.

19 Besides France, Haiti was coveted by other European powers (notably Spain and Germany) and by the United States. As per the U.S. Department of State Office of the Historian, *Milestones in the History of U.S. Foreign Relations*, President Woodrow Wilson sent in 1915 the United States Marines into Haiti 'to restore order and maintain political and economic stability in the Caribbean. This occupation continued until 1934'.

20 See, for example, The Empire of Necessity: Greg Grandin, *Slavery, Freedom, and Deception in the New World*, Metropolitan Books, 2013, 360p.

21 Olivier de la Granville, *Economic Growth: A Unified Approach*, 2nd edition, Cambridge University Press, 2016.
22 See, for example, *ILO 2012 Global Estimate of Forced Labour*: www.ilo.org/forcedlabour.
23 Michael J. Sandel, *Justice: What's the Right Thing to Do?*, Farrar, Straus and Giroux, 2009, p. 211/308.
24 See, for example, Bruce Cumings, *Dominion from Sea to Sea: Pacific Ascendency and American Power*, Yale University Press, 2010, 641p.; also Howard Zinn, *A People's History of the United States: 1492 – Present*, 1980 revised in 2003; Noam Chomsky, for example his *Hopes and Prospects*, Haymarket Books, 2010, 327p.; Jacques Barzun, *From Dawn to Decadence – 1500 to the Present*, Harper Collins Publishers, 2000, 877p.; in addition to the works of other eminent essayists, journalists, pamphleteers or novelists, such as Mark Twain and Thomas Paine.
25 See, for example: http://en.wikipedia.org; www.portaloceania.com; and 'Indigenous Australian', *The Economist*, 28 January 2017, p. 42.
26 The King George III *Royal Proclamation of 1763*, the *US Indian Removal Act of 1830*, the *Canadian 1857 Civilization of Indian Tribes Act*, and their subsequent amendments). The U.S. seventh president Andrew Jackson (with two-term presidency starting in 1829) had owned hundreds of slaves who picked cotton on his plantations. He called on Congress to allocate land west of the Mississippi to ruthlessly uprooted Native Americans from their ancestral lands in the South East of the USA. He had forced Indian Americans to trek to reservations with thousands dying of cold or exhaustion.
27 See 'Arthur Manuel – Leader from Canada's First Nation', *The Economist*, 28 January 2017, p. 74.
28 BBC, 24 November 2017, and other media.
29 United Nations Economic and Social Council, *Preliminary Study of the Impact on Indigenous Peoples of the International Legal Construct Known as the Doctrine of Discovery*, submitted by the Special Rapporteur Tonya Gonnella Frichner at the eighth session of the Permanent Forum on Indigenous Issues, 4 February 2010, pp. 1–2/22p. [E/C.19/2010/1]; see also Seth Adema, *The Christian Doctrine of Discovery: A North American History*, Christian Reformed Church, November 2013, 42p.; and Steve Newcom, 'Five Hundred Years of Injustice', *Shaman's Drum*, Fall 1992, pp. 18–20 http://ili.nativeweb.org/sdrm_art.html.
30 Sources: The Chicago Online Bibliography of Mamluk Studies of the Middle East Documentation Center at the University of Chicago offers comprehensive bibliographies of all primary sources relating to the Mamluk sultanate of Egypt and Syria: ref. http://mamluk.uchicago.edu.
31 See, for example, James Miller, *Examined Lives: from Socrates to Nietzsche*, Farrar, Straus and Giroux, 2011, 422p.; and Alan Rayan, *On Politics: A History of Political Philosophy from Herodotus to the Present*, Liveright/Allen Lane, 2012, 1152p.
32 Martha C. Nussbaum, *Frontiers of Justice – Disability, Nationality, Species Membership*, Harvard University Press, 2006, pp. 410–411/487.
33 Peter Singer, *The Most Good You Can Do – How Effective Altruism is Changing Ideas About Living Ethically*, Yale University Press, 2015, pp. 4–5/211p.
34 See his book: *Education of a Christian Prince*, published in Basel, 1516.
35 Quote from *The Discourses* of Machiavelli as translated by A. Gilbert, and published by Duke University Press, 1965, reproduced in: '*Niccolò* Machiavelli', Stanford Encyclopaedia of Philosophy, 8 September 2009, 21p.; see also Lawrence Freedman, *Strategy: A History*, Oxford University Press, 2013, 751p.; and http://plato.stanford.edu/entries/machiavelli/.
36 Jeremy Bentham, *An Introduction to the Principles of Morals and Legislation*, J. H. Burns and H. L. A. Hart, eds, Clarendon Press – Oxford, 1996 p. 12/343.
37 Ibid., pp. 38–41.

38 Michael J. Sandel, *Justice: What's the Right Thing to Do?*, Farrar, Straus and Giroux, 2009, p. 53/308p; see also, Sherma Folland, Allen C. Goodman and Miron Stano, *The Economics of Health and Health Care* – Chapter 18, 'Equity, Efficiency, and Need', Pearson Education, Inc., 7th edition, 2013, pp. 389–410.

39 Roger Crisp, *Mill on Utilitarianism*, Routledge, 1997, p. 17/232.

40 Cited by Paolo Savona, 'On the Definition of Political Economy and on the Method of Investigation Proper to It: Reflections on the Bicentennial of the Birth of John Stuart Mill', *The Journal of European Economic History*, Capitalia, Rome, Winter 2005, pp. 573–598; for an insightful analysis of J. S. Mills' philosophy, compared with the philosophies of other leading thinkers in the era of 'Enlightenment', see also John Rawls, *Lectures on the History of Political Philosophy*, ed. Samuel Freeman, Harvard University Press, 2007, pp. 251–316/476p.

41 See the works of Nobel laureate Herbert A. Simon relating to *bounded rationality*.

42 Gary S. Becker: 'The Economic Way of Looking at Life', *Nobel Lecture*, 9 December 1992: www.nobelprize.org/nobel_prizes/economic-sciences/laureates/1992/press.html; and *The Economics of Discrimination*, University of Chicago Press, 15 August 1971, 178 p.; also 'The Great Trailblazer: Economists Everywhere Should Mourn the passing of Gary Becker', *The Economist*, 10 May 2014, p. 65.

43 See Michael J. Sandel, *What Money Can't Buy – The Moral Limits of Markets*, Farrar, Straus and Giroux, New York, 2012, p. 130/244.

44 See his *Sketch for a Historical Picture of the Progress of the Human Mind* which was published posthumously in 1795.

45 James B. Allen, *The Psychology of Happiness in the Modern World – A Social Psychological Approach*, Springer Publishing Co., 2018, p. 360/381p.

46 The suffrage of women in France had to await the late date of 21 April 1944 ordinance of the French Provisional government led by General De Gaulle, while other countries had enfranchised women much earlier (e.g. Turkey did so in 1934).

47 James Miller, op. cit., pp. 39–40.

48 By Luis Filella, 2007, for the United Nations Children's Fund, also available at www.unicef.org.

49 See, for example, the International Museum of the Red Cross and the Red Crescent in Geneva: www.micr.ch.

50 For example, J. C. Sharman, *The Despot's Guide to Wealth Management: On the International Campaign against Grand Corruption*, Cornell University Press, 2017, 261p.

51 Derek Bok, *The Politics of Happiness*, Princeton University Press, 2010, 262p.; also Francis Wade, 'Bhutan's Gross National Shame – 1990s Pogroms against Ethnic Nepalese Still Cast Shadow over Bhutan's *Happiness*', Damak/Nepal, 14 July 2014 in: www.ucanews.com/news/bhutans-gross-national-shame/71401.

52 Joseph Fisher, *BBC News*, 28 September 2017; and 'Getting Myanmar Wrong', and 'The Rohingya Diaspora – Unwanted Everywhere', *The Economist*, 28 October 2017, p. 51 and 46, 27 January 2018 – respectively.

53 See, for example, OECD, *Settling In: OECD Indicators of Immigrant Integration 2012*, 3 December 2012, 173p.

54 See, for example, Commission on Legal Empowerment of the Poor and United Nations Development Programme, *Making the Law Work for Everyone*, vol. 1, 2008, 97p.; and Gerald J. Beyer, 'Economic Rights – Past, Present, and Future', in Thomas Cushman, ed., *Handbook of Human Rights*, Routledge, 2014, article on pp. 291–310/744p.

55 See, for example, Amartya Sen, *Identity and Violence – The Illusion of Destiny*, Norton, 2007, 215p.; and Amine Malouf, *In the Name of Identity: Violence and the Need to Belong*, English translation of *Les Identités meurtrières*, 1998; translated by Barbara Bray, 2000, ISBN 0-14-200257-7.

56 Hansard, 11 November 1947.

57 Peter J. Katzenstein, ed., and author of 'The West as Anglo-America', in: *Anglo-America and its Discontents – Civilizational identities beyond West and East*, pp. 2–3/317p. Citing John Charmley, author of *Churchill: The End of Glory – A Political Biography*, Faber & Faber, 19 February 2009, 776p.
58 Tom Heyden, director of the Peace and Justice Resource Center, 'The 10 Greatest Controversies of Winston Churchill's Career', *BBC News Magazine*, 22 January 2015.
59 See, for example, The U.S. Senate Intelligence Committee Report on Torture, *Committee Study of the Central Agency's Detention and Interrogation Program*, Senate Select Committee on Intelligence [Author], Dianne Feinstein [Foreword], Amazon, 30 December 2014; also 'Torture by Another Name: CIA Used "Water Boarding" on at Least 12 DETAINEES', *Guardian*, 17 October 2015.
60 See, for example, the well-documented report on *Françafrique*: http://fr.wikipedia.org; and http://en.wikipedia.org; also Paul Melly, *The Cosy Relations between France and Africa*, BBC, 13 September 2011, 4p.
61 Congressional sources and news agencies.
62 Chas W. Freeman, former U.S. Ambassador, *The Challenge of Asia*, Speech to the Camden Conference, Main-U.S.A, 17 February 2011, 10p.
63 Richard N. Haass, President of the Council on Foreign Relations, 'The Age of Non-polarity – What Will Follow U.S. Dominance', *Foreign Affairs*, May/June 2008.
64 See for example, Bruno Arcidiacono, *Cinq types de paix – Une histoire des plans de pacification perpétuelle, XVII-XXe siècles* [in French] – title translated: *Five Types of Peace – A History of Perpetual Pacification Plans, XVII – XXth Centuries*, The Graduate Institute Publications, Geneva, 2011, 486p; Peter Singer, *Famine, Affluence, and Morality*, [with a Foreword by Bill and Melinda Gates, p. vii-viii], Oxford University Press, 2016, 86p.; and *SIPRI Yearbooks* of the Stockholm International Peace Research Institute: www.sipriyearbook.org. The SIPRI organization has published data on military expenditures worldwide since 1949 and has analysed their implications for global peace.
65 See Paul S. Rowe, 'Christians in The Middle East – Lebanon', in: *Encyclopedia of Modern Ethnic Conflicts*, 2nd edition, vol. 1, ABC-CLIO, 2016, pp. 464–466/847p. for vols. 1 and 2.
66 Salim al-Hoss (previously a professor at the American University of Beirut) had served five stints as Prime Minister of Lebanon during the turbulent civil war years of 1975–1990 with its appalling destructions and mass murders of an estimated 200,000 people, out of a population of approximately four million inhabitants (see, for example, Marie-Joelle Zahar, 'The Lebanon Civil War, 1975–1990', in Joseph R. Rudolph Jr., ed., *Encyclopedia of Modern Ethnic Conflicts*, vol. 1, 2nd edition, ABC-CLIO, 2016, pp. 346–364/411p.).
67 His speech as President of the Arab Anti-Corruption Organization, delivered in Kuwait, 17 November 2008, reproduced in English in his book 'Lights within the Nation's Vastness', All Prints Distributors & Publishers, Beirut: www.all-prints.com, pp. 301–302; ref. also: www.arabanticorruption.org; additional information is available through 'Transparency International – The Global Coalition against Corruption': www.transparency.org; see also 'Business in Lebanon', *The Economist*, 28 February 2015, pp. 33–34.
68 See, for example, Adeel Malik and Bassem Awadallah, *The Economics of the Arab Spring*, Oxford Centre for the Analysis of Resource Rich Economies, December 2011, 31p.: www.economics.ac.uk.
69 Figures on Palestinian refugees are 'guess-timated'. The Lebanese authorities along with the Palestinian Authorities agreed on 2 February 2017 to carry out a comprehensive and accurate census of Palestinian refugees who are cramped in delimited camps living in dire conditions.
70 See, for example, Jim Muir, 'Lebanon Grants Palestinian Refugees Right to Work', *BBC News*, 17 August 2010.

71 See UN High Commissioner for Refugees, *Global Trends – Forced Displacement in 2015*, pp. 18–21/66p.

72 ILO, *Assessment of the Impact of Syrian Refugees in Lebanon and Their Employment Profile*, Geneva, 2014, 48p.; also Press Conference of Minister of Social Affairs Waël Bou Faour and Minister of Health Rachid Derbas, *L'Orient Le Jour*, Beirut, 5 December 2014; and Amnesty International, *Left Out in the Cold – Syrian Refugees Abandoned by the International Community*, 5 December 2014, 38p; www.amnesty.org.

73 See, for example, Julia Tierney, 'The Diaspora, Debt, Dollarization: Unravelling Lebanon's Resilience to a Sovereign Debt Crisis', *Jadaliya ezine*, 25 May 2015, in: www.jadaliyya.com/pages/index/23250/the-diaspora-debt-and-dollarization_unraveling-leb and Rosalie Berthier, '*Abracada … Broke – Lebanon's Banking on Magic*', 9 May 2017, 16p. in: www.synaps.newtwork/abracada-broke.

74 Keynote Speech by former Prime Minister of Lebanon Fuad Siniora, 'Outlook for the Arab World in the 4th Anniversary of the Arab Spring', *UAE Energy Forum*, Abu-Dhabi, 13 January 2015.

6 Towards an overarching strategy

This monograph's quintessence can be encapsulated into three central issues:

The *first* main issue attempts to fathom the state of *wellbeing* by seeking to disentangle the fundamental and varied components of that multifaceted complex phenomenon.

The *second* issue examined in this monograph concerns conventional definitions of *wellbeing*. It questions the *raison d'être* of focusing exclusively on such parameters as income, consumption of goods and services, expenditures, technological change, and the like. Other factors, notably universal fundamental values, should be prominently included.

The *third* issue is concerned with building an archetype that is sufficiently comprehensive to serve as a composite all-embracing benchmark for evaluating significant changes in the wellbeing of the globe's stakeholders. Such a novel comprehensive benchmark offers us a lens that can help us to deepen and improve our understanding of changes facing humankind, and to manage judiciously the current abode of humans and other species.

The following terminal chapter offers forward-looking views regarding the above-mentioned issues.

Diagnosing the 'State of the Globe'

The terrestrial globe is currently and for the foreseeable future the sole dwelling available to humankind. Fallout of human activities can readily migrate across frontiers. They can thus cover large areas of the globe or its totality, thereby impacting life (e.g. in matters of climate change, weapons of mass destruction, pandemics, toxic products, etc.). These existential catastrophic risks cannot be addressed by the few. They require global cooperation for effectiveness sake. Indeed, lest they get lethally contaminated by the ills of the distressed, the currently rich, secure, and healthy people cannot ignore other people's calamities.

The globe needs therefore to be examined continuously in order to diagnose eventual ailments and weaknesses, to correct nefarious practices and morbidities that could lead to potential disasters, and to examine sound and prudent courses of behaviour. Factually based data should help policy-makers to reach seasoned judgements and judicious decisions that protect the globe and preserve the livelihood of its species.

Calamities can be avoided thanks to truthful information. This is increasingly available (through censuses, surveys, polls, satellite pictures, telecommunications, and other means of measurement). In all circumstances, one has to differentiate the *true* from the *fake*, and the *partial* or *fragmented* information from the *holistic*. One-sided, partial, or unauthenticated information could lead humans to make erroneous judgements, as illustrated by the allegory on the elephant (summarized in Exhibit 6.1).

The senses can transmit fragmentary information that could lead humans to reach unsound judgements and to make flawed decisions. The genuine understanding of phenomena calls for comprehensive, accurate, and objective documentation – along with coherent reasoning – to avoid the distortions of fragmented or illusory perceptions. All possible means of human knowledge (senses, intuition, reason, experience, logic, introspection, etc.) can help us reach *truth*. As new facts come to light, analysts should be able to fill in lacunae, correct past faulty interpretations, and resolve controversies or polemics. *Truth* is multifaceted; it gains from improved methodologies and tools that objectively collect, record, analyse, or synthesize information *in toto* on valid sound bases.[1]

Exhibit 6.1 In search of incontestable truth: the partial and the holistic

A parable generally attributed to Buddhist tradition, states that the followers of a wise king queried him about *truth*. He reportedly told them the story of a few persons struck by the handicap of impaired sight. These persons were invited to describe what they had *touched* – each touching a specific part of a creature until then unknown to them [it was an *elephant*].

The above-mentioned persons had to rely on the limited information each had already gained through their other unimpaired senses. The first person who stroked the tail opined that it was a *rope*; the second person who touched the belly called it a *pot*; the third person who examined the trunk thought it was a *pestle*; and so on. All their surmises turned out to be 'scraps of truth', since each person made use of *incomplete* information. They all missed the 'holistic truth'.

Source: adapted by the author from the source: *The Soka Gakkai Dictionary of Buddhism*: www.sglibrary.org

The above-mentioned 'elephant' metaphor was cited by U.S. Congressman Tom Davis in commenting on the problems of opacity or distortion created by the fragmentation of the U.S. financial regulatory system among several agencies. Each law-enforcement agency, operating separately, captures only a partial view of the financial sector's complex conditions. Indeed, a *bitty* approach of financial regulations is likely to produce distorted views of the sector's performance, risks, flaws, or abuses.[2] A holistic approach is therefore required to reach a full grasp of phenomena under scrutiny. Indeed, focusing on a *fraction* of a phenomenon while occulting other parts would convey an incomplete-cum-false picture. For the truthful grasp of a phenomenon, *fragmented*, or *partial* information needs therefore to be completed by a full synthetic/holistic approach that seizes the subject matter from different perspectives and offers a *comprehensive understanding*. With such *understanding*, policy-makers supported by solid scientific research could formulate *rational* policies and practices capable of being implemented to change current predatory life styles into wholesome ones. Such a change presumes foresight and an indefectible commitment on the part of those who wield power to serve the common good.

Many governmental and non-governmental institutions collect, store, and disseminate extensive reliable data susceptible of being used to map, store, monitor, and evaluate information on changes in the 'State of the Globe'. They include international organizations (such as the World Bank), academic institutions and research centres (such as the *Center for International Development at Harvard University*), media (e.g. *Economist*), business groups, think tanks, etc. The 189 *World Bank* member countries (plus 28 other economies with populations of more than 30,000) are classified so that data users can aggregate, group, and compare statistical data of interest. By tracking all major situations in which *vulnerabilities* and/or *opportunities* are emerging, we could obtain an integrated multifaceted 'State of the Globe' report that evaluates significant changes. This will prove a welcome complement to existing *partial measurement* techniques.

For an illustration of a 'partial measurement' technique, one can mention the 'carbon footprint' index that applies to countries, cities, enterprises, institutions, etc. The said index measures the relative dependence of economic actors on 'dirty' high carbon fossil fuels (coal and/or petroleum), instead of 'green' energy (such as solar and wind farms). Among the respected indices in this field, we can mention: Leadership in Energy and Environmental Design (LEED), the Siemens Green City Index, the STAR (Sustainability Tools for Assessing and Rating Communities) System, Oil Change International, etc.[3]

The proposed 'State of the Globe' can be initially a sketchy incomplete portrait in view of the absence of reliable and comprehensive data. In the absence of accurate information on certain key features of the globe (e.g. changes in the desertification), a surrogate can be used (e.g. changes in green spaces). Estimates will be subject to correction if and when accurate information becomes available to correct errors and/or fill in gaps.

The publication of the report on the 'State of the Globe' could be made on an annual basis for some data (e.g. per capita income, growth or regression rates in the production or consumption of basic commodities, births/deaths rates, accidents/criminal records, employment, pollution, etc.), and over longer periods for other data (e.g. detailed population censuses). Past data from censuses or surveys can be updated, corrected and/or completed as reliable data become available. Thanks to the great strides made by 'information systems' and the enormous capacity of contemporary computers to crunch vast numbers and inputs, yearly reporting becomes quite feasible. For the sake of collecting and analysing data objectively, it may be worthwhile to envisage that such a report on the 'State of the Globe' be researched and published under the aegis of an international neutral multi-talented multifaceted agency, such as the United Nations University.

In assessing changes in global wellbeing over time, we could start with a period that ushered momentous transformations, and for which reliable data are reasonably available. It is plausible to consider the period on the eve of the take-off of the *Industrial Revolution* (in the late eighteenth century in England) as a base period. Current and future changes in the composition of 'clusters of wellbeing' of the proposed normative archetype (ref. Exhibit 1.1) will then be measured and evaluated, by reference to the base period (namely the start of the *Industrial Revolution*).

The careful investigation of positive and negative factors that have affected the globe (or parts thereof) could enable human groups to draw lessons from *past* crises or calamities in the hope of avoiding or effectively controlling *future* ones. Existing indicators of progress (or regression) in wellbeing will have to be carefully chosen, duly fine-tuned or corrected, and properly weighted. Researchers have a vast field of investigation with potentially productive results for the overarching goals of protecting life and prosperity in our planet. Within these goals, the eradication of *destitution* and the taming of *aggressiveness* are likely to remain humanity's top twin grails![4] Issues raised in this monograph will further enlighten our reflections on humanity's prospects with respect to progress in wellbeing.

Science and universal values working in tandem

Progress encompasses all domains of human activity. Judging from the experiences and achievements so far realized by the human species, one can argue that humans have progressed in a ratcheting-up process in selected fields. This concerns notably the fields of science and technology. *Science* can be defined as 'the attempt to understand and explain natural phenomena by using systematic, preferably measurable, observation or experiment, and to apply reason for the knowledge thereby obtained to infer testable laws and make predictions or retrodictions'.[5] *Technology* stands for the tools used in the practical application of scientific knowledge. Decision-makers and analysts in business and government often consider that cutting edge scientific-technological know-how represents 'the decisive competitive factor' for wealth-creation over the long term in a modern economy.[6]

Global cooperation in the scientific-technological field is a potent factor for alleviating poverty, protecting health, and advancing human wellbeing.[7] Conversely, scientific-technological advances could be used to exploit, dominate, or annihilate other humans or living creatures. *Progress* needs therefore to be anchored in universal socio-ethical values, around which all humans should adhere at all times and in all places – despite cultural, philosophical, ideological, or spiritual differences.[8] *Scientific-technological progress* devoid of fundamental *universal values* can lead humans astray; this is why the two forces need to be interlocked. Otherwise, technological progress could be a source of harm and regression if it falls in the hands of evil persons.

To ascertain their validity and predictability, scientific findings need to be continuously corroborated by evidence from additional research buttressed by empirical observations that probe more deeply and more widely the investigated phenomena. For the sake of truth, science requires the continuous verification of hypotheses or theories through comprehensive empirical observations, in order to confirm valid interpretations that decode reality and offer workable solutions to encountered problems. Previous scientific findings have, therefore, to be validated by completed data, updating, and/or re-examination of hypotheses. This should well lead to the reinterpretation or revision of hitherto held verisimilitudes, views or beliefs resulting from 'partial' knowledge, egregious errors, or flawed analyses. Indeed, knowledge can be obtained through additional evidence thanks to appropriate tools for collecting data, ascertaining their authenticity and accuracy, and analysing and synthesizing them objectively.

Proclaimed truths in various fields are often provisional and need to be subjected to continuous scrutiny in order to avoid surmises, truncated information, faked data, or manipulated information. Errors, imperfections or lacunae can be addressed in due course, as more accurate or comprehensive data are collected and analysed, and as evidence is sifted and evaluated by sound methodologies. Yet, it is not unusual to find widespread lack of transparency or unreliable figures (some would say cheating for self-interest) by state and private groups. This has been well illustrated by reference to world oil with respect to its supply and demand, oil reserves, production costs, profits, etc.[9]

Humans are increasingly expanding their knowledge in all domains, thereby reducing the scope for conjecture or speculation, and relying on the scientific method based on the 'right to doubt', inquisitiveness, and testing. It is important to admit, in genuine humility, that a vast range of phenomena, despite giant strides in the advancement of erudition and science, will forever remain inexplicable or unknowable – i.e. beyond the perception or grasp of human mind, senses, and/or consciousness. Past and current limitations on humans' capability of comprehending phenomena have not deterred individuals from pursuing their natural curiosity for learning, using new approaches and tools, direct and indirect, to discover, identify, measure and evaluate diverse phenomena.

In all circumstances, one should admit that there are limits to the effectiveness of various cognitive techniques that are currently available or being developed by epistemologists. Our senses and our intellect are incapable of comprehending the totality of phenomena affecting humans and the cosmos. Given the human make-up, some realities tend to elude our intelligence, perception, or senses. Among scholars who have propounded the holistic approach, one can cite Edgar Morin's work on epistemology, *La Méthode*.[10]

Phenomena in various fields, notably in the social and cultural, are influenced by dynamic and complex intractable forces not readily conveyable into deterministic quantitative models. A few such phenomena are unpredictable, while others are not amenable to accurate measurement. Reason is incapable of grasping and/or analysing logically all phenomena, and vast domains are not accessible to the human mind or senses. No matter how learned they become, humans cannot reach the state of omniscience. Their faculties (reason and senses), aided by their most sophisticated tools, do not allow them to fathom or comprehend fully all aspects of the universe's components.

Systems of beliefs tend to address certain phenomena (such as the metaphysical ones) which cannot be perceived or comprehended through the senses and reason. They are generally based on dogma, and their precepts or prescriptions need not be corroborated by *scientific evidence*. The latter calls for *inquisitiveness*, *doubt*, and *testing* in the process of discovering 'truth'.[11] In the absence of scientifically investigated and demonstrated rational explanations of reality, some turn to spiritual, mystical, shamanistic, or animistic interpretations. A few thinkers consider that in the pursuit of truth, certain current *scientific laws* are tentative and are subject to further testing to confirm their validity.[12]

Gurus and other charismatic individuals have, since ancient times, inspired disciples and communities to follow teachings that are not based on natural laws. Religious faith, as conveyed by scriptures, is generally based on absolute trust in dogmatic beliefs. Depending on cultures, these beliefs comprise: spiritual revelations, worship of one or multiple deities, shamanism, miracles, mysteries, ghosts, angels, magic, mysticism, myths, legends, animistic traditions, superstition, and other transcendental, supernatural, or conjectural beliefs. Systems of beliefs do not require scientific verification or testing by their adherents; they are generally based on dogma. If misused, these systems of belief can lead to fundamentalism, bigotry and intolerance vis-à-vis rival systems.[13]

Over the centuries, humanity's challenges have become increasingly interconnected and complex. They currently present the risk of having local problems grow into serious crises that migrate to other regions of planet Earth, and possibly threaten humanity at large. This applies to various vital domains such as: economic and social crises (e.g. widespread famines), threats to health (e.g. pandemics), security catastrophes (e.g. global nuclear cataclysm), human rights abuses (genocides, and crimes against humanity), nature's upheavals (earthquakes, flooding, severe climatic upheavals, asteroid crashes, etc.), energy crises, or dangerous industrial/urban waste (that could stifle living creatures, destroy the productivity of land, the potableness of water, the quality of seas and oceans, or the salubriousness of habitat).

Mutating characteristics: a business leadership's model

The phenomenon of human wellbeing has multiple dimensions. Throughout this book's analyses, we have been concerned with improving the *quality of life* for humankind. The latter involves improvements in business/economic life, as well as improvements in other domains such as health, intellect, emotions, behaviour – to mention a few. In this section, we focus on the challenge of mutating human characteristics from the standpoint of business/economic achievements. More specifically, we focus on 'model-characteristics' of business leadership that could be developed in humankind to enhance economic prosperity and people's wellbeing.

Leaders can be generally identified by reference to a few key characteristics. Hereafter, we focus on those in the socio-economic field. These persons are recognized by: their clear vision and their effective strategies; their capability to innovate or apply profitably others' innovations; their aptitude at recruiting, training, and retaining human talents in their enterprise; their capacity at overcoming crises; and their genuine concern for the fair treatment of their stakeholders.[14] Business leaders do not constitute a homogeneous cohort – whether in their thoughts, strategies, styles of command, and/or in other respects. The pith of leadership is in germinating ideas and actions that can improve the status quo. Leaders inspire and spark energies to attain ambitious goals. Their achievements owe much to their creative visions, and their rigour in implementing high standards of governance.

In an open and competitive market (i.e. assuming the absence of monopolistic practices), profits generated over the long term by a given company in a given country could be used as an indicator of success, signifying that consumers/users approve of the firm's products or services. Nevertheless, the *fair* split of benefits among its various categories of stakeholders (entrepreneurs, investors/owners, lenders, managers, various categories of employees, suppliers, contractors or subcontractors, and other concerned parties) is a challenging operation for business leaders. To avoid crippling disputes, *fair* sharing among *stakeholders* can be judged by reference to a few criteria. These include adequate compensation for efficiency, innovation, judicious risk-taking, bearing hardships, assuming demanding responsibilities, loyalty, and ethical behaviour. To reach a balanced split of value-created among stakeholders, soundly based and rigorously conducted investigations should help.[15]

In a multilateral and multi-stakeholder open world economy, the value creation chain is likely to span several business entities (the final seller, along with various intermediaries and sub-contractors) operating in several jurisdictions before reaching the ultimate consumers. The higher the number of independent jurisdictions in the supply chain, the higher is the scope for potential risks that could escape transnational systematic regulatory compliance (e.g. regarding forced labour victims, honest reporting, pollution controls, quality of products, safe and salubrious working conditions, money laundering, and other problems). Malpractices are likely to occur when regulatory loopholes blur the traceability of a complex product that has been handled through multiple business entities or channels, and has been the subject of successive industrial transformations in separate jurisdictions. Indeed, several companies (notably trans-national corporations) take advantage of locating their business activities or booking their transactions in 'offshore' jurisdictions that have no or little regulations that protect all stakeholders' legitimate rights, notably those of host governments' fiscal rights and workers' decent employment conditions.[16]

Under public opinion pressures, the International Chamber of Commerce has recommended a code of conduct for its members that (largely composed of sizeable trans-national firms). These firms have in their supply chains sub-contractors operating in various jurisdictions. Central management of a trans-national corporation may lose track in comprehensively monitoring all the activities relating to its products (with its multiple intricate sources of suppliers/ sub-contractors in a globalizing world economy). A few of these sub-contractors may seek to evade regulations, and their dereliction of duties is occasionally condoned by local authorities. Indeed, the writ of the federal or central governments does not reach local jurisdictions – for reason of corruption, organized crime, bureaucratic gridlocks, and other constraints.

A few trans-national companies may have little incentive to eradicate shabby practices or abuses by their sub-contractors or suppliers, especially if such behaviour is tolerated by host governments. Abuses would include: employees' over-work at miserly pay; exposure to toxic products, hazardous waste, and/or accident-prone unsafe equipment; unsafe working conditions (sweatshops, dangerous mines, time-worn structures, exposure to severe climatic conditions); slummy polluted neighbourhoods; discrimination against women; bonded 'child and adult' labour; sub-quality products; and other violations of laws and good practices. These problems have been abundantly reported.[17]

Codes of conduct become meaningfully effective if they are coupled with governmental regulatory agencies' rigorous sanctions for abuses (e.g. in matters of workers' exploitation and other human rights violations, bribe solicitation or extortion, and other issues – as adopted by the 42 governments of the OECD in their *Guidelines for Multinational Enterprises*, updated on 25 May 2011.[18] According to the International Chamber of Commerce:

> Companies are responsible for ensuring the quality and safety of their products, and for minimizing the negative environmental impact of these products especially when they reach the end of their life-cycle. A number of sectors have already voluntarily integrated this aspect of 'customer responsibility' in their approach to product design and management, such as white goods manufacturers and car manufacturers, while in some jurisdictions these requirements are even mandated by law.[19]

Numerous individuals are happier to take hold of their lives through launching their own businesses. Their independence in running their own business gives meaning to their life. Several quarters praise the significant role of these entrepreneurial '*self-employed*' (usually micro-small businesses) in so far as they generate benefits for themselves and for their stakeholders – through *innovation*, *job creation*, *GDP growth*, and the *spread of wealth*.[20]

Entrepreneurial business leaders (often subject to encomiums) are a breed of pioneers who seek to *change* things for the better, using inter alia *innovations* (technical or managerial, small or blockbuster). They are generally highly motivated promethean individuals whose *raison d'être* and deep *pleasure* is in their quest to create. Innovations need not necessarily be generated by business leaders themselves; they can be bought from third parties (inventors, researchers and developers, patents' owners, and others).

Entrepreneurs have to be distinguished from *replicators* of existing business models or run-of-the-mill *imitators*. In their bandwagon behaviour, the imitative persons seek primarily their own employment. A high-intensity motive for entrepreneurs is the realization of high net profits from the success of their activities. They hope to realize these profits in due course (i) by converting their privately owned enterprise into one with publicly traded shares, or (ii) by selling their business to another business group. Legislation in various countries levies lower taxes on entrepreneurs' capital gains realized from the total or partial sale of their enterprises, compared with revenues obtained from salaried work or the payment of pensions. Such differentiation is intended to favour risk-taking in entrepreneurial activities.[21]

Entrepreneurs are likely to flourish in propitious environments, as expressed by Peter Nijkamp:

> ... the entrepreneur is increasingly conceived of as the critical change agent who has to reach the highest performance in a competitive system. He or she has to face externalities of various kinds (e.g. in industrial districts), but is also the creator of new initiatives ... From a spatial perspective the entrepreneur has to excel in terms of local embeddedness, global orientation, exploitation of proximity advantages, use of clustering and network principles and access to advanced knowledge circuits.[22]

Among the often-cited interpretations of the entrepreneurial function, one could refer to Joseph Schumpeter's works. He considers entrepreneurs as creators-innovators-developers whose impact shows up in disruptive innovation that replaces existing products or processes by new ones. He argues that

> the function of the entrepreneurs is to reform or revolutionize the pattern of production ... by exploiting an invention or, more generally, an untried technology possibly for producing a new commodity or producing an old one in a new way, by opening up a new source of supply of materials or a new outlet for products, by reorganizing an industry and so on.[23]

Reflecting on the history of the productive apparatus, Schumpeter argues that

> the opening up of new markets, foreign or domestic, and the organizational development from the craft shop and factory to such concerns as U.S. Steel illustrate the same process of mutation ... that incessantly revolutionizes the economic structure *from within*, incessantly destroying the old one, incessantly creating a new one. This process of Creative Destruction is the essential fact about capitalism.[24]

One should note that the introduction of *new* products can enlarge the spectrum of choices available to users or consumers, without necessarily 'destroying' the demand for already existing products or processes of production so as to make them ipso facto obsolete. Moreover, entrepreneurs can promote the development of 'new needs' for consumption or use that did not exist before; they can also reduce the economic 'life span' of their existing products (i.e. programme their 'obsolescence' over relatively short periods) in order to sustain or increase their sales with new products whereby manufacturers build the expiry of their products so that consumers will be forced to replace them.

Programmed obsolescence has been resorted to by major transnational companies such as Apple, Samsung, Epson, HP, Brother, and Canon. France is the only country so far [2018] to have in its judicial arsenal a law [effective 2015] that condemns *programmed obsolescence* as a crime [with the culprit company being fined up to 5 per cent of its annual sales and the responsible executives facing up to two years jail term]. French prosecutors have launched a probe against some of the above-mentioned companies, starting at the end of 2017.[25] The Italian authorities, through their antitrust/consumer-protection investigations, have sought since January 2018 to find out whether some of the above-mentioned companies espoused 'a general commercial policy taking advantage of the lack of certain components to curb the performance times of their products and induce customers to buy new versions'.[26] Fines, according to Italy's national consumer code, could well run into millions of euro.

Categorization of business leaders based on one or few characteristics blurs the uniqueness of each entrepreneur by reference to strengths or weaknesses.[27] Possibly, an indispensable feature of *enduring leadership* is 'enlightened judgement'. While extolling the above characteristics of an entrepreneurial person, it is not uncommon to find entrepreneurs lacking in skills to manage judiciously all aspects of a complex enterprise (that comprise material, human, and financial resources; clientele; government relations; research and development; etc.).

No two business leaders are identical with reference to their character, mettle, motivation, style of leadership, or approach to their stakeholders. Entrepreneurs, in particular, have diverse idiosyncrasies with respect to their innate personal characteristics and talents, acquired skills, or styles of behaviour. They can have a mixture of positive and negative characteristics that could well change over time. Some characteristics are generally considered positive (e.g. avant-gardist, perfectionist, patient, appreciative, responsive, decisive, reflective, empathic, charismatic, readily reactive to changes in environments or contexts, susceptible to drawing lessons from past experiences, etc.). Other characteristics are mostly viewed as negative (e.g. abrasive, irascible, bombastic, obsessed by hubris status, authoritative, manipulative, greedy, egomaniac, inconsistent, inconsiderate, callous, etc.). Authors of biographies could diverge in their interpretations of events and in their evaluation of the characteristics of any given person.[28]

Nevertheless, to be considered a *business paragon* or *icon of achievement*, a few inter-related key clusters of characteristics are deemed pivotal, taken together.

Six clusters of factors are proposed hereafter as fundamental to the locus of business leadership and entrepreneurship: (1) *vision and ambition* that enhance capabilities of seizing or creating opportunities, (2) *unfailing intrepidness* in pursuing tenaciously goals coupled with resilience in overcoming setbacks or crises, (3) *sound strategies* that allow balanced partaking in value creation among stakeholders, (4) *strong motivation* in the pursuit of set goals, (5) *sustainable performance*, and (6) *ethical concerns*. These six pillars could serve in building a composite benchmark for the measurement of the quality of persons at the helm of businesses.

First: vision and ambition

A potential 'business leader' can be distinguished from the rank and file by reference to key characteristics, innate and/or acquired. Among these one can list an insatiable curiosity to probe, combined with an auspicious flair and intuition for *spotting, seizing, and/or creating opportunities*. The said entrepreneur does not await passively such opportunities. As a bellwether resourceful leader, she/he can separate the wheat from the chaff. Thinking 'out of the box', iconoclastic entrepreneurs have a natural inclination to disregard 'conventional wisdom'. Often called unorthodox or maverick, such entrepreneurs have the courage to depart from current methods or techniques, of production or management. As trailblazers, they overcome prevailing resistance to change, complacency and faintheartedness by supporting novel bold projects, and seek to develop them as new paths to of wealth creation. They are capable of extracting profit-making solutions out of current problems.

Entrepreneurs can use novel technologies or ameliorate existing ones. Although an entrepreneur need not be an inventor of new technologies, she/he has nevertheless the capacity of comprehending existing and evolving technologies and putting them to optimal use. In seeking higher levels of efficiency and performance, entrepreneurs' inventiveness can also focus on the judicious re-organization or re-structuring of their business activities.

An 'entrepreneurial leader' has therefore the capacity of converting an embryonic model into a successful going concern. Starting with a blueprint, the entrepreneur's next stage is to create a workable prototype. Her/his subsequent challenge would then be to produce efficiently and for profitable commercialization the refined model. In proposing concrete workable solutions, the entrepreneur relies on relevant insights, inventiveness and experiences. Honed by common sense, careful reasoning, and various expertise, her/his performance will be evaluated by reference to the criteria of growth in sales and net profits over the medium-long term. In the field of business creativity, examples of serial innovators have been studied by researchers, and due attention has been given to those with *breakthrough* innovations compared with *small* ones whose cumulative impact could, nevertheless, be quite significant.

An 'entrepreneurial leader', with a creative vision and sound strategies, aims therefore at surpassing the performance of her/his closest competitors.

Second: intrepidness

Another characteristic of an 'entrepreneurial leader' is that of a *resolute character that does not dither*. S/he craves to realize her/his project, and accept for that purpose to bear willingly and for a while personal sacrifices (in material resources, rest, or leisure). Their sacrifices do not wipe out their own perception of the subjective worth of their activities which they deem superior to those of salaried people.[29] Such creative risk-daring entrepreneurs will try to tap resources from their families, their circle of acquaintances, and potential partners – before seeking funds from risk capitalists. The trials and tribulations of starting a new business require tenacity, endurance, and unwavering commitment over the medium/long term to her/his chosen project, regardless of the vagaries of unfolding circumstances. Steadfastness and perseverance need not preclude flexibility in re-adapting the project in line with new unfolding conditions.

The above-mentioned characteristic of intrepidness is undergirded by ambition, zeal, a well-founded appetite for risk-taking, and avoidance of procrastination. Knowing that risk is an integral part of existence and without being reckless or feckless, the entrepreneur's intrepidness needs to be underpinned by knowledge, will, resoluteness, enthusiasm, and genuine pleasure derived from 'expected successes' in the fructification of the targeted project. A successful entrepreneur generally does not buckle under the strain of work pressure and has the capacity to withstand crises. She/he derives considerable satisfaction from overcoming obstacles to achieve the desired objectives. *Intrepidness* calls for *persistence* on the part of entrepreneurs. Barring delusional objectives, *persistence* will be rewarded by expected (a) *financial returns*, (b) satisfaction in being in the *driver's seat* to run one's enterprise, (c) recognition and esteem expressed by stakeholders, family, and/or the community; and (d) genuine wellbeing.[30]

Third: sound strategies

Far from buccaneering oligarchs or crony capitalism,[31] a role model 'entrepreneurial leader' is recognized for her/his sound conduct. That conduct becomes a vital strategic *asset* that enhances the economic performance of the enterprise, as it gains in image and goodwill vis-à-vis customers, employees, partners, regulatory agencies, and others. In particular, customers' loyalty to the firm is bound to increase when the quality and other terms of the product are respected; employees' fair treatment is likely to pay off with responsible work and less squandered time; partners, contractors, and financial intermediaries are likely to treat the firm favourably; regulatory agencies are likely to avoid harassing law-abiding firms with superfluous controls; etc.

Observance of ethical principles in business encompasses multiple dimensions. These include delivering products as contracted, the decent treatment of workers-collaborators (not as underlings but as essential contributors to wealth creation), the balanced allocation of benefits and costs among stakeholders, and the effective compliance with legal-civic responsibilities. Predatory and vampire-like practices are thus shunned – such as the (a) exploitation of users, consumers, workers, or sub-contractors (through monopolistic practices, constraint of trade, usury, corruption, counterfeiting, cheating, or abuse of human rights), health problems and accident injuries, or (b) degradation of the ecosystem (through pollution and contamination of the environment, waste of resources, and other negative externalities). By complying with good governance, and honouring commitments, an entrepreneur infuses stakeholders with trust, and motivates them to exercise their best efforts in furthering the prosperity of the enterprise.

Business ethics and codes of conduct could be likened to an intangible productive asset – other things remaining equal. Indeed, such conduct can generate the trust of customers who will maintain their loyalty to the firm's products, and will incentivize key contributors to that firm's value creation, such as workers/collaborators, partners, financiers, etc.[32]

Fourth: strong motivation

Researchers in psychology have probed the forces that underpin human behaviour. Abraham Harold Maslow (1908–1970) pioneered a theory of a hierarchy of human needs and the positive motives for their satisfaction. He argues that humans are first and foremost motivated by satisfying their biological and physiological needs (air, food, drink, shelter, temperate climate, sleep, sex, etc.). This is followed by four supplementary layers of needs to be satisfied, ranked sequentially as follows: safety, belongingness to a group, esteem, and finally self-actualization and fulfilment.[33] Quoting one scholar,

> ... many critics have claimed that in placing self-actualization over, say, the need for love and the need to belong, Maslow was favouring Western-style individualism over the more relationship-oriented view of human life and human needs one finds in many other cultures.[34]

Other scholars have developed similar paradigms of human motivation, emphasizing certain factors in the light of their own experiences and research. Indeed, the universe of leadership is protean, boasting singular humdinger personalities for those who outshine. We present hereafter three such *entrepreneurial models*: (i) the *egocentric*, prompted essentially by 'self-centred control' over their business in the expectation of increasing their gain; (ii) the *stakeholders-inclusive*, motivated by the entrepreneur's quest for a 'balanced satisfaction' of customers, employees, investors, and other stakeholders; and (iii) the *community-driven* when the entrepreneur's top priority is 'service' to a praiseworthy cause of a group of people or to society at large.

i Self-centred egotistic entrepreneurs, albeit multifarious, have in common the primacy of self-promotion. Thanks to an acute sense of pride in their personal success, they often have an insatiable desire to perform (measured by generating income and wealth for themselves). With a proclivity for elitist self-esteem verging occasionally on narcissism, the said entrepreneurs focus primarily on their own interests, relegating the legitimate interests of other stakeholders, with whom they have difficulties in empathizing.

Many researchers have acknowledged that the pursuit of *personal gain* is a high-intensity motivation in business creation and development. The fundamental challenge, however, is to guard against the possibility that this pursuit could fall onto the slippery slope of *hubris and greed* (as business leaders get lured and mesmerized by personal gain much in excess of their contribution to the value pie), *foolhardy risks* (objectively unjustified, and resulting from presumptuous arrogance), *short-termism* (favouring immediate benefits at the expense of sustainable benefits), and/or *predation* (encroaching on other stakeholders legitimate rights). Egocentric entrepreneurs could encounter difficulties in: recruiting and retaining *talented collaborators*, forging mutually beneficial and stable relationships with *reliable partners* and *subcontractors*, or winning the *loyalty of consumers/users* – all these parties fearing becoming prey. This category of egocentric entrepreneurs is less likely to accept advice to readily correct their methods or practices.

ii Stakeholder-inclusive entrepreneurs are recognized for their due consideration towards their stakeholders. They are typically driven by a culture of inclusiveness, fairness, and partaking among all stakeholders. In so doing, these entrepreneurs attract and keep talents, earn the loyalty of collaborators, build mutually beneficial and reliable business relations among partners and contractors, and satisfy consumers' legitimate expectations. Modern organizational theory of strategic management has emphasized the positive role of 'balanced partaking' among *stakeholders* thus:

> The conventional notion that the corporation should create wealth only for its shareowners is incorrect. The corporation should be redefined to emphasize its relationships with and responsibilities toward *all* [*sic*] stakeholders, both voluntary and involuntary ... The stakeholder model of the corporation fits in with broadly accepted normative and ethical considerations.[35]

Stakeholder-inclusive entrepreneurs are characterized by a sense of responsibility extending beyond their own narrow self-interest. They endeavour to balance stakeholders' interests with appropriate compensation in order to serve the long-term goals of their enterprise. They are concerned with 'proportionality' of benefits skilfully and subtly distributed among their stakeholders. Though difficult to calibrate, attain, and/or maintain durably in a dynamic world, an entrepreneur's managerial philosophy based on team work and balanced sharing of the value pie with her/his diverse stakeholders strengthens the zeal of all parties concerned in the pursuit of performance goals. Judicious compromises reduce sources of conflict between management and workers or employees, enhance productivity, eliminate despondency or neglect, and protect against stress, anxiety, or sickness.

Empirical evidence has shown that business leaders who embrace 'process fairness' reduce discontent, enhance efficiency, generate support for new strategic initiatives, and promote an environment of creativity and performance. Business leaders' *balanced and fair* distribution of the 'net value created' among stakeholders (commensurate with each party's contribution over time) is nevertheless a difficult task to implement.[36]

iii Community-driven entrepreneurs or business leaders generally espouse the goal of *service to a given community*, or a segment thereof. Also called 'social entrepreneurs' (in so far as they seek innovative solutions for solving society's most pressing problems), their activities can be illustrated by such priorities as: (a) non-polluting sustainable projects, (b) micro-business, (c) gender and ethnic equality, (d) salubrious affordable housing, (e) decent jobs for poverty alleviation, (f) mutual help within the community, (g) fair trade, (h) needed infrastructures, (i) healthy quality products at reasonable prices, and other praiseworthy missions (local or extra-local). Social entrepreneurs are distinguishable from the category of unpaid volunteers or charity dispensers, in so far as they are generally innovative in running their activities and expect to be reasonably remunerated for their services. Yet, they are less driven by sole pursuit of personal profit or by cupidity, and more by purpose. Indeed, they seek compensation for their services at more moderate levels, compared with the self-centred entrepreneurs bent on maximizing their own benefits.

Several scholars have analysed the motives, strategies, and accomplishments of these entrepreneurs where the spirit of 'doing good' is omnipresent. *Community-driven* entrepreneurs have generally a modest parsimonious lifestyle, in comparison with self-centred counterparts. They normally derive deep personal satisfaction from their community-activities. Heightened recognition and prestige conferred by the general public onto these entrepreneurs' valuable role in society could attract others to follow suit.[37] One should emphasize that activities favouring a specific portion of a community could be at variance with serving the *common good* of the whole community, should *needier* members be excluded from these activities.

Distinctions among business leaders with respect to their motivations (the self-centred, the stakeholders-inclusive, or the community-driven) are not always clear-cut. Each of the above-mentioned business behaviours can be *rationalized* by the entrepreneurs concerned as serving best their enterprise. Some entrepreneurs may change their behaviours over time, prompted by a variety of motives.

Fifth: sustainable performance

The attractiveness of a business project is measured by reference to multiple criteria, often inter-related. Chief among the commonly used criteria by the business community is the project's *financial returns* distributed to investors, calculated over various time horizons, depending on the *investors'* preferences. Criteria of concern to other stakeholders comprise notably (a) terms of employment and compensation for *workers/employees*, (b) the uninterrupted satisfaction of *consumers'* exigencies, and (c) significant contributions to the *community* through local employment, tax payments, and positive externalities (such as easy access to health-care centres, public transport, and other infrastructures).

The results obtained by start-up entrepreneurs are mixed. One researcher (Shikhar Ghosh, senior lecturer at Harvard Business School) estimated that three-quarters of their funders in the United States had failed to recuperate their invested capital. His research covered over 2,000 companies that had received venture capital funding of at least $1 million from 2004 to 2010. Specifically,

> ... if failure means liquidating all assets, with investors losing all their money, an estimated 30% to 40% of high potential U.S. start-ups fail. If failure is defined as failing to see the projected return on investment – say a specific rate or date to break even on cash flow – then more than 95% of start-ups fail.[38]

The above-mentioned financial performance does not take into consideration costs other than the financial ones (i.e. besides the loss of investments). Non-financial costs include: absence of social life, insomnia, angst, breakdown of social relations, alienation of collaborators, risks of divorce and family estrangement, dysfunctional attitudes, addiction to alcohol or drugs, loss of friends and mentors, loss of credibility vis-à-vis funders, nervous breakdowns, and other problems.

Reducing business leadership to the above-mentioned pillars could be limiting. Indeed, many analysts and research institutions have identified other key factors to account for diverse situations and complex reality.[39]

Sixth: ethical concerns

Leadership in business needs to be underpinned by ethical values. Creators and developers of businesses cannot be solely motivated by profit-making for themselves and the other shareholders. Many have given their *social responsibility* a high importance. This concern gets translated in such matters as protection of employees with respect to offering decent working conditions, ethnic diversity, environmental salubrity, gender equality, gay rights, combatting discriminations (religious or racial discrimination, or xenophobia), etc.

Some business leaders view social responsibility not just as an intrinsically desirable ethical goal. They consider it also a vital source of harmony and motivation for their workers and employees to create value for their enterprises.[40]

In the 'Mutating characteristics' section (p. 243), we have reviewed human superior achievements in one domain, namely that of business. Some scholars have argued that science can enable us to make comprehensive enhancements in all attributes or characteristics of existing humans so as to produce a new 'species' that is *permanently superior* to the existing one. That jump into a superior creature shows up in the important characteristics – notably in wholesomeness, life longevity, superior intellect, benevolent sentiments, etc. The challenges facing the creation of the *transhuman* species are reviewed hereafter in the next section.

Beyond the *Anthropocene* era and the transhuman ambitions

Humans are entering a new geological age, the *Anthropocene*, defined as the period during which human activity has had a harmful influence on planet Earth's climate and environment. Several intellectuals (hailing from geology, ecology, biology, genetics, engineering, neurology, psychology, sociology, cosmology, philosophy, ethics, etc.) believe that the *Industrial Revolution* has produced a considerable negative impact on the functioning of the Earth (for example through *greenhouse* warming and climate change). Humans have been responsible for accumulated waste, rapid depletion of finite resources, rising anthropogenic pollution owing to CO_2 emissions, significant reductions in biodiversity, notable reductions in arable and forested lands, desertification, etc. Some scientific researchers fear that: 'Global warming and many other human-driven changes to the environment are raising concerns about the future of Earth's environment and its ability to provide the services required to maintain viable human civilizations.'[41]

Visions of the future regarding 'human progress in wellbeing' stretch from the *overly optimists* on one extreme, to the *utter pessimists* on the other extreme. The *overly optimists* belong to the 'transhumanists' group who believe that

> nanotechnologies will be embedded in our brains and other organs; our genes will be redesigned to eliminate aging and maybe even death by natural causes; synthetic biology will compensate for the diminishment of Darwinian-evolved biodiversity … Humans will colonise and terraform Mars and eventually Earth-like planets throughout the galaxy …

The *utter pessimists* group belongs

> to the eco-apocalyptic vision [in which] the ocean will acidify and stagnate; sea levels will rise precipitously; cycles of flood and drought will intensify; crops will fail; diseases will proliferate; resource wars will ensue; nation states will evolve into failed states; the human population will crash; the remnants will be led by sociopathic warlords; and an irreversible Dark Age will descend on what remains of humanity.[42]

Several thinkers believe that:

> … there is no steady accretion of advances towards greater civilization or even human decency over a long period of time. It can all be taken away

> terrifyingly quickly [as the return of torture in America, justified by the war on terror] ... Advances in science and technology do not run in parallel with improvement in civilizational values, and the growth in human knowledge does not go with any increase in reasonableness.

John Gray characterizes the quintessence of the human species as 'predatory' owing to its inexorable drive for the *egocentric domination* of planet Earth. He uses for that characteristic the term 'homo rapiens' speculating that 'Earth may have no choice but to evict us over the long term.'[43]

In the same vein as that espoused by John Gray, ecologists argue that giving overriding primacy to the satisfaction of human needs (namely the *anthropocentric*) at the expense of all the other constituents of planet Earth is a threat to both *human survival* and *nature's integrity*.[44] *Anthropocentric* environmentalists support 'a sustained, healthy, and beautiful environment ... because it is essential to human well-being. They argue the value of nature is thus derived from how it affects humans.'[45]

Pessimistic views regarding humankind's have been expressed by other contemporary thinkers, among whom one could cite Pankaj Mishra. In his richly referenced book *Age of Anger*, he laments the state of the world in the early twenty-first century, where:

> endemic war and persecution have rendered an unprecedented sixty million people homeless. Endless misery provokes many desperate Latin Americans, Asians and Africans to make the risky journey to what they see as the centre of successful modernity. Yet more and more individuals and groups – African-Americans in American Cities, Palestinians in Occupied Territories, Muslims in India and Myanmar, to African and Middle Eastern refugees in European camps and asylum-seekers imprisoned on remote Pacific Islands – are now seen as superfluous.[46]

Transhumanist thinkers argue that it is possible to transmute permanently the human species through genetics, and cutting-edge technology. They believe that the human species can break away from its current biological limitations, and enhance permanently its physical, psychic, mental, emotional, and moral characteristics. Accordingly, they seek to stave off ageing, raise significantly human intelligence and capabilities, sustain youthfulness, elongate healthy life, eliminate involuntary suffering, control aggressive feelings, strengthen emotional wellbeing, avert various categories of diseases or vulnerabilities, exercise their creative leadership, or augment resilience. Such speculations of mutating to the 'better' were already expressed in ancient times (similar to the aspirations of *Gilgamesh* [two parts divine and one part human] in accordance with the Akkadian-Sumerian epic poem dating prior to the twenty-first century BC).

In modern times, one could refer to the fictional creation of a new humanoid out of body parts, as per Mary Shelley's novel *Frankenstein; or, The Modern Prometheus* [1818]. According to Mary Shelley's tale, Victor Frankenstein, the scientist, confects that humanoid who turns out devoid of ethical values. That creature strikes a chord with the underside of current scientific-technological progress in artificial intelligence and artificial life.[47]

Some thinkers believe in eugenics, genetic engineering, and similar approaches aimed at changing human biological characteristics for the better.[48] A few espouse *meliorism* with the belief that the world tends to improve and that humans can aid in its betterment.

The term 'transhumanism' was coined by the biologist Julian S. Huxley (1887–1975) in his essay [pp. 13–17] within the collective work titled *New Bottles for New Wine*, published by Chatto and Windus in 1957 in London. Its aim is to transform the human condition by making widely available sophisticated technologies that greatly enhance human intellect and physiology. Nick Bostrom characterizes contemporary *transhumanism* as an interdisciplinary approach aimed at:

> radical extension of human health-span, eradication of disease, elimination of unnecessary suffering, and augmentation of human intellectual, physical, and emotional capacities. Other transhumanist themes include space colonization and the possibility of creating super intelligent machines, along with other potential developments that could profoundly alter the human condition … Transhumanism advocates the well-being of all sentience, whether in artificial intellects, humans, and non-human animals (including extraterrestrial species, if there are any). Racism, sexism, speciesism, belligerent nationalism, and religious intolerance are unacceptable. In addition to the usual grounds for deeming such practices objectionable, there is also a specifically transhumanist motivation for this. In order to prepare for a time when the human species may start branching out in various directions, we need to start now to strongly encourage the development of moral sentiments that are broad enough to encompass within the sphere of moral concern sentiences that are constituted differently from ourselves.[49]

A few researchers have proposed techniques that enable robots' *artificial intelligence* to be programmed to behave in accordance with moral standards.[50] Ideally, moral standards incorporated in robots' *artificial intelligence* should be guided by UDHR's norms.

Commenting on the essence of the transhumanist approach, one researcher in the field has found that:

> Apart from their focus on morphological freedom and avoidance of harm, transhumanists often make a much stronger, positive moral claim: we should promote people's wellbeing. While there are diverging views of what constitutes wellbeing or good life, there is a consensus that normative reasons speak in favour of a clever use of technologies for this purpose.[51]

The claim of some thinkers that 'moral' enhancement could be realized is uncertain (compared with 'physical' and/or 'intellectual' enhancement). Indeed, it is debatable whether science and technology can enhance moral qualities of the 'new humans'. Moreover, it is difficult to reach worldwide consensus regarding the criteria for ascertaining whether morality has been enhanced (or degraded) in parallel to changes in physical or intellectual capacities. This was clearly conveyed by Karen Gloy in her paper 'Post-humanistic Thinking and Its Ethical Evaluation.' According to Gloy:

> The discussion about gene manipulation, computer and nanotechnology, as well as artificial intelligence research and their consequences, splits participants in the discussion into two groups of proponents and opponents. The proponents are fascinated by the possibilities that open up, believing in progress, optimistic and entirely caught by the immanent necessities of these sciences and practices, affirm and support that field of research, while their opponents, worried and anxious regarding the unforeseeable and uncontrollable consequences along with the radical changes in thinking and acting, as well as the loss of order, criticize and try to impede these branches of science.[52]

Some social and political thinkers question the desirability of progress-driven policies that focus on changing current conditions substantially. One such thinker argues:

> The antimodern condition is therefore a statement against progress and the idea of human perfectibility. It is profoundly anti-utopian in that it rejects the idea that we should sacrifice the present in favour of the future. History tells us that the search for human perfectibility is both futile and dangerous. Moreover, we only have one life, and we have ends to meet in the present so why should we sacrifice this for a hypothetical future? ... The key problem with modernity is that it forces us always to look forward and never to accept where we are now. But the failure that naturally follows creates a sense of anxiety. We are told that we should aspire to change, but we tend to fall short and so judge ourselves, and others, harshly.[53]

Various thinkers query whether enhancement should or could be *comprehensive*, and whether it is realizable at the same pace for all humans – in contra-distinction to the enhancement of selective factors at different paces as relevant to each individual. Furthermore, the moot issue remains 'to what *praise-worthy* end should we enhance human capabilities'? By tinkering around with human biology, there are potential risks of producing sub-human species or monstrous beings? Would the hubris of some transhuman thinkers-cum-scientists land us into uncharted territories whose grave ethical consequences cannot be fathomed?[54]

Socially responsible persons do not relapse into indifference, complacency, despondency, sluggishness, or fatalism vis-à-vis catastrophes or tragedies. Such persons would overcome apathy and immobility, and would endeavour unflaggingly to influence the course of events to improve life's conditions on our planet. The moot question is whether such exemplary persons could command clout that exceeds that of the cynics, in order to tip the balance towards sustainable progress. Swinging passively between *gloom* and *glow*, or *dystopia* (a society characterized by misery, squalor, oppression, disease, bleakness, and other cataclysms), and *utopia* (a happy society of harmonious relations and mutual respect) is not uncommon. With no illusion for a panacea or a fit-for-all solution, global cross-disciplinary research in which all centres of learning, private and public, get involved and interconnected (possibly under the broad aegis of the UN University) could open up new paths and horizons susceptible to help us improve our comprehension of complex phenomena aimed at preventing regression, and consolidating and furthering worldwide sustainable progress.

Could possibly human psyche morph for the better – away from domination, abuse, turpitudes and other grave crimes – and in favour of global wellbeing? Or is the human species' predicament perennially subject to the roller coaster cycles of recurrent 'progress-stagnation-regression'? A few thinkers have doubted the likelihood of an uninterrupted positive evolution of mankind along the overarching goals of global wellbeing. They argue that the predicament of humans is that of continuous transgression of universal ethical values and that their prosperity is transient. They argue that human civilizations are bound to wane, and ultimately decay and terminate in ruin.

Taking stock of civilizational achievements over the past two millennia, a few thinkers have concluded that humanity has progressed – both materially and morally. Quantitative economic historians have the conviction that economic development has been dazzling. This is notably the position of Angus Maddison and his school of thought and research that grew from his works at the OECD, and at the University of Groningen/The Netherlands.[55]

Another scholar considers that 'aggressive/violent social behaviours' have fallen and will continue to do so. This is notably the stand of Steven Pinker in his voluminous richly documented book *The Better Angels of our Nature – The Decline of Violence in History and its Causes*.[56] His concluding reflexion is:

> Yet while this planet has gone cycling on to the fixed law of gravity, that [human] species has also found ways to bring the numbers down, and allow a greater and greater proportion of humanity to live in peace and die of natural causes. For all the tribulations in our lives, for all the troubles that remain in the world, the decline of violence is an accomplishment we can savour, and an impetus to cherish the forces of civilization and enlightenment that made it possible.[57]

Pinkers' judgement is shared by other thinkers, chief among them John Hands. In the latter's view:

> A basic duality in human nature has been evident from the emergence of humans, manifested in such things as cooperation versus competition,

> selflessness versus selfishness, and compassion versus aggression. It has been seen as a conflict between good and evil ... But this conflict is not static. Reflective consciousness has been evolving at an ever increasing rate from its emergence and is changing the balance in this duality. While the aggressive competitive instinct remains a powerful but decreasing force shaping human evolution, it has been countered by an increasing comprehension that peaceful cooperation is the only way for the human species to survive and continue to evolve.[58]

From his vantage position, U.S. former President Barak Obama has offered a similar view. He argues:

> I believe that overall, humanity has become less violent, more tolerant, healthier, better fed, more empathetic, more able to manage difference. But it's hugely uneven. And what has been clear throughout the 20th and 21st centuries is that progress we make in social order and taming our baser impulses and steadying our fears can be reversed very quickly. Social order starts breaking down if people are under stress. Then the default position is tribe – us/them, a hostility toward the unfamiliar or the unknown.[59]

The author of this book recognizes that the human species has an *ambivalent* and *complex* nature that can be driven by opposing *destructive* and *constructive* forces that coexist simultaneously within the same individual, although varying in significance. Should the goal of preserving planet Earth from doom prevail among humans, the globalization of welfare will then be the desirable path in which humans and nature can live in mutually beneficial symbiosis as proposed in our normative archetype (ref. Exhibit 1.1). *Artificial intelligence, (AI)* can help in this process, although one should not exaggerate its 'mutating impact' in increasing permanently the human brain's capacity.

Indeed, AI has led to the development of robotics (i.e. the use of automated machines that replace more or less complex human functions). The design, construction, and operation of AI machines generally require sophisticated computer systems for their control, sensory feedback, and information processing. One eminent scientist, Stephen Hawking (professor of cosmology at Cambridge University) warned that 'the development of full artificial intelligence could spell the end of the human race'.[60] Hawking along with several other thinkers fear that AI could lead to *dystopia* – namely an undesirable or frightening community characterized by dehumanization, environmental disasters, totalitarian regimes, and other cataclysms.

The speculative apocalyptic prediction neglects the fact that artificial intelligence – despite the accelerating power of computing – fails to produce the human mind's capabilities of 'understanding and consciousness' – according to Mark Bishop, professor of 'cognitive computing' at the University of London.[61]

Comprehension, reflection, discernment, judgement, conscience, ethical evaluation, artistic appreciation, the exercise of free will, and the manifestation of complex emotions (including positive and negative impulses) – are essentially unique attributes of the human species as we know it today; even the most sophisticated robots cannot reproduce the foregoing human traits. Robots' artificial intelligence is based on models that use past experiences. This intelligence cannot handle 'rationally' totally new situations or unknown problems that have not been already envisaged by the authors of robot models. Moreover, artificial intelligence could malfunction because of a few uncontrollable factors, such as defects in programming or cyber-attacks by adversaries.

Scientific-technological progress on its own is not a panacea. It needs to be coupled with other challenges encountered by humanity, and in particular in the field of observance of *universal fundamental human rights* [whose proxy is the UDHR] in an environment of *peace and security*. This book has examined a few benchmarks considered essential prerequisites for a humanist-driven wellbeing. This raises the fundamental question of the extent to which humans – given their rational and non-rational characteristics – are likely to learn from past calamities by avoiding dismal repeats. In the judgement of some historians, progress in various wakes of life is likely to continue.[62] Other thinkers are cagier.[63]

While it is recognized that human perfectibility is not nigh, progress based on enhancing *human capabilities* is foremost among developmental goals. Scientists have managed so far to increase considerably human capabilities, notably with reference to: improved health; imperviousness to pain; life longevity; protection from various ailments or dangers; and accurate and enhanced productivity of tasks through digitalization, automation, and robotization.[64] The considerable advances in scientific knowledge were not, however, paralleled by similar advances in ethical behaviours and values. We cannot metamorphose the intrinsic characteristics of complex human nature (enhancing its positive components and/or neutralizing the negative ones). Nevertheless, technology can empower people, thereby producing *super-humans* (as judged notably by their physical, intellectual, and other existing and potential capabilities.[65]

Thanks to advances in science and technology, a few philosophers and futurologists will continue to ponder on the possible emergence of a *post-human species*, possibly 'superior' compared with the current human species.[66] However, and as pointedly expressed by Nicholas Agar, 'the danger of modifying ourselves to better fit our wellbeing technologies is that we cannot be sure exactly what we will lose. We are complex beings. We lack full understanding of our own complexity.'[67]

Several thinkers and political leaders advocate *global security* with a peaceful world free from massively destructive weapons (e.g. thermo-nuclear, biological, or chemical). Their utterances have remained lofty theoretical goals. Promises of redeploying funds away from building military arsenals and waging wars – to the benefit of development programmes aimed at (i) eradicating poverty, (ii) reducing inequalities, and (iii) strengthening resilience – all are likely to remain humanity's grail. For an indication on the cost of recent wars, 'the U.S. has spent and taken obligations to spend approximately $4.4 trillion on the wars in Iraq, Afghanistan and Pakistan [from 11 September 2001 till 2014] not including the money requested for FY2015'.[68]

Our analyses in this book have sought to offer a variety of views on progress and wellbeing. We have attempted to identify their core components. Individuals may then assign weights to each component in line with their self-enlightened interests. Accordingly, some would feel 'happy' by accumulating riches or wielding a lot of power. Others would be deeply satisfied with readily accessible simple pleasures, such as walking in nature marvelling at beautiful scenery, or sharing sweet moments of conviviality with family or friends. As such, it is unrealistic to advocate a generally applicable model of *wellbeing* whose components satisfy all human beings in all respects. Indeed, definitive causality links between high incomes on one hand and wellbeing/happiness on the other hand have proven fallacious.[69]

Reflecting on future human behaviours, several 'realist' thinkers who disregard ethical considerations, believe that the human species is likely to strengthen its ascendancy over the Earth's ecology, with the fallout from human activities provoking the extinction of several species. A balance is likely to be reached when human interests and welfare oblige us to establish harmonious relations with other stakeholders of planet Earth. Humans will then be obliged – for the sake of their survival and welfare – to halt climate warming, thawing of ice caps, rising sea levels, the acidification of oceans, and their other depredations of planet Earth.

Whether we are making steady continuous and unimpeded progress in all categories of our normative archetype (ref. Exhibit 1.1) is subject to speculation and controversy. *Transhumanists*, however, believe that the human species is on the path of transmuting into *superior* beings (in matters of biological, mental, psychic, or ethical conditions) through science, technology, and other disciplines. Other thinkers believe that the foregoing desiderata smack of utopia and hubris. This book's analyses – it is hoped – could widen the scope of reflections and exchanges in the search for improved approaches that reduce bellicosity and protect a decent life with dignity in a flourishing planet Earth.

Notes

1 See, for example, Gerd Gigerenzer and Reinhard Selten, eds, *Bounded Rationality – The Adaptive Toolbox*, The MIT Press, 2002, 396p.

2 *Hearings on the Financial Crisis and the Role of Federal Regulators*, U.S. House of Representatives, 23 October 2008.

3 See, for example, Benjamin R. Barber, *Cool Cities – Urban Sovereignty and the Fix for Global Warming*, Yale University Press, 2017, 207p.

4 The *Oxford Advanced Learner's Dictionary*'s defines *grail* as: 'a thing that you try very hard to find or achieve, but never will'.

5 See John Hands' widely researched and richly documented *Cosmosapiens – Human Evolution from the Origin of the Universe*, Duckworth Overlook, 2015, p. 3/674p.

6 See, for example, Helmut Ortner, 'The Origin of the "Knowledge Economy"', *The Journal of European Economic History*, Rome, Capitalia, Fall 2006, pp. 427–461.

7 See, for example, Annals of the New York Academy of Sciences, *Progress in Convergence: Technologies for Human Wellbeing*, eds William Sims Bainbridge and Mihail C. Roco, vol. 1093, December 2006, 367p.

8 See, for example, François Jullien, *De l'universel, de l'uniforme, du commun et du dialogue entre les cultures* [*Universality, Uniformity, Commonality, and Dialogue among Cultures*], Fayard, 2008, 266p.

9 See, for example, 'Oil Data: Is It Becoming More Reliable?', *Middle East Petroleum and Economic Publications (Cyprus) Ltd*, 23 September 2016, pp. 19–21, www.mees.com.

10 Also see Edgar Morin's paper on 'Restricted Complexity, General Complexity', at the *Colloquium on the Intelligence of Complexity: Epistemology and Pragmatism*, Cerisy-La-Salle, France, 26 June 2005, 25p. – translated from French by Carlos Gershenson.

11 See, for example, Richard Dawkins, *The God Delusion*, Houghton Mifflin, 2008, 463p.

12 See, for example, Rupert Sheldrake, *The Science Delusion*, Coronet, 2012, 400p.

13 See, for example, Martha C. Nussbaum, *The New Religious Intolerance – Overcoming the Politics of Fear in an Anxious Age*, Harvard University Press, 2012, 285p.; also Narendra Dabholkar, Founder of *The Committee for the Eradication of Blind Faith*, cited by *The Economist*, 14 September 2013, p. 90.

14 See, for example, Richard L. Miller, 'Leadership – Theory and Practice', in Stephen F. Davis and William Buskist, eds, *21st Century Psychology – A Reference Handbook*, vol. 2, Sage Publications, 2008, pp. 152–162.

15 See, for example, Ian Dew-Becker and Robert Gordon, 'Where Did the Productivity Growth Go? Inflation Dynamics and the Distribution of Income', *NBER Working Paper No. 11842*, December 2005; Emmanuel Saez and Thomas Piketty, 'The Evolution of Top Incomes: A Historical and International Perspective', *NBER Working Paper No. 11955*, January 2006; also Branko Milanovic, *Global Inequality: A New Approach for the Age of Globalisation*, Belknap – Harvard University Press, April 2016, 320p.

16 See for example the reports of Verité, a 'global NGO with a mission to ensure that people around the world work under safe, fair, and legal conditions': *Strengthening Protections Against Trafficking in Persons in Federal and Corporate Supply Chains*, January 2015, 152p. – www.verite.org.

17 See, for example, Denis G. Arnold, 'Working Conditions: Safety and Sweatshops', pp. 628–653; and Lisa H. Newton, 'Environmental Ethics and Business, pp. 658–676, in George G. Brenkert and Tom L. Beauchamp, eds, *The Oxford Handbook of Business Ethics*, Oxford University Press, 2010, 733p.; also 'The Trouble with Outsourcing', *The Economist*, 30 July 2011, p. 58; and 'Supply Chains in China – Core and Periphery', *The Economist*, 6 March, 2010, p. 67.

18 See: www.oecd.org; see also: The World Bank Group, *Living Our Values – Code of Conduct*, 2013, 43p., www.worldbank.org/ethics.

19 International Chamber of Commerce, *ICC Guidance on Supply Chain Responsibility*, Paris, 10 October 2007, 12p. (www.iccwbo.org); see also Paul Redmond, 'International Corporate Responsibility', in: *The Sage Handbook of Corporate Governance*, op. cit., pp. 385–611.

20 See, for example, Paul Vandenberg, *Poverty Reduction through Small Enterprises*, Working Paper, International Labour Office, Geneva, 2006, 59p.; IBM, *Global Innovation Outlook 2.0*, March 2006, 49p.; and the International Finance Corporation, 'IFC SME Ventures Fund': www.ifc.org.

21 'Can Entrepreneurship Be Fostered?', *World Development Report 2013*, p. 114.

22 *Entrepreneurship, Development and Spatial Context*, p. 292/271–293p.; in Naudé, op. cit.

23 Joseph A. Schumpeter, *Capitalism, Socialism, and Democracy*, 3rd edition, Harper & Row, 1950, p. 132.

24 Ibid., p. 83.

25 https://phys.org/news/2017-12-epson-apple-french-legal-pressure.html.

26 *Reuters*, 18 January 2018.

27 See, for example, 'Deluded Bosses – Who Is behind Me?', and 'Leaders Need to Learn to Beware of Their strengths', *The Economist*, 8 June 2013, pp. 63 and 64 respectively.
28 See, for example, the biographical accounts of the co-founder of Apple: Walter Isaacson, *Steve Jobs*, Simon & Schuster, 2011, 656p.; and Brent Schlender and Rick Tetzeli, *Becoming Steve Jobs: The Evolution of a Reckless Upstart into a Visionary Leader*, Crown Business, 2015, 464p.
29 Amorós and Bosma, op.cit., p. 11 and 64.
30 See Daniel V. Holland and Dean A. Shepherd, 'Deciding to Persist: Adversity, Values, and Entrepreneurs' Decision Policies', *Entrepreneurship – Theory and Practice*, March 2013, pp. 331–358.
31 Crony capitalism has grown out of cosy connections to the authorities. Unlike innovative entrepreneurs whose income derives largely from creativity, the beneficiaries from these connections extract *rent* thanks to their 'special' privileged relations with ruling class. The latter offer concessions, licences, or exclusive business rights in such fields as natural resources, telecoms, real estate, gambling, defence, subsidized funding, privatizations of enterprises, monopolistic business rights, etc. A crony index was developed for that purpose by *The Economist* (see: 'Our Crony-Capitalism Index', 7 May 2016, pp. 46–48; also: economist.com/cronyindex2016).
32 See, for example, Anne T. Lawrence and James Weber, *Business and Society – Stakeholders, Ethics, Public Policy*, 14th edition, McGraw-Hill International Edition, 2014, pp. 68–113/551p.; and Gordon L Clark, Andreas Feiner, and Michael Viehs, *From the Stockholder to the Stakeholder – How Sustainability Can Drive Financial Outperformance*, University of Oxford, September 2014, 58p.
33 Maslow's hierarchy of needs was first proposed in his 1943 paper entitled 'A Theory of Human Motivation', originally published in *Psychological Review*, 50, pp. 370–396.
34 Michael Slote, *Human Development and Human Life*, Springer, 2015, p. 15/52p.
35 James E. Post, Lee E. Preston, and Sybille Sachs, *Redefining the Corporation, Stakeholder Management and Organizational Wealth*, Stanford University Press, 2002, pp. 32–33/376p.; see also R. E. Freeman, *Strategic Management: A Stakeholder Approach*, Pitman, Boston, 1984; and R. Edward Freeman and John McVea, 'A Stakeholder Approach to Strategic Management', in *Handbook of Strategic Management*, Blackwell-Wiley, June 2005; and: http://papers.ssrn.com.
36 See, for example, Joel Brockner, 'Why It's So Hard to be Fair', *Harvard Business Review*, March 2006, pp. 122–129; and Hossam Zeitoun, *Corporate Governance Modes, Stakeholder Relations, and Organizational Value Creation*, University of Zurich, Doctoral dissertation in Business Administration, 26 October 2011, 123p.
37 See, for example, Leonardo Becchetti and Carlo Borzaga, eds, *The Economics of Social Responsibility – The World of Social Enterprises*, Routledge, 2010, 258p.; and Jost Hamschmidt and Michael Pirson, eds, *Case Studies in Social Entrepreneurship and Sustainability*, Greenleaf Publishing Ld., 2011, 452p.; also Ehaab Abdou, A *Practitioner's Guide for Social Entrepreneurs in Egypt and the Arab Region*, The American University in Cairo – John D. Gerhart Center for Philanthropy and Civic Engagement, October 2010, 90p.
38 See Deborah Gage, 'The Venture Capital Secret: 3 Out of 4 Start-Ups Fail', *Wall Street Journal*, 20 September 2012.
39 See, for example, Diego B. Avanzini, 'Designing Composite Entrepreneurship Indicators', and Sameeksha Desai, 'Measuring Entrepreneurship in Developing Countries', in Wim Naudé, ed., *Entrepreneurship and Economic Development*, Palgrave Macmillan, 2011, 373p. – pp. 37–93, and 94–107 respectively.
40 See, for example, 'CEOs and Society – America Inc Gets Woke', *The Economist*, 2 December 2017, pp. 55–57.
41 See, for example, Will Steffen, Paul J. Crutzen, and John R. McNeill, 'The *Anthropocene*: Are Humans Now Overwhelming the Great Forces of Nature?' (2007), in

Peter Newell and J. Timmons Roberts, eds, *The Globalization and Environment Reader*, Wiley Blackwell, 2017, pp. 27–42/454p.

42 J. Baird Callicott, 'Worldview Remediation in the First Century of the New Millennium', in Serpil Oppermann and Serenella Iovino,eds, *Environmental Humanities – Voices from the Anthropocene*, Rowman & Littlefield, 2017, pp. 133–154/373p.

43 John Gray, interviewed by Richard Lofthouse, 'Forget Your Delusions and Be Happy', in *Oxford Today*, Michaelmas Term 2015, vol. 28 no. 1, pp. 34–37; www.oxfordtoday.ox.ac.uk; also John Gray, *Black Mass – Apocalyptic Religion and the Death of Utopia*, Penguin Books, 2008, 342p.

44 Andrew Heywood, *Politics*, 3rd edition, Palgrave Macmillan, 2007, p. 65 and 445/478p.

45 Dale Murray, *The Global and the Local – An Environmental Ethics Casebook*, Brill, 2016, p. 19/522p.

46 Pankaj Mishra, *Age of Anger*, Allen Lane, 2017, pp. 328–329/406.

47 See, for example, a selection of latest books on the subject of *science fiction* and the *contemporary progress in genetics and robotics* in: 'Mary Shelley and "Frankenstein" – The Monster in the MIRROR', 17 February 2018, pp. 73–74.

48 See, for example, Raymond Kurzweil, *The Singularity Is Near, When Humans Transcend Biology*, Viking, 2005, 652p.

49 Nick Bostrom, 'Transhumanist Values', in Frederick Adams, ed., *Ethical Issues for the 21st Century*, Philosophical Documentation Center Press, 2003; reprinted in *Review of Contemporary Philosophy*, vol. 4, May (2005).

50 See, for example, Simon Parkin, 'Teaching Robots Right from Wrong', *The Economist 1843*, June and July 2017, pp. 68–73.

51 Robert Ranisch, 'Morality', pp. 149–172, in Robert Ranisch and Stephan Lorez Sorgner, eds, *Post- and Transhumanism – An Introduction*, Peter Lang, 2014, 313p.

52 Part of the collective work Irina Deretic/Stefan Lorenz Sorgner, eds, *From Humanism to Meta-, Post- and Transhumanism*, Peter Lang, 2016, pp. 219–220/381p.

53 Peter King, *The Antimodern Condition – An Argument Against Progress*, Ashgate, 2014, p. XI, and p. 114 and 116/128p.

54 One scholar offers the following view:

> Imagine for a moment that you were told to improve a text you have written by replacing each word of the text with another better word. While each word on its own seems to have improved, the overall text will have lost its meaning. In this sense the text is no longer authentic. This example illustrates the importance of considering the text holistically. In an analogous way, it is crucial to look at the human holistically when attempting to assess the morality of human enhancement … Technological progress promises to make us better. But, as the line between human enhancement and dis-enhancement, and between human, post-human, or sub-human become more and more blurry, it will become more and more difficult to understand what 'better' actually means.

Johann A. R. Roduit, *The Case for Perfection – Ethics in the Age of Human Enhancement*, Peter Lang, 2016, pp. 115–116 and 118/130p. One needs to admit that there is no clear-cut definitive and universal single answer to 'what "*better wellbeing*" stands for'.

55 See also Johan Norberg, *Progress – Ten Reasons to Look Forward to the Future*, Oneworld, 2016, 246p.

56 Published by Allen Lane, New York, 2011, 802p.

57 Pinker, p. 696.

58 See John Hands, *Cosmosapiens – Human Evolution from the Origin of the Universe*, Duckworth Overlook, 2015, p. 556/674p.

59 'President Obama's Interview with Jeffrey Goldberg on Syria and Foreign Policy', *The Atlantic*, April 2016.

60 BBC News – Technology, 'Stephen Hawking Warns Artificial Intelligence Could End Mankind', 2 December 2014; see also Nick Bostrom, *Superintelligence – Paths, Dangers, Strategies*, Oxford University Press, 2014, 328p.
61 See *The Independent*, 7 December 2014.
62 See for example Johan Norberg, *Progress: Ten Reasons to Look Forward to the Future*, Oneworld, 2016, 246p.
63 See, for example, Gregory Treverton – Chairman, National Intelligence Council, *Global Trends: Paradox of Progress*, January 2017, 226p. www.dni./nic//globaltrends.
64 See, for example, Gail Dixon and Paul Parsons, *50 Science Ideas You Really Need to Know*, Quercus Publishing Plc, 2016, 207p.
65 See, for example, Sebastian Thrun, 'Technology Gives Us Super-Human Powers', *Bulletin*, 3, 2016, Credit Suisse, pp. 22–27.
66 See, for example, David Roden, *Post Human Life – Philosophy at the Edge of the Human*, Routledge, 2015, 211p.
67 Nicholas Agar, *The Sceptical Optimist – Why Technology Isn't the Answer to Everything*, Oxford University Press, 2015, p. 194/206p.
68 Professor Neta C. Crawford, Boston University, 25 June 2014; www.costofwar.org. Some aid institutions warn that progress in reducing global poverty and disease is in jeopardy (see, for example, Bill and Melinda Gates Foundation, *Goalkeepers – The Stories Behind the Data*, 2017, 42p.
69 See, for example, Carol Graham, *Happiness around the World –The Paradox of Happy Peasants and Miserable Millionaires*, Oxford University Press, 2009, 249p.; Paul Dolan, *Happiness by Design, Finding Pleasure and Purpose in Everyday Life*, Allen Lane, 2014, p. xx/235p; and Sonja Lyubomirsky, *The Myths of Happiness*, Penguin Books, 2013, 298p.

Epilogue

Science and ethics 'working in tandem' – humanity's vital engine for socio-economic progress in wellbeing[1]

Taking stock of the historical evolution of mankind's *wellbeing* in its multiple dimensions, analysts have offered different evaluations on this evolution. They stretch from the euphoric to the despairing.

As things stand now (i.e. in the first quarter of the twenty-first century) by comparison to earlier periods, it is reasonable to conclude that great strides have been made towards the realization of goals in certain domains, notably that of 'science and technology', through an additive process.

In other domains, and in particular in that of respecting rigorously 'humanitarian universal values', the pace of progress has generally lagged behind that of 'science and technology', and has suffered from multiple reverses – even in countries dubbed as 'ethically advanced'.

The preceding statement elicits an important query: Can we extricate, neutralize or control human nature's destructive impulses in order to open-up and fructify potential trails of future comprehensive and inclusive progress in wellbeing solidly-based on 'universal values'?

The foregoing query deserves the relentless pondering and the diligent response of researchers, policy makers, decision makers, and ordinary citizens. As put by a Nobel Prize laureate, we can call for that purpose on several disciplines, including the discipline of

> Economics [which] works toward the common good; its goal is to make the world a better place … It analyses situations in which individual interest is compatible with the quest for collective well-being, as well as those in which, by contrast, individual interest hinders that quest.[2]

In the current 'era of globalization', many people have emphasized the desirability of the goal of 'economic growth'. Judging by this criterion, one could state that the evolution of 'economic growth' over the past two centuries has been momentous, benefiting rising proportions of humans considerably. This is evidenced by the continuous increase in per capita wealth and income worldwide, longer and healthier lives, vast scientific discoveries, wider and readily accessible knowledge, higher comfort in habitat, more leisure time, and other benefits.

Economic growth's achievements, however, have been realized with significant collateral *costs*. Fallout comprises: greenhouse emissions, accumulation of toxic wastes, excessive depletion of scarce natural resources, land-water-air pollution, and other enduring noxious collateral damages. These socially-harmful problems have been perpetrated by negligent egotistic and venal individuals or groups.

Businesses can have better opportunities to serve their stakeholders and to prosper over the long term, should they be guided by standards of good governance (not only regarding their own operations, but also in relation to their global value chains), Codes of good conduct and principles of good governance have been proclaimed by several prominent parties, such as United Nations agencies (along with other international organizations) and diverse professional groups. They generally call for ending antisocial reprehensible practices, and for promoting accountability, transparency and respect of laws. The condemned practices comprise notably: forced adult and child labour, neglect in the protection of health-cum-safety problems that affect workers and their families, spread of graft and corruption, and various other abuses of 'universal human rights'.[3]

Some thinkers seek to bridge the gap between progress in 'science and technology' on one hand, and progress in the implementation of 'universal values' on the other hand. These thinkers have espoused the *Transhumans'* movement whose ambition is to transform 'via science' humans into a *superior* species with respect to the two categories of (i) improved physical-mental-psychic capabilities (in health, life longevity, intellectual capacity, etc.), and (ii) sounder moral qualities. The realization of such an overreaching goal of *superior humans* is likely to remain a subject conjecture. Other thinkers claim that parallel improvements *in intelligence and moral behaviours* have been also realized along with *material progress* over the past two centuries.[4] Though difficult to measure, Pinker argues that people are growing 'more intelligent and more humane [*sic*]'!

At the opposite of the argumentation of Pinker, British philosopher John Gray considers improvements in moral behaviour 'illusionary'; he portrays humanity as a ravenous species engaged in wiping out other forms of life on planet Earth. Gray writes

> Human knowledge tends to increase, but humans do not become any more civilized as a result. They remain prone to every kind of barbarism, and while the growth of knowledge allows them to improve their material conditions, it also increases the savagery of their conflicts.[5]

In wrapping-up the monograph's analyses, this author recognizes the vanguard role of (a) *science* and (b) *ethics working in tandem*. Both aim at serving the overarching goal of an all-inclusive progress in wellbeing, covering current and future generations. Human wellbeing lies in the harmonious symbiosis of *material* and *moral* factors. Expressed differently, *universal values* need to be implemented for the sake of humanity's wellbeing – ratcheting-up continuously in an *additive and irreversible* fashion similarly to the progress in 'science and technology'. That challenge merits the relentless top priority attention of creative intellectuals and innovative practitioners who can influence the evolution of wellbeing on planet Earth positively.

The proposed periodic 'State of the Globe' (ref. Chapter 6) can serve all parties concerned in their evaluation of the overall evolution of conditions on planet Earth. Hopefully, humans who have power, foresight and stamina are collectively able to steer away humankind from planetary existential disasters.

Notes

1 Zuhayr Mikdashi (23 March 2018).
2 Jean Tirole, *Economics for the Common Good*, Princeton University Press, 2017, p. 5/563p.
3 See for example: Norichika Kanie and Frank Biermann, eds, *Governing through Goals – Sustainable Development Goals as Governance Innovation*, MIT Press, 5 May 2017, 333p.
4 See Steven Pinker, *Enlightenment Now: The Case for Reason, Science, Humanism and Progress*, Viking/Allen Lane, 2018, 576p.; and the book's 'Lead Review', *The Economist*, 24 February, 2018, pp. 67–69.
5 Ref. John Gray, *Black Mass – Apocalyptic Religion and the Death of Utopia*, Penguin Books, 2008, p. 265/342p.

Index

Page numbers in *italic* denote figures.

Taylor & Francis Group
an informa business